CHANGING CLASS
EDUCATION AND SOCIAL CHANGE IN POST-APARTHEID SOUTH AFRICA

CHANGING CLASS

EDUCATION AND SOCIAL CHANGE IN POST-APARTHEID SOUTH AFRICA

EDITED BY LINDA CHISHOLM

Zed Books
London & New York

HSRC PRESS
Cape Town

First published in South Africa in 2004 by HSRC Press
Private Bag X9182, Cape Town, 8000, South Africa
www.hsrcpublishers.ac.za

Published in the rest of the world in 2004 by Zed Books Ltd.
7 Cynthia Street, London N1 9JF, UK, and
Room 400, 175 Fifth Avenue, New York, NY 10010, USA

© 2004 Human Sciences Research Council

All rights reserved. No part of this book may be reprinted or reproduced or utilised in any form or by any electronic, mechanical, or other means, including photocopying and recording, or in any information storage or retrieval system, without permission in writing from the publishers.

Cover by FUEL Design
Production by comPress

Distributed in South Africa by Blue Weaver Marketing and Distribution,
PO Box 30370, Tokai, Cape Town, 7966, South Africa.
Tel: +27 +21-701-4477
Fax: +27 +21-701-7302
email: booksales@hsrc.ac.za

Distributed in the USA exclusively by Palgrave Macmillan,
a division of St Martin's Press, Inc.,
175 Fifth Avenue, New York, NY 10010

In South Africa
ISBN 0 7969 2052 4 PB

In the rest of the world
ISBN 1 84277 590 1 HC

Contents

List of figures and tables		vii
Acknowledgements		x
Abbreviations and acronyms		xii

Introduction Linda Chisholm 1

SECTION 1 CHANGING CONTOURS 29

Chapter 1 The development challenge in post-apartheid South African education 31
Haroon Bhorat

Chapter 2 Balancing public and private resources for basic education: school fees in post-apartheid South Africa 57
Edward Fiske and Helen Ladd

Chapter 3 'Constituting the class': an analysis of the process of 'integration' in South African schools 89
Crain Soudien

Chapter 4 Educational de/centralisation and the quest for equity, democracy and quality 115
Suzanne Grant Lewis and Shireen Motala

Chapter 5 The new face of private schooling 143
Jane Hofmeyr and Simon Lee

SECTION 2 CHANGING LANDSCAPES 175

Chapter 6 Multilingualism and education 177
Thobeka Mda

Chapter 7 Political change, curriculum change and social formation, 1990 to 2002 195
Ken Harley and Volker Wedekind

Chapter 8 Assessment, qualifications and the NQF in South African schooling 221
Johan Muller

Chapter 9	The case of teacher education in post-apartheid South Africa: politics and priorities *Yusuf Sayed*	247
Chapter 10	Teacher unions, policy struggles and educational change, 1994 to 2004 *Logan Govender*	267
Chapter 11	Changes and continuities in South Africa's higher education system, 1994 to 2004 *Jonathan D Jansen*	293

SECTION 3 CHANGING MARGINS — 315

Chapter 12	Don't bite the hand that feeds you: South African education NGOs in a period of change *Seán Morrow*	317
Chapter 13	The state of play in early childhood development *Kim Porteus*	339
Chapter 14	Youth development in transition, 1992 to 2004 *Margaret Perrow*	367
Chapter 15	Adult basic education and social change in South Africa, 1994 to 2003 *Ivor Baatjes and Khulekani Mathe*	393
Chapter 16	The education business: private contractors in public education *John Pampallis*	421

About the authors — 435

Index — 437

List of figures and tables

Figures

Figure 5.1	Independent schools in South Africa, 2003	153
Figure 5.2	ISASA's member schools, December 2002	157
Figure 8.1	Mean scores for Numeracy, Literacy and Life skills by province in the Grade 3 systemic assessment, 2001	234
Figure 8.2	South Africa's performance on the Grade 4 MLA Numeracy test, 1995	236

Tables

Table 1.1	A snapshot of key labour market trends: 1995 to 2002	33
Table 1.2	Employment and economically active population (EAP) shifts, by race and gender: 1995 to 2002	36
Table 1.3	Employment and EAP shifts, by education level: 1995 to 2002	37
Table 1.4	Sectoral share of employment, 1995 and 2002	38
Table 1.5	Share of employment by three skills categories and main sector (percentage)	40
Table 1.6	Unemployment rates by race and gender, 1995 and 2002 (percentage)	42
Table 1.7	Unemployment rates by education level, 1995 and 2002 (percentage)	43
Table 1.8	Tertiary unemployment rates, by race, 1995 and 2002 (percentage)	44
Table 1.9	Unemployment for degreed workers: African and white, 1995 and 2002	45
Table 1.10	Degreed unemployed distribution by field of study and race (percentage)	46
Table 1.11	Distribution of unemployed by age cohort and education level	48
Table 1.12	Distribution of unemployed by period of search and age cohort (percentage)	49

Table 1.13	Unemployed who have worked before: when last was this? (percentage)	50
Table 1.14	Literacy levels of the unemployed	51
Table 1.15	Distribution of the unemployed across wage-earning households	52
Table 2.1	Students in independent schools, 1995 and 2000	59
Table 2.2	School fees charged, primary schools and secondary schools, Eastern Cape and Western Cape, 2001	61
Table 2.3	Public expenditure on education, selected countries	63
Table 2.4	Estimates of national enrolment rates	68
Table 2.5	Enrolment rates, Eastern Cape and Western Cape, 2001	70
Table 2.6	Percentage of students with fee exemptions, primary and secondary schools by former department, Western Cape, 2002	73
Table 2.7	Public and private resources in primary schools, by former department, Western Cape, 2001	75
Table 2.8	Resources in secondary schools, by former department, Western Cape, 2001	76
Table 2.9	Summary of determinants of matriculation pass rates, Western Cape, 2001: impacts on the weighted pass rate	77
Table 2.10	Aggregate spending on education, 1997/98 to 2002/03	80
Table 2.11	Determinants of matriculation pass rates, Western Cape, 2001	83
Table 3.1	Extent of changes in selected schools in five provinces (percentages)	97
Table 3.2	Percentage of Gauteng learners by 'race' groups	98
Table 3.3	Total percentage of Gauteng learners by 'race' groups in public and independent schools	98
Table 3.4	Learner demographic profiles	99
Table 3.5	Percentage of African learners in selected KZN schools	100
Table 5.1	Enrolment in independent schools by racial group	158

LIST OF FIGURES AND TABLES

Table 8.1	Senior Certificate Examination results, 1994 to 2002	230
Table 8.2	Number of Grade 3 learners that participated in the Grade 3 systemic assessment mainsteam study, 2001	233
Table 10.1	Union membership	274
Table 10.2	Total number of teachers in mainstream schools by gender in 2001	276
Table 12.1	Role of women in education NGOs	323
Table 13.1	ECD provisioning: access, state subsidisation, expenditure	348

CHANGING CLASS

Acknowledgements

Many people contributed to ensuring that this book saw the light of day. I owe a special debt to Mokubung Nkomo who encouraged and supported the idea when I first arrived at the Human Sciences Research Council (HSRC). Many thanks to the authors for their contributions and the readers, Pam Christie, Elaine Unterhalter and Bruce Fuller, for their constructive comments on the chapters. Ben Fine, Jonathan Jansen and Elaine Unterhalter all helped improve the Introduction: all errors remain mine. Mary Ralphs of the HSRC Publishing Division has been an excellent editorial manager, and John Daniel and Garry Rosenberg provided a steady steering hand. This book is written in honour of all those who have worked to build a democratic intellectual and educational culture in South Africa.

Abbreviations and acronyms

ABE	Adult basic education
ABET	Adult basic education and training
ACE	Accelerated Christian Education
ACSI	Association of Christian Schools International
AETASA	Adult Educators and Trainers Association of South Africa
ALN	Adult Learning Network
ANC	African National Congress
BHE	Branch for Higher Education
C2005	Curriculum 2005
CASS	Continuous Assessment
CEM	Council of Education Ministers
CEPD	Centre for Education Policy Development
CHE	Council on Higher Education
CIE	Catholic Institute for Education
Cosatu	Congress of South African Trade Unions
COTEP	Committee for Teacher Education Policy
CTA	Common Tasks of Assessment
CUP	Committee of University Principals
DACST	Department of Arts, Culture, Science and Technology
DET	Department of Education and Training (previous apartheid department for Africans in urban areas)
DoE	Department of Education
DoF	Department of Finance
DoL	Department of Labour
DPW	Department of Public Works
ECD	Early childhood development
EFA	Education For All
ELP	Expected Levels of Performance
ELRC	Education Labour Relations Council
EMIS	Education Management Information System

ABBREVIATIONS AND ACRONYMS

EPU	Education Policy Unit
ERS	Education Renewal Strategy
ETDP	Education, Training and Development Practices
ETQA	Education and Training Quality Assurance
FET	Further Education and Training
FTE	full-time equivalent
GDE	Gauteng Department of Education
GEAR	Growth, Employment and Redistribution (Programme)
GENFET	General and Further Education and Training
GET	General Education and Training
GETC	General Education and Training Certificate
GNU	Government of National Unity
HAI	Historically advantaged institution
HDI	Historically disadvantaged institution
HECOM	Higher Education Committee
HoA	House of Assembly (previous apartheid department for whites)
HoD	House of Delegates (previous apartheid department for Indians)
HoR	House of Representatives (previous apartheid department for coloureds)
HRD	Human Resources Development
HRDS	Human Resources Development Strategy
IAYD	Integrated Approach to Youth Development
IDT	Independent Development Trust
IEA	International Association for Educational Achievement
IEB	Independent Examinations Board
ISASA	Independent Schools Association of Southern Africa
ISC	Independent Schools Council
JEP	Joint Enrichment Project to the Language Plan Task Group
JET	Joint Education Trust
JLC	Joint Liaison Committee
JMB	Joint Matriculation Board

LACs	Learning Area Committees
LANGTAG	Language Plan Task Group
LEAF	Leadership Education and Advancement
LiEP	Language in Education Policy
LPHE	Language Policy for Higher Education
M&E	Monitoring and Evaluation
MEC	Member of the Executive Council
MLA	Monitoring Learner Assessment (Study)
MTBPS	Medium Term Budget Policy Statement
MTEF	Medium Term Expenditure Framework
MYIP	*Multi-Year Implementation Plan*
NAISA	National Alliance of Independent School Associations
NAPTOSA	National Professional Teachers' Association of South Africa
NATU	National Teachers' Union
NCHE	National Commission on Higher Education
NECC	National Education Crisis (later Co-ordinating) Committee
NED	Natal Education Department (previous apartheid department for whites in Natal)
NEPA	*National Education Policy Act*
NEPI	National Education Policy Investigation
NEST	New Era Schools Trust
NGO	Non-Governmental Organisation
NNSSF	National Norms and Standards for School Funding
NPO	Non-Profit Organisation
NQF	National Qualifications Framework
NSB	National Standards Body
NSDS	National Skills Development Strategy
NSF	National Skills Fund
NSFAS	National Student Financial Aid Scheme
NSTE	National System of Teacher Education/Norms and Standards for Teacher Education
NTB	National Training Board
NTUF	National Teachers' Union Forum
NUE	National Union of Educators
NYC	National Youth Commission

ABBREVIATIONS AND ACRONYMS

NYDF	National Youth Development Forum
NYP	National Youth Policy
OBE	Outcomes-based education
PALCs	Public Adult Learning Centres
PANSALB	Pan South African Languages Board
PBO	Public Benefit Organisation
PRAESA	Project for the Study of Alternative Education in South Africa
PSCBE	Public Service Co-ordinating Bargaining Council
PTSA	Parent Teacher Student Associations
QA	Quality Assurance
QC	Quality Assurance Committee
RDP	Reconstruction and Development Programme
RNCS	Revised National Curriculum Statement
RNE	Royal Netherlands Embassy
SAAIS	South African Association of Independent Schools
SABJE	South African Board of Jewish Education
SACE	South African Council for Educators
SACOL	South African College for Open Learning
SACP	South African Communist Party
SACTE	South African College for Teacher Education
SADTU	South African Democratic Teachers' Union
Safcert	The South African Certification Council (initially Board)
SALDRU	South African Labour Development Research Unit
SANLI	South African National Literacy Initiative
SAOU	Suid-Afrikaanse Onderwysersunie
SAPSE	South African Post Secondary School Education
SAQA	South African Qualifications Authority
SASA	*South African Schools Act*
SCOPA	Standing Committee on Public Accounts
SDA	*Skills Development Act*
SDPU	Skills Development Policy Unit
SETA	Sector Education and Training Authority

SGB	School Governing Body and also Standards Generating Body
SO	Specific Outcomes
TED	Transvaal Education Department (previous apartheid structure)
TIMSS	Third International Maths and Science Study
UDD	Universal Declaration on Democracy
UNDP	United Nations Development Programme
UNISA	University of South Africa
UP	University of Pretoria
UPE	University of Port Elizabeth
USAID	United States Agency for International Development
UYF	Umsobomvu Youth Fund
WCED	Western Cape Education Department
Wits	University of the Witwatersrand, Johannesburg

Introduction

Linda Chisholm

Ten years after the ending of apartheid, questions are being asked about what substantive change has been achieved. Where better to look than at education, where the intentions and effects of apartheid were most insidious and overt and the efforts to change most visible and dramatic?

Since 1994, there has been a significant refashioning of the education and training landscape in South Africa. Eighteen racially-divided departments have been restructured into nine. Education budgets are designed in principle to achieve equitable outcomes and overcome the racial disparities that marked apartheid budgeting allocations. Education control has been decentralised, and schools, colleges, technikons and universities have been opened to all races. Curricula, their review and design, have been revamped, and management and administration reorganised. Novel forms of assessment, qualification and certification have been introduced through an entirely new body, the National Qualifications Framework (NQF). Teacher education is now provided under the auspices of the higher education sector. Higher education itself has been reorganised. A new multilingual language policy has been articulated for schools. Skills levies and Sector Education and Training Authorities (SETAs) have been brought into being to provide training for workers. Substantially altered educational philosophies now suffuse policy documents.

But what has changed in practice? How are these changes to be interpreted? And why have they changed the way they have? What is the relationship of that change in particular areas of education to broader processes of economic and social change? If apartheid was immanent in everything about the way education was shaped, practised and deployed, then how does the new society embed contemporary forms of education both as an outcome of, and factor in, the transition from apartheid? And how does the new education, in turn, influence social development? These are the big and broad questions that stimulated the writing of this book; the chapters were written with them in mind. Not all the chapters adopt the same approach. Indeed, in an edited book of this length it is not possible to explore all the dimensions of the education-society relationship. Many of the chapters do, however, reflect on the deeper changes that have and have not occurred through and in education as a consequence of, in response to, or in shaping, wider social changes. They look at the contribution of education to social change as much as that of social change to education. By analysing change, the areas of continuity become visible; by analysing continuities, the areas that have changed are highlighted.

Different writers were invited to reflect on what has changed in particular areas in education over the last ten years. Draft abstracts and papers were discussed at two workshops. In these, the bigger picture and common themes began to emerge, and chapters were recrafted in the light of these discussions. Although each chapter provides a wealth of factual information, they all go beyond a simple balance-sheet of achievement and failure. Such analyses, drawn to celebration or regret, will be all too common in national assessments of progress since 1994. The chapters in this book seek instead to present a multifaceted picture of change and continuity. They are grouped into three broad sections: those that give a sense of the changing shape, outline and character of the education system and its relationship to society; those that shift the focus to changing alignments in the classroom, union meetings and the lecture hall; and those that turn our gaze to those at the margins – women caring for pre-school children; NGOs (non-governmental organisations); poorly-educated, unemployed youth and their organisations; illiterate and unskilled adults. The book also includes a chapter on a phenomenon apparently on the margins, but central to how education is being reconfigured – private contracting in public education.

This introduction briefly discusses the main themes and conclusions of the book in the first two sections and then discusses the chapters in terms of them.

Changing class

The title, *Changing Class*, suggests both the active process of effecting change within social classes and classrooms and the nature and process of that change. The book examines the relationships between changing classes and classrooms. It provides an analysis of educational trends and developments over the past decade, in the context of the legacy left by apartheid. It examines an interrelated set of terrains which have been the focus of policy and intervention and that impact on classrooms. Classrooms are here broadly understood as educational spaces within schools, colleges, universities, organisations and movements.

The notion of education as a 'system of provision' is a suggestive one for framing the nature of the analysis. In this approach, education not only involves a range of activities from the building of schools to the setting of curricula; it also interacts with the panoply of economic, social, political and cultural relations and is heavily involved in a range of social structures, relations and processes and their associated conflicts (Fine 2002: Chapter 10; Fine & Rose 2001: 4). Concepts of class, power, conflict and inequality are critical in this approach. It diverges most significantly from that of human capital theory, perhaps not the only, but a significant approach to contemporary education (Unterhalter 1998). It differs from human capital theory in so far as it aims to provide an analysis not only of the contribution of education to economic growth but of the underlying issues and full range, impact and consequences of the policies set in place since 1994. As such, it also provides an implicit critique of human capital theory.

Human capital theory is linked to the market-friendly policies that have been pursued with great force over the last decade, both globally and in South Africa. South Africa has become integrated into the global economy on terms that initially included extending the principles of the private sector to public spheres such as education. This has included greater reliance on notions of choice, but also a renewed commitment to, and articulation of, approaches to education such as human capital theory. These were first touted decades earlier but were subjected to signficant critique. These revitalised approaches echo those policies that have informed educational reform in many other parts of the world since the 1980s (see for example Fiske & Ladd 2000; Gewirtz, Ball & Bowe 1995; Whitty 1997). Amongst other things, criticisms quickly emerged that such policies were achieving macroeconomic targets at the expense of employment and equity (Habib 2003: 235). While South Africa's embrace of the market in education is tempered by the manifest need for intervention to achieve equity, human capital theory has enjoyed a relatively uncritical acceptance.

South Africa's transition to democracy occurred at a junction when the Washington consensus on pro-market policies was breaking down under the impact of a decade of criticism. It nonetheless was an influence, albeit not the only one, on South Africa's unfolding education and training policy in the first few years after 1994. In the theoretical rationale for policies embodied in the Washington consensus, markets will function well if left to themselves. Market imperfections may emerge, and if they do, the role of the state is to correct them. In principle, by reducing the role of the state and providing for greater choice, the state intends to achieve greater equality. Equilibrium will be derived from the pursuit and optimisation of individual choice. Individual behaviour and choice, based on the notion that individuals make decisions to maximise their welfare or utilities, thus lead to social change and social benefit. During the 1990s, this consensus broke down and a new, post-Washington consensus emerged. Its key features include an acceptance of the complementarity of states and markets and the role of custom and tradition. The problem, as Fine points out, is that its policy principles continue to be based on those of neoclassical economics and the methodological individualism of mainstream economics, which pays scant attention to the complexity of social and historical context and consequences of market processes (Fine 2001: 144). This is nowhere more evident than in the application of human capital theory to education.

Human capital theory posits that improving individual educational attributes will lead to economic growth. On the surface this is a concept with which few can disagree, in the sense that it may denote the wish for education and economic growth and a link between the two. As a descriptive wish, there is little harm in it. As an analytical tool and basis for making educational decisions, however, it is deeply problematic. The concept is usually applied in a manner that removes from the analysis of national education systems their history, social and economic content, complexity and interrelatedness with socio-economic and political structures, processes and struggles. The social struggles and relations that shape outcomes are not reducible to individuals maximising their utilities or to imperfections arising from a market which, if left to itself, would function perfectly and reward all, requisitely educated and trained, with economic and social benefits. This book demonstrates the flaws of such an approach by engaging in a full social analysis of education which takes its historical roots seriously (see also Unterhalter 2003). Thus, for example, with reference to this book, in order to understand what has changed, why and how, it is not enough to look at the relationship between the inputs and outputs of the system. Educational systems and their relationships to society are far more complex than this. Both inputs and outputs are situated within complex social, political and economic environments that have an impact on both, as well as the relationship and outcomes.

The role of the state is important in this analysis. The 1990s saw a sustained discussion of the role of globalisation in national development. At first, globalisation was seen as substantially eroding the role of the state which simply became regarded as the conduit for establishing global rules to ensure open markets at the national level. This was followed by some appreciation for the resilience of the national state or even contestation over global processes by national states in the adoption of new ideas and practices. South Africa provides a case for analysis of these broader trends, for it remains true that even as international borrowing or transfer is not a new phenomenon in South Africa, they continue to be 'indigenised by local social relations deeply fractured by the politics of racial power' (Chisholm 2002: 95). Put differently, the way that new global rules and related ideas are played out on the South African stage depends on the way they are taken up by local social actors in the context of historically-established social relations.

In the case of the analysis of the state, it is also important to acknowledge that the state is not homogenous and that there are differences and power struggles within the state as government, and within government, between departments and individuals. Chapters in this book also reveal contradictory dimensions within the same department: an educational state simultaneously withdrawing from direct control through decentralisation and playing a strong interventionist role through the restructuring, for example, of teacher and higher education. It is, however, also a state confronted not least by major problems in the skills base on which it is able to draw, as well as its authoritarian inheritance. The state itself is complex and operates in a complex environment. But dealing with the state alone takes us only part of the way towards an understanding and account of the unfolding character of education in post-apartheid South Africa. An understanding of changing social relations is also needed.

Several of the chapters suggest that South Africa's macroeconomic policy over the last decade has had marked and unintended effects in education. It is not difficult to provide evidence for the proposition that, even as the stated intent of post-apartheid's education policy-makers has been to reconcile the interests of competing and unequal social classes and races, those of a new deracialised middle class have come to predominate. The education budget has been reorganised, but it has not expanded. School financing policy has provided targeted funding for the poor but has protected public schools for the middle class. Curricula have promoted philosophies and forms of education which shift the goals of schooling but they also facilitate middle-class leadership and its creative self-expression. Decentralisation of schools has democratised local control but has given the middle classes the greatest command over how schools are run and what they can buy for their fees. Desegregated, formerly white, Indian and coloured schools have opened 'the doors of culture and learning' (ANC 1955) but have integrated only a minority of African children. They are offered the values and practices of middle-class schools which officially promote 'non-racialism' and gender equity but in practice are far from race-blind or gender-sensitive. Assessment practices have broadened but hide continuing inequalities of performance. Language policy recognises African languages but has enabled middle classes, and particularly white, English-speaking middle classes, to exercise choice and discretion in selection of the medium of instruction and, in so doing, to maintain their social dominance. The private school sector has mushroomed and includes many poorer African children, even as elite private schools have maintained their privilege. Higher education has also deracialised but simultaneously become more selective and competitive, regulating entry through its portals to the middle class in more stringent ways. On a somewhat different note, the position of teachers, as members of the middle class, has both improved and changed in relative terms.

Teacher education has shifted from its college base to higher education, the traditional locus for the creation of the professional salariat of the society. Expectations of teachers are different from what they were under apartheid and this is reflected in new approaches to teacher education curricula. Through the Education Labour Relations Council, teacher unions collectively enjoy recognition and have the ability to improve members' conditions of work. But this has to be balanced against the shift in the relative social status of teachers, which has negatively affected their ability to intervene in policy.

It is not surprising, in this overall analysis, that adult literacy classes have faltered, youth development has suffered, early childhood development remains under-resourced and that rural poor communities struggle with inadequate resources.

The major conclusion emerging from the book is both simple and dramatic. Educational development and the emerging system have favoured an expanding, racially-mixed middle class. In relative terms, serving the racially-mixed middle class necessarily gives whites an initial advantage. Some evidence does, however, also exist of growing intraracial class differentiation (Nattrass & Seekings 2001; 2002). Education plays a role in this differentiation. Favouring the middle class may not have been the conscious intent of policy; indeed, the stated intent has been the opposite: redress for the poor. Whatever the reasons for the gap between intent and outcomes, there is no doubt that the resulting social change is considerable in achievement and direction, but is characterised by the putative and loose coupling of a democratic project of deracialisation with neo-liberalism and 'the deracialisation of the apex of the class structure' (Daniel, Habib & Southall 2003: 20).

In drawing attention to the role of social class in education, the intent is not to assign blame and responsibility to one class for how South Africa has unfolded since 1994. What is at issue is analysis of the social significance of this class in South Africa's history and contemporary education, its relationship to other social classes, its raced and gendered character and the relationship of the nature of social change to the character of changing class and race relationships.

Although the power of corporate capital in South Africa is far from diminished, and the organised working class continues to contest and shape this power and the nature of the post-apartheid settlement, their influence on education was greatest at the moment of the shaping of policy. South Africa's NQF created through the *National Education Policy Act*, is widely seen as the product of the peculiar alliance that developed between them during the transition period of 1990 to 1994 (Allais 2003: 308/9). The NQF was predicated on the notion of the integration of education and training, an initially exciting idea whose assumptions about the relationship between education and economic growth soon chimed with the assumptions of human capital orthodoxy. Once this orthodoxy was in place, corporate capital appeared to retreat from attempting to influence the shape and direction of educational change. As Baatjes and Mathe suggest in their contribution to this book, there is evidence of precious little real concern even with minimal skills training of workers. This is not surprising when the changing nature, even transformation of South African corporate capital into a global operator, with shallow roots in South Africa and borderless horizons in the search for skills, is taken into account. The greater interest, as Bhorat shows, is in skilled labour, and accordingly higher education, also the new mantra of the complex of institutions around the World Bank purveying educational ideas. The educational aspirations of the organised working class have by contrast apparently become ensnared and institutionalised in the complex bureaucratic maze established by the NQF.

In this context, it is possible to argue that the middle class in South Africa has asserted itself. This middle class is heterogenous, consisting of a managerial and professional salariat within both the public and private sectors. It is internally divided, not least by history, and is continually shaped and recreated in its interactions with the external environment. Unravelling its particular role and aspirations in determining the shape of education in post-apartheid South Africa is thus not a simple matter. As a heterogenous and racially-segmented entity, the aspirations of its constituent elements are not singular. It is also not desirable to separate out its influence (or lack of influence) from that of other classes, whose role has been and continues to be equally powerful.

Neither this Introduction nor the authors tries to provide a definition of this middle class. It is clear that a great deal more mapping of this class in the contemporary period needs to be done. Full account must be taken of its own economic and social history, and similarities and differences from middle classes in other contexts (see, for example, Ball 2003 for an analysis of the class strategies of the middle classes in education in the United Kingdom). An important starting point must be Harold Wolpe's pioneering work on race and class in South Africa (1988). In a remarkable critique of studies which alternately emphasise only continuities or discontinuities between different historical periods, he argued that:

> ... an understanding, in any given period, of the political conjuncture requires an analysis which on the one hand is historically specific and on the other hand is not reduced solely to a descriptive account of struggles and events. To achieve this, it is necessary to analyse not only the prevailing struggles but also the structural conditions which mark the character of a period and provide the

specific context against which the content and direction of political conflicts can be understood. (1988: 3)

It is important not to over-simplify the issue; drawing attention to class is not to say that the racial base has disappeared and class determines social outcomes. Neither race nor racism has disappeared. Gender remains largely invisible. Race, class and gender remain powerfully articulated. And, as Soudien, drawing on Wolpe, demonstrates in this volume, we need to be aware of how 'our explanations of the realities we confront will always be grasping or incomplete', and how discourses of race, class and gender can 'displace complexity', shaped as they are by our 'representational modalities' and 'the multiple conscious and unconscious positions of privilege we call upon as we pronounce and enunciate'. But what we have to recognise, as he says, is that 'race, class, gender and language in South Africa are implicated in a complex of signs that are part of a process of profound social realignment in the country.'

A relatively new dimension of South Africa's middle class is that of the black middle class. The historical role of South Africa's black middle class has been traced in various social histories (see, for example, Kuper 1965; Marks 1986; Marks & Rathbone 1982). Using broad brushstrokes, it is possible to say that these social histories have explored the making of this class through mission education in the nineteenth century up to the middle of the twentieth century; and its frustration in the greater part of the twentieth century through the social segregation and legal framework of dispossession and disablement established by apartheid's political, economic, educational and social edifice. They have explored its essentially dependent position in relation, on the one hand, to a much more powerful white middle and upper class, its power secured through apartheid, and on the other to the broad mass of urban and rural working poor, marginalised and unemployed people. It was brutally suppressed in the 1950s and 1960s. Some of its members fled into exile and regrouped or sought a diminished place within the racial and balkanised political and economic framework created under apartheid. This class was and is neither united nor monolithic racially, ethnically or politically. Different choices were made and different political and social trajectories were and are possible within this class. Since 1990, the consolidation of a new racially-mixed middle class may owe something to new alliances between black and white as well as between new political elites and elites created by the apartheid state.

The democratisation of South African society and the dismantling of apartheid have enabled this class and indeed many sections of South African society to blossom and flourish. It has played a key role in building a new social order and shaping it in distinctive ways. Of course, it has not done this alone. This new black middle class has managed its historically dependent position in relationship to other classes in such a way that it has secured a base from which to transform both itself and the wider society. The chapters in the first section reveal important aspects of this process.

Filling out the theme of middle-class attainment reveals that the bigger picture is one of enormous complexity and diversity across provision as a whole, as is revealed in each of the areas investigated. Tensions and contradictions abound, and both positive and negative lessons can be extracted from the chapters. Several of the chapters cast fresh light on the past decade and provide new perspectives on institutional histories. One of the most compelling issues is that of gender. Much recent work suggests that access for both boys and girls is an achievement of the last decade. Girls in particular are doing well and staying in school (DoE 2003; Perry 2003; Subotzky 2003). When this information is disaggregated, it becomes clear that these trends correspond to racial hierarchies of historically established privilege. The relationship between these trends and the known high levels of gender violence and abuse in the society are unclear. However, there is some work to suggest that schools can be not only spaces safe from domestic violence, and thus promote achievement and success in school, but also unsafe spaces in so far as girls' vulnerability to abuse by male teachers is concerned (HSRC 2001). Another question is around what happens to girls when they leave school. Historically they have entered gender-specific forms of work and faced glass ceilings. The chapter by Govender, for example, reveals how the unions have played a major role in ensuring gender parity in conditions of work, taken up gender issues and made them central to their campaigns on HIV/AIDS, and struggled to ensure that women occupy leadership positions in the unions. The chapter raises questions about the impact of these campaigns over the last ten years.

Similarly, a number of chapters reflect on how social actors have responded to changed conditions. A complex story emerges of the extent to which parents, teachers and learners are acting on and in their changed contexts, institutions, and classrooms in order to ensure better life chances through education. One of the most telling in this regard is the chapter by Margaret Perrow which documents in great detail the way that youth working in and through the youth development organisation, the Joint Enrichment Project (JEP), have strug-gled to continue to make the organisation work for them in very changed circumstances from those of the late 1980s and early 1990s. Perrow tells the story of their negotiations and compromises with the new social order in the attempt to find some foothold in it. Baatjes and Mathe also record the rise and fall of adult literacy NGOs in the context of a dramatic decline in funding, the institutionalisation of adult education agendas by a new instrumentalism based on the human capital orthodoxy, and the continuing efforts to assert an emancipatory agenda within the context of civil society.

In highlighting the theme of 'changing class' the book draws attention to one major aspect of the transition: the way in which the conditions of market capitalism have resulted in an imperfectly realised democratic project. Despite the best will and policies in the world, an education system has unintentionally emerged that privileges a deracialised middle class. In this regard, it could be argued that social theory that privileges concepts of class, power, conflict and inequality has more to say about the unfolding character of South African education than does human capital theory.

Education and social change

That class is a critical component of the reconfigured education system is clear. The economic and political context of educational change at the national level must also play some role in explaining this unfolding character. This context is crucial to understanding the broad parameters of social change. Its key elements included a process of national reconciliation based on a historic compromise between old and new ruling elites accompanied by the creation of conditions for the globalisation and further intensification of South African capital. This involved, amongst other things, an unprecedented penetration of regional markets on the one hand and, on the other, a continuing and relentless decline of jobs, not only in mining and farming but also in the financial and services sectors inside South Africa. The creation of a democratic state committed to reliance on the market and fiscal austerity enabled political incorporation, but little respite from poverty and unemployment, as the chapter by Bhorat shows. New national and provincial governments were also hampered across the decade, as predicted in 1993 by the Macroeconomic

Research Group, by the institutional incapacity to deliver, arguably one of the greatest challenges in post-apartheid South Africa (Fine 2001: 163; MERG 1993; see also Nzimande & Mathieson 2000).

Given this context, how have discussions on education and social change in South Africa been conducted and how do the authors in this book approach the issue? The theme of education and social change has been heavily explored both internationally and locally. A veritable industry has emerged in the last two decades around different ways of defining, researching, analysing and understanding processes of change in and around education. Much of the literature has focused on 'educational reform', 'innovation', 'transition' and 'transformation' (see, for example, Fullan 1991, 1993; Griffin 2002; Halsey, Brown, Lauder & Wells 1997; Hargreaves 1998; Mebrahtu, Crossley & Johnson 2000). These concepts have shaped the subjective as well as analytical perspectives with which the relationship of education to broader social processes has been discussed. The latter have included, pre-eminently, globalisation, changing forms of work, and transitions from authoritarian to democratic rule in many parts of the world. The impact and ramifications of the marketisation of education have been seen as a dimension of both the dismantled liberal, democratic, welfarist European governments, as well as of the newly-established liberal, democratic governments and education policy regimes of Eastern Europe and many African countries.

Central to the notion of marked social change is a sense of historical difference, whether this be described as 'transition', 'reform' or 'transformation'. The focus on 'change', 'transition', 'reform' and 'transformation' in the 1990s often involved an ahistorical use of these concepts, innocent of their political and ideological content or context. The use of these terms interchangeably has tended to empty them of specific meaning. To signal and, hopefully, to avoid this danger, the term 'social change' is used throughout this volume. There was, otherwise, no effort to fix one approach to social change amongst contributing authors, so that the concept of 'social change' is used in different ways. Some authors emphasise the role of social *reproduction* within a broader process of social transformation, while others focus on policies in this period as a source of significant, not necessarily anticipated, social change over the longer term. Some emphasise the interrelationship of continuity and change, and yet others the potential of education, such as adult basic education, to serve as vehicles for radical discontinuities. In short, the term 'social change' is variously deployed to emphasise diversity and complexity, contradictions and tensions and, not least, specificity in studying a society seeking to emancipate itself from the inheritance of apartheid.

The use of social change in this way represents a sea change in approach as it succeeds two decades or more of writing on the role of education in South Africa as either legitimating inequality or as a weapon of change. Neither approach on its own is entirely satisfactory. An emphasis on the role of education as a mirror of social inequality cannot account for those instances where education has been a force and vehicle for change. But an emphasis on the role of education as an agent of transformation at the expense of a consideration of its role in maintaining the status quo is equally inadequate. 'Education,' as Nasson and Samuel observed in 1990, 'is particularly equipped both to maintain the existing social order and also to promote varying kinds of change or mobility'(1990: 1). Or, as Nasson put it in relation to the question of social change, 'education might be seen as an important participating force, but not as an arbitrating one' (1990: 103). He cites Robinson, writing almost a decade earlier, in 1982, as saying that 'although education cannot transform the world, the world cannot be transformed without education' (Nasson 1990). A combination of the two approaches is preferable to each on its own, regardless of the period under discussion. This combination should also take care not to read change as good and reproduction as bad under all circumstances. Above all, we need to locate the forces at work in their specificity.

Thus, for some, the negotiated transition of elite-pacting consolidated a social democratic order within which education could and did begin to play a role in promoting upward social mobility (Adam & Moodley 1993; Van Zyl Slabbert 1992; Webster & Adler 1995 for a critique). For others, at the opposite extreme, the international neo-liberal, Washington consensus combined with a new and compliant national bourgeoisie created the conditions for little change to occur through and in education which continued to reflect wider social inequalities (Bond 2000; Marais 2001). There may be truth in both these perspectives. There has been both change and continuity. The transition to democracy has consolidated elites. Although this has been and continues to be a contested process, these elites have accommodated to the power and interests of corporate capital and social inequalities do continue to widen. But some have benefited and others not. This link requires a consideration of more than policy and a focus on the role of social actors. While the parameters of social action are set by international and local contexts, new social forces are shaping the social environment and new possibilities are being created within these parameters for some.

To date, writing on South African education following the transition has focused on the paradox of change and non-change. This literature has not reflected much on the relationship between the changing political economy of race, class and gender and the unfolding character of education. Following the initial euphoria after 1994, and the adoption of market-oriented policies, framed within a discourse of emancipation from authoritarian apartheid controls, critical work began to appear in the latter part of the 1990s. Both the experience of government as well as the increasingly apparent, 'profound shift away from the original premises that had been established by the democratic movement in the early 1990s' (Kraak & Young 2000: 2) resulted in writers beginning to probe the processes by which this shift had occurred and the reasons for it. The shifting gaps between principle and practice, between policy and implementation, and between researchers and policy-makers came under scrutiny. Concern focused on the nature of change: its limited extent was variously interpreted as non-change, symbolic change, and failed implementation.

Two basic approaches, linked to critiques of globalisation and drawing on postmodernism, have informed this interrogation of 'change': those that focus on the nature of the state and bureaucracy and those that focus on policy. Those explanations that focus on the state and bureaucracy make one of two arguments. The first argument emphasises the neo-liberal character of the state operating in a global context where the marketisation of education and the imperative towards fiscal austerity form part of the constraining environment within which education policy reform occurs. Fiscal constraints, lack of capacity and contradictions between different policy goals all contribute to the failures of implementation (Motala & Pampallis 2001).

The second argument emphasises the role of the state and bureaucracy as agents of change and sees them in a more benign way as directing – and limiting – social change. Fleisch's semi-autobiographical work exemplifies this kind of approach (2002). Neither argument focuses on the relationship between reconfigured relations within the state and social class, although Fleisch does refer to the critical role of 'former activists-turned-bureaucrats' within the new bureaucracy. It is necessary to add to these analyses a sense of the real politics and conflicts that attend the policy process.

The second type of explanation focuses on policy. Some see the shift as a simple process of loss of idealism and greater realism about what is achievable, deploying concepts such as 'policy maturation' and 'policy slippage' (Kraak & Young 2000: 10). By far the most influential has been that of Sayed and Jansen (2001) and Jansen (2000). Sayed highlights the tensions and contradictions in the different discourses shaping and underpinning policy whereas Jansen develops the notion of 'policy as symbolism'. Education policy, Jansen argues, 'is best described as a struggle for the achievement of a broad political symbolism that would mark the shift from apartheid to post-apartheid society' (2000: 46). Non-change in South African education is largely the consequence of policy being political symbolism: 'every single case of education policy-making demonstrates, in different ways, the preoccupation of the state with settling policy struggles in the political domain rather than the realm of practice' (2000: 46). The consequences of this are, he argues, negative for education: 'the reliance on political symbolism as the overarching framework for education policy-making effectively rules out any major transformation of education in South Africa's future ... But schools will not change and education quality will not improve' (2001: 6). This argument is appealing, but it may also be necessary to look at who has benefited and who has not, as well as at the real and material effects on teachers, parents and classrooms of decisions that regulate the content and control of, spending on, and access to, education.

Rather than trying to explain why or whether or not there has been change in the contemporary period, Kallaway's authors (2002) begin a process of re-interpreting earlier periods of South Africa's history. Observing the deep continuities that exist between approaches to policy in earlier and contemporary periods (and particularly the policies of the 1980s' National Party and the 1990s) Kallaway raises profound questions about the relationship between the past and the present (2002: 1–94).

Seen against the broad backdrop of history and South Africa's changing political economy, the authors in this volume examine the consequences of the 'uncertain framework of political and moral compromise that formed the background' to South Africa's transition to democracy (Kallaway 2002: 10). They show how the market-friendly orientation of the state has been a major factor in shaping unfolding policy and the character of change. The state and bureaucracy are seen as key players, but not as independent from the changing political economy and the role played by a broader array of social actors. These can exist inside and outside the state and act as classed, raced and gendered beings who themselves have changed in the context of broader social change.

Changing contours

The first five chapters in this book look at the changing contours of the system in its interaction with wider social change. These papers are not *about* the expanded middle class, but they reveal its impact and role in key areas of education and so draw attention to it.

Haroon Bhorat's opening chapter underscores the fact that South Africa's transition has been a pre-eminently political one: the economic consequences of apartheid are still acutely present. His examination of labour market trends in the past decade shows that the most significant shift has been the rising demand for skilled labour across all races coupled with the surprising new phenomenon of graduate unemployment and continued high levels of unemployment amongst educated youth and poorly-educated adults. His chapter suggests a growing bifurcation between those endowed with economic and educational advantages and those without. Those with these advantages are able to benefit from new opportunities afforded by a change of political climate. As he puts it, 'the winners have been the highly skilled while the losers have been almost without exception unskilled workers.'

One of the most controversial educational policies in the last decade has been that relating to school fees. Fiske and Ladd take an in-depth and sober look at the consequences of this policy. They show that South Africa adopted fees for a number of reasons including limited public funding available for education, pressures for local control and the argument made by two international consultants that fees would keep the middle class in the public school sector. Using data from the Eastern Cape and Western Cape, they argue that fees *did* keep the middle class in the public school sector but were not responsible for keeping children out of primary school. The private school sector remains small, enrolling only 2.1 per cent of South Africa's learners. However, fees are charged according to income. As a result, social class reinforces inequalities by enabling wealthier schools to appoint more teachers who are responsible for improved quality and they also force parents to select schools on the basis of fees. Fees have done little to help historically disadvantaged schools: they have not freed up more funds for redistribution. They have not enabled schools to become more efficient in so far as poorer schools have found it difficult to collect fees, use scarce resources to do so and generally end up with too small a revenue to make any difference to the overall budget and operations of the school. Formerly disadvantaged schools thus continue to suffer from inadequate resources. To address the situation, the authors suggest that schools continue to be given a certain baseline allotment as they currently are, but that in addition they can choose between either setting fees and doing with the fees what they want or, in lieu of charging fees, receiving an extra allotment of teachers.

Crain Soudien's chapter both brings into sharp relief the extent of deracialisation of schools and introduces subtle new ways of understanding integration. He shows that the overwhelming movement has been of Africans into formerly English-speaking white, Indian and coloured schools. There has been virtually no movement in the opposite direction, towards African schools. Large chunks of the system remain mono-racial. In those small pockets where classrooms are mixed, the dominant mode of 'integration' has been assimilation into the dominant ethos, which is also usually race-, gender- and class-inflected. He finds little evidence for the existence of anti-racist schools. And he draws attention to the 'distinct realignment of socio-economic groups' taking place through the schools 'with the large-scale exodus of middle class black parents and their children out of the former DET and HoD and HoR systems into the former white systems'. This drift towards a new middle-class alignment has, he argues, also been facilitated by the *South African Schools Act*. The establishment of School Governing Bodies (SGBs) has 'projected parental identity around a restrictive middle class notion of who parents were', and the cultural and financial resources they can draw on. The result is a domination of SGBs in poor schools by principals and teachers and in formerly white areas by white, middle-class parents. In this way, the new and enlarged middle class has driven the nature of the new system but it has apparently also been accepted by the poor.

Whether decentralisation through the *South African Schools Act* and establishing SGBs has indeed enhanced equity, democracy and quality – the goals of the policy – is the subject of the chapter by Grant Lewis and Motala. Making sense of a disparate local literature, they argue that these goals have not been met, except in resource-rich contexts. They reflect on the limited nature of the research in South Africa, which has focused on whether implementation has been faithful to the original intentions, and propose moving away from analysis of policy intents to researching, analysing and understanding local practice in terms of 'theories of action'. Despite the evidence they provide of implementation not achieving stated goals, they do not see any real possibilities for reversing this process of decentralisation. Hofmeyr and Lee's contribution on the growth of private schooling in low-fee, black, independent schools sees this also as something that is not likely to be reversed. This change has been as dramatic as that of decentralisation through SGBs. Hofmeyr and Lee show that, although this sector remains extremely small within the overall system, by 2004 it had grown to almost three times the size it was in 1990. Their work, like that by Fiske and Ladd, suggests that the middle class has chosen to stay in public schools rather than move to the private sector. Instead of a neat dichotomy between public and independent schools, they see a 'continuum' of schools in which the parallels are greater between the privileged public and private schools and the poorer public and private schools than between public and private alone. Like decentralisation, this is an area that needs much more research and analysis both for its substance as well as for its implications.

Together the chapters mentioned so far paint a picture of an expanded, mixed middle class that patronises a public school system that is internally differentiated by race but also increasingly by class. Similarly, the private sector in schools has grown but so too has the gap between rich and poor in this sector.

Changing landscapes

The chapters in the second section of this book look at the stuff of education: language policy, curriculum and assessment processes, teacher education, unionisation and higher education.

Language policy in education and curriculum were vehicles for the intellectual dispossession that characterised apartheid. Reversing the damage of apartheid education has been the task of the entire educational edifice, but perhaps language, curriculum and assessment have been critical, as they set the goals and parameters within which teachers and administrators operate. The repression and restrictions of apartheid also weighed heavily on unions and in higher education. The chapters in this section provide an analysis of the nature and direction of change since 1994. The changes they reveal are ambiguous and contradictory.

Mda's chapter problematises current multilingual policies in education and looks at how English, despite being spoken as a first language by a minority, still shapes conceptions of what is desired. Her chapter traverses a difficult, contested and multifaceted terrain with great simplicity. She speaks to the multilingual classrooms that prevail in urban and multicultural schools, but also raises critical questions regarding language policy in rural areas. Harley and Wedekind's chapter is concerned with the contradiction between the approach to Curriculum 2005 (C2005), introduced in schools from 1997, in well-resourced and poor schools. In the former it appears to be used effectively and in the latter it is seen primarily as an instrument for social and political action. They explain this in terms of C2005 being essentially a political rather than a pedagogical project. In addition, they argue that strong historical continuities exist between C2005 and what was common practice in formerly white schools and strong discontinuities exist between the historically disadvantaged schools and the new expectations. They argue, on the one hand, that the practice of the new policy has had the effect of undermining the policy vision in the majority of schools and, on the other, that learner-centredness is not foreign to the middle classes with its belief in individual autonomy. They argue that social reproduction is clearly taking place through the curriculum, but that this fit is not a functional one.

Each chapter in the book uses a slightly different form of periodisation, consistent with conceptions of key developments in each period. Muller introduces a three-phase periodisation to trace the history and tensions inherent in the assessment and qualifications system bequeathed by apartheid and transformed into the NQF. His chapter deals with a complex set of changes, their interrelationships, successes and failures in three main periods: what he calls 'relative policy stasis' between the 1980s and 1994; 'policy reform and increased tension' in phase two, 1994 to 2000; and 'the advent of systemic reform and quality assurance in phase three, 2000 to 2002. Underlying the discussion is the tension in the effort to integrate education and training manifested in the NQF. Muller distinguishes and describes the conflicts between what he calls the administrative and pedagogical progressives in the Departments of Labour and Education (DoL, DoE) respectively, who are associated with promoting either centralised or decentralised forms of assessment. In the context of an unresolved tension between diagnostic and systemic assessments, he shows how assessments of learner performance have uniformly shown not only low achievement in numeracy, literacy and life-skills, but also revealed that South African performance in these areas is amongst the lowest third on the African continent. He concludes that, 'with the present direction in place, there will be class differentiation of outcomes and hence an exacerbation of disadvantage, progressive rhetoric notwithstanding, although this disadvantage will be kept more invisible than it should be by the continued lack of performance data that only comprehensive systemic assessment can provide'.

The whole world in which teachers, their educators and unions move has changed. Realignments have occurred at every level. Govender argues that the face of unions has shifted dramatically as well as their relationship with government. In 2002, the South African Democratic Teachers' Union (SADTU) membership stood at 210 235, the National Professional Teachers' Organisation of South Africa (NAPTOSA) membership at 95 988 and the Suid Afrikaanse Onderwysersunie (SAOU) at 41 315. The chapter tracks the changing relationships and shifting fortunes of SADTU, NAPTOSA and SAOU showing how they and their members have benefited from a new labour relations dispensation, recognition by the DoE, and substantial sources of income. Major challenges for all unions remain gender and HIV/AIDS. The chapter concludes that 'a powerful teacher union presence in the policy domain, with the potential to influence issues of economic and social justice, has become a reality'.

Sayed's contribution argues that changes in teacher education have been amongst the most significant that have occurred since 1994. The restructuring, amalgamation and incorporation of teacher education into universities, as well as the reorientation of curricula, have had massive implications for expectations of what teachers and teacher education should do. These changes in teacher education have bucked much of the international trend. Policy in this domain has been far from symbolic; he describes them as 'substantive and fundamental' and as having major long-term implications. This is all the more so if account is taken of the numbers of teachers and college trainers who were made redundant by the changes and who reappear in Bhorat's unemployed graduates. Change and continuity are two sides of the same coin, as Jansen shows.

Jansen is concerned with both change and continuity. His chapter concludes that the consequence of changes in higher education over the last ten years has been permanent alteration of social relationships within universities, the political relationship between government and universities, and the economic relationship between universities and their competitors. In this assessment, the continuities are as strong: the profile of academic staff remains largely white and male, and institutional cultures have remained more or less the same. Here a similar dynamic seems to be operating as in schools, where the assimilationist dynamic that Soudien describes reinforces the dominant class and racial character of particular institutions. And even as student bodies may have become more diverse, this has not been matched by a similar process in staff profiles.

Changing margins

In a book of this kind there are silent changes that are difficult to capture. Anyone with a history in the decades before 1990 will remember the power and significance of civil society, school, youth and higher education student organisations. Education was an arena for the mobilisation and political expression of entire generations (Badat 1999). Today, as Jansen's chapter demonstrates, they play a very different role. That they are on the margins of a new system is, however, clear, as is demonstrated in the next set of chapters which deal sequentially with the overall NGO scenario, the field of early childhood development (ECD), youth development, and adult education. A final chapter, on private contracting, links the worlds of government, NGOs and the private sector. Each chapter says something about state–civil society relationships and how they have unfolded over the past decade. The chapters in this final section deal with some of those for whom the changes have not been as positive and beneficial as they may have been for the middle class. As these chapters indicate, the social actors within each of the spheres discussed have responded to changes in ways that reveal resilience and adaptation to changed circumstances.

Even within these *milieux*, there are those who have benefited and those who have not, as Morrow shows in his chapter on educational NGOs. Formerly sites of resistance and incubators of change and alternatives to dominant codes and practices, NGOs have been forced to compromise with the new business and/or education-speak in order to survive. As donor funding has gone to government, many NGOs have died. Some survived and adapted to a more commercial environment than the one in which they were formed. In some respects more dependent and compliant than in the apartheid years, their role in South Africa, as Morrow shows in his overview, cannot be compared with either that of the large charity-NGOs or of NGOs in other African countries. As such, they currently constitute a defensive space from which contradictory positions and practices are articulated. If NGOs are a small and beleaguered shadow of their former selves, then the student and youth movements in schools, communities and universities which so profoundly marked South Africa's history in the last three decades of the twentieth century have all but disappeared into the ranks of South Africa's reconstituted middle and working classes.

Porteus's chapter is concerned with the peripheral placement of ECD in the first decade of post-apartheid South Africa. She neatly contrasts two models of care: an institutional model, preferred by the Department of Finance (DoF) but not supported by either research or a pilot project, and a community-based model, in which women in informal settings take care of children. Emerging policy towards the end of the millennium has prioritised the institutional Reception Year as the preferred model, but under-investment raises questions about the feasibility of this model. The chapter also discusses why the Reception Year became the preferred model. In the context of this argument she presents a wealth of information on the situation of children in poverty in South Africa and the various policy, pilot and research initiatives undertaken to address ECD.

At the outset of the book, Bhorat draws attention to the substantial levels of unemployment amongst relatively well-educated youth. Perrow looks at youth development in South Africa through the lens of the unfolding history of JEP, an NGO which took up youth issues in the key period of South Africa's transition. She argues that the material reality of most young people, especially poor, black youth, has not changed dramatically since 1992, and that the organisations representing their interests at national level have undergone significant shifts linked to broader contextual changes. The history of JEP reflects the patterns that have affected the youth sector. One of the main shifts over the decade was that youth issues were brought within the ambit of the central state after 1995. She shows how, as the external political and social climate changed, JEP underwent corresponding discursive shifts. In successive periods over the last decade it articulated a discourse of collectivity and resistance, systemic capacity-building and individual skill-development, a 'development discourse' of productivity, accountability and efficiency, and a self-reflexive discourse of individuation and strategising in a competitive free market.

The chapter by Ivor Baatjes and Khulekani Mathe focuses the lens on a field which had a small but vibrant NGO community at the outset of democracy. The chapter looks at changes in the sector in the light of the notion that adult education can be an agent for social change. It contrasts two approaches to adult education: emancipatory and instrumentalist adult basic education (ABE). It argues that the ability of ABE to be a vehicle for social change has been severely constrained by the dominance in the last decade of instrumentalist approaches to ABE. These have seen the simultaneous rise and fall of ABE NGOs, institutionalisation and formalisation of adult basic education and training (ABET), the failure of state-sponsored mass ABE campaigns, and continued poor quality and level of ABE provision. Institutions established to promote skills development amongst workers, the SETAs, have to date not delivered on their promise. On-the-job and college-based skills development training are not dealt with in any great depth in this book (see Cosser, McGrath, Badroodien & Maja 2003; McGrath, Badroodien, Kraak & Unwin 2004). The chapters by Bhorat, Baatjes and Mathe point to the significance, possibilities and limitations of changes introduced through the SETAs. And Perrow provides a perspective on how training and development institutions such as NGOs have responded to changed external forces. In this bleak environment, organisations and agencies concerned with literacy of adults have re-emerged: connecting with organisations in civil society, they are revitalising the radical tradition in ABE.

Pampallis's contribution focuses on those professional NGOs and private companies that provide services to government, and on how this relationship has developed over the past decade in a mutual process of changed state operations and changed positionings of NGOs and the for-profit sector. He poses the question as to whether government should seek to encourage and support the non-profit NGO sector by favouring NGOs in the awarding of tenders or by subsidising them in some other way. His chapter is also of relevance to all local NGOs that have been forced to reorient themselves to some form of 'service-delivery' for government in implementing its programmes. He argues that in addressing the medium- to long-term policy issues, the education authorities and the government need to engage in some reflection on what is to become of the small but growing industry that has been spawned. A whole cadre of skilled education professionals – consultants, trainers, managers, analysts, researchers, evaluators, assessment specialists and others – has developed outside of the public education system and is being supported to a large extent by foreign funding. This is untenable and undesirable. The chapter raises questions about the changing nature of the state and civil society in South Africa and returns us to the first chapter which draws attention to the high demand for skilled labour of all colours in the context of major and sustained unemployment amongst South Africa's black youth.

Conclusion

As in periods before it, the conscious intent of policy has been contradicted by its outcomes. But this does not mean that there has been no 'change' or 'transformation'. The social position of some individuals and the racial composition of South Africa's classes have changed. The context within which they act has changed. The underlying rationale for policy and action has changed. This in turn has influenced individual and social strategies and choices, as much in policy as in practice. The outcome has been a reconfigured and realigned system, which officially gives opportunities to all but, in practice, allows the middle classes to benefit from them while the urban and working poor struggle to do so within contexts of severe social and economic deprivation.

Many classrooms, or sites of education, have experienced the impact of these changes in dramatic form – whether in the form of changed racial and class composition, the pressure to implement a host of new policies, or reflect new entrepreneurial modes of conducting educational activities. Many others still look the same in practice – in the nature of educational practices and social relationships inside them, as well as the extent to which social class, poverty and inequality reach into and out of classrooms. The challenge is not only to appreciate the links between education and social change over time but also to address its consequences in all its ramifications. If a new social order is being established through education, and education is helping to shape this new social order, then there remains a powerful role for education to challenge the old, the continuing and the new inequalities and injustices.

The conceptual tools for such an analysis lie in a full appreciation of the structural conditions within which these changes have occurred, the agency of social actors, and the nature of education systems as comprehensively contextual systems of provision rather than decontextualised processors of a limited range of inputs.

References

Adam, H & Moodley, K (1993) *Negotiated Revolution: Society and Politics in Post-Apartheid South Africa*. Johannesburg: Jonathan Ball

Allais, SM (2003) The National Qualifications Framework in South Africa: A Democratic Project trapped in a Neo-Liberal Paradigm, *Journal of Education and Work,* 16: 305–324

African National Congress (1955) *The Freedom Charter*

Badat, S (1999) *Black Student Politics: Higher Education and Apartheid. From SASO to SANSCO 1968–1990*. Pretoria: HSRC

Ball, SJ (2003) *Class Strategies and the Education Market: The Middle Classes and Social Advantage*. London and New York: Routledge Falmer

Bond, P (2000) *Elite Transition: From Apartheid to Neo-Liberalism in South Africa*. London: Pluto Press

Chisholm, L (2002) Continuity and Change in Education Policy Research and Borrowing in South Africa. In Kallaway, P (ed) *The History of Education under Apartheid 1948–1994*. Cape Town: Pearson Education

Cosser, M; McGrath, S; Badroodien, A & Maja, B (eds) (2003) *Technical College Responsiveness*. Cape Town: HSRC Publishers

Daniel, J; Habib, A & Southall, R (eds) (2003) *State of the Nation: South Africa 2003–2004*. Cape Town: HSRC Press

Department of Education (2003) *Education Statistics in South Africa at a Glance in 2001*. Pretoria: Government Printers

Fine, B (2001) *Social Capital versus Social Theory: Political Economy and Social Science at the Turn of the Millennium*. London and New York: Routledge

Fine, B (2002) *The World of Consumption: The Material and Cultural Revisited*. London: Routledge

Fine, B & Rose, P (2001) Education and the Post-Washington Consensus – *Plus ca Change?* In Fine, B; Lapavitsas, C & Pincus, J (eds) *Neither Washington nor Post-Washington Consensus: Challenging Development Policy in the Twenty First Century*. London: Routledge

Fiske, E & Ladd, H (2000) *When Schools Compete: A Cautionary Tale*. Washington: Brookings Institution Press

Fleisch, BD (2002) *Managing Educational Change: The State and School Reform in South Africa*. Johannesburg: Heinemann

Fullan, Michael G (1993) *Change Forces*. London: Falmer Press

Fullan, Michael G with Stiegelbauer, S (1991) *The New Meaning of Educational Change*. Second Edition. New York: Teachers College Press

Gewirtz, S; Ball, SJ & Bowe, R (1995) *Markets, Choice and Equity in Education*. Buckingham, Philadelphia: Open University Press

Griffin, R (2002) *Education in Transition: International Perspectives on the Politics and Processes of Change*. Oxford: Symposium Books

Habib, A (2003) State-Civil Society Relations in Post-Apartheid South Africa. In Daniel, J; Habib, A & Southall, R (eds) *State of the Nation. South Africa 2003–2004*. Cape Town: HSRC Press

Halsey, AH; Brown, P; Lauder, H & Stuart Wells, A (1997) *Education: Culture, Economy, Society*. Oxford: Oxford University Press

Hargreaves, A (ed) (1998) *International Handbook of Educational Change*. London: Kluwer Academic Publishers

Human Sciences Research Council CYFD (2001) *A Study of School Responses to Violence and Harassment of Girls*. Pretoria: HSRC

Jansen, J (2000) Rethinking Education Policy-Making in South Africa: Symbols of Change, Signals of Conflict. In Kraak & Young (eds), *Education in Retrospect*. Pretoria: HSRC

Jansen, J & Christie, P (1999) *Changing Curriculum: Studies on Outcomes-Based Education in South Africa*. Cape Town: Juta

Kallaway, P (ed) (2002) *The History of Education under Apartheid 1948–1994: The Doors of Learning and Culture shall be Opened*. Cape Town: Pearson Education

Kraak, AH & Young, M (eds) (2000) *Education in Retrospect*. Pretoria: HSRC

Kuper, L (1965) *An African Bourgeoisie: Race, Class and Politics in South Africa*. New Haven: Yale University Press

Macroeconomic Research Group (MERG) (1993) *Making Democracy Work: A Framework for Macroeconomic Policy in South Africa*. Cape Town: Centre for Development Studies

Marais, H (2001) *Limits to Change: The Political Economy of Transition*. Second Edition. Cape Town: University of Cape Town Press and London: Zed Books

Marks, S (1986) *Ambiguities of Dependence: State, Class and Nationalism in Early Twentieth Century Natal.* Johannesburg: Ravan Press

Marks, S & Rathbone, R (1982) *Industrialisation and Social Change: African Class Formation, Culture and Consciousness, 1870–1930.* London: Longman

McGrath, S; Badroodien, A; Kraak, A & Unwin, L (eds) (2004) *Shifting Understandings of Skills in South Africa.* Cape Town: HSRC Press

Mebrahtu, T; Crossley, M & Johnson, D (2000) *Globalisation, Educational Transformation and Societies in Transition.* Oxford: Symposium Books

Motala, E & Pampallis, J (2001) *Education & Equity: The Impact of State Policies on South African Education.* Johannesburg: Heinemann

Nasson, B (1990) Education and Poverty. In Nasson, B & Samuel, J *Education: From Poverty to Liberty; Report for the Second Carnegie Inquiry into Poverty and Development in Southern Africa.* Cape Town: David Philip

Nasson, B & Samuel, J (1990) Introduction. In Nasson, B & Samuel, J *Education: From Poverty to Liberty; Report for the Second Carnegie Inquiry into Poverty and Development in Southern Africa.* Cape Town: David Philip

Nattrass, N & Seekings, J (2001) Democracy and Distribution in Highly Unequal Economies: The Case of South Africa, *Journal of Modern African Studies*, 39(3): 471–499

Nzimande, B & Mathieson, S (2000) Educational Transformation in South Africa's Transition to Democracy. In Mebrahtu, T; Crossley, M & Johnson, D (eds) *Globalisation, Educational Transformation and Societies in Transition.* Oxford: Symposium Books

Perry, H (2003) Female Performance in the Senior Certificate Examination: Excellence Hiding behind the Averages, *Edusource data News* 39: 14–25

Sayed, Y & Jansen, J (2001) *Implementing Education Policies: The South African Experience.* Cape Town: University of Cape Town Press

Subotzky, G (2003) Addressing Equity and Excellence in Relation to Employment in Higher Education, *Edusource data News* 38: 1–13

Unterhalter, E (1998) Economic Rationality or Social Justice? Gender, the National Qualifications Framework and Educational Reform in South Africa, 1989–1996, *Cambridge Journal of Education*, 28 (3): 351–368

Unterhalter, E (2003) The Capabilities Approach and Gendered Education. An Examination of South African Complexities, *Theory and Research in Education*, 1: 7–22

Van Zyl Slabbert, F (1992) *The Quest for Democracy*. Johannesburg: Penguin

Webster, E & Adler, G (1995) Challenging Transition Theory: The Labour Movement, Radical Reform and the Transition to Democracy in South Africa, *Politics and Society*, 23 (1): 76–106

Whitty, G (1997) Creating Quasi-markets in Education: A Review of Recent Research on Parental Choice and School Autonomy in Three Countries. In Apple, MW (ed) *Review of Research in Education*, 22: 3–47. Washington DC: American Education Research Association

Wolpe, H (1988) *Race, Class and the Apartheid State*. London: James Currey, OAU & Unesco Press

Section 1

Changing contours

Chapter 1: The development challenge in
post-apartheid South African education   31

Haroon Bhorat

Chapter 2: Balancing public and private resources for
basic education: school fees in post-apartheid
South Africa   57

Edward Fiske and Helen Ladd

Chapter 3: 'Constituting the class': an analysis of the
process of 'integration' in South African schools   89

Crain Soudien

Chapter 4: Educational de/centralisation and the quest
for equity, democracy and quality   115

Suzanne Grant Lewis and Shireen Motala

Chapter 5: The new face of private schooling   143

Jane Hofmeyr and Simon Lee

CHANGING CLASS

1 The development challenge in post-apartheid South African education

Haroon Bhorat

Introduction

Following the onset of democratic rule in South Africa in April 1994, it soon became clear that the transition was a political one, in the narrowest sense of the term. Specifically, the new South African government has been, and indeed continues to be, beset with the longer term and more inertial consequences of apartheid. These consequences can be represented generically as the economic outcomes engendered by the policy of legislated racial exclusivity. Nowhere is this challenge more acute than within the arena of the labour market. The ability of the domestic economy to generate a sufficient quantum of jobs has constantly come under policy-makers' scrutiny.

This chapter documents and identifies key trends in the labour market. It begins by questioning the notion of jobless growth as characteristic of the post-apartheid labour market, and goes on to explore just how poor employment growth has been over the last decade. It examines the nature of employment trends by race, gender and sector and contrasts these with the educational characteristics of the unemployed. Using the October Household Survey for 1995 and Labour Force Survey of 2002, the chapter argues that the most significant shift in the labour market over the last ten years has been the rising demand for skilled labour across all races, coupled with the surprising new phenomenon of graduate unemployment and continued high levels of unemployment amongst poorly-educated youth and adults.

The chapter concludes with a brief analysis of the challenge for education and skills development. The implications for all levels of the education system are explored in greater depth in succeeding chapters.

Post-apartheid trends in the labour market

The democratic government inherited a labour market that had been subject to the long-run effects of both structural shifts and technological change in the domestic economy. The former was represented by the shift in output away from the primary sectors, toward the services sectors, while the latter has of course been manifest in the onset of the microelectronics revolution as well as significant increases in capital-labour ratios. The labour market consequences have been an increase in the demand for highly-skilled workers, combined with large-scale attrition at the bottom-end of the labour market.[1] The post-apartheid period has also been marked by the addition of one crucial causal variable – the relatively poor performance in economic growth. There can be no doubt that this low level of output expansion has impacted negatively on the propensity of the economy to create employment. We turn now to consider some of the labour market shifts in greater detail, against the backdrop of these tepid growth levels.

Table 1.1 on the next page presents a snapshot of the key labour market statistics for the period 1995 to 2002. Concentrating on the labour force data according to the expanded definition of unemployment (the 'unofficial' definition), it is evident that over this period, the economy created about 1.6 million jobs. While the sectoral and skills detail of this growth did of course vary, it is clear that the notion of aggregate 'jobless growth' in the South African economy is erroneous. The economy, in the aggregate, has been creating jobs rather than shedding them.

It is important though to try to place this absolute expansion of employment into context. Specifically, it is necessary to assess the number of jobs that were created relative to the new entrants that came into the labour market annually between 1995 and 2002. The data indicates that between 1995 and 2002, the number of new entrants increased by about five million individuals. This has meant, therefore, that about 3.4 million individuals – some of whom were first-time entrants into the labour market – have been rendered or have remained jobless since 1995. As a result of this employment performance, unemployment levels increased to over seven million individuals in 2002.

Table 1.1 A snapshot of key labour market trends: 1995 to 2002

Category	1995	2002	Change	Change (percentage)	Target growth rate	Employment absorption rate
Employment	9 557 185	11 157 818	1 600 633	16.75		
Unemployment (expanded definition)	3 883 819	7 288 833	3 405 014	87.67		
Labour force	13 441 004	18 446 651	5 005 647	37.24	52.38	31.98
Official Definition Estimates						
Employment	9 557 185	11 157 818	1 600 633	16.75		
Unemployment (strict definition)	1 909 468	4 271 302	2 361 834	123.69		
Labour force	11 466 653	15 429 120	3 962 467	34.56	41.46	40.39

Sources: October Household Survey, 1995 and Labour Force Survey, February 2002 (see statssa.gov.za)
Notes:
1. The Official Definition Estimates are based on the assumption of the strict definition of unemployment, and hence conceive of a labour market that excludes the discouraged workseeker.
2. The 1995 data has been re-weighted with the 1996 census weights to ensure comparability across the two time periods.

Much of the debate around employment trends in the post-apartheid period has become anchored around the notion of 'jobless growth' – that in combination with unspectacular economic growth, jobs have been simultaneously shed across most sectors in the economy. The initial data here makes it plain that the economy did not experience an absolute decline in employment. Put differently, the notion of 'jobless growth' characterising post-1995 employment trends is simply wrong. However, while South Africa did not have jobless growth in this period, it clearly had employment growth that was insufficient relative to the growth in the labour force.

The data from Table 1.1 suggests that while employment grew at 17 per cent over the period, if all the new entrants were to have been placed into employment since 1995, employment would have needed to grow by 52 per cent over the period. In other words, in order to maintain unemployment at its 1995 levels, employment should have risen by just over three times the existing rate. In terms of the employment absorption rate, the data suggests that over the period the economy has been able to provide 32 jobs for every 100 economically active individuals in the labour market. Even by the strict definition of unemployment, which is government's official representation of the labour market, the economy has created only 40 jobs for every 100 members of the labour force.

How poor has employment growth been?

The figures earlier clearly point to the growing numbers of unemployed individuals, as a result of employment growth not keeping pace with the growth in the labour force. An important point of departure in this regard is to examine national economic growth rates over this period. Data reveals that over the 1995–2002 period, economic growth rates hovered in a band between 0.8 per cent and 4.3 per cent, with an annualised mean of 2.8 per cent over the period. Employment growth over this period grew, as indicated earlier, by 16.75 per cent – which is a mean rate of about 2.1 per cent per annum. In very simplistic terms this comparison indicates that for the level of output growth[2] recorded for the economy, employment expansion has not been as dismal as often indicated.

The critical caveats to the above representation are fourfold. Firstly, the relationship between output and employment will, and indeed does, vary across sectors. Hence, we may find that sectoral output growth in some sectors results, through changing factor proportions, in a relatively inelastic employment response. A sectoral division of the employment-output relationship may therefore reveal 'jobless growth' in some sectors. It remains important to keep in mind that while in the aggregate, the employment performance of the economy has not been as abysmal as often indicated, the sectoral details may in some cases reject this notion. Secondly, the growth in employment may be primarily a function of informal sector expansion. Output growth may in fact be associated with growing informal employment, but aggregate contraction of formal sector employment.[3] Thirdly, the growth in employment recorded is for all workers, irrespective of their supply characteristics. The nature of employment growth may be biased towards skilled and semi-skilled workers, with unskilled workers still losing their jobs over this period. Put differently, the basic output-employment relationship referred to above may mask specific skills preferences in the labour demand trajectory of the economy. Finally, the above estimates do not reveal anything about possible changes in the quality of employment. Quality of employment may be affected through, for example, the increased prevalence of part-time work, reduction in benefits offered to the workforce, greater outsourcing and so on.

Ultimately, though, the aggregate data suggests that while there has been employment expansion since the first majority government, we need to be mindful that in terms of the economically active population and its growth over time, this job performance has been far from adequate. What this suggests is that the current level and trajectory of economic growth has not been conducive to employment expansion. While this analysis falls well short of providing formal output-employment elasticities it provides fairly powerful, albeit initial, evidence for the fact that the growth-employment relationship in this seven-year period has been notably inelastic. Put differently, the economy's low and single-digit growth rates have been consistently unable to act as a generator of a sufficient quantum of employment in the domestic economy. In addition to the problem of low growth inhibiting labour demand expansion, significant labour supply-side constraints also inhibit employment.[4] These are manifest in the form of inadequate supply characteristics amongst a large number of the unemployed in the face of what has now been well documented for South Africa as skills-biased employment growth.

Employment trends by race, gender and sector

In attempting to provide a more textured analysis of employment patterns since 1995, Table 1.2 on the following page gives employment and labour force shifts by race and gender. In terms of the figures for employment by race, it is evident that for all groups the demand for labour increased. Hence, the highest increase in percentage terms was for Indian workers, followed by African, coloured and then white workers. The racial distribution of the total employment shift between 1995 and 2002 therefore indicates that all groups gained from employment. In terms of the gender results, female employment grew by 33 per cent over the seven-year period, while the figure for males was 6 per cent.

As noted above, however, what is critical are the relative employment shifts, as these calculations are better measures of labour market performance amongst the various cohorts under scrutiny. Using the approach identified above, while all employment growth rates were positive, the relative labour demand shifts, as approximated by the employment absorption rate, yield

Table 1.2 Employment and economically active population (EAP) shifts, by race and gender: 1995 to 2002

Category	Employment change	EAP change	Target growth rate	Change in employment (%)	Employment absorption rate
Race					
African	1 151 396	4 118 973	66.88	18.69	27.95
Coloured	136 292.9	346 494.9	30.96	12.18	39.33
Indian	136 942.3	242 044.3	68.65	38.84	56.58
White	141 178.6	254 630.6	13.22	7.33	55.44
Other	34 823	43 504	n.a.	n.a.	n.a.
Gender					
Male	352 642	1 846 391	31.74	6.06	19.10
Female	1 247 401	3 158 069	84.45	33.36	39.50
Total	1 600 633	5 005 647	52.38	16.75	31.98

Sources: October Household Survey, 1995 and Labour Force Survey, February 2002
Notes:
1. 'Other' for Unemployed in 2002, includes an unspecified category.
2. For 2002, 590 (1 187) individuals who were employed (in the labour force) for the weighted sample had an unspecified gender.

contrasting results. For example, while the African growth rate was higher than white employment growth, the employment absorption rate tells a very different story. The relative performance of African employment, when considering the new African entrants into the labour market, was actually far poorer. While African employment should have grown at about 67 per cent to absorb all the new entrants, white employment only needed to expand by 13 per cent. The gap between the actual and desired job performance for Africans (27.95 per cent) was far wider than that for white workers (55.44 per cent). Put differently, employment was generated for about only 28 per cent of all new African entrants into the labour market, relative to 55 per cent of new white entrants. The generic point though is that while positive employment growth was reported for all race groups, relative to the growing labour force, all races yielded poor or inadequate labour demand growth. The gender figures reinforce the importance of concentrating on relative employment shifts: despite the high growth in female employment, the employment absorption rate for this cohort was still about only 40 per cent, although notably much higher than for men at 19 per cent.

Table 1.2 also yields an important consideration with regard to the growth-employment relationship: that the benefits to growth in terms of employment gains are almost always unevenly distributed. They will be unevenly distributed according to race, gender, age, education and perhaps most obviously, location. In Table 1.3, the data by education level shows for example that while 64 out of every 100 tertiary-educated individuals found employment in the 1995 to 2002 period, this figure dropped to 35 for those with a matric and 14 for those with incomplete secondary education.

Table 1.3 Employment and EAP shifts, by education level: 1995 to 2002

Education level	Employment Change	Change (%)	EAP Change	Change (%)	Target growth (%)	Empl. gap (%)
No education	-40 741	-5.25	-68 325	-5.92	-8.81	59.63
Primary	353 393	16.15	969 692	28.80	44.30	36.44
< Matric	253 612	8.52	1 789 828	40.06	60.14	14.17
Matric	569 706	27.15	1 612 411	57.63	76.84	35.33
Tertiary	428 386	29.74	669 302	43.50	46.47	64.00
Unspecified	36 277	46.50	32 739	28.41	41.96	110.81
Total	1 600 633	16.75	5 005 647	37.24	52.38	31.98

Sources: October Household Survey, 1995 and Labour Force Survey, September 2002
Note: The matric category includes individuals that may have a National Technical Certificate (NTC III) qualification. Incomplete secondary education includes individuals who may have a NTC I or NTC II qualification.

In this instance, the point is that economic growth has disproportionately managed to create employment for more educated individuals. This explains the racial and to some extent the gender figures noted in Table 1.2. But here lies a crucial sub-text in this argument: that economic growth is a necessary condition for employment growth, but it is clearly not a necessary *and* sufficient condition for employment growth that is at the same rate as the growth in the labour force. Additionally then, what the data suggests is that while greater output expansion is clearly a requisite for employment growth, the rapid growth in the labour force *together* with a labour force that in most cases possesses inadequate supply characteristics, remain critical obstacles to long-run, sustainable employment growth in the domestic economy.

CHANGING CLASS

In trying to provide some detail on the unevenness in these employment patterns, we attempt a brief analysis of the changing nature of sectoral employment patterns. Table 1.4 provides an overview, at the main sector level, of the changing allocation of employment. In terms of absolute employment, all sectors witnessed an increase in employment, with the exception of Mining and Quarrying, Community services, and Post and Telecommunications. The latter is predominantly represented by the public sector. Within this short time-period, there were also noticeable shifts in sectoral allocation of employment.

Table 1.4 Sectoral share of employment, 1995 and 2002

Main sector	1995	Share	2002	Share	Percentage change
Agriculture, Fishing & Forestry	1 184 712	0.12	1 477 255	0.13	24.69
Mining & Quarrying	593 000	0.06	481 343	0.04	-18.83
Manufacturing	1 420 956	0.15	1 596 496	0.14	12.35
Utilities	84 041	0.01	84 550	0.01	0.61
Construction	433 492	0.05	527 678	0.05	21.73
Internal trade	1 650 017	0.17	2 191 347	0.20	32.81
Transport & Communication	469 200	0.05	550 918	0.05	17.42
Transport	329 194	0.03	434 613	0.04	32.02
Post & Telecommunications	140 006	0.02	116 305	0.01	-16.93
Finance, Real estate & Business services	582 897	0.06	1 023 373	0.09	75.57
Community, Social & Personal services	2 952 269	0.31	3 117 365	0.28	5.59
Domestic services	800 887	0.08	1 132 666	0.10	41.43
Community services (excl. Domestic services)	2 151 382	0.23	1 984 699	0.18	-7.75
Other producers	186 601	0.02	107 493	0.01	-42.39
Total	9 557 185	1.00	11 157 818	1.00	16.75

Sources: October Household Survey, 1995 and Labour Force Survey, February 2002
Notes:
1. For 2002, 'Community services' is the sum of community service and employment in private households.
2. 'Other producers' refers to those not classified, exterior organisations, foreign governments and other producers.
3. Mining figures for 1995 adjusted using official Chamber of Mines figures, given the exclusion of hostel dwellers in the 1995 October Household Survey.

While most sectors yielded unchanging shares of employment since 1995, there was a reallocation of employment away from Community services (23 per cent to 18 per cent) and Mining and Quarrying (6 per cent to 4 per cent), toward the Internal trade (17 per cent to 20 per cent) and Finance, Real estate and Business services sectors (6 per cent to 9 per cent). In terms of the former sectors, the restructuring exercise within the public sector, as well as the continued pressure on the viability of a number of mining enterprises, has contributed to this declining contribution to aggregate employment. The economy's long-run pattern of output expansion in the services sectors is again revealed here. A prime example of this expansion is to be found in the Finance, Real estate and Business services sector, where employment almost doubled over the seven-year period. Differential output expansion at the sectoral level is one of the key reasons that aggregate economic growth will deliver an uneven growth in employment. The long-run labour demand trajectory of the economy will thus hinge on the nature and extent of long-run output expansion at the sectoral level.

It is important to bear in mind that, together with output expansion at the sectoral level, what is also relevant in terms of labour demand patterns, is the particular configuration of skills needs that can be identified within each sector. This provides another important layer in understanding the unevenness of economic growth at the sectoral level. Table 1.5 on the next page documents the changing nature of employment by three broad skills categories at the main sector level. The national figure reflects the continuation of the long-run labour demand trend, namely that output growth continues to be skills-biased. Despite the evidence garnered of aggregate employment growth, the share of unskilled workers in the labour force declined by four percentage points, from 31 per cent in 1995 to 27 per cent in 2002, while the share of skilled and semi-skilled employment both increased by two percentage points.

In turn, it is evident that at the sectoral level, these patterns of declining proportions of unskilled workers and higher shares of semi-skilled and skilled employees are reinforced. In Manufacturing for example, the share of skilled workers in employment increased from 6 to 10 per cent, while that of unskilled workers declined from 19 to 15 per cent. There was then essentially a redistribution of jobs within Manufacturing away from unskilled workers, toward skilled workers. This pattern is replicated noticeably in sectors that reported a reduction in aggregate employment in the previous table. In

Table 1.5 Share of employment by three skills categories and main sector (percentage)

Main sector	Year	Skilled	Semi-skilled	Unskilled
Agriculture	1995	0.01	0.22	0.77
	2002	0.01	0.56	0.43
Mining & Quarrying	1995	0.04	0.77	0.19
	2002	0.04	0.89	0.07
Manufacturing	1995	0.06	0.74	0.19
	2002	0.10	0.75	0.15
Utilities	1995	0.06	0.79	0.13
	2002	0.09	0.82	0.08
Construction	1995	0.06	0.74	0.19
	2002	0.06	0.74	0.20
Internal trade	1995	0.14	0.66	0.20
	2002	0.10	0.60	0.30
Transport & Communication	1995	0.15	0.73	0.11
	2002	0.22	0.67	0.11
Transport	1995	0.19	0.69	0.12
	2002	0.23	0.64	0.12
Communication	1995	0.05	0.83	0.10
	2002	0.17	0.78	0.05
Finance	1995	0.17	0.77	0.06
	2002	0.25	0.67	0.08
Community services	1995	0.13	0.71	0.15
	2002	0.19	0.70	0.11
Private households	1995	0.00	0.03	0.97
	2002	0.00	0.16	0.84
Unspecified	1995	0.07	0.35	0.17
	2002	0.05	0.17	0.04
Total	1995	0.09	0.59	0.31
	2002	0.11	0.61	0.27

Sources: October Household Survey, 1995 and Labour Force Survey, February 2002
Notes:
1. 'Skilled' refers to ISOC (International Standard Occupational Classification) codes 1 and 2; 'Semi-skilled' refers to ISOC codes 3 to 8 and 'Unskilled' refers to ISOC code 9, excluding code 9999.
2. 1995 'Unspecified' includes armed forces who number 17 399.
3. For 1995 and 2002, 'Unskilled' includes domestic workers.
4. 'Private households' for 2002, and 'Domestic services' for 1995, were treated as synonymous here.

Mining and Quarrying, Communication and Community services there has been a movement away from unskilled workers toward semi-skilled and/or skilled employees. Interestingly, in the Internal trade sector, the reverse seems to have occurred, where the share of skilled workers declined and that of unskilled employees increased. A telling statistic is that in 7 of the 12 sectors, there was a decline in the share of unskilled workers.

Table 1.5 suggests a dual challenge for the domestic economy, in terms of producing an adequate economic growth strategy. Firstly, there is the challenge of converting the current low and erratic levels of economic growth to higher and more consistent rates of output expansion. Secondly, it remains likely that the nature of labour demand uptake as a result of economic growth will continue: namely, the disproportionate uptake of semi-skilled and skilled workers, relative to unskilled workers. This unevenness of growth requires the upgrading of the supply characteristics of those individuals entering the labour market each year in search of employment.

The supply characteristics of the unemployed

The supply-side of the labour market was alluded to in the previous section, in terms of the tepid employment performance of the economy, which has ultimately resulted in a rising number of jobless in the society. We attempt here a more nuanced assessment of the key markers of the unemployed. In particular, we try to focus on the supply characteristics of the unemployed and how these may in turn be a contributory factor to the economy's poor labour absorption capacity.

Table 1.6 on the next page provides unemployment rates by race and gender for 1995 and 2002. As indicated earlier, the low employment absorption figures for the economy have meant that unemployment levels and rates have risen in this post-apartheid period. Specifically, the national unemployment rate, according to the expanded definition, has risen by about 10 percentage points from 29 to 39 per cent. This remains an astounding reflection of this economy's inability to engender sufficient employment.

The figures also reveal the maldistribution of unemployment incidence by race. African unemployment rates by 2002 stood at 47 per cent compared with 9 per cent for white workers. Interestingly, the female unemployment rate is

Table 1.6 Unemployment rates by race and gender, 1995 and 2002 (percentage)

Year	1995	2002
Race		
African	36.16 (0.010)	46.62 (0.005)
Coloured	22.15 (0.011)	29.59 (0.011)
Indian	13.41 (0.017)	24.57 (0.018)
White	4.79 (0.004)	9.17 (0.005)
Gender		
Male	22.68 (0.009)	33.84 (0.006)
Female	37.32 (0.011)	45.32 (0.004)
Total	29.24 (0.097)	39.51 (0.005)

Sources: October Household Survey, 1995 and Labour Force Survey, February 2002
Notes:
1. The 'Other' category for race groups as well as the 'Unspecified' categories for race and gender are excluded in the estimates for 2002.
2. Standard errors are in parentheses, and are corrected according to frequency weights, the primary sampling unit and sampling stratification.

in fact lower than the African unemployment rate. White unemployment rates increased at the fastest pace during this period, as they almost doubled from 4.8 per cent in 1995 to 9.17 per cent in 2002. While the absolute rate for whites is still much lower than for Africans, this change is indeed a new phenomenon in the post-apartheid labour market.

These employment trends reaffirm the trend of skills-biased employment shifts across all main sectors of the economy. One would therefore expect that the supply characteristics of the unemployed in terms of educational levels would match well with these labour demand preferences. Table 1.7 presents unemployment rates by education level for 1995 and 2002.

The figures are startling. They suggest firstly that unemployment levels across all education categories (except for the 'no schooling' cohort) increased – a fact we would expect, given the evidence by race and gender. However, it is clear that the largest percentage growth in unemployment is found amongst workers with a matric or a tertiary qualification. In these two categories, unemployment levels grew by 56 per cent for the unemployed with a matric and by 139 per cent for those with a tertiary qualification. This is manifest in a significant increase in unemployment rates in the period, where matric unemployment rates went

Table 1.7 Unemployment rates by education level, 1995 and 2002 (percentage)

Education level	1995	2002
No schooling	33.12 (0.019)	32.30 (0.012)
Primary	35.49 (0.013)	41.38 (0.010)
Incomplete secondary	33.85 (0.009)	48.39 (0.005)
Matric	25.28 (0.013)	39.51 (0.010)
Tertiary	6.44 (0.005)	15.37 (0.006)
Total	29.24 (0.097)	39.51 (0.005)

Sources: October Household Survey, 1995 and Labour Force Survey, February 2002
Notes:
1. *The 'Unspecified' education category was omitted for the 2002 estimates.*
2. *'Tertiary' for 1995 captures individuals with a diploma/certificate with Grade 11 or lower; 'Diploma/certificate' with Grade 12 or a degree.*
3. *'Tertiary' for 2002 captures individuals with the above qualifications, but with an additional 'Post-graduate degree or diploma' category added.*
4. *Standard errors are in parentheses, and are corrected according to frequency weights, the primary sampling unit and sampling stratification.*

from 25 to 40 per cent and tertiary unemployment rates from 6 to 15 per cent. In the latter case, this represents more than double the unemployment rate over the seven-year period. In contrast, despite the fact that the absolute unemployment rates are lower in the remaining education categories, the rate of increase over the time period was not as significant as the two high-end qualifications. The high unemployment rates for matriculants can be (and have been in the past) explained by the low labour absorption capacity of the economy – the poor employment growth trends outlined earlier. However, the high unemployment levels amongst degreed individuals is a surprise, and puzzling. This is more so given the skills-biased employment shifts noted for the long-run in South Africa.

The apparently contradictory results are, perhaps, explained to some degree by the following two tables. Table 1.8 provides tertiary unemployment rates by race, while Table 1.9 provides the unemployment rates for workers with a degree only. In the first of these tables, the racial unevenness in tertiary unemployment rates is telling. While there were increases in the tertiary unemployment rates across all racial groups, the burden of graduate unemployment has been borne by African individuals.

Table 1.8 Tertiary unemployment rates, by race, 1995 and 2002 (percentage)

Race	1995	2002
African	10.01 (0.011)	25.95 (0.009)
Coloured	8.49 (0.019)	9.86 (0.020)
Indian	5.56 (0.013)	8.21 (0.017)
White	2.26 (0.004)	4.63 (0.005)
Total	6.44 (0.005)	15.37 (0.006)

Sources: October Household Survey, 1995 and Labour Force Survey, February 2002
Note: Standard errors are in parentheses, and are corrected according to frequency weights, the primary sampling unit and sampling stratification.

The figures show that the unemployment rate for African individuals with a tertiary qualification went up from 10 per cent to 26 per cent over this period – an increase of about 160 per cent. While the absolute levels of white unemployment continue to remain much lower than the levels of all other race groups, the rate more than doubled over this period. It is the key result for Africans, however, that feeds the national unemployment rate increase, from 6 per cent to 15 per cent. The trend of growing national tertiary unemployment rates is thus essentially explained by growing joblessness among the African degreed population. These figures for tertiary workers capture individuals with a variety of qualifications including, for example, diplomas with or without a matric, technikon qualifications, and a university degree. Unemployment rates for workers with university degrees only are represented in Table 1.9.[5]

In the first instance, the figures indicate that there is an upward bias in the tertiary category when non-degreed workers are included. The figures for African and white participants therefore indicate that the estimates for individuals with degrees only lie below the tertiary aggregates.

For example, for African participants with a degree or post-graduate degree the unemployment rate stood at 16.41 per cent in 2002, compared with a 26 per cent unemployment rate for all tertiary qualified African participants. The figures for whites were 3.15 per cent and 4.63 per cent respectively. However, despite these lower unemployment rates for degreed workers, it needs to be noted that the rate of increase in numbers of unemployed was greater for degreed workers. Hence the number of white unemployed increased by 141 per cent over the seven-year period and more than quadrupled for African

Table 1.9 Unemployment for degreed workers: African and white, 1995 and 2002

	African	White
Unemployment numbers		
1995	8 834	5 645
2002	45 959	13 597
Change (percentage)	420.25	140.87
Unemployment rates		
1995	5.87 (0.015)	0.01 (0.006)
2002	16.41 (0.018)	3.15 (0.008)

Sources: October Household Survey, 1995 and Labour Force Survey, February 2002
Note: Standard errors are in parentheses, and are corrected according to frequency weights, the primary sampling unit and sampling stratification.

graduates. Both these figures are higher than the overall changes for African and white workers with a tertiary qualification. Indeed, while the figures from Table 1.8 suggest a growing unemployment problem amongst participants with some tertiary qualification, the figures here are more worrying. They suggest that the labour market is being marked not only by a growth in tertiary unemployment levels, but also, as a sub-set, by a growth in the number and rate of unemployed individuals with a degree or post-graduate degree. Put differently, there can be no doubt that we are witnessing the beginning of a graduate unemployment problem in South Africa.

A university degree remains a heterogeneous product, in that individuals will accumulate these degrees in different fields of study as well as at institutions of differing quality (perceived or actual). In trying to determine the distribution of these degreed unemployed according to fields of study, we exploit an excellent question in the Labour Force Survey that asked all respondents to identify their field of study, if they had a tertiary qualification. Table 1.10 presents the results on the sample of unemployed with university degrees only. The aggregate (total) figures indicate that the majority of the unemployed with degrees are in the Education, Training and Development field. This matches well with the public sector restructuring process, and suggests that teachers have borne the brunt of the restructuring in the public sector.

This dominance of Education, Training and Development as a field of study for the degreed unemployed seems to be concentrated amongst African and coloured participants. Interestingly, the aggregate data, as well as that for

Table 1.10 Degreed unemployed: distribution by field of study and race (percentages)

Area of study	African	Coloured	Indian	White	Total
Communication Studies & Language	4.33	0.00	100.00	7.35	5.58
Education, Training & Development	32.87	41.37	0.00	10.47	28.04
Manufacturing, Engineering & Development	3.9	0.00	0.00	0.00	2.87
Human & Social Studies	8.55	0.00	0.00	14.66	9.50
Law, Military Science, Security	5.22	22.18	0.00	3.75	5.48
Health Sciences & Social Services	11.43	36.45	0.00	10.57	12.08
Agriculture & Nature Conservation	2.2	0.00	0.00	0.00	1.62
Culture & Arts	6.62	0.00	0.00	3.92	5.74
Business, Commerce & Management Studies	21.5	0.00	0.00	30.32	22.46
Physical, Mathematical, Computer & Life Sciences	3.39	0.00	0.00	13.92	5.53
Physical Planning & Construction	0.00	0.00	0.00	5.02	1.10
Total	100.00	100.00	100.00	100.00	100.00

Source: Labour Force Survey, February 2002

whites, show that the unemployed with degrees in Business, Commerce and Management Studies constituted a fairly significant share of degreed unemployment within those cohorts. The third dominant field of study (for Africans and the aggregate estimates) was Health Sciences and Social Services. Again, this may be picking up the contraction of employment opportunities within the public health service. A degree in Human and Social Studies was also fairly dominant, as about 10 per cent of the national sample of degreed unemployed had accumulated human capital in this area. Ultimately then, the data suggest that, of the unemployed with degrees or post-graduate degrees, those in Education, Training and Development; Business, Commerce and Management Studies and Health Sciences account for about 63 per cent of the sample of degreed unemployed individuals.

This points to two key deductions. Firstly, it is evident that the process of public sector restructuring has resulted in this poor employment performance amongst African workers, with a large share of these individuals being teachers and other large share occupations within the public sector, such as nurses. Secondly, the data point provisionally to the importance of ensuring that the institutions of supply, namely the universities and technikons, are producing graduates with a skills profile that matches current demand trends. This conclusion is derived particularly from the surprisingly large share of unemployed graduates with a commerce degree. This tentative evidence suggests that either institutions of higher education may not be matching their curriculum design effectively enough with the labour demand needs of employers or that the quality of degrees is poor, or both.

The unemployable

The seven-year analysis above has reinforced results from longer run studies around the notion of skills-biased employment shifts in the domestic economy. The winners have been the highly skilled while the losers have, almost without exception, been unskilled workers. In terms of the unemployed, this means that those individuals who are not skilled or, put differently, have low levels of education will in all probability not get a job. Furthermore, those who are older and not well-educated will most likely never obtain a job in their lifetime. In contrast, young unemployed individuals with some form of education can be trained up and provided with some of the skills that firms may find useful. It needs to be remembered that whilst both these groups are officially unemployed, they present very different employment probabilities. In this context, the unemployed youth with some level of secondary education may, with the help of a skills development programme for example, find some form of employment. However, the middle-aged unemployed with very low levels of formal education will in all likelihood never find employment in their lifetime.

If one dissects the unemployed in this way, the unemployed youth are a distinct category from the older unemployed. This has led to the notion that the latter cohort are in fact *unemployable* rather than unemployed (Bhorat 2000). However, no detailed empirical analysis has in fact gone into assessing whether the cohort of older unemployed are in fact distinct from the unemployed youth. We briefly attempt an introductory analysis testing this hypothesis of the 'unemployable'. Table 1.11 splits the unemployed into two categories: 'non-youth' and 'youth', where the former are the unemployed aged 40 and above, and the latter under the age of 40. This division is utilised as the starting point for beginning to assess the different attributes of the older unemployable workers relative to their younger counterparts.

Firstly, it is clear from Table 1.11 that of the 7.3 million unemployed recorded for February 2002, about 1.3 million are 40 or older. This reinforces the point that the economy's unemployment problem has a very strong youth dimension. The key attribute differentiating these two cohorts of workers though, is their level of education. Table 1.11 makes it plain that the non-youth unemployed have a distinctly lower level of human capital accumulation than the youth: 54 per cent of the non-youth, about 705 000 individuals, have accumulated between zero and seven years of education (primary schooling or less), while the figure for the youth is less than half this, at 24 per cent.

Table 1.11 Distribution of unemployed by age cohort and education level

Education level	Non-youth	Youth	Total
No schooling	187 058	163 620	350 678
Percentage	*14.37*	*2.73*	*4.81*
Primary	518 693	1 276 156	1 794 849
Percentage	*39.85*	*21.31*	*24.62*
Incomplete secondary	445 270	2 582 593	3 027 863
Percentage	*34.21*	*43.13*	*41.54*
Matric	90 741	1 651 610	1742351
Percentage	*6.97*	*27.58*	*23.90*
Tertiary	46 627	292 771	339 398
Percentage	*3.58*	*4.89*	*4.66*
Unspecified	13 092	20 602	33 694
Percentage	*1.01*	*0.34*	*0.46*
Total	1 301 481	5 987 352	7 288 833
Percentage	*100.00*	*100.00*	*100.00*

Source: Labour Force Survey, February 2002

Put differently, while about 33 per cent of the youth unemployed have a matric or tertiary qualification, only about 11 per cent of the older unemployed possess these qualifications. The above analysis on employment trends since 1995, and longer-run analyses for South Africa, underline the notion of employment growth at the top-end of the occupational ladder. Skilled (better educated) workers have a significantly higher probability of employment than less skilled (or less educated) workers. Given this, with a lower level of education and being older, the non-youth cohort of the unemployed are faced with vastly lower probabilities of employment than the unemployed youth. More specifically, we can perhaps nuance our definition of who the 'unemployable' are more than likely to be: the data suggest that those jobless individuals over the age of 40 with primary schooling or less best reflect the core of individuals in the labour market who, given the economy's labour demand trajectory, are not likely to get a job in their lifetime.

We attempt here a brief assessment of the other attributes of the cohort of unemployed aged 40 and over with primary schooling or less, identified as the 'unemployable'. Their characteristics are then compared against those of the unemployed youth. Table 1.12 presents the period spent searching for a job by the two groups of unemployed. The figures across both cohorts point to the strong structural nature of South Africa's unemployment problem. About 38 per cent of the 'unemployable' and 39 per cent of the youth unemployed have been searching for a job for one year or more. Indeed, the predominant search period, across both cohorts, is three years or more.

Table 1.12 Distribution of unemployed by period of search and age cohort (percentage)

Period of search	Unemployable	Youth	Total
Less than 1 month	4.38	4.81	4.72
1 to less than 2 months	2.09	3.59	3.36
2 to less than 3 months	1.78	3.20	3.00
3 to less than 4 months	1.67	1.94	1.94
4 to less than 6 months	1.24	1.98	1.89
6 months to less than 1 year	2.74	5.64	5.26
1 to 3 years	11.00	16.94	16.12
3 years or more	27.14	22.00	23.18
Don't know	0.24	0.24	0.23
Unspecified	47.47	39.67	40.31
Total	100.00	100.00	100.00

Source: Labour Force Survey, February 2002

The response rate for this question in the survey was very poor. Close to half of the 'unemployable' did not respond compared with about 40 per cent of the youth unemployed. If we assume, however, that the distribution of the search period would remain the same with all observations included, then the table points clearly to the fact that the mismatch between demand and supply affecting the domestic economy has continued to filter down into the younger age cohorts who have been searching for similar periods to the 'unemployable'.

In trying to understand previous economic activity we took the above sample of unemployed and those who reported having worked previously, and asked when last it was that they worked. Table 1.13 presents the results from these two questions. There is here a distinct difference in the past economic activity of the unemployable when compared with the youth unemployed.

Table 1.13 Unemployed who have worked before: when last was this? (percentage)

Time period	Unemployable	Youth	Total
1 week to less than 1 month	1.15	2.72	2.23
1 to less than 2 months	2.20	3.67	3.15
2 to less than 3 months	2.74	4.37	3.75
3 to less than 4 months	1.55	3.48	2.79
4 to less than 5 months	1.46	2.56	2.19
5 to less than 6 months	1.33	2.52	2.11
6 months to less than 1 year	4.68	9.95	8.30
1 to less than 2 years	8.92	15.25	13.31
2 to less than 3 years	10.80	12.07	11.72
3 years or more	55.04	31.76	38.77
Don't know	0.84	1.41	1.30
No response	9.28	10.23	10.39
Total	100.00	100.00	100.00

Source: Labour Force Survey, February 2002

The data reveal that about 66 per cent of the unemployable who had worked before, had done so two years or more previously. This figure compares with 44 per cent for the youth unemployed. This result tangentially suggests that a large number of the unemployable had in fact been employed as labourers and would have lost their jobs as structural changes and technological shifts in the domestic economy impacted on low-skilled employment.

Perhaps the most critical reflection of the likelihood that these 'unemployable' individuals will never find a job in their lifetime, is found in Table 1.14. It reports on literacy levels for the two cohorts. Respondents were asked if they could read or write in at least one language. Remembering that the unemployable are already pre-defined as individuals with primary schooling or less, these figures are particularly important as they test functional literacy levels.

Table 1.14 Literacy levels of the unemployed

Literacy	Unemployable	Youth	Total
Read in (at least) one language			
Yes	524 397	5 800 676	6 905 932
Percentage	*72.95*	*96.88*	*94.75*
No	194 446	185 819	382 044
Percentage	*27.05*	*3.10*	*5.24*
Total	718 843	5 987 352	7 288 833
	100.00	*100.00*	*100.00*
Write in (at least) one language			
Yes	518 824	5 790 814	6 889 753
Percentage	*72.17*	*96.72*	*94.52*
No	199 752	195 778	398 053
Percentage	*27.79*	*3.27*	*5.46*
Total	1 301 481	5 987 352	7 288 833
	100.00	*100.00*	*100.00*

Source: Labour Force Survey, February 2002

Within the group of unemployable, about 27 per cent of the sample could not read in any language, while 28 per cent were unable to write in any language. These individuals amounted to about 200 000 amongst the unemployable. In addition, amongst the youth, less than five per cent were functionally illiterate. This result brings into sharp contrast the notion of the youth unemployed as against the 'unemployable'. Even within this latter cohort of workers with primary schooling or less, there exists a further sub-group whose levels of illiteracy would surely render it impossible to legitimately expect them to take up long-term employment in an economy that places a premium on highly skilled job-seekers.

One of the important policy issues that arises from these descriptors of the unemployed, is the survival strategies of the unemployed in terms of the households to which they attach themselves. Are the unemployed primarily found in households with no access to wage income or in households with one or more wage earners? Or are they evenly spread across all types of wage earning households? While in some quarters the relationship between the employed and unemployed has often been cast as conflictual in nature, it is obvious that income entering the households will be the key mechanism for ensuring the survival of the unemployed. With this in mind, Table 1.15 examines the distribution of the unemployed, 'unemployable' and youth unemployed across wage-earning households. The latter are defined according to the number of wage earners within each household, ranging from no earners to three or more wage earners in a household.

Table 1.15 Distribution of the unemployed across wage-earning households

Number of earners in household	Number of unemployed	Share of unemployed (%)
National estimates		
0	3 570 244	48.98
1	2 864 673	39.30
2	683 409	9.38
3+	170 507	2.33
Total	7 288 833	100.00
Youth		
0	283 4491	47.34
1	2 389 743	39.91
2	614 050	10.26
3+	149 068	2.49
Total	5 987 352	100.00
Unemployable		
0	446 299	62.09
1	225 804	31.41
2	36 498	5.08
3+	10 242	1.42
Total	718 843	100.00

Source: Labour Force Survey, February 2002

At the national level and using the expanded definition of unemployment, the data suggests that 49 per cent of the unemployed do not have access to a wage earner within a household. Alternatively, 51 per cent of the unemployed have access to at least one wage earner in a household, with the majority located in a one-wage earner household. The figures for the youth unemployed essentially mimic those of the national estimates. In terms of the unemployable though, there is a notable shift. Over 62 per cent of the unemployable do not have access to a wage earner within the household. Conversely, 38 per cent of the unemployable have access to at least one wage earner within a household. The data then simultaneously suggest that on the one hand, large sections of the unemployed (and significant sections of the 'unemployable') are supported by wage earners within the same household, while on the other hand, equally significant shares of the unemployed (and a disproportionate segment of the unemployable) are not supported by wage income.

While additional data analysis is required, it is clear that within the zero wage earner households, it is state transfers such as the old age pension, child support grant and so on that would be the main source of income to these households. Other important flows would be remittances, inter-household transfers and unrecorded economic activity. For the 'unemployable', the figures suggest that a disproportionate number of these individuals are forced to rely on income entering the household from sources generated through activities outside the labour market. More generally, though, the table makes it plain that any wage moderation policy that does not engender expanded employment opportunities will make the unemployed worse off, through increased household poverty levels.

Conclusion

This chapter has attempted to present some of the key empirical co-ordinates that define the South African labour market in this post-apartheid period. The data show that the notion of 'jobless growth' for the South African economy is clearly erroneous. The important caveat to this reasoning, though, is that the labour force has simultaneously grown at a higher rate than employment. In net terms then, employment expansion has been relatively poor. On the back of unspectacular economic growth, this result is not surprising. However, the cohort analysis of employment and labour absorption trends did make it clear that the labour market challenge cannot be overcome purely through the growth process. The chapter also attests to the notion of the 'unemployable' as a distinct, more disadvantaged cohort amongst the unemployed. It is the unemployable who should be viewed as a target for poverty alleviation strategies rather than labour market interventions, given the high probability that they will not find employment in their lifetimes.

In terms of labour market interventions, however, it is clear that the second segment of the unemployed consists of better-educated and younger participants. It is these individuals whose current labour supply characteristics, marked most obviously by their formal qualifications, do not match with the labour demand needs of the economy. The South African government, through the Department of Labour, has already embarked on such a strategy in a generic sense. This strategy is captured under the banner of the *National Skills Development Strategy* (NSDS). The NSDS is legally anchored in the *Skills Development Act* (SDA), 1998, and administratively run through the Skills Development Planning Unit (SDPU). The purpose of the Sector, Education and Training Authorities (SETAs), created via the SDA, is to utilise the levies provided for in the SDA to narrow this gap between demand and supply. Put differently, the brief of the SETAs is to ensure that the supply characteristics of workers is upgraded through the process of education and training, in a manner that meets with firms' labour demand needs. It is only in meeting such needs of firms that the SETAs can be said to have succeeded in their tasks. Ultimately then, through the machinery provided by the NSDS, unemployed youth can be targeted for skills upgrading. Given the manner in which the strategy has been set up though, the unemployed will only be targeted through the National Skills Fund. (See also Baatjes & Mathe and Perrow, in this volume.)

Given the unevenness of the economy's growth generation – both in terms of sectoral expansion and skill requirements – a fair degree of intervention is required on the labour supply side. Put differently, the simultaneous existence of a skilled labour shortage and unskilled labour surplus, points to the importance of adhering to a policy framework that emphasises both the need to kick-start economic growth as well as ensure that the characteristics of the suppliers of labour match those in demand by growing sectors.

Notes

1. For a historical account of these shifts and their impact on the South African labour market, see Bhorat (2000), Bhorat & Hodge (1999) and Edwards (2000).
2. 'Output growth' refers to the growth rate, over any specified period, in the value of goods and services produced either nationally or sectorally by an economy. The standard measure of this output is Gross Domestic Product (GDP).
3. The poor coverage of the informal sector in the October Household Survey for 1995 makes this comparison of formal versus informal sector employment growth very difficult to determine. However, there would seem to be indicative evidence that both organic growth in informal employment and better capturing by Statistics South Africa (StatsSA), have yielded a rapid expansion in informal employment.
4. In a labour market context, 'demand and supply side' refers to the demand for labour (from employers) and the supply of labour (through the economically active population).
5. Note that in the October Household Survey, 1995, there was only a category for a university degree, whereas in the Labour Force Survey, 2002, this was split into 'a degree' and 'a post-graduate degree'. We combined these two categories from the Labour Force Survey, 2002, to enable a comparison with the 1995 figures.

References

Bhorat, H & Hodge, J (1999) Decomposing Shifts in Labour Demand in South Africa, *South African Journal of Economics*, 67(3): 348–380

Bhorat, H (2000) The Impact of Trade and Structural Changes on Sectoral Employment in South Africa, *Development Southern Africa*, Special issue, September 17(3): 437–466

Edwards, L (2000) Globalisation and the Skill Bias of Occupational Employment in South Africa. Unpublished paper. University of Cape Town

CHANGING CLASS

2 Balancing public and private resources for basic education: school fees in post-apartheid South Africa

Edward B Fiske & Helen F Ladd

Introduction

Determining the right balance between public and private resources in the provision of primary and secondary resources is high on the global policy agenda. In formalising the global commitment to universal basic education, the 1990 World Conference on Education for All in Jomtien, Thailand, made it clear that national governments in developing countries typically lack the tax-generated resources to fund education at an adequate level. Jomtien thus established a context for the discussion of school fees and other user charges in developing countries. Such fees are controversial, though, and recent years have brought growing international efforts to abolish them, especially at the level of primary education.

It should come as no surprise that in the mid-1990s, when South Africa was abandoning its apartheid past and embarking on the difficult process of restructuring its education system to serve the needs of the new democracy, policy-makers had to grapple with how best to balance reliance on public and private resources. Consistent with South Africa's progressive new Constitution, which identified basic education as a right for all citizens, the new government abolished the racially-defined departments of education, established a single education system and made nine years of education compulsory, the first time that any education had been compulsory for Africans. At that same time, the post-apartheid government made an explicit decision to encourage public schools to supplement public funds with school fees. It did so despite the declared aspirations and promises of the African National Congress (ANC) during the final years of the apartheid period that all children should have access to a free basic education. South Africa has continued that policy in spite of the current global pressure to eliminate fees at the primary level. However, fee policy remains a topic of current debate and was the subject of significant attention in a March 2003 Department of Education (DoE) report to the Minister of Education.[1]

In this chapter, we examine the South African experience with school fees in the context of the international debate about such charges. We address three main questions. First, what economic and political pressures induced South Africa to turn to school fees as a significant revenue source for its newly-reconstituted school system? Second, was the decision to rely on fees a sound one? In answering this question, we take into account both what was known at the time and how things have played out over time. Third, is it time to revisit the fee policy, and, if so, what changes might be appropriate?

Much of our empirical analysis is based on school-level data from two South African provinces, the Eastern Cape and Western Cape. The Eastern Cape was formed primarily from two of the homelands created by the apartheid government and pieces of white South Africa and has struggled with the problems of inadequate resources and a weak governmental infrastructure. The Western Cape, by contrast, is a wealthy province that includes the city of Cape Town and that inherited a strong governmental structure from the apartheid era. We supplemented the data with interviews during the first half of 2002 with national and provincial policy-makers as well as with school principals and other educators in the two provinces.

We show that South Africa adopted a fees-based policy for a variety of reasons, including the limited availability of public resources and the pressure for local control over education. Most decisive in taking this decision, though, was the argument that charging fees would forestall a flight of the middle class to private schools, thus providing continuing political support for the state education system and avoiding the creation of yet another bifurcated educational system in South Africa. Our analysis indicates that the fee policy succeeded in keeping students in the public school system and, contrary to the effects of fees in many other developing countries, apparently did not significantly keep children out of primary school. At the same time, the fees have affected the way in which students sort themselves among schools, with class beginning to replace race as the primary determinant of who is able to access the formerly white schools. Furthermore, fees have reinforced the advantages enjoyed by the formerly white schools without at the same time increasing the resources available to schools serving historically disadvantaged students. We conclude that it would be appropriate at this time to consider changes to the fee policy that would benefit the historically disadvantaged schools.

Public and private funding in post-apartheid South Africa

The architects of post-apartheid South Africa understood that a restructured state education system would be just as critical to the building of a new and democratic social order in South Africa as its predecessor had been to the sustaining of apartheid.

Thus, central to the new South African democracy were the constitutional guarantee of a basic education for all – subsequently defined as nine years of compulsory education – and the deracialisation and unification of the education system. Unification was accomplished in part by establishing a single national education system and by defining only two types of schools, public and independent. The wording of the *South African Schools Act* (SASA) with respect to independent, or private, schools, specifies that any person may establish and maintain such a school albeit 'at his or her own cost' (RSA 1996).[2]

Table 2.1 Students in independent schools, 1995 and 2000

	Students in independent schools		All students		Independent students/ all students (%)	
	1995	2000	1995	2000	1995	2000
Eastern Cape	n.a.	8 049	2 233 997	2 105 579	n.a.	0.4
Gauteng	85 727	117 531	1 427 872	1 554 495	6.0	7.6
Western Cape	16 366	28 133	885 416	916 387	1.8	3.1
South Africa	n.a.	243 732	11 897 965	11 836 906	n.a.	2.1

Sources: South Africa Survey 2001/2002, South African Institute of Race Relations 2001: 252 and 254 for all student figures other than the 1996 entries for all students. That entry is from the South Africa Survey 1997/98. South African Institute of Race Relations 2001: 143. Note that the 1995 ratios were calculated using the 1996 estimates for all students.
Notes:
1. The figures for enrolment in independent schools are not strictly comparable. The 2000 figures are from the DoE and the 1995 figures are from the Education Foundation. The independent school figures include students in independent primary, secondary, combined, intermediate and middle schools. Total students include learners from Grades 1 to 12, pre-primary enrolments, pupils with special needs at public schools, and pupils at combined, intermediate, and middle schools.
2. n.a. signifies not available.

As shown in Table 2.1, which is based on official data from the national DoE, only 2.1 per cent of students in the country as a whole were enrolled in such schools in 2000.[3] We note, however, that the percentages were higher in the wealthier provinces of Western Cape and Gauteng, and increased in those provinces between 1995 and 2000. The Western Cape, which includes Cape Town, and Gauteng, which includes Johannesburg and Pretoria, are home to many of the country's political decision-makers, a fact that is relevant for a major argument for school fees, discussed below.

Responsibility for overseeing the operation of the state education system was assigned to the Departments of Education in the nine newly-established provinces, while the task of managing local schools was vested in each school's elected school governing body (SGB), which by design is dominated by parents (RSA 1996: 16). These SGBs were given a variety of responsibilities, from the setting of admissions policy subject to non-discrimination requirements to making recommendations to the provincial Department of Education regarding the appointment of teachers and staff (RSA 1996: 14). Of central importance to this study is the mandate:

> A governing body of a public school *must take all reasonable measures within its means to supplement the resources supplied by the State* in order to improve the quality of education provided by the schools to all learners at the school. (RSA 1996: 21, emphasis added)

This provision refers not only to school fees but also to voluntary contributions from the community. The setting of school fees is optional in the sense that a school can impose such fees only when authorised to do so by a majority of parents attending a budget meeting at the school (RSA 1996: 21). Once a fee is approved, however, all parents are required to pay it except those who, under a provision added in 1998, are exempted from doing so by action of the SGB because of their low income. Although a child cannot be denied admission for failure to pay the fee, schools can sue parents for non-payment (RSA 1996: 5, 23). Money collected from school fees is put into a school fund that can be used for any school purpose, including the hiring of additional teachers. Teachers hired out of locally-raised funds are referred to as school governing body – or SGB – teachers.

Table 2.2 shows the amounts and variation in the fees charged by schools in the Eastern Cape and the Western Cape in 2001. In the very poor Eastern Cape fees were low and nearly two-thirds (63 per cent) of primary school students attended schools paying fees of less than R25 per year. Fees were generally higher

Table 2.2 School fees charged, primary schools and secondary schools, Eastern Cape and Western Cape, 2001

	Eastern Cape		Western Cape	
Fee range (Rand)	Percentage of students	Cumulative percentage	Percentage of students	Cumulative percentage
Primary schools				
0–25	62.7	62.7	6.2	6.2
26–50	18.4	81.1	21.7	27.9
51–100	5.6	86.7	29.6	57.6
101–250	4.1	90.7	21.1	78.6
251–1 000	3.7	94.4	6.8	85.4
1 001–2 000	2.9	97.3	7.4	92.8
>2 000	2.7	100.0	7.2	100.0
Secondary schools				
0–25	2.0	2.0	0.0	0.0
26–50	27.6	29.6	2.6	2.6
51–100	28.2	57.8	12.7	15.3
101–250	28.7	86.5	32.6	47.9
251–1 000	6.3	92.8	28.9	76.8
1 001–2 000	2.0	94.8	5.6	82.4
>2 000	5.2	100.0	17.6	100.0

Source: Calculated by the authors based on data provided by the Eastern and Western Cape DoEs. Excluded from the table are all the combined schools, of which there are many in the Eastern Cape. Most of the combined schools in the Eastern Cape are in the former Transkei homeland. Many of those schools did not report fees.

in the Western Cape, where the typical, or median, primary school student was subject to a fee in the range of R51 to R100. Some public primary schools in both provinces had quite high fees. More than 5 per cent of the students in the Eastern Cape and more than 14 per cent of those in the Western Cape faced fees of over R1 000.

The fees are uniformly higher for secondary schools. The median secondary school student in the Eastern Cape faced a fee of between R51 and R100, while his or her counterpart in the Western Cape encountered a fee of over R250. Close to 18 per cent of the secondary school students in the Western Cape faced fees that were greater than R2 000.

To put these fees in perspective, we estimate that average, per pupil public spending on behalf of students in the Western Cape in 2001 was about R3 600 for primary school students and about R4 000 for secondary school students. Thus a fee of R100 would augment spending by about three per cent at the primary level. The median fee at the secondary level of about R250 would increase spending by about 7 per cent, while a fee of R2 000 would do so by about 50 per cent. Later in this chapter, we say more about the relative magnitude of the fees for various types of schools.

Why were school fees permitted and encouraged?

International experience suggests that the major reason for the widespread practice of school fees in developing countries is the inability of the governments of such countries to provide free basic education at public expense. Although insufficient public funding was certainly a relevant factor in South Africa, it was only one of several forces or considerations favouring the use of fees, including political economy considerations that reflected the legacy of apartheid.

Limited availability of public resources

Once it took power, the ANC and its allies soon recognised that there would be insufficient public funds to equalise public funding at anywhere near the level needed to provide the quality of education to all students that had previously been available to white students. With whites in 1993 accounting for only 17 per cent of the total population of South Africa, any redistribution of funds from the former white schools to the rest of the schools across the country would be spread so thinly that it would do little to enhance the education available to the historically disadvantaged schools.

A widely-held position at the time was that the new government should view education as an investment in South Africa's future and hence direct substantial sums of money to schooling for the long-deprived black majority. Such arguments were thwarted, though, by evidence that, as shown in Table 2.3, South Africa was already spending a larger share of its gross national product (GNP) on education than the international average for developing countries. When it became clear that additional public funds would not be forthcoming, the only alternative seemed to be to harness the private sector and to allow schools to charge user fees. In recognition of this reality, the 1995 Committee

BALANCING PUBLIC AND PRIVATE RESOURCES FOR BASIC EDUCATION

to Review the Organisation, Governance and Funding of Schools (henceforth referred to as the Hunter Report) laid out three policy options, all of which called for school fees in some form to supplement public funding.

Table 2.3 Public expenditure on education, selected countries

Country	As percentage of GNP	As percentage of total government expenditure	Percentage spent on primary and secondary schooling
Industrial country average	5.4	n.a.	n.a.
Developing country average	3.6	n.a.	n.a.
Sub-Saharan Africa country average	5.5	n.a.	n.a.
South Africa	7.1	22	81
Thailand	3.8	19	73
Malaysia	5.3	16	71
Brazil	1.6	n.a.	56
Turkey	3.3	n.a.	69
Chile	2.9	13	68
Sri Lanka	3.2	9	72
Zimbabwe	8.3	n.a.	79
Zambia	2.6	9	66
India	3.8	12	64

Source: UNDP, Human Development Report 1997, Table 15 cited in Seekings (2001)

Promotion of local control

The shape of the new education system was extremely important to both black and white people. As apartheid began to unravel in the late 1980s and early 1990s, the national government, anticipating a shift of political power from white to black hands, transferred ownership of the physical property of the formerly all-white schools to the parents in these schools and granted them significant authority to run their own affairs, including the right to augment public revenues by charging fees to parents (Karlsson, McPherson & Pampallis 2001: 146). Despite the concerns of the ANC and its allies that such powers would perpetuate apartheid differences, black architects of the new democratic order, operating within the context of a Government of National Unity (GNU), did not seek to roll back local control of schools. Both white Afrikaners and black people understood that a peaceful transition from one of the most unfair political, social and economic systems in the world to a new democratic order by necessity involved compromise. One such compromise was that white people would be permitted to retain significant control over their schools.

The case was also made that black people should have control over their schools as well. During the struggle against apartheid, many African people had viewed schools as instruments of the apartheid government and thus as institutions to be distrusted and scorned. One way of overcoming this deeply-rooted distrust of schooling, many people believed, was to give ownership and control of the schools back to local school communities. Although school fees need not be part of a self-governing package, they were seen as a way of giving local governing bodies both discretionary funds and a major incentive to use funds wisely. For this reason, advocates of more efficient schooling in South Africa typically supported greater reliance on school fees (Crouch 1995).

Mobilisation of private resources to achieve egalitarian goals

The democratic movement initially opposed school fees but eventually came to accept arguments that, by providing local schools with an independent source of revenue, fees paid by wealthier communities would release scarce state funds for poor schools, thereby promoting more equal educational opportunity (Donaldson 1992; Pampallis 1998). This argument for fees emerged most clearly in the Hunter Report's preferred 'partnership funding' option, which called for a combination of obligatory fees and voluntary contributions to supplement public funding of schools for non-personnel purposes. The authors proposed that very poor families pay no fees and that others be required to pay fees based on a sliding scale related to their family income. The collection of obligatory fees was intended to help poor students both by freeing up public funds to be distributed to schools serving poor students and by making it possible for children from poor families to have access to a range of public schools, rather than being restricted to low-quality schools with no school fees.

To policy-makers at the time, perhaps the most persuasive case for school fees came from Luis Crouch and Christopher Colclough, a pair of international consultants. They argued that if schools were not allowed to charge fees and use them for purposes such as the hiring of additional teachers, the quality of the formerly white schools would deteriorate. That, in turn, would induce many key 'opinion and decision-makers' to pull their children out of the public school system and enrol them in private schools. Once outside the state education system, the consultants argued, families would have little reason to exert political pressure for more public spending on education. As with the Hunter Report itself, the consultants were careful to emphasise that the argument was not an elitist one designed to privilege the middle class but rather a means of improving schools for the poor (Crouch 1995).

The two consultants proposed a fee policy similar to the one that was subsequently embodied in the 1996 *South African Schools Act*, and their work proved to be compelling to policy-makers (Pampallis 1998). This policy called for the governing body of each school to be empowered, indeed encouraged, to charge fees after discussion with the parents. Both Colclough and Crouch recommended that children from families with incomes below some national threshold be exempt from school fees. Such a policy was not immediately adopted, but in 1998 a provision was added that required school governing bodies to issue full or partial exemptions from fees for families whose annual income fell below thresholds defined by the size of the school fee. To offset any incentive for schools to exclude exempted children, both consultants suggested that richer schools should be required to reserve a certain number or proportion of spaces for non-fee-paying students. That provision, however, has not been enacted (Colclough; Crouch 1995).

Allowing schools to charge fees thus provided a mechanism to enhance limited public resources in a way that respected the agreements already reached between whites and the ANC regarding local governance. It also served to maintain support for the state education system among privileged classes that were no longer defined primarily by race. As Karlsson, McPherson and Pampallis have noted, by joining with whites to preserve the independence and quality of the former Model C schools, black political leaders were able 'to silently permit their own class interests to be taken care of without confronting (clashing with) their own, largely poor, constituencies' (Karlsson et al. 2001: 151).

South Africa's approach to fees in an international context

South Africa's decision to permit local governing bodies to impose compulsory school fees came in the early 1990s, shortly before global sentiment began to mount in opposition to such a policy. Unicef has organised a campaign to eliminate primary-level fees and other costs in Africa, and in 2000 a group of non-governmental organisations (NGOs) and teachers' unions formed a Global Campaign for Education around the belief that 'free, quality basic education for every girl, boy, man and woman is not only an essential right but an achievable goal'. In April 2000 representatives from 185 countries, including South Africa, meeting in Senegal, approved the Dakar Framework for Action as a means of assuring that by 2015 all children should 'have access to, and complete, free and compulsory primary education of good quality (Unesco 2000a: 32).

The principal argument in the international literature for abolishing fees is that they are a major cause of non-enrolment among the poor. Researchers have identified a number of countries where the elimination of fees has had a positive impact on student enrolment, albeit sometimes at the cost of lower school quality. When the government of Malawi fulfilled an election campaign pledge in 1994 by abolishing school fees and enacting a policy of Free Primary Education (FPE), primary school enrolment soared by more than 50 per cent, from approximately 1.9 million in 1993–94 to nearly 3 million the following year (Kadzamira & Rose 2001). Similarly, when Uganda eliminated tuition fees for primary schools in 1997 under its Universal Primary Education (UPE) initiative, school enrolment increased by 70 per cent (Hillman & Jenkner 2002). The most recent country to curtail school fees is Kenya, where the newly-elected president, Mwai Kibaki, fulfilled his own campaign promise by eliminating the fees that students had been required to pay in the country's 17 500 primary schools. The response was an immediate surge in enrolment that forced some schools to put new students on a waiting list for the next term.

Although the fact that fees deter enrolment among the poor in some situations would seem indisputable, international studies suggest that there are limitations on the extent to which the elimination of such user charges will solve the problem of non-enrolment. For one thing, fees are not the only influence that can deflate demand for education among the poor. Other obstacles include the opportunity costs of having children in school rather than working in the home or fields, expectations of low economic returns from a primary education, social norms that discriminate against girls and the burdens families face in dealing with AIDS. If demand for education is low for such reasons, eliminating fees may have little effect on parents' decision to send their children to school.

While research shows that the widely-held argument that fees prevent large numbers of families from enrolling their children in primary school is compelling in many, if not most, developing countries, it is by no means clear that this proposition applied to South Africa in the 1990s. To this issue we now turn.

The impact of fees on access to schooling in South Africa

As far as we can tell, under-enrolment of children at the primary level was not a serious problem in South Africa in the mid-1990s when the new funding policies were introduced. Nor does it appear to be a big problem today. By contrast, at the secondary level, many potential students are not in school, and the drop-out rate appears to have risen over time. Hence, it is hard to rule out fees as one of the factors affecting secondary school enrolments, though other factors may play a greater role.

Estimates of national enrolment rates for primary school students are presented in Table 2.4. We report a variety of estimates in order to emphasise the difficulty of determining a precise estimate of the overall enrolment rate and to highlight different definitions of the concept.[4] The first column presents three estimates of the proportions of students by age who were enrolled in school in 1995. This measure, we believe, is the best one for addressing questions about access to school. The first entry, which is based on enrolment data from the national Education Management Information System (EMIS) and national demographic data from a different source, indicates that close to 100 per cent of children aged 7 to13 were enrolled in school in 1995. This figure could well overstate the enrolment rate, since schools may inflate their enrolments to obtain more funding. The second estimate of 96.2 per cent may provide a better estimate not only because the numerator and the denominator are from the same source, the Stats SA 1995 October Household Survey, but because the enrolment data are not subject to the biases inherent in the EMIS data. Providing additional credibility to that estimate is the third

Table 2.4 Estimates of national enrolment rates

	Proportion of 7–13-year-olds enrolled	Gross (by grade)	Net (age appropriate by grade)
EMIS/DIB95	0.998		
OHS 95	0.962		
SALDRU	0.953*		
EFA 1997 (Grades 1–7)		0.965**	0.871**
EMIS 1999 (Grades 1–7)		1.06	0.933
EMIS 1999 (Grades 8–12)		0.89	0.614

Definitions and sources: Entries in the first two rows were calculated by the authors from data reported by age of student in Luis Crouch and Thaba Mabogoane (1997: Table 1). In row 1, the enrolment data are from the education management information system (EMIS) and the population data are from the Demographic Information Bureau (DIB) Data Set. In the second row, the data are from Enrolment and Population, 1995 October Housing Survey (OHS), Stats SA. The South African Labour and Development Research Unit (SALDRU) estimates were reported in Crouch (1999: Table 6). EFA 1997 data was reported in Ministry of Education (2000) Education for All: The South African Assessment Report (March), Table 4. EMIS 1999 gross enrolment figures were reported in EduSource Data News, No. 33: Table 3. The net figures were estimated by the authors based on information in the same source (Table 2) on appropriately-aged learners as a percentage of total enrolment for the year 1998. The percentages are 88 per cent for primary school students and 69 per cent for secondary school students. The gross enrolment rate is defined as the total number of students enrolled in the specified grades divided by the estimated number of children in the appropriate age range for those grades. The net enrolment rate is the number of children of the appropriate age enrolled in the specified grades divided by the estimated number of children in the appropriate age range.
Notes:
* 7–15-year-olds.
** Entries exclude students in independent schools.

entry, which is based on a separate survey by the Southern Africa Labour Development Research Unit (SALDRU). The slightly lower estimate of 95.3 per cent could reflect the fact that it includes 14- and 15-year-olds, who have somewhat lower enrolment rates than the 7- to 13-year-olds in the previous two estimates.[5]

Columns 2 and 3 report enrolment rates by grade. The gross enrolment rate is the ratio of the total number of students enrolled in the relevant grades to the total number of children in the appropriate age range for those grades. Because the numerator includes both under-age and over-age children, the gross enrolment rate can exceed one. The net rate counts in the numerator only those enrollees who are in the appropriate age range for those grades and hence, in the absence of data errors, should not exceed one. Differences between the net and gross enrolment rates may provide useful information on how well the education system is working. To the extent that differences reflect high retention rates, for example, systems with large differences between gross and net enrolment ratios might be viewed as inefficient in the sense that they require more resources to get a typical student through the system.[6]

As of 1999, the estimated net enrolment rate in South African primary schools was about 93 per cent. This estimate may be somewhat high because it is based on school enrolment data that may be somewhat inflated, or it could be misleadingly low because it excludes any 12- and 13-year-olds who have already progressed on to Grade 8. In any case, this rate is high in comparison to net enrolment rates in other countries. The EFA 2000 Assessment, which examined the status of basic education in 180 countries, reported that the net enrolment rate for all countries in 1998 was 84 per cent, with rates ranging from 82 per cent in less developed regions to 98 per cent in more developed ones. The average rate for countries in sub-Saharan Africa was only 60 per cent (Unesco 2000b). In addition, the various estimates of South African enrolment rates provide no evidence of a decline in enrolment over time. What is striking about the data in Table 2.4 is the significant drop in the net enrolment rate that occurs between the two levels of schooling – from over 90 per cent at the primary level to about 62 per cent at the secondary level.

Table 2.5 reports our own comparable estimates of enrolment rates for the Eastern and Western Cape. The observation that the estimated enrolment rates for the Eastern Cape by age (column 1) and the net rate by grade (column 3) at the primary level are greater than one, suggests that the enrolment figures for that province may be somewhat inflated. If we take the Western Cape figures roughly at face value, it appears that 100 per cent of all 7- to 13-year-olds were in school in 2001, and that about 94 per cent of them were enrolled in primary grades. This figure is misleadingly low, however, because of the relatively recent change in the school-entering age from age six to age seven. As shown by the adjusted figure for the Western Cape in column 3, adding in the 13-year-old students in Grade 8 implies that 99 per cent of the students aged 7 to 13 were in the appropriate set of grades.

Based on these admittedly imperfect estimates of enrolment rates, it would be difficult to argue that school fees have kept significant numbers of South African children from enrolling in primary schools. This outcome may be attributed in part to the existence of national policies designed to minimise the effects of fees on poor families. These include the prohibition against

Table 2.5 Enrolment rates, Eastern Cape and Western Cape, 2001

	By age (7–13)	Gross (by grade)	Net (age appropriate by grade)
Eastern Cape			
Grades 1–7	1.07	1.25	1.04
Grades 8–12	–	0.82	0.59
Western Cape			
Grades 1–7	1.01	1.07	0.94 (0.99)*
Grades 8–12	–	0.82	0.66

Source: Calculated by the authors based on data from the Eastern Cape and Western Cape DoEs.
Definitions. By age: Total number of children aged 7 to 13 enrolled in school based on EMIS data divided by the total number of children that age in the province according to Statistics South Africa's Labour Force Survey. Gross: Total number of students enrolled in the specified grades based on EMIS data divided by the estimated number of children in the appropriate age range for those grades.
Net: Number of children of the appropriate age enrolled in the specified grades divided by the estimated number of children in the appropriate age range in the province.
Note: *The first entry is based on the assumption that the age appropriate range for Grades 1 to 7 is 7 to 13. This figure understates enrolment because some 13-year-olds were in Grade 8 in 2001. This situation reflects the fact that the entry age for students in earlier years had been age 6. If we include the 13-year-olds in Grade 8, it appears that 99 per cent of the 7- to 13-year-olds were in school in an appropriate grade.

denying admission to children who cannot pay fees and the introduction in 1998 of a fee exemption policy for low-income families. According to that policy, a child is eligible for a full exemption if the combined gross income of the parents is less than 10 times the annual school fee per learner, and the child is eligible for a partial exemption if the income is between 10 and 30 times the amount of the school fee. As we will show, however, the fee exemptions have not been widely used even in situations of widespread poverty.

Other factors may also help account for the limited impact of fees as a deterrent to enrolment in primary schools. For one thing, our interviews with the principals of schools serving poor students suggest that most of them face major difficulties in collecting their published fees even when they are as low as, say, R20 per year. Such principals typically report that, despite time-consuming efforts on the part of themselves and their teachers to pressure parents into paying, they are fortunate to collect the designated fee from even a minority of families. Although schools have the option of taking non-paying parents to court, such an approach is not worth the time and effort involved given the small amounts that would be realised if successful. Thus, through informal realities and practices, many low-income families in poor communities may well pay little or no school fees.

The lower school-enrolment rates at the secondary level provide greater leeway for the possibility that school fees have kept some students out of school. However, snapshots at one point in time are hard to evaluate at the secondary level because, in contrast to the situation at the primary level, there is no clear goal such as 100 per cent enrolment in developing countries to serve as a basis of comparison. In data not shown here we take a more longitudinal perspective and document rising drop-out rates during the late 1990s in the Western Cape, a finding that could be consistent with a negative effect of fees. The problem is that other factors are at work as well. Of particular concern is the increased pressure being placed by the national DoE on secondary schools to increase their pass rates on the matriculation exam. One way for schools to do so is to encourage students not likely to pass to drop out of school, and anecdotal evidence suggests that this may be happening.

The impact of fees on enrolment patterns

While it is not at all clear that fees at the primary level have deflated the overall enrolment rate in South Africa, they appear to have significantly affected enrolment patterns among schools. That is because parents who accept the need to pay fees tend to sort themselves into schools partly in line with the fees that they are willing and able to pay. In schools serving richer communities, both the level of fees and the collection rate are generally much higher than in schools serving the poor. Hence, the students who attend those schools are either middle-income students whose parents can afford the fees or lower-income students who are accepted by those schools and who are eligible for a full or partial fee exemption. Fees thus constitute an incentive for parents to sort themselves out by income in their selection of schools.

There are two sets of factors at work here. The first is the preferences of low-income families for certain types of schools, such as those within walking distance or those with particular types of educational programmes combined with their ability and willingness to pay the fees charged by a particular school. The second factor is the decisions that school governing bodies make regarding their general admissions policies. As noted by both Crouch and Colclough, school governing bodies have incentives to minimise the admission of low-income students eligible for fee exemptions in order to avoid substantial cross-subsidies of such students by the more affluent parents. Though schools have to be careful not to discriminate against such students in an unlawful way, there is little doubt that many schools consider a family's likely ability to pay their fees when making admissions policies.

Table 2.6 provides information on the patterns of school fees and fee exemptions for schools in the Western Cape grouped by former education departments of the apartheid era. While the schools no longer serve students only of a designated race, as of 2001, there was still a strong correlation between the former department in which a school was located and the race of the students that it served. As shown in Fiske and Ladd (2002), it appears that over 99 per cent of the students in the schools served by the former national Department of Education and Training (DET) were black in 2001 and that over 91 per cent of the students in the schools served by the former House of Representatives (HoR) were coloured. The formerly white schools served by the House of Assembly (HoA) exhibited greater overall racial diversity, with about 65 per cent of their students still white in 2001, 30 per cent coloured and about 5 per cent black.[7]

The top two rows of Table 2.6 show that the average annual fees at the primary level ranged from R45 in the DET schools to over R2 000 in the former white schools. At the secondary level they ranged from R105 to R2 700 respectively. In the absence of fee exemptions, the high fees in the former white schools would put them out of the range of all but middle- and upper-middle-class families.

Exemption patterns are shown in the bottom two panels of Table 2.6. We continue to group schools by former department and by whether they are primary or secondary schools. In addition, we categorise each school into one of five fee quintiles ranging from low fees to high fees. A close look at Table 2.6 (and in particular at the numbers in parentheses) will reveal that, not surprisingly, the DET schools are disproportionately found in the low fee quintiles while the white schools are disproportionately in the high fee quintiles. We divided schools in this manner because of our prediction that the incentive for families to apply for fee exemptions would be greater when the fee is higher and the school more likely to try to collect it.

Table 2.6 Percentage of students with fee exemptions, primary and secondary schools by former department, Western Cape, 2002

	DET (black)	HoR (coloured)	HoA (white)	Total
Average annual fee charged (in Rand)				
Primary	45	99	2 077	443
Secondary	105	333	2 701	1 126
Percentage of students with fee exemption (no. of schools in parentheses)				
Primary schools (by fee quintile)				
1 (low)	1.9 (67)	3.6 (159)	–	2.5 (226)
2	1.7 (37)	1.7 (188)	–	1.7 (225)
3	4.3 (6)	1.9 (219)	–	2.1 (225)
4	13.3 (4)	2.3 (218)	10.6 (2)	2.7 (225)
5 (high)	0.0 (1)	1.3 (26)	4.1 (197)	3.7 (226)
Total	2.5 (115)	2.2 (810)	4.1 (199)	2.5 (1 127)
Secondary schools (by fee quintile)				
1 (low)	0.9 (46)	1.7 (20)	0.0 (2)	1.1 (68)
2	2.5 (9)	3.6 (56)	0.0 (1)	3.4 (66)
3	–	4.0 (63)	–	4.2 (66)
4	–	3.8 (15)	6.9 (51)	5.9 (66)
5 (high)	–	–	5.1 (65)	5.1 (65)
Total	1.2 (55)	3.6 (154)	5.7 (119)	3.7 (331)

Source: Calculated by the authors based on data provided by the Western Cape DoE.
Notes: DET signifies Department of Education and Training, HoR House of Representatives, and HoA House of Assembly. Included in the totals are three primary and three secondary schools formerly run by the House of Delegates (HoD) for Indian students that are not shown separately. Excluded completely from the table are three primary schools without fee data and three HoR secondary schools without fee data.

Of interest are the levels and patterns of the percentages of students in each cell who receive exemptions from fees. In primary schools, only 2.5 per cent of the families overall and 4.1 per cent in the former white schools receive fee exemptions. We interpret the 4.1 per cent figure to mean that the other 95.9 per cent of the students in the former white schools can afford the high fees charged by those schools. A similar pattern emerges at the secondary level, where we find that only 5.7 per cent of the students in the former white secondary schools receive full or partial fee exemptions.

Thus, either as a result of the fee policy or other factors, the former white primary and secondary schools have become schools open primarily to those with relatively high incomes, whether they be black or white. This pattern suggests that to some extent race is being replaced by economic class as the determinant of who is able to go to the formerly white schools.

Impact of fees on school quality

School fees may affect school quality directly by giving the schools that are able to levy fees the opportunity to purchase additional resources, such as teachers, that may enhance student performance. As argued by the international consultants, school fees may also exert an indirect effect by keeping key decision-makers engaged in the public schools. We examine both mechanisms in this section.

Direct effects on school quality

School fees will directly affect school quality only to the extent that they permit schools to significantly augment the resources provided by the state. As shown in Table 2.7 for primary schools and Table 2.8 for secondary schools in the Western Cape, this criterion is met only for the former HoA (white) schools. The first row of Table 2.7 reports, by former department, the average fee charged per learner, and the second row, the average total public spending per learner. Assuming that all fees were collected and that there were no fee waivers, fee revenue for the DET (black) schools would account for only one per cent of their total revenues. In contrast, the average fee of R2 077 per learner in the former white schools would augment total public funding in those schools by 54 per cent.[8]

The bottom half of Table 2.7 translates these monetary figures into the quantity of teachers and teaching qualifications. The availability of fee revenue permitted the typical black primary school to hire less than a fifth of an additional teacher while the typical white school was able to hire close to four additional teachers, which as shown in the second row, expanded their publicly funded teaching force by close to 30 per cent. The final three rows of the table provide information on the student-teacher ratios and the qualifications of state-funded teachers. For reasons we have discussed elsewhere, the white schools were somewhat advantaged in terms of both the quantity and quality of state-funded teachers. They had slightly lower learner-to-teacher ratios, teachers with higher average qualifications (as measured on the 10 to 17 scale),

Table 2.7 Public and private resources in primary schools, by former department, Western Cape, 2001

	DET (black)	HoR (coloured)	HoD (Indian)	HoA (white)	Total
Resources per student (Rand)					
Annual fees charged	45	99	327	2 077	443
Total public funds per learner	3 002	3 613	4 142	3 857	3 594
Teachers and teacher qualifications					
SGB teachers (number per school)*	0.16	0.29	1.33	3.82	0.90
SGB teachers as a percentage of state-paid teachers	0.60	2.20	12.50	28.50	6.30
Learners per state-paid teacher	38.40	36.30	37.10	35.90	36.60
Average qualifications**	13.41	13.10	13.51	14.05	13.30
Percentage of unqualified teachers	6.50	20.90	9.40	0.80	15.00

Source: Calculated by the authors based on data provided by the Western Cape DoE.
Notes:
* All teachers hired by SGBs divided by the number of schools in the cell.
** Based on a scale of 10–17, where 13 represents a qualified teacher.

and a smaller proportion of under-qualified teachers.[9] Similar patterns emerge in Table 2.8, which shows that the former white schools had sufficient fee revenue to expand their teaching staff by over 29 per cent.

Although it might seem reasonable simply to assume that these resource differences would translate into differences in educational quality, that assumption has been contested in other contexts and is worth investigating using South African data.[10] To that end, we have used the statistical tool of multiple regression analysis to examine the relationship between teaching resources and educational outcomes in South African secondary schools. We use as our outcome measure, the matriculation pass rate for twelfth graders in each school, with the passes of students who did sufficiently well on the exam to qualify for university weighted at 1.33, an ordinary pass.[11] We undertake this analysis cautiously and in full recognition of its limitations.[12] Nevertheless, we believe the analysis is useful, particularly for making the case that the

Table 2.8 Resources in secondary schools, by former department, Western Cape, 2001

	DET (black)	HoR (coloured)	HoD (Indian)	HoA (white)	Total
Resources per student (Rand)					
Annual fees charged	105	333	283	2 701	1 126
Total public funds per learner	3 402	3 972	3 803	4 419	4 034
Teachers and teacher qualifications					
SGB teachers (number per school)*	0.13	0.94	0.67	5.96	2.60
SGB teachers as a percentage of state-paid teachers	0.40	3.00	2.50	29.50	9.40
Learners per state-paid teacher	33.60	33.20	35.30	32.40	33.10
Average qualifications**	13.83	14.10	14.17	14.48	13.30
Percentage of unqualified teachers	2.60	0.80	1.20	0.00	0.90

Source: Calculated by the authors based on data provided by the Western Cape DoE.
Notes:
* All teachers hired by SGBs divided by the number of schools in the cell.
** Based on a scale of 10–17, where 13 represents a qualified teacher.

ability of some schools to hire SGB teachers appears to improve educational outcomes. Importantly, we use a direct measure of those teachers, expressed as a proportion of state-funded teachers, rather than the fee itself, as the main variable of interest. At the same time, we include in the model the school fee as a measure of the affluence of the student body.

Table 2.9 summarises the results for two specifications of the model: a basic model that includes four teacher variables and three control variables, and a second model that includes all of those variables plus indicator variables for the former education department of each school. The full equations are reported in Table 2.11 (on p. 83). Of most interest are the estimated impacts of the teacher variables. The numerical entries in the table indicate the effects on the (weighted) matriculation pass rate of a difference in each variable, which for illustrative purposes we defined as equal to the difference between the average value of the variable in the former white school and that in the former DET schools. Thus, for example, the first entry indicates that the advantage to the former white schools of having a lower learner-to-teacher ratio raised the (weighted) matriculation rate by 1.2 percentage points. The relatively small magnitude of this effect largely reflects the observation that the learner-to-teacher ratio for state-provided teachers does not differ much across white and black schools, as is shown both in the previous table and in parentheses under the variable name in the first column.

Table 2.9 Summary of determinants of matriculation pass rates, Western Cape, 2001: impacts on the weighted pass rate

	Basic model	Model with former education departments
Teacher variables*		
Learner-to-educator ratio (-1.2)	1.2	0.6
Average qualifications (0.65)	7.9	6.2
Percentage unqualified teachers (-2.6)	4.1	1.7 (not significant)
SGB teachers as % of state-funded teachers (29.1)	7.5	5.3
Control variables**		
Community poverty	negative	negative
School fees charged	positive	positive
School resources (non-teacher)	not significant	not significant
Ex-HoA (white)	–	base
Ex-DET (black)	–	negative
Ex-HoR (coloured)	–	negative
Ex-HoD (Indian)	–	not significant
No. of observations	277	277
Percentage of variation explained (adjusted)	62	67

Source: Based on the regression results reported in Table 2.11. The weighted pass rate is the number of students who passed the matriculation exam as a fraction of all students who took the exam, with those who received endorsements for university entrance weighted at 1.33, an ordinary pass.
Notes:
*For each variable the entries are the estimated effects on the weighted pass rate of the difference in the average for the variable in the former white (HoA) schools and the former black (DET) schools. See Table 2.8 for the averages by former department. The magnitudes of these differences are in parentheses below the name of each variable.
**For the first three variables, the entries indicate the direction of the impact on the weighted pass rate as the value of the variable is larger. For the former departments, the entries are the direction of impact relative to the base category of former white schools.

Much larger are the effects on matriculation rates of the advantage that the white schools enjoy with respect to teacher qualifications (7.9 percentage points) and SGB teachers as a share of state-funded teachers (7.5 percentage points). We interpret these as the effects of teaching resources rather than simply as the effects of having more affluent students since we have included as control variables two measures of income: (1) an index of the poverty of the school community and (2) the level of fees charged, which, as we noted earlier, serves as a proxy for the family income of the students in the school. The addition, in column 2, of indicator variables for the former education departments reduces the magnitudes of the estimated effects of the teacher variables, but three out of four of them are still statistically significant.[13] This finding suggests that even for comparisons among schools within a particular former department, the quantity and quality of teachers are positively associated with student outcomes. Relative to the teacher characteristics in an average school, a higher learner-to-teacher ratio is associated with a lower (weighted) pass rate; a more highly qualified group of teachers is associated with a higher pass rate; and, finally, a larger proportion of SGB teachers raises the pass rate.

Thus, while we are reluctant to interpret these results as conclusive proof that the number and quality of teachers matter, they are certainly consistent with that presumption. According to the estimated model, schools with more state-funded teachers or higher quality teachers generate better educational outcomes than do other schools. In addition, all else held constant, the more that schools are able to augment their state-funded teachers with SGB teachers, the better are their educational outcomes.

Indirect effects on school quality

The findings that emerge in Tables 2.7 to 2.9 are also relevant to the indirect mechanism through which fees might affect school quality. First, the assertion of the international experts that giving schools the authority to set fees would allow the former white schools to retain much of the quality they enjoyed during apartheid appears to have been accurate. That maintenance of quality in turn could well be a major explanation for the low rates of flight to the private schools that we documented in Table 2.1. Second, by confirming the proposition that variations in both publicly-funded and privately-funded resources affect school quality, the previous analysis also highlights the importance of maintaining strong public support for education funding, particularly for teachers.

Nonetheless, one prediction of the international consultants appears to have been thwarted in practice. That prediction was that if the key decision- and opinion-makers were induced to keep their children in public schools, public funding for education would be higher than it would have been without their engagement. In fact, it turned out that there was virtually no leeway for such opinion-makers to have much impact on the amount of public resources available for education. That was true for two reasons, both related to the global economy.

The first and most important was the introduction of the macroeconomic strategy, known as Growth, Employment and Redistribution (GEAR), in 1996. This conservative shift in economic policy was largely motivated by the desire to convince international investors that the new South Africa could manage its fiscal affairs in a responsible manner consistent with the 'Washington consensus' view that fiscal restraint and economic efficiency were to be pursued by developing countries at all costs. Though paying lip service to the more expansive goals of the earlier Reconstruction and Development Programme (RDP), GEAR kept interest rates high and focused attention on reducing the deficit rather than on promoting economic growth. The expected new foreign investment, however, did not prove to be forthcoming, and the result was a significant slowdown in the economy that was far greater than would be predicted by the slowdown in the world economy (Weeks 1999). The combination of fiscal austerity and the economic slowdown left little leeway for additional public spending of any type.

The second factor to affect education spending was the international benchmarking that we mentioned earlier. Because South Africa was already spending a higher share of its gross domestic product (GDP) on education than most other developing countries, policy-makers were not willing to spend more than seven per cent of GDP on education, despite arguments by some that the legacy of apartheid required special efforts in the area of education and that early investments in education would ultimately generate large social returns. Even under that constraint, growth in real (that is, adjusted for inflation) spending could have occurred provided the economy had grown as it was expected to do under the RDP.

The trends in education spending during the late 1990s are shown in Table 2.10. Total spending, including both national and provincial spending, increased by only 14 per cent between 1997/98 and 2000/01, with a similar increase projected between that year and 2002/03. During the same period, however, prices were rising at a faster rate, as shown for two price deflators at the bottom of the table. Thus the 14 per cent increase in actual spending translates into a decline in real spending. Spending at the provincial level, which accounts for over 85 per cent of total education spending and for all spending on primary and secondary schools, also declined in real terms. Only the inflation-adjusted spending of provinces on ordinary public schools appears to have increased, but even that increase was tiny.

Table 2.10 Aggregate spending on education, 1997/98 to 2002/03

	1997/98	1998/99	1999/2000	2000/01*	2001/02**	2002/03**
Total spending						
National and provincial	44.50	45.10	46.70	50.70	54.80	58.40
(Index)	(1.00)	(1.02)	(1.05)	(1.14)	(1.23)	(1.31)
Provincial spending						
Total	38.50	38.70	39.80	43.30	46.90	50.10
(Index)	(1.00)	(1.01)	(1.04)	(1.12)	(1.22)	(1.30)
Ordinary public schools	28.70	30.60	33.70	36.80	38.30	40.70
(Index)	(1.00)	(1.06)	(1.17)	(1.28)	(1.34)	(1.42)
Price deflators						
GDP index	1.00	1.06	1.13	1.22	1.31	–
Government services Index	1.00	1.09	1.16	1.24	1.34	–

Source: Source of spending data: RSA National Treasury, Intergovernmental Fiscal Review, 2001. Deflators are implicit price deflators for gross domestic product (GDP) and for government services.
Notes:
* = preliminary.
** = estimate from the medium term forecast.

Overall evaluation

Several general conclusions emerge from this analysis regarding South Africa's decision to encourage schools to levy fees. On the positive side, this policy appears to have successfully induced most middle-class families to keep their children in the public school system. That is an important achievement in light of South Africa's apartheid history and the values implicit in the new democracy. In replacing the fragmented education system under apartheid, it was essential for the new government to avoid setting up yet another bifurcated system of education. Moreover, permitting the former white schools to charge school fees headed off the temptation to seek equity by destroying the islands of educational excellence that existed under apartheid. South Africa needed all the trained workers and citizens it could muster, and it made little sense to undermine the quality of the 'good' schools, especially at a time when the constituency of those schools was being widened to include all races.

Contrary to the expectations of the international consultants, however, the fee policy did little, if anything, to help the historically disadvantaged schools. The policy as implemented included no explicit provision to free up more funds to be distributed to historically disadvantaged schools, as would have been the case under the preferred option of the Hunter Report, and the GEAR economic policy provided little leeway for public funding on education to respond to political pressures for greater spending. Moreover, the argument that school fees would induce schools serving low-income students to become more efficient turned out to be flawed because such schools found it difficult to collect fees, used scarce resources to do so, and generally ended up with fee revenue that was too small a portion of the overall budget to have much effect on the overall efficiency of school operations. The formerly disadvantaged schools continue to suffer from inadequate resources. We have made the general case for this conclusion elsewhere (Fiske & Ladd 2002).

Revisiting the balance between public and private funding in South Africa

At the time of writing, nine years had passed since South Africa began the ambitious task of replacing apartheid-era social, political and economic systems with new institutions committed to democratic and equitable principles. For the reasons discussed earlier, it made sense for the country to rely on both the public and private sectors to marshal the resources needed for the reformed state education system. Nevertheless, the fact remains that, as a fundamental human right, basic education is more appropriately financed by broad-based taxes on the entire community than by a method that relies partially on user charges paid by parents (Hillman & Jenkner 2002: 10, 24–25). The challenge for South Africa now is to move in that direction.

One possible strategy is for the government of South Africa to continue providing a baseline allotment of teachers to all public schools, based, as now, primarily on the number of learners enrolled in each school. Schools would then be given the following two choices.

1. They could continue to set school fees at whatever level they chose and to use the fee revenue as they wished, including to hire additional teachers.
2. Alternatively, they could give up the right to charge fees in return for a guaranteed additional number of supplemental teachers (and associated classrooms, if necessary), beyond their basic government funded allotment. A more flexible version of this option would give schools the freedom to decide whether to spend the additional government resources on teachers or on other inputs.

Most likely, schools serving the wealthier families would choose the first option on the grounds that maintaining the quality of their schools was worth the cost of the additional fees even at the loss of some public funding. Poorer schools, in contrast, would be likely to choose the second option. The overall result would be that additional public funds would be channelled to the needier schools without interfering with the power of the wealthier schools to use private funding to maintain school quality.

This proposal reflects, in part, the spirit of the partnership-funding approach initially proposed in the Hunter Report but, unlike this report, extends the principle beyond non-personnel spending to the hiring of teachers. Such a policy would not keep the former Model C schools that once served the white elite from having far greater access to resources than other schools. It would, however, most likely reduce some of the current fee-related disparities in quality among wealthy and poor schools by enhancing the teaching staff of the poor schools. In doing so it would address what appears to us to be the more urgent priority, which is to find ways for getting more resources to the schools serving low-income and historically disadvantaged families.

Table 2.11 Determinants of matriculation pass rates, Western Cape, 2001[a]

	Basic I	With former department II
Teacher variables		
Learner-to-educator ratio	-0.0097**	-0.005**
	(6.00)	(2.56)
Average qualification of teachers[b]	0.122**	0.095**
	(3.04)	(2.49)
Percentage of teachers underqualified[c]	-0.016**	-0.0065
	(3.10)	(1.30)
School governing body teachers (share)[d]	0.258**	0.181*
Family income		
Community poverty	-0.528**	-0.285
	(6.59)	(3.25)
Annual school fee	0.000013**	0.000014**
	(2.12)	(2.25)
Other control variables		
School resources	-0.161	-0.138
	(0.96)	(0.88)
Former white (base)	–	Base
Former DET (black)	–	-0.285**
		(5.52)
Former HoR (coloured)	–	-0.121**
		(3.14)
Former HoD (Indian)	–	-0.011
		(0.08)
Constant	-0.308	-0.089
	(0.59)	(0.16)
No. of observations	277	277
Adjusted R²	0.62	0.67

Notes: Dependent variable is weighted matriculation pass rate.
a. Dependent variable is the number of students who passed the matriculation exam as a fraction of all students who took the exam, with those who received endorsements for university entrance weighted at 1.33, an ordinary pass.
b. Based on teacher qualification scale that runs from 10–17.
c. Full qualification is matriculation plus three years which translates to 13 on the teacher qualification scale.
d. SGB teachers as a fraction of government funded teachers.
Equations were estimated by ordinary least squares; t-statistics are in parentheses,** indicates statistical significance at the five per cent level and * at the ten per cent level.

Acknowledgements

This chapter is part of a larger research project on South Africa's efforts to make its education system more equitable and democratic. The larger project was supported by a Fulbright grant to Helen Ladd that enabled the two authors to spend six months at the University of Cape Town in 2002. The authors are extremely grateful to the Fulbright Association, to the Department of Economics at the University of Cape Town and to the Spencer Foundation, which provided supplemental funds for the research. In addition, the authors appreciate the able research assistance of Steven Kent and Richard Walker, and the co-operation of Education Department officials in the Western Cape and Eastern Cape, who provided the school level data for those provinces.

Notes

1. That report recommends that the DoE more stringently monitor fee-setting processes and provide fairer and more effective exemptions processes that are fully integrated into government's programmes to alleviate poverty (DoE 2003).

2. *South African Schools Act* of 1996: 24. In fact the independent schools receive some public subsidies. Before 2000, all registered independent schools received a provincial subsidy on a sliding scale with the poorest schools obtaining the most and the well-endowed schools the least. Since 2000, the wealthier schools receive no subsidy. If an independent school's fees are more than 2.5 times the average provincial *per capita* norms and standards expenditure on public pupils, then it receives no subsidy. Schools with fees below that level continue to obtain a subsidy with the poorest schools obtaining the maximum amount of 60 per cent of average provincial *per capita* (non-teacher) spending on public schools.

3. The estimates in Table 2.1 exclude students in unregistered independent schools. According to Hofmeyr and Lee (this volume), the total number of private schools, including unregistered schools, could be twice as large as the total reported by the DoE. Because unregistered schools are likely to be smaller than registered schools, however, the proportion of students in all independent schools reported in the table most likely underestimates the number of students in independent schools by a smaller proportion than for the number of schools. Hofmeyr and Lee also emphasise that, contrary to the perception that the independent sector caters to wealthy, white students, the sector is now mainly religious and community-based, serves a predominantly black clientele, and typically charges low school fees.

4. The publication of the 1996 census raised some serious questions about the validity of the figures reported in the first column of Table 2.4. Although the census reported no enrolment figures for students in the 7 to 13 age range, its estimate of the proportion of 7- to 24-year-olds in school suggested a much lower enrolment rate for the younger ages than is consistent with the figures reported in the table. Careful analysis by Crouch (1998) suggests that the census may well have seriously underestimated the school enrolment figures. He argues, and we agree, that the figures in the table are the more believable figures, largely because they emerge from different sources, one based on a full census of schools and two from separate household surveys. Because the census is self-administered to a larger degree than is either Statistics South Africa's October Household Survey (OHS) or the SALDRU survey, it is subject to greater misinterpretation.

5. Based on EMIS/DIB data, enrolment ratios for 14- and 15-year-olds were 0.91 and 0.88, and on 1995 OHS data were 0.97 and 0.94 (Crouch & Mabogoane 1997, Table 1).

6. Care is required, however, in interpreting the differences. At a minimum a distinction should be made between over-age students who were retained and those who dropped out of school for non-school reasons – such as to take care of an ailing parent or to earn income – and then returned to school. Also, the presence of under-age children in primary school could well reflect the absence of other childcare options for parents.

7. These are estimates because many schools in the Western Cape did not report racial breakdowns and the estimates vary by primary or secondary school (see Fiske & Ladd 2002). Also, we have left out the Indian (HoD) schools because of their small number. See also Soudien in this volume who argues that, nationally, children classified black appear to constitute a larger proportion of the total school population in former Indian and coloured schools than in former white schools.

8. Because the entries in the first row of Table 2.7 represent the fees charged per student, rather than the fees collected by the schools, they most likely understate the true disparities in fee revenue across types of schools. That conclusion follows because of the greater ease with which the former white schools can collect the fees they charge. Working in the other direction, however, is the fact that fee exemptions are more common in the former white schools than in the schools of the other departments.

9. Fiske & Ladd (2002). The minimum level for a qualified teacher is 13, which represents matriculation (formerly called Standard 10) plus three years of additional training.

10. The proposition has been frequently contested in the US context by Eric Hanushek based on meta-analyses of studies of the effects of resources. (See, for example,

Hanushek, 1986 and 1997). His conclusions have been challenged, however, by other more sophisticated meta-analyses (Hedges, Laine, and Greenwald 1994). That resources mattered during the apartheid period in South Africa has been demonstrated quite convincingly by Case and Deaton (1999).

11. The results are similar, but slightly less strong, when the dependent variable is not weighted. When ordinary pass rates are used, much of the variation at the high end of the distribution is lost because many schools have pass rates of 100 per cent.

12. The outcome measure is quite crude, and ideally, one should control for the achievement of students as they enter the school in Grade 8 and include a more complete set of control variables. In addition, one must be aware of the potential for some reverse causation in the sense that the higher-qualified teachers may choose to teach in the schools with higher matriculation pass rates. At the same time, the inclusion of the two income-related variables (school poverty and the school fee) does a reasonably good job of controlling for family background characteristics that play such an important role in educational outcomes, and thereby help to keep the reverse causation problem to a minimum.

13. The insignificance of the share of unqualified teachers in this equation reflects the high correlation between the value of that variable and the former department of the school.

References

Case, A & Deaton, A (1999) School Inputs and Educational Outcomes in South Africa, *Quarterly Journal of Economics*, 114: 1047–1084

Colclough, C (no date) Notes on a Scheme for School Fees, to be Introduced Voluntarily by Schools

Crouch, L (1995) School Funding Options and Medium-Term Budgeting for Education in South Africa. Consultant's Report prepared for the DoE. November

Crouch, L (1999) Education Data and the 1996 Census: Some Crucial Apparent Problems and Possible Strategies for Resolution, *Edusource Data News* 24: 10–16

Crouch, L & Mabogoane, T (1997) Aspects of internal efficiency indicators in South African schools: analysis of historical and current data, *Edusource Data News* 19: 4–28

Crouch, L & Mabogoane, T (1998) No Magic Bullets, Just Tracer Bullets. Unpublished manuscript

Department of Education (2003) *Report to the Minister: A Review of the Financing, Resourcing and Costs of Education in Public Schools.* 3 March

Donaldson, A (1992) Financing Education. In McGregor, R & McGregor, A (eds) *McGregor's Educational Alternatives*. Kenwyn: Juta

Fiske, E & Ladd, H (2002) Financing Schools in Post Apartheid South Africa: Initial Steps Toward Fiscal Equity. Paper prepared for International Conference on Education and Decentralisation: African Experiences and Comparative Analysis, Johannesburg, 10–14 June. Forthcoming in Conference Volume. (Also available as a Sanford Institute Working Paper. Duke University, Sanford Institute of Public Policy)

Hanushek, E (1986) The Economics of Schooling: Production and Efficiency in Public Schools, *Journal of Economic Literature*, 24(13): 1141–1177

Hanushek, E (1997) Assessing the Effects of School Resources on Student Performance: An Update, *Educational Evaluation and Policy Analysis*, 19(2): 141–164

Hedges, L; Laine, R & Greenwald, R (1994) Does Money Matter? A Meta-Analysis of Studies of the Effects of Differential School Inputs on Student Outcomes, *Educational Researcher*, 23(3): 5–14

Hillman, A & Jenkner, E (2002) *User Payments for Basic Education in Low-Income Countries*. International Monetary Fund Working Paper

Hofmeyr, J & Lee, S (this volume) The New Face of Private Schooling. In Chisholm, L (ed) *Education and Social Change in post-apartheid South Africa*. Pretoria: HSRC

Hunter, P (1995) *Report of the Committee to Review the Organisation, Governance and Funding of Schools*. First Text Copy Edition. Pretoria: DoE

Kadzamira, E & Rose, P (2001) *Educational Policy Choice and Policy Practice in Malawi: Dilemmas and Disjunctures*, Institute of Development Studies Working Paper 124, University of Sussex

Karlsson, J; McPherson, G & Pampallis, J (2001) A Critical Examination of the Development of School Governance Policy and its Implications for Achieving Equity. In Motala, E & Pampallis, J (eds) *Education & Equity: The Impact of State Policies on South African Education*. Cape Town: Heinemann

Pampallis, J (1998) Decentralisation in the New Education System: Governance and Funding of Schooling in South Africa 1992–1997. In *Democratic Governance of Public Schooling in South Africa*. Durban: University of Natal Education Policy Unit

Perry, H (1996) *Summary of Luis Crouch's report (November 1995) on the School Review Committee's proposals for school funding*. Johannesburg

Republic of South Africa (1996) *South African Schools Act*, No. 84 of 1996. Pretoria: Government Printers

Seekings, J (2001) *Making an Informed Investment: Improving the Value of Public Expenditure in Primary and Secondary Schooling in South Africa.* Report for the Parliament of South Africa, commissioned by the Standing Committee on Public Accounts.

Unesco (2000a) *Dakar Framework for Action.* Paris: Unesco

Unesco (2000b) *Final Report of the World Education Forum.* Paris: Unesco

Weeks (1999) Stuck in Low Gear? Macroeconomic Policy in South Africa, 1996–98, *Cambridge Journal of Economics,* 23: 795–811

3 'Constituting the class': an analysis of the process of 'integration' in South African schools

Crain Soudien

Introduction

Any discussion that seeks to delve into issues such as 'community', 'integration', 'the nation' and so on, cannot but begin with the caution that history and the broad social sciences constitute a *constructed* field. Whether one takes the approach of consensus and leans towards what has come to be understood as the 'liberal' view of society, namely, that of a presumptive sense of coherence (and asks what constitutes 'the community'; how 'the nation' is imagined; what divisions and fractures exist within the nation, group or community; what is to be 'integrated' or unified) or the more critical approach of rights and justice (and asks how rights are to be distributed or redistributed) will always depend, as Carr (1964) would have said, on *who* the historian or the social commentator asking the question is.

Mindful of Carr's injunction, this chapter seeks to provide an explanation of how South African schools are dealing with the challenge of integration. The broad argument that it will make is that the notion of 'integration' depends on how the concept of difference is defined. The chapter works mainly with the dominant approach to difference in South Africa, that of race. It tries to show, as an attempt to engage with the question of how education is contributing to social change in South Africa, that the most critical outcome of the process of integration has been that of assimilation. While there has been a flight of children out of the former black schools, there has been no movement whatsoever in the direction of black schools. It is also argued that children of colour have moved in large numbers towards the English-speaking sector of the former white school system. This clearly suggests that the social nature of the education system has changed quite dramatically. The change, however, has been complex and has made it possible for the expanded middle class, which now includes people of colour, to consolidate its position of privilege. Working-class and poor people, conversely, continue to experience high degrees of vulnerability and even discrimination.

The chapter begins with a discussion of the different ways in which the field of difference has been conceptualised and understood in South Africa. It proceeds to suggest that there are difficulties that come with the conventional understandings of difference in South Africa and, using the notion of 'scapes', or ways of seeing, points to a more complex way of looking at how integration might be approached.

Race, class and notions of difference

One of the most important scholars of social difference in South Africa, Harold Wolpe (1988), argues that neither race nor class, by itself, is capable of explaining the nature of the South African social formation and the ways in which privilege, power and position are distributed. Neither is able to grasp the entire story of social division, the hierarchies that operate within society and, critically, how rights accrue or are denied. Explaining South Africa and seeking to resolve the injustices and inequalities would require more than working through issues of race and/or class. In his work he makes the crucial point that the formation and maintenance of racial groups and division in South Africa is a process that takes place in specific contexts that are subject to both centrifugal and centripetal pressures. Allied to these is the crucial element of politics, which operates often independently from other factors but always in some form of articulation with them. This combination of the instances of race, class and politics produces effects and outcomes that are, moreover, ongoing and always in flux. They produce differentiations within groups, fracturing their homogeneity. Privileging race, therefore, as a category of analysis, underplays the ways in which a whole range of conditions and processes influence the sense of cohesiveness and fragmentation within groups. Class analysis too, he continues to argue, suffers from a similar insularity and reductionism. As a result of this reductionism, little room is allowed for non-class effects. 'It is clear,' says Wolpe, 'that this analysis provides no conceptual basis for an analysis of the specific conditions in which racial categorisations come to provide the content of class struggles and/or the basis of organisation of interests in a manner which both cuts across class divisions and yet may serve to sustain, change (for example, racialisation or deracialisation) or undermine them' (1988: 15).

The value of Wolpe's work is that it calls into question the ways in which discourses of race and class have been mobilised to understand South Africa. In his text, *Race, class and the apartheid state*, he implicitly argues against the dominant iconographic systems of South Africa, particularly those of race, and looks to more complex ways of understanding social difference in South Africa. In attempting to analyse post-apartheid South Africa there is much to work with. The racial discourse of apartheid has been sustained and carried into the new South Africa, even as the new state has struggled to assert itself. The new reform agenda has remained firmly within the discourse of race. This is manifest in policies of affirmative action, immigration and social renewal.

While recognising how and why the language of race retains its pertinence, of concern in thinking about questions of integration, is the question of how the theory we use is able to engage with and even displace the power/knowledge couplet of race (and even class). How do we write in ways that will subvert the power that comes with the language of race?

Part of an answer is recognising that our explanations of the realities we confront will always be grasping or incomplete. They construct and constitute the reality as we speak it. They hold versions or interpretations of what is out there and present these as the truth. They are unable to recognise the multiple social contingencies that enter our processes of making meaning. Instead, our statements of what reality is depend on unproblematised portmanteau theories that are allowed to define and to normalise what clearly is partial and incomplete. Forgotten are the stratagems and artifices of our representational modalities within these grand theories, forgotten are the multiple conscious and unconscious positions of privilege we call upon as we pronounce and enunciate.

Towards a new space

In attempting to move to a more self-conscious theoretical position, one which is aware of how we take position within the structures and narratives of our own social analyses, we need to develop a social criticism that is alert to the shifting relationship between cultural difference, social authority and political discrimination; one that can deal with the dominant rationalisations of self and other. Such an approach would need to be aware of how much the ways in which we speak, our theories and languages of description, can be mobilised for the dominant project of race and class. It has the potential to open up ways of seeing that take us beyond the stereotypical ways in which difference is understood. Critically, it unmasks the arbitrary ways in which the mark of the stereotype is assigned to each of us, particularly the racial, class, cultural and gender values that define who we are. It has the potential to help us work in new productive spaces where we can confront processes of social and individual meaning-making – culture – in our lives and recognise how those processes continually produce new forms of oppression and emancipation, and how each of us is implicated in these processes. From such a position we can develop a project of emancipation that is fundamentally conscious of the complex ways in which we are positioned and position ourselves. We can begin to see each other in our heterogeneity and to deal with, and not disavow, the proclivity within us to 'other' as we socially identify. The power of such an approach is to force us to realise the limitations of consensual and collusive theories of community embodied in notions of race, class, gender, culture and so on.

Taking this into thinking about the questions of unity or integration in South Africa, we clearly have a long way to go. Critically, therefore, if we are seeking to enter a new social space where notions of 'unity' and 'integration' drive social policy, what realities, we must ask, are we to unify and to integrate? Can it be *any* reality? *All* realities? And once we have unified or brought them together, what notions of self and group do we use that will remain just and fair, sensitive to the multiple ways in which individuals and groups seek to be represented, and yet at the same time, critical and alert to the political and ideological artifices that go with building polities?

Working with notions of integration – integration-scapes

In terms of the arguments above I want to suggest that there are two ways of proceeding. The first is to develop an approach that tries to work with the notion of multiplicity and brings together, as far as is possible, the range of factors that *can* be identified within a given context. The second is to work with the dominant languages of description in their attenuated form, or insofar as they attempt to articulate with other ways of seeing.

The first approach could be described as the contingent model and the second as the dominant factor model. Elements of both models were used in the

Education Inclusion and Exclusion in India and South Africa Project reported in an Institute of Development Studies (IDS) Bulletin (Subrahmanian, Sayed, Balagopalan & Soudien 2003). The contingent model clearly carries more possibilities in terms of its aims of uncovering the complex and multiple forms of identification and identity that would have to be revealed and would need to be mediated in a common social space. The second is more limited in so far as its logic tends to insulate the major factor, even when its dominance is in doubt.

For pragmatic purposes, however, I am electing to work with the dominant factor model simply because there is available material to work with. Attempting to work in an integrated factor framework, at this stage, is not viable, if only because the existing material on integration, as it has been understood and assembled, does not easily lend itself to thinking of complexity and contingency.

Having made the decision to use the dominant factor approach, I am proposing that a suitable way forward might be to work in a number of what one might call 'scapes' where the dominant factor can be seen to be at work. Scapes are used here as ways of seeing. They frame the objects that come into view in particular kinds of ways. Reality and an explanation of what reality constitutes are defined in relation to the dominant factor. Having assembled these scapes we might then see how we can reach *towards* a contingent model by articulating the different scapes in an integrated analysis.

Important about such an approach is that:
- It acknowledges, in its very genesis, its limitations and the possibilities for being recruited into use by the dominant project.
- It recognises its dependency on certain representational strategies, chief amongst which are reductionism and essentialism.
- It declares its culpability as a discursive framework for defining reality.

What are the scapes that we can describe? The most obvious are those of race, class and gender. Allied to these are cultural scapes, language scapes, religious scapes, age scapes, sexual orientation scapes, physical ability scapes, intellectual ability scapes, nationality scapes, health scapes (including HIV/AIDS) and a whole range of others that have yet to be specified.

Taking this approach is, of course, not without its difficulties. While it attempts to suggest a way through the thickets of the school integration discussion, there are certain immediate challenges that it throws up. Predictably, the first and most important is that of attempting to develop a series of ways of seeing in an analytic space where particular perspectives have been privileged and others disallowed. Given this, we have to accept that some scapes will be considerably fuller, better-constructed and more accessible than others. Other scapes will be, in their turn, either darker or emptier. This clearly suggests opportunities for developing new lines of research and investigation. These are not pursued in this work. The next section of the chapter, therefore, seeks to work with the dominant scapes of race and class. The discussion draws on work carried out both by myself and colleagues as well as by a range of researchers working in the field.

The race scape

The race scape is, of course, dominant within the repertoire of school integration analyses and studies both in South Africa and elsewhere in the world. In many ways, the South African debate has depended on the discussion as it has unfolded in the United States and to a lesser degree in the United Kingdom. In the United States, where it has attracted both the best and the worst theorists of schooling and equality, the genre has literally exploded. In South Africa it has achieved prominence in a field that remains frustratingly slim, under-researched and heavily dependent on the terminology, the typologies and modes of analyses of North Americans.

Studies that take race explicitly as their focus in South Africa include the work of Lemmer and Squelch (1993), Dekker and Lemmer (1993), a landmark report conducted for the Human Rights Commission by Vally and Dalamba (1999), a forthcoming doctoral thesis by Tihanyi (2003), Zafar's (1998) work on integrating public schools, and a study published by the Education Policy Unit at the University of Natal arising from a Master's thesis by Naidoo (1996). A larger corpus of work which looks more generally at school relations rather than race only is also available in the work of Christie (1990), Gaganakis (1990), Carrim (1992), Soudien (1996, 1998a, 1998b), Carrim & Soudien (1999), Chisholm (1999), Dolby (2001) and Soudien & Sayed (2003). Other studies, such as that of Hofmeyr (2000), touch on the subject. There are undoubtedly many more studies and commentaries on the matter. These, however, represent the most significant in the field.

The dominant theoretical approach within this body of work is that of social construction. As is to be expected, no works in the South African literature explicitly approach race from the primordialist perspective (even though those beliefs may exist, and may parade as social constructionism). In relation to social construction, positions vary from the Marxist to those leaning towards what was earlier described as contingency theory.

The consequence of this approach is to understand integration, and its opposite, desegregation, in distinctive kinds of ways. As Naidoo says, integration 'requires fundamental changes in ... personal attitudes and behaviour patterns. It requires major changes of deep-seated attitudes and behaviour patterns among learners and teachers of minority and majority groups' (1996: 11). In this approach, integration is when groups with their cultures come together. The interesting thing for this discussion is not what happens when bodies meet, but that which occurs when the cultural auras or cultural universes around people come into contact with each other. People are assumed to be carrying their universes around them as they engage and negotiate with each other.

How they deal with each other, carrying these universes with them, is the interest of those who work with race. Following the work of sociologists and psychologists, integration occurs only when positive interaction occurs (see Rist 1979). What counts is not physical contact but how yielding and open to engagement the universes people are carrying around with them are. As Naidoo says, 'the current ethos of a school, the nature of the interaction and existing patterns and institutional features and policies of school may limit or facilitate such integration' (1996: 11). These orientations make possible, essentially, three different approaches to integration, namely, assimilation, multicultural education and anti-racist education. These approaches, from the perspective of equality and justice, represent a continuum of possibilities in which one can see degrees of accommodation and integration.

The least accommodative and integrative is the assimilationist position. In this position the values, traditions and customs of the dominant group frame the social and cultural context of the school. Quoting Gillborn, Naidoo explains that key to the assimilationist project are the presumptions that subordinate groups represent a threat to the standards of the dominant group and that the dominant group is culturally superior (1996: 12).

By contrast, the consequences of assimilationism for subordinate groups are dire. They are expected both to give up their own identities and cultures and, critically, to acknowledge the superiority of the culture, and by implication, the identities of the groups into whose social context they are moving.

In response to the oppressiveness of assimilationism, especially in the United States and the United Kingdom, a more accommodative policy was developed called multiculturalism. Central to multiculturalism was the idea that the school had to accommodate the different cultures brought into it. Arising in response to the demands of politically subordinate groups, it essentially sought to make the point that all cultures were equally valid and had to be respected in the school context.

Not unexpectedly, multiculturalism drew the ire of critics from both the right and the left. Right-wing critics, such as Hirsch (1987) and Ravitch (1990) in the United States, argued that it undermined the inclusivist nature of the great American culture and sought to infuse into it inferior standards. Critics on the left saw it, *inter alia*, as a weak, and in the end racist, alternative to real democracy in so far as it paid lip service to the rights of the subordinate, and was also a way of continuing to shore up half-baked and stereotypical notions of culture. They argue that the so-called respect for other cultures fails to engage with the complex ways in which individuals and groups develop attitudes to one another. While cultures are celebrated, the processes through which those cultures are delineated and then hierarchalised never come into view. They call, therefore, for a perspective that engages directly with processes that make meaning. Theirs, they argue, is an anti-racist programme that directly attacks the othering implicit and embedded in dominant culture.

These three approaches are evident and have been used in most studies working in the race scape in South Africa. Interestingly, most studies come to much the same conclusion, namely, that the integration process in South Africa has followed a decidedly assimilationist route.

In what follows an attempt is made to show how these studies come to this conclusion. Before this is done, a point of clarification about the empirical strength of the data available to us is necessary. As things stand, essentially because the new government has officially abolished racial categories (even though this policy is inconsistently followed), not all schools or provincial authorities collect statistics about their learners in terms of race. Where information is collected in this way, it has happened, one hopes, as a result of individual decisions at schools, hopefully with the consent of parents and learners. Official statistics that reflect the racial demography of schools are not uniformly available. Annual reports of provincial governments, as a result, do not systematically include integration as an aspect of schooling experience. While the reports might make mention of racism and racial incidents at schools, they do not deal with race as a demographic factor. The result of this is that we do not know in a precise and accurate way what has happened in terms of racial integration in South African schools.

One source of empirical data is a research-led body of evidence on learner migration carried out by the Human Sciences Research Council (HSRC) (Sekete, Shilubane & Moila 2001). Another is a set of statistics provided to the Human Rights Commission study (Vally & Dalamba 1999). Fleshing out this picture are a number of studies where estimations of integration have been made based on a number of sources.

The Sekete et al. study, based on a survey of 120 schools (79 returns) in five provinces, showed that enrolments had changed dramatically (2001: 33). In response to the question of the extent to which changes had occurred in their schools, respondents reported as shown in Table 3.1.

Table 3.1 Extent of changes in selected schools in five provinces (percentages)

	None	Minor	Moderate	Major	n.a.
Enrolments have changed in terms of their racial composition	6.8	16.1	31.2	29.3	16.2
The schools admission policy has changed to accommodate learners from different residential backgrounds	10.4	11.4	27.7	39.7	10.8
The number of learners coming from other than the school's immediate neighbourhood has changed	5.2	19.3	36.2	33.1	6.1

If one accepts that almost 75 per cent of schools are formerly designated as black and that, as is argued later, very little change would have happened in these schools in terms of demographics, the extent of the changes signalled in the table is considerable. In response to all three questions about the extent of change, as is shown in Table 3.1, more than 60 per cent of the respondents acknowledged that either moderate or major changes had taken place in their schools.

The 1999 Vally and Dalamba study (see Table 3.2) shows that across the former House of Assembly (HoA) schools that served pupils classified white, the House of Representatives (HoR) system that served pupils classified coloured and the House of Delegates (HoD) system that served pupils classified Indian, all in the Gauteng region, the number of children classified African (black) was significant. What is clear is the strength of the movement into the former Indian and coloured schools.

Table 3.2 Percentage of Gauteng learners by race groups

	Ex-DET 'African'				Ex-TED 'white'				Ex-HoR 'coloured'				Ex-HoD 'Indian'			
	A	W	C	I	A	W	C	I	A	W	C	I	A	W	C	I
Grade 1	100	0	0	0	16	75	2	6	9	0	91	0	61	0	22	17
All Grades	100	0	0	0	22	72	3	2	31	0	67	0	45	0	5	50

Note: Tables 3.2 and 3.3 use the following abbreviations: A (African), W (white), C (coloured) and I (Indian).

These statistics need to be read in conjunction with those captured in Table 3.3 that show the breakdown of learners by race in the entire system for Gauteng.

Table 3.3 Total percentage of Gauteng learners by race groups in public and independent schools

	All public schools				Independent (subsidised)				Independent (non-subsidised)				Total			
	A	W	C	I	A	W	C	I	A	W	C	I	A	W	C	I
Grade 1	77	16	5	2	55	37	2	6	80	18	2	0	76	17	5	2
All Grades	71	21	5	2	57	35	2	5	86	12	1	0	70	22	5	3

Studies examining other provinces support the trends noted in Gauteng. The Inclusion and Exclusion Project (Soudien & Sayed 2003) looked at 14 schools (fictitious names provided) located in the provinces of KwaZulu-Natal, the Eastern Cape and the Western Cape. Based on estimates provided by school principals, the schools' demographic profiles are shown in Table 3.4.

Table 3.4 Learner demographic profiles

Name of school (fictitious)	Ex-depart-ment	Enrolment (%) TOTAL	A	W	C	I	Medium of instruction	Social context
Ruby Primer	HoR	300	60	40			Afrikaans	Poor working class
Lagaan Primary	HoD	800	15		5	80	English	Middle class
Bass Secondary	HoD	1 200	80			20	English	Stable working class
Dover High School	HoD	+/-900	80			20	English	Middle class
Amazon Secondary	HoD	+/- 1 000	80			20	English	Stable working class
Marula Primary	HoD	520	60		10	20	English	Poor working class
Basildon Primary	DET	414	90				English	Middle class
Divinity Technical	DET	+/-700	100				English	Stable working class/lower middle class
Bongalethu Secondary	DET	1 001	100				English	Working class poor
Siyafika Secondary	DET	1 020	100				English	Working class poor
Eastdale Primary	HoA	+/- 600	60	40			English	Upper middle class boys
Oasis Senior Primary	HoA	+/-700	20	10		70	English	Middle class
Valley Primary	HoA	600		90	10		English	Middle class
North City High	HoA	800	0	90	10	0	Afrikaans	Middle class

What is interesting about this set of data is how complex schools' population mixes have become. While the national evidence, as argued earlier, of the nature and the extent of the movement of South African boys and girls across their apartheid divides is not available, the assumption that the strongest movements have occurred from black to white schools is open to question. It would appear that the movement from formerly black schools to Indian and coloured schools has been as strong as, if not stronger than, that of black people into formerly white schools. Black students have been migrating into Indian and coloured schools closest to their homes and convenient for purposes of travel. In the Cape Town area, for example, former Indian and coloured schools located on bus and train routes from the townships have been the recipients of considerable numbers of black students. While anecdotal evidence seems to suggest also that there has been a domino effect in this process with coloured and Indian students moving further up the transport line to former white schools, the reality seems to be that the demographic profiles of former coloured and Indian schools have changed significantly with some schools' pupil rolls being up to 50 per cent black.

This evidence is supported by Naidoo's work in KwaZulu-Natal (KZN) which shows that the percentages of children classified black in former Indian schools are more than twice those in the former white schools from the former Natal Education Department (NED) (see Table 3.5).

Table 3.5 Percentage of black learners in selected KZN schools

Ex-Department	School			Area					Medium of instruction	
	High	Prim	Total	Dbn	PMB	Newcastle	Port Shep	Rich. Bay	Eng	Afrik
Ex-NED	17	10	14	17	10	15	30	10	21	<1
Ex-HoD	41	28	35	35	35	38	30	30	35	n.a.
Average	29	19	24	26	23	27	30	20	28	<1

Interesting about the Naidoo study is the suggestion that the levels of integration in smaller towns are lower than those in the metropolitan areas. Evident in both smaller towns and the metropolitan areas is the large enrolment of children classified black in former HoD schools.

Hofmeyr's study in the Carletonville area, carried out over three years, shows evidence of large movements from former Department of Education and Training (DET) schools (2000). Interesting about this study, and also suggested in the Soudien and Sayed (2003) and Tihanyi (2003) studies, is that former white schools have not uniformly become majority black. While this is certainly not the basis for making definitive statements, it appears that English-speaking former HoA schools are more popular amongst black learners and parents.

The actual patterns of migration are important to track and understand. Fiske and Ladd (in this volume) use Western Cape data to show how learners are migrating from black to Indian and white schools. The evidence provided by Tihanyi, as well as Gauteng data, shows a different pattern. Learners and their families are making important decisions about what they perceive to be in their best interests. Noteworthy are the following:

- The flight of students out of former black schools. There has been no parallel movement whatsoever of children classified coloured, white and Indian into former black schools. The schools that are integrating, therefore, are all the non-former DET schools.
- Children classified black appear to constitute a larger proportion of the total school population in former Indian and coloured schools than in former white schools.
- Children classified black, it would appear, are not entering Afrikaans-speaking former white schools in significant numbers.

Why these particular patterns are arising deserves more detailed study than is possible here. Briefly, however, it is clear that the flight of black children out of the former DET system has much to do with the recent history of turbulence within that system and the perception, as many commentators suggest, of higher standards in the other systems (see, for example, Sekete et al. 2001). This is especially the case with regard to the former HoD schools. While former white schools are regarded in the same light, the perception that they are expensive has limited the movement of students into them. Following these comments, it is true to say then that particular kinds of schools are not attracting large numbers of previously disqualified learners. Why this is so undoubtedly has to do with issues of physical, financial and linguistic access. These issues were explored in the Soudien and Sayed (2003) study and will not be pursued here.

A further point to note before looking at the outcomes of the studies is the degree to which the schools retain the racial profiles of their former authorities as far as teachers are concerned. Former Indian schools remain largely Indian with respect to their teachers, former white schools largely white and former coloured largely coloured (Soudien & Sayed 2003).

Having outlined the patterns of movement in the system, it is now necessary, on the basis of the existing research, to make some comments about what is happening in these schools.

In none of the studies is there evidence of what the literature calls the anti-racist school. Instead, all the studies concur on the distinct tendency towards assimilationism. This is even the case in the examples of the politically conscious schools my own work has looked at (see Soudien 1996). This is an important point around which to pause because it talks to the issue of those individual teachers and schools in the system who deliberately and consciously work for and project themselves as subverters of the dominant order (see Weider 2001a, 2001b and 2002). There remains a strong tradition in the country of individuals who have valiantly sought to make what they teach the subject of their own, and their pupils', interrogation. In many instances, however, these individuals, unless they were supported by organisations, such as was the case with the Teachers League of South Africa, burned themselves out in their efforts. The schools which presented themselves as radical schools were also, and still are, complex and contradictory places. While these schools promote a strong non-racial ethos, and present themselves as 'schools for people' and not 'schools for coloureds' or 'schools for black', they do not have the analytic sophistication to engage with issues of identity. Much of their engagement with race is polemical rather than substantial and interrogative. They end up, as a result, working with notions of identity that young people are simply required to take on. Following this, Naidoo says explicitly that all the schools in his study followed an assimilationist approach (1996: 28). The Vally and Dalamba study comes to a similar conclusion: 'the predominant trend in school desegregation is the assimilationist approach, or as one student emphasised: "I feel that if pupils from other races want to come to our school then they must adjust to the culture and norms of the school."' (1999: 24).

Vally and Dalamba suggest that some schools have begun to espouse a multicultural perspective (1999: 32). Providing evidence for this statement they quote teachers in schools who make comments such as the following:

> We are fortunate to have a rich diversity of cultures in our school. We respect and recognise the different cultures and ethnic groups and promote tolerance and understanding amongst them. In the beginning we had problems, mainly due to preconceived perceptions and judgements amongst different cultures, a general insecurity in the community and a lack of experience of how to deal with problems.

Testimony like this is certainly not in short supply in all the studies and, clearly, it is important to recognise that multiculturalism, as described earlier, enjoys a great deal of respect in schools and might even be practised. Tihanyi (2003: 15), for example, chose to place two of her schools in a category she referred to as 'deracialised multiculturalism'. She comments: 'Two former Model C schools and the private school I visited (Acacia and Main Street High and Table Mountain Grammar School) use the language of multiculturalism and inclusivity to describe the process of racial integration.' Quoting a personal interview with the principal of Table Mountain Grammar School, as follows:

> It is important that everyone celebrates ... diversity and be proud of being 'coloured' or black, and these are the things from my culture that I'm proud of and not feel inferior to any culture in any way, and not sort of think that this one is better than the other. It isn't that at all ... they're different, and one should be proud of the differences.

Tihanyi (2003: 15) goes on to say:

> My first impressions, indeed, validate this statement: I saw faces of many colors among the well-dressed and seemingly cheerful students, who, as they chatted and laughed with one another, gave a picture of relaxed race relations. Unlike Mountain Side, which had no whites, in these schools white students are the majority, usually followed by a sizeable group of 'coloured,' and a few black students.

> Most white students say that race relations are good at their school – even that race does not 'exist'. Some students of colour share this opinion, while others notice subtle signs of what they see as racial discrimination on the part of teachers and fellow students. When it comes to recess, a look at the school yard showed me the clear lines of separation that keep students in racially divided groups. However, students insist that this has nothing to do with race; it is cultural, they say, people who share the same culture feel comfortable with one another.

Without denying the existence of these forms of address to race in many schools, many forms of multiculturalism are in effect variations of assimilationism. They are rooted in the presumption that the dominant culture is an unquestionable good. The incoming children might be allowed to perform in their so-called native guises for special occasions, but they operate under the protection of the dominant culture. A principal makes the point very clear: 'I wish South Africa could visit us and see how things should be done ... We are a veritable United Nations. You have taught us about your cultures ... we thank you that you have lead (sic) us unscathed into the new South Africa' (Vally & Dalamba 1999: 32).

In closing my discussion of this scape I want to suggest that assimilationism is overwhelmingly hegemonic as a practice of integration in schools. In attempting to develop a framework for understanding schools under this rubric we can begin to identify the different kinds of assimilationism that might present themselves in schools. Towards such a typology, it is possible to identify assimilationism as it plays itself out in a variety of ways in the complex environment of former Indian and coloured schools, in English-speaking former white schools that have remained largely white, in English-speaking schools that have become majority black schools and in Afrikaans-speaking former white schools. Former black schools, because they have not experienced the movement of new constituencies into their classrooms, clearly fall outside the scope of the discussion in this scape (racial as this reality might be, of course).

As the work of Tihanyi (2003), my own work on so-called black children in a so-called coloured school (1996), the work of Naidoo (1996), Vally and Dalamba (1999) and Soudien and Sayed (2003) suggest, there is a deep resentment in many schools of the so-called newcomers. This manifests itself in the ways children play, formal ceremony at school and pedagogical practice and amounts to what I call *aggressive assimilationism*. This kind of assimilationism is brusque, characterised by high degrees of intolerance and often violence.

Less aggressive are the forms of assimilationism evident in schools with political histories, such as former Indian and coloured schools, where issues of race are seldom addressed. This form of assimilationism I refer to as *assimilationism by stealth*. My own study of a high profile former coloured school with a strong political pedigree (see Soudien 1998c) describes the particular conceits that circulate in schools such as these where the incoming so-called black children are recruited into new 'non-racial' identities that have never been opened up to inspection.

The final form of assimilationism is most evident in former white English-speaking schools and is what I call *benign assimilationism*. This form of assimilationism looks like multiculturalism because there is an attempt to acknowledge the cultural diversity of the school's learners. The schools in this category deliberately have cultural evenings, unlike the schools in the two previous categories, and present themselves as self-consciously inclusive. The intent of this policy, in so far as it leaves the dominant relationships in the school untouched, is an assimilationist one.

The class scape

Untangling race from class in the South African context is clearly undesirable. There are, however, distinct ways in which schools behave that can be perceived to be, and understood to be, the actions of class agents rather than simply those of race agents.

Few studies on school integration (or desegregation), or schools as a site for social cohesion, approach the matter from an explicitly class perspective. This is essentially because class has been used in education, following the work of theorists such as Bowles and Gintis (1976), for making sense of the school as a medium for social differentiation. In this explanation, school allocates people to specific class positions. It is a sorting agency rather than an integrative agency. While this use of class makes sense, there are critical ways in which perspectives based on class underestimate how class structures and class influences work to maintain, in an integrating way, the cohesion of society. The work of Althusser is crucial here. He tried to explain how ideology worked in society through what he called 'ideological state apparatuses'; they transmit ruling class ideology and maintain the subject class in its subordinate position.

Moving from this point of departure, class provides an important framework for understanding how integration is being conceptualised and effected in South Africa. Central to the race scape I argued earlier, was the project of assimilationism into the cultural universe of the dominant order. What the class scape offers is a way of understanding how domination is being *rearticulated* in an extra-race way around integration. Integration in this approach is decidedly not *unity* and *social harmony*. It is not the assertion of the cultural values of the dominant group that is important to understand, but the modalities of the dominant group as it seeks to maintain its hold on the social order. For this order to survive, it is important that the dominant group wins people over to the class project. Critical, therefore, is its attempt to construct a social consensus in which classes occupy and *accept* their places. *Social cohesion* is important. Based on the dominance of the socially privileged or the elite class, the social objective of the class project is the shaping and reconfiguration of society. This dominance, however, is not that of the so-called whites, but a new elite comprising the core of the old white elite and selected elements from amongst the former subordinate black groups. School in this project is about nurturing this class and its interests, in the face of threats to the hegemony of the class.

In the racial scape it was possible to show the dimensions of the integration process amongst different racial groups. How integration manifests itself in terms of class is less obvious. What one can say, however, is that a distinct realignment of socio-economic groups is taking place in the schools, with the large-scale exodus of middle-class black parents and their children out of the former DET and HoD and HoR systems into the former white system. A domino effect appears to be playing itself out within the school system (Soudien & Sayed 2003). When the apartheid system began breaking down, the flow of children within the system took place in fairly predictable ways. Previously-excluded black, coloured and Indian children moved in large numbers into the formerly white schools. Black children began to move into formerly Indian and coloured schools. For black schools, significantly, this amounted to a flight of the more economically stable elements within their midst, leaving those schools largely with the poorest members of the community. This is about class following its own interests. Naidoo's work supports this line of thinking. He suggests that the process of integration followed distinct socio-economic paths in KwaZulu-Natal in both ex-NED and ex-HoD schools (1996).

Important to understand here are the complex ways in which class supplants and displaces race as a means of determining the social character of schools. The relatively low numbers of black students entering elite schools, and the high numbers entering poor schools reflect, one might argue, the objective and ideological situations in which the different classes find themselves. It is not possible, for reasons that are explored later, for poorer children to move into wealthier schools in large numbers, even if the system is supposed to admit any child if a place exists for him or her. Many things happen in wealthy schools that conspire to keep out the poor child. What this suggests is the bedding down of new class processes or new social alignments within the schooling system that are producing new and distinctive class forms. It is out of these that one can say that there is a reconstituting of the class.

How this process is happening is important to understand. It happens around what Marxists call the 'objective' forces that are active in society and around the ideological mechanisms the middle class has at its disposal.

In terms of objective forces, the social and economic resources families have access to is a major structural determinant in where they send their children. While it is true that the flight from township schools has, as Sekete et al. (2001) say, a great deal to do with the search for better education, it also has to do with costs and with what parents know. Black parents are choosing to send their children away from the township, but invariably they send their children to modest former white, coloured and Indian schools. School fees are a major determinant in guiding parents' decisions. In all of the schools in the Soudien and Sayed (2003) study, finances prove to be either exclusionary or inhibitory. A whole range of filtering mechanisms is used in these schools. Before children are admitted, even in the elite black schools, parents are often required to pay a deposit of 50 per cent of the annual fee. Where parents are tardy in paying, a variety of shaming devices are used. In places school reports are withheld until fees are paid. Aside from these mechanisms, often fees are pitched at extremely high levels. In the case of Eastdale College, an elite Eastern Cape school, parents have to 'be able to afford it' in order for their young ones to be part of the school.

Parents also depend a great deal on their own children for making these decisions (Sekete et al. 2001: 60). Their children would have heard about the class devices at schools and would have urged them not to risk the kinds of embarrassments that went with being poor in a more wealthy school. These factors do not operate for middle-class parents, by contrast. Middle-class parents spare no costs in the decisions they make. In the 1990s, people classified black became the largest constituency in both subsidised and non-subsidised independent schools in the Gauteng province (Vally & Dalamba 1999). While there may be a flight of people classified white into the independent school sector, one could similarly say that there has been a rapid increase of black, middle-class numbers in non-DET schools. This increase has been facilitated by the abolition of the *Group Areas Act*. Middle-class, former-white areas have experienced significant increases in inflows of black people. In the case of at least one private school in the Johannesburg area, the governors actively encouraged black parents to buy property in the area of the school. In all the former black schools virtually every single teacher had his or her children in a former white or coloured or Indian school. At the Bongalethu School in Mdantsane, Eastern Cape, teachers spoke explicitly of the class decisions they had made for their children. They could not be expected, they argued, to keep their children in the conditions that existed in the townships (Soudien & Sayed 2003).

The drift towards a new middle-class alignment has also been facilitated by the direction being taken in the policy domain. Central in this large body of legislation and policy directives is the *South African Schools Act* (SASA), which was passed in 1996. By the time the new government came into power in 1994, governance infrastructures in black schools had all but collapsed. As part of the process of rebuilding the school system, the government passed the Act as an attempt to give parents the responsibility of managing the schools their children attend and of officially legitimating parental participation in the life of the school. The Act required that schools establish school governing bodies (SGBs), which were to be composed of parents, teachers, students (in the case of secondary schools) and members of the school support staff. This structure was required to develop school policy across a whole host of areas and to ensure that the school managers would carry out this policy. Achieving this, however, was compromised by the way in which the new legislation framed identities in the schools, particularly parental identities. The Act projected parental identity around a restrictive middle-class notion of who parents were and how they functioned. Central to this notion were particular understandings of how time is used, what domestic resources are available for the schooling process, how much cultural capital parents can draw on in relating to school and so on. The upshot of the practice, as a result, was that in black schools, SGBs continued to be dominated by their principals or their teachers. In formerly white schools, middle-class white parents dominated.

This approach of the state was complemented by practices that were emerging in schools, especially in the governance of schools. Soudien and Sayed (2003) documented many instances where the schools not only retained but nurtured practices that effectively sidelined poorer people. Valley Primary in Cape Town maintained its middle-class character through the invocation of gender and the deployment of gender identities within the school. These allowed the school to draw on existent and strongly encoded social structures within the school, many of which were not as familiar and accessible to parents who were not white and middle class. For example, The Mother Programme and The Catering Committee were exclusively run by women. This assumed that most mothers who had children at the school were not working or should not be working. Projecting these approaches as 'family orientated' allowed the school to assimilate newer parents, and even non-middle-class parents into its social project. Poorer parents thus had access and rights of way in the school, but decidedly so on the school's terms.

The situation at Eastdale College in the Eastern Cape was similar. The school had effectively assimilated parents into a middle-class settlement based on a particular image of what the school stood for. This was particularly clear in the consistent and seamless representations of parents of their 'responsible parent' identities. At a former white primary school in Durban, parents were convinced by the school that they were *buying* into a way of doing things that was in their children's interests. The school convinced them that the package – effectively a commodity – it was offering was what their children needed to succeed in the world of work (Soudien & Sayed 2003).

This discussion suggests that a particular kind of class settlement is taking place in schools that is being actively driven by the middle class. Conscious of its position within the new South Africa this class is constructing a new concept of integration and even a new concept of its identity around the notion of 'good schooling'. Largely led by the old white middle class, this class operates on the basis of buy-in of the new middle classes into the new settlement. This buy-in comes with the acquiescence of the new elite. Soudien and Sayed (2003: 39) describe the situation at a former middle-class, white primary school in Durban called Oasis, where the settlement pivoted on the maintenance of 'standards': 'At Oasis in 1991, the school accepted the first persons of colour, 22 "Indian" and 3 African learners. These learners were carefully selected; "We took the cream of the crop," said a teacher.' Though parents' and learners' racial identities, religious and cultural backgrounds were different, their socio-economic status was very much the same. There was amongst parents an agreement about what constituted 'good' education and where 'good' education could be obtained. For the class the priority would be to preserve the character and traditions of the 'good' schools for the maintenance of what they perceived to be quality.

Important also about this new settlement is the way in which the position of the poor and their schools is fixed. Given the stipulations of the *South African Schools Act*, particularly its discursive constructions of the ideal parent, and the ways in which the wealthy have erected barriers to entry for the disadvantaged, poor schools have, by and large, accepted the *modus operandi* of the new system. Driven, therefore, as the new settlement has been by the new and enlarged middle class, the poor have, one could suggest, also bought into the way in which the system operates.

Other scapes

Clearly, as this chapter has sought to argue, one can delineate difference in a number of other ways in South Africa. The most immediate of these are gender, language and religion, but include also region and geographical location (urban and rural) and a number of other less obvious ways. Important about these are the complex ways in which they determine and configure access to rights and opportunities. Clear examples which demonstrate these realities are rural schools and boys' or girls' schools. Less clear but equally if not more powerful is the medium of instruction of a school. Medium of instruction, particularly English, defines, for large numbers of children in South Africa, the degree to which, epistemologically, they have access to and understand what they are being taught. For many, because their English language competence is so poor, exclusion is a structural experience.

Conclusion

I have tried to argue in this chapter that we are constrained by the dominant languages of description that exist within our sociological repertoires. These dominant languages predefine what can and can't be seen. The argument of this contribution is that there exist multiple ways in which society experiences difference but that within these, certain ways are privileged. As they are elevated in importance they become normative and so come to condition how social differentiation in everyday discourse is approached. Race, as a result, becomes the almost unchallenged lens through which South African difference is understood. By using scapes this essay has sought to work with a recognition of this form of discoursing and to point out some of its limitations.

Reality, however, does not operate in scapes. It exists out there in a swirl of events and phenomena which language seeks to tame or call to order. Language, in this sense, is a device which seeks to approximate the 'facts' of experience. Recognising this, the challenge is how we might begin to talk to encompass, as efficaciously as we can, the complexity of this swirl that surrounds us and that is who we are.

In attempting to make a comment about the social reconstruction process taking place in South African education, it is necessary to say that, while our languages will always be inadequate and while we might demur at the reductive and essentialising discourses of race, class and gender, we cannot but acknowledge the large role these forces play in our everyday lives. Displace complexity as these discourses do, there are ways in which we can see patterns of what one might call *contingency* emerging. One can argue that race, class, gender and language in South Africa are implicated in a complex of signs that are part of a process of profound social realignment in the country. This realignment is not simply a racial or a class or a gender realignment but is pivoted on the contingencies of the new post-apartheid landscape in which dominance is reinterpreting itself and is being reinterpreted. These contingencies are forcing groups and individuals to re-evaluate and reposition themselves in relation to the range of social differences which surround them and in relation to the problem of having to work out new positions of power and authority. Emerging out of this is a reconfiguration and, in some instances, a reworking of hegemonic practices.

Critical in working through the scapes is recognising how much dominant practices in each of them have essentially remained as they were and how apposite the notion of assimilationism is, whether one is talking of race, class, language or gender, for understanding the social processes underway in each. The story of education in the new South Africa is, in these terms, essentially a story of the reconfiguration of dominance in relation to race, class, gender and language dominance. Dominant practices have adjusted to the contingencies, but the presumptions upon which they have been premised have remained unchanged. The existing ways in which things are done are 'virtuous', in and of themselves. Dominant racial groups, dominant classes, dominant genders and dominant languages have had to make space for new constituencies but they have done so on their own terms. Important in understanding the contingencies here are recognising the political dynamics, the strategic occupation of space – agency – by groups, particularly previously excluded groups, and the strategic yielding of space by others. The continuation of domination is always a contingent moment.

Using this argument, integration in education in South Africa can be argued to be a process of accommodation in which subordinate groups or elements of subordinate groups have been recruited or have promoted themselves into the hegemonic social, cultural and economic regime at the cost of subordinate ways of being, speaking, and conducting their everyday lives.

References

Bowles, S & Gintis, H (1976) *Schooling in Capitalist America: Educational Reform and the Contradictions of Economic life.* London and Henley: Routledge and Kegan Paul

Carr, EH (1964) *What is History?* New York: Alfred Knopf

Carrim, N (1992) *Desegregation in Coloured and Indian Schooling.* Johannesburg: Education Policy Unit, University of the Witwatersrand

Carrim, N & Soudien, C (1999) Critical Anti-Racism in South Africa. In S May (ed) *Critical Multiculturalism: Multicultural and Anti-Racist Education.* London: Falmer Press

Chisholm, L (1999) Change and Continuity in South African Education: The Impact of Policy, *African Studies,* 58 (1): 87–103

Christie, P (1990) *Open Schools: Racially Mixed Catholic Schools in South Africa, 1976–1986.* Johannesburg: Ravan Press

Dekker, E & Lemmer, E (eds) (1993) *Critical Issues in Modern Education.* Durban: Butterworths

Dolby, N (2001) *Constructing Race: Youth, Identity and Popular Culture in South Africa.* Albany: State University of New York Press

Gaganakis, G (1990) Perceptions of Black Pupils in Non-Racial Private Schools in Johannesburg. Unpublished M.Ed. thesis, University of the Witwatersrand

Hirsch, ED (1987) *Cultural Literacy: What Every American Needs to Know.* Boston: Houghton Mifflin

Hofmeyr, J (2000) The Emerging School Landscape in Post-Apartheid South Africa. Unpublished mimeo

Lemmer, E & Squelch, J (1993) *Multicultural Education: A Teacher's Manual.* Halfway House: Southern Book Publishers

Naidoo, J (1996) *Racial Integration of Public Schools in South Africa: A Study of Practices, Attitudes and Trends*. Durban: University of Natal Education Policy Unit

Ravitch, D (1990) Diversity and Democracy: Multicultural Education in America, *American Educator*, 14 (1): 16–48

Rist, R (ed) (1979) *Desegregated Schools*. New York: Academic Press

Sekete, P; Shilubane, M & Moila, B (2001) *Deracialisation and Migration of Learners in South African Schools*. Pretoria: HSRC

Soudien, C (1996) Apartheid's Children. Unpublished doctoral dissertation, State University of New York at Buffalo

Soudien, C (1998a) 'We know why we're here': The Experiences of African Children in a 'Coloured' School in Cape Town, South Africa, *Race, Ethnicity and Education*, 1 (1): 7–29

Soudien, C (1998b) Equality and Equity in South African Education. In Cross, M & Mkwanazi Twala, Z (eds) *Unity, Diversity and Reconciliation: A Debate on the Politics of Curriculum in South Africa*. Cape Town: Juta

Soudien, C (1998c) Our School is not Coloured: Struggling with Identity at City Central, Cape Town, South Africa. In Bak, N et al. (eds) *Going for the Gap*. Cape Town: Juta

Soudien, C & Sayed, Y (2003) Integrating South African Schools: Some Preliminary Findings, *IDS Bulletin*, 34 (1): 29–42

Subrahmanian, R; Sayed, Y; Balagopalan, S & Soudien, C (eds) (2003) Education Inclusion and Exclusion: Indian and South African Perspectives, *IDS Bulletin* 34 (1)

Tihanyi, K (2003) Racial Integration and Implications for Reconciliation in Post-Apartheid South Africa: An Ethnographic Account of High School Students' Experiences. Unpublished dissertation presented to the Faculty of the Graduate School of Cornell University in partial fulfilment of the requirements for the degree of Doctor of Philosophy

Vally, S & Dalamba, Y (1999) *Racism, 'Racial Integration' and Desegregation in South African Public Secondary Schools*. A Report on a Study by the South African Human Rights Commission

Weider, A (2001a) White Teachers/White Schools: Oral Histories From the Struggle Against Apartheid. Unpublished mimeo

Weider, A (2001b) A Principal's Perspective of School Integration: The First School to Integrate in Cape Town, South Africa, *Equity and Excellence in Education*, 34 (1): 58–63

Weider, A (2002) Informed by Apartheid: Mini Oral Histories of Two Cape Town Teachers. In *The History of Education Under Apartheid: 1948–1994*. Cape Town: Pearson Education

Wolpe, H (1988) *Race, Class and the Apartheid State*. Paris: Unesco

Zafar, S (1998) *School-Based Initiatives to Address Racial and Cultural Diversity in Newly integrating Public Schools*. Durban: University of Natal Education Policy Unit

4 Educational de/centralisation and the quest for equity, democracy and quality

Suzanne Grant Lewis and Shireen Motala

Introduction

Decentralisation of school finance and governance is a prominent illustration of efforts in South Africa to promote social change since 1994. Whether it has involved the transfer of budgeting and service delivery to provinces or the devolution of responsibility for governance and financing to the school level, it has been justified on the grounds of achieving economic growth, democratisation, equity and redress. Today, however, questions are being raised about the ability of decentralisation to affect positive social change and to realise all these goals.

Educational decentralisation in South Africa reflects tensions and contradictions in the demands on the government on the one hand to be globally competitive and on the other to attend to redress and equity. Not surprisingly, despite the intention to establish a uniform system of governance and funding norms, schools and school-level actors have experienced the devolution of school governance and financing in a variety of ways, reflecting in part their different historical and material conditions. Surprisingly, the bulk of policy and research over the last ten years has focused on the form rather than on the substance of policy. The emphasis has been on the implementation of formal rules and roles rather than on how the policy is put into practice and how school-level actors have experienced decentralisation in terms of its expressed goals. Research to date has thus taught us little about the impact of the policy, but there are sufficient questions being raised to warrant the Review of School Governance.[1]

This chapter starts with a brief historical account of factors contributing to the development of a decentralised school governance and financing policy. It then discusses local debates on educational decentralisation, organising them around the three related discourses of governance, democracy and equity. With this backdrop in place, it analyses existing empirical evidence of the impact of school-level decentralisation on the goals of reducing inequities through local financing, promoting democratic participation and improving the quality of education available. Whereas Fiske and Ladd, in this volume, examine the background and consequences for equity of a fees policy in schools, this chapter considers the impact of decentralisation more broadly and in relation to the promotion of democratic participation and quality schooling. Several arguments are developed under these themes, drawing on existing evidence and highlighting the limitations of extant research. Overall, the chapter argues that the goals of decentralisation for improved equity, expanded democracy and improved quality have not been met, except in resource-rich contexts. The chapter concludes that the need for more empirical work should not be more of the dominant effort to assess policy fidelity. Rather, a different approach is required if we are to deepen our understanding of decentralisation policy in practice.

Circumstances leading to the policy

Analyses of educational decentralisation in other parts of the globe suggest the value of understanding policy rationales and associated assumptions (Bray 1999; Hanson 1997; Welsh & McGinn 1998). It is clear that educational decentralisation generally, and devolving power to schools specifically, is almost always motivated by economic and political aims.[2] Pedagogical rationales have been far less common although it is familiar rhetoric to claim that decentralisation will improve the quality of education (Fiske 1996).

South Africa's decentralisation of education is motivated by political and economic considerations. Politically, the post-apartheid government was committed to devolving power to the people and meeting 'the aim of redress and equity in the provision of quality education' (DoE 1998: Section 34). Economically, the government found itself with insufficient financial resources to meet the educational needs of the country. A number of writers have pointed to the dialectic between South Africa's macroeconomic commitments, education policies and the shifting paradigms in the broader world represented in the shift from the Reconstruction and Development Programme (RDP) to the Growth, Employment and Redistribution (GEAR) Programme (Badat 1997; Chisholm 1997; Chisholm & Fuller 1996; de Clercq 1997; Fiske & Ladd in this volume; Weber 2002).

The two education policy instruments of interest in this context are the *South African Schools Act* (SASA) (RSA 1996c) and the *National Norms and Standards for School Funding Act* (NNSSF) (DoE 1998). The *South African Schools Act*, among other things, provides for the establishment at all public schools of school governing bodies (SGBs) composed of the principal and elected representatives of parents, teachers, non-teaching staff, and (in secondary schools) learners. A basic set of functions and powers are assigned to all SGBs, including the determination of admissions policy, the recommendation to the province of teaching and non-teaching appointments, the financial management of the school, the determination of school fees and additional fundraising. Additional powers can be assigned if the governing body meets certain criteria. Under the Act, SGBs are juristic persons. Parents must be in the majority and chair the body.

The emergence of SGBs as vehicles for the decentralisation of power to schools was an outcome of the macroeconomic policy shifts – and their global influences – as well as a contestation between old and new orders in the education policy process. Two traditions borne of different racial experiences, the democratic movement of the Parent Teacher Student Associations (PTSAs) and the National Party's Model C schools for white communities, set public expectations and framed discussions regarding new school governance structures. In former black, coloured and Indian schools, management councils were formed with parent representatives but these councils were advisory only and lacked legitimacy as the members served at the pleasure of the principal.[3] As dissatisfaction with the apartheid schooling system grew during the 1980s, the National Education Crisis Committee (NECC) called for the establishment of PTSAs with broad-based representation, including parents, teachers and learners. Local participation in school governance remained a key element as the NECC further defined its vision of governance in the National Education Policy Investigation report on governance and administration (NEPI 1992).

Decentralisation was touted as an efficient management solution by the National Party's 1992 Education Renewal Strategy (ERS). The ERS proposed a single education system for the country, with management councils in each school on which parents were given greater power than teachers. That same year the strategy was translated into practice for white schools as the Model C design, and by 1993 about 96 per cent of white schools had chosen this option (Karlsson, McPherson & Pampallis 1999). These schools had significant autonomy and were empowered by law to set policies, such as language requirements for admission which served to exclude children of certain backgrounds (Carrim & Tshoane 2000). Model C schools received a state subsidy and covered the remainder of their costs through school fees that effectively excluded working class and unemployed South Africans. The ERS had no mechanisms for redress or redistribution of resources.

Under the new government, the 1995 *White Paper on Education and Training* (RSA 1995) was the first policy statement to argue for SGBs, with membership drawn from the school community and with attention to race and gender representation. Following this, the Hunter Committee was convened and tasked with reviewing the organisation, governance and funding of schools (DoE 1995). A protracted, contested process followed, which saw expression in two more draft white papers, a debate in the media that focused on the future of white schools, extensive consultation and negotiation, and numerous drafts of the *South African Schools Act* (Karlsson et al. 1999: 8–10).

One of the most contentious issues was and continues to be that of funding, as it involves trying to reconcile the need for equity and improved quality with insufficient state funding. SASA establishes the principle that the state is obliged to fund public schools on an equitable basis 'in order to ensure the proper exercise of the rights of learners to education and the redress of past inequalities in education provision' (RSA 1996c: Section 34). At the same time, the government made clear the difficulties inherent in an open-access education system and called for a strategic partnership between role-players (or 'stakeholders' as they are commonly called), including the government. Within this process, government has stated that it can provide the basic minimum, and that anything beyond this is the responsibility of parents. Under SASA, all SGBs are expected to supplement state funds in order to improve the education that they offer, either through school fees or other forms of fund-raising:

> A *governing body* of a *public school* must take all reasonable measures within its means to supplement the resources supplied by the state in order to improve the quality of education provided by the *school* to all *learners* at the *school*. (RSA 1996c: Section 36 emphasis added)

Issued two years after SASA was passed, the *National Norms and Standards for School Funding* regulations (DoE 1998) provided the instruments to address inequalities among schools within provinces. In the first instance, it provides for exemption from fees for parents who are unable to afford them. In the second and third, capital expenditure on new schools or additional classrooms and facilities is to be based on a ranking of geographical areas by need. Provincial education departments are required to direct 60 per cent of their non-personnel and non-capital recurrent expenditures towards the poorest 40 per cent of schools. This funding covers three categories of expenditure: maintenance of school buildings, municipal services and utilities, and learning support materials. Provinces must compile a list of schools based on the community's socio-economic levels of development and physical resources at the school.[4] Provinces are free to develop their redistribution mechanism within the national government framework and at least two different models are being attempted (Wildeman 2000b). These three redress mechanisms illustrate the centralising/decentralising tension evident in the national policy. The central government efforts to assure the population that redress will occur are accompanied by restrictions on provincial authority.

Debates surrounding the introduction and implementation of policy

A discussion of the evolution of South African debates on educational decentralisation cannot be separated from a discussion of international influences. One outcome of globalisation is global competitiveness in education, which places economic performance, accountability and quality at the centre of educational change efforts. Pursuing finance-driven reforms, states are under enormous pressure to increase public spending on education and to investigate other sources of income to fund expansion (Carnoy 1998). As a result, they tend to focus on decentralisation, which places such self-managing schools under severe financial pressure (Fullan 1998). Globalisation, then, has created a set of premises that have made schools within its range more global (through international comparisons), as well as more local (in terms of financial reliance) than ever before (Fullan 1998; West & Hopkins 1996).

Governance

Despite our participation in this global project of decentralisation, the term 'decentralisation' is rarely used in South African education policy documents. Instead, decentralisation discourse is framed within conceptualisations of governance, democracy and equity. These three themes, discussed below, have their own interacting discourses, which serve to pull the transformation project in a number of competing directions (Porteus 2001; Sayed 2002). We argue that although equity concerns are losing ground at present, support for democratic participation is largely through attention to form, not function.

The term 'governance' gained currency in international discourse as part of the neo-liberal framework and the New Policy Agenda (Elmore 1993; Osborne & Gaebler 1992). This agenda argues that countries must have democracy and 'good' governance, with the associated claims that there is consensus on how 'good' is defined and that the term is a neutral, indeed universal, one despite being shot through with ideological meaning. Development 'experts' optimistically refer to good governance as the 'missing link' to economic growth and economic reform in the developing world (UNDP 2002).

The neo-liberal definition of governance that has ascended takes good governance to mean a reinvented and efficient form of government in a market-oriented society (Stoker 1996). It carries the expectation that government will think critically about what it can and cannot provide efficiently, be open to private contracting (or 'outsourcing'), fiscal restraint, the identification of new sources of funding, and generally take a new look at 'how we do business'. Responsibility for the 'social' is relegated away from the central state and towards localities and private citizens.

In South Africa, the post-1994 governance debate has focused on form, that is, the formal articulation of rules, roles and responsibilities. The policies related to governance largely articulate the structure, roles and functions of different levels of government: their composition, powers, channels of accountability, and rules guiding their operations. Perhaps as a consequence, writings exploring the success of school governance in South Africa have largely focused on the formal form and the ability of SGBs to meet legislative prescriptions (Kgobe 2002; McPherson & Dhlamini 1998; Motala, Porteus & Tshoane 2002). Little attention has been paid to their functioning, the exercise of authority or the distribution of voice, which are arguably the critical issues (McLennan 2000). Researchers, we contend, have been preoccupied with *policy fidelity* rather than with understanding how opportunities for greater local engagement are being seized to transform schools. We hope that over time this will change and in our conclusion suggest how to make a shift in the focus of the research.

Democracy

Democracy and democratic participation are very much part of the decentralisation discourse. In employing decentralisation in the service of democracy, South Africa aligns itself with the Universal Declaration on Democracy (UDD), which states that:

> Democratic institutions and processes must also foster decentralised local and regional government and administration, which is a right and a necessity, and which makes it possible to broaden the base of public participation. (UDD 1997: Para 23)

In the wake of the destructive impact of apartheid on authority structures and school-community relations, the South African government recognised the need for new structures and procedures to elicit and facilitate local participation. However, there does not appear to be recognition that the representative democracy being promoted through SGBs is a system of competition for power and influence, that is, a decidedly political one. While the official policy discourse on democracy through school governance appears decidedly apolitical, the policy in practice is strikingly aware politically as it moves political competition to local sites and in so doing deflects pressure from the centre. This will be discussed more fully later in the chapter.

Scholars are questioning the dominant models of democracy, including the Western liberal model, represented in SASA. Democracy is assumed to be rationalist, essentialist and universalist, yet experience is 'of alterity, othering, heterogeneity, dissonance and resistance' (Benhabib 1996: 5). Benhabib asks, 'Does democracy rest on homogenising models of identity?' (1996: 5). SASA appears to homogenise each of the groups represented on SGBs – parents, teachers, and learners. Clearly a choice was made to base representation on stakeholder group identities rather than on ideas or views (Phillips in Benhabib 1996) or, as one might reasonably expect in post-apartheid South Africa, race, class or gender.

Like the concern raised earlier about governance, there is a similar worry that in the push for democratic participation through local governance structures, most of the attention has been on economic processes and administrative efficiency (UNDP 2002: vi). Some of the efforts to monitor policy implementation have confused form with function, failing to heed UNDP's warning to not equate the holding of elections with the establishment of a functioning democracy.

Finally, several critics have interrogated SASA's concept of participation, drawing on the international effort to problematise the concept (Rahnema 1992). Sayed (1999: 30) and Soudien (this volume) suggest that SASA's emphasis on parental participation could advantage middle-class communities. Grant Lewis, Naidoo and Weber (2002) argue that SASA assumes receptivity of parents to responsibilities, conceiving of participation as a rational and morally correct act. Sayed and Carrim (1997a: 30) suggest that inclusiveness is tied to discourses of democracy, and that in practice such inclusiveness works in ways that may further marginalise black working-class and rural families. The criticism of how school governance and financing policies are related to democratic participation is, however, primarily conjectural. Empirical work has provided little insight into either the nature of participation or how participation and accountability are understood and practised by various SGB members.

Equity

International analyses have given considerable attention to the equity impacts of shifts in authority through decentralisation policies (Bray 1999; Chubb & Moe 1990; Fuller & Clarke 1994; Sayed & Carrim 1997a and b). Equity reforms in post-apartheid South Africa in the late 1990s were intended to equalise funding among provinces, schools and socio-economic groups. In broad terms, equity was to be achieved through the redistribution of human, physical and resource inputs. The government's expression of equity has come to be framed in specific ways, consistent with neo-liberal theories: universal access, but restricted through user fees; school governance with privatisation, decentralisation and prominent market features; top-down decision-making which implicates school communities in teacher retrenchments and cost-cutting.

Much of the equity discourse has focused on school financing. The critical educational literature in South Africa has two main aspects: the devolution of power to provinces and to schools. The main critiques have focused on the overall macroeconomic framework, whether expenditure on social spending is sufficient, whether greater efficiency is required and the overall tension between meeting social development goals while retaining fiscal targets (Badat 1997; Chisholm, Motala & Vally 1999; Patel 2002; Vally 2000;

Wildeman 2000a and b, 2002a and b). The debate has centred around social reconstruction on the one hand and the needs of the market on the other (Porteus 2001; Sayed 2002). On the efficacy of the specific mechanism, there appears to be no easy answer but it is the subject of ongoing review for government and independent researchers. An underlying concern appears to be whether decentralisation mechanisms can work in a highly disparate and poverty-laden context and whether provincialisation actually works to reduce disparities both inter- and intra-provincially (see also Wildeman and Fiske & Ladd in this volume).

In sum, the formation of local governance bodies in schools represents a possible vehicle for increased participation, equity, and quality improvement, but there is a perception that SGBs will not lead to the desired outcomes. One of the most critical concerns is that this configuration of funding and governance policies, in the context of the deep inequities between schools and communities, will in fact work to perpetuate or deepen inequities rather than challenge them. The recent Human Development Report cautions:

> ... while democracy can promote equitable development, the goals of democracy and equity should be considered largely independent – with both requiring a dedicated effort and political will. (UNDP 2002: 60)

We turn to examine the evidence on whether the policies have succeeded in meeting the professed outcomes.

The differentiated impact of the policy on equity, democracy and quality

Crouch (2002), Motala (2003) and Patel (2002) argue that the education system post-1994 is a truly decentralised system and goes beyond what is described as 'deconcentration' in the literature. Certainly, South Africa has moved faster and further than any other sub-Saharan African country in introducing school-based governance and financing on a national scale (Naidoo 2001).

In our effort to understand the devolution of governance and financing to the school level, we do not focus on determining whether decentralisation has been achieved, since that examines the means rather than the end. Instead, we examine to what extent the decentralisation efforts have promoted the goals of decentralisation, namely, reduced inequities, expanded democratic participation and improved quality. We concentrate in particular on school-level empirical evidence from studies of school governance and financing, since a synthesis of these disparate studies is in order. We supplement this data with other forms of evidence, including legislative amendments.

For a country with over 27 000 primary and secondary schools, the existing school-based research is disappointing in its scope and depth. Existing school-based empirical work on SASA has accorded the provinces of KwaZulu-Natal and Gauteng the most attention. Much more work remains to be done. (See Bischoff & Phakoa 1999; Bischoff & Sayed 1999; Chakane 2002; GDE 2001; Hyslop 1999; Karlsson 2002; Khulisa 1999; Mashele & Grobler 1999; McPherson & Dlamini 1998; McPherson & Naicker 2002; Simkins 2002.) We turn now to the first of the three policy outcomes.

Reducing inequities through financing at the local level

The key question is whether devolved financing mechanisms have led to greater equity within and across provinces and schools. In reviewing the school-based research we consider whether schools have managed to utilise financial resources, both government and private, to improve conditions. We draw the following conclusions:
- Innovative national and provincial financing formulas have had important redistributive effects but have not managed to address backlogs.
- Institutional co-ordination across different levels of governance is needed to strengthen the specific allocation of funds at the school level so they may begin to meet the policy goals of equity, redress, democracy and quality.
- The lack of agreement on what constitutes 'adequacy' and minimum learning conditions hinders progress on equity.
- The effective transfer of responsibility for redress to the local level, through fund-raising and decisions on the usage of funds, may be contributing to increased inequity, given the huge variability of infrastructure provision and teacher quality. In this regard the concept of self-managing schools and Section 20 and Section 21 status requires review.

The first level of decentralised financial control is through the inter-provincial formula outlined in the *National Education Policy Act* (RSA 1996b). Recent analyses of provincial data have argued that significant progress has been made towards a fairer distribution of public funds across provinces (Fiske

& Ladd 2002: 23). But there are several indications that the inter-provincial formula has been unable to address historic inequities (See DoE 2003 and Patel 2002).

The second key form of devolved financial responsibility for equity and redress has been the redistribution of non-personnel expenditure. While provinces have been successful in allocating the non-personnel expenditure according to need, the differences between provinces are stark: the allocation to the poorest school in the Northern Cape is slightly higher than the allocation to the least poor school in Mpumalanga, for example. Historical disparities in the funding of schools were based on race and region, with secondary learners being funded at a higher level than primary school learners. The availability of more funds has resulted in better targeting and distribution within provinces, in particular for the three poorest learner quintiles. However, insufficient allocations made to middle quintile schools remain a problem and these schools continue to bear the brunt of the redress aspects of the funding norms (Wildeman 2002a). Schools in higher socio-economic quintiles (as determined by the school funding norms) were better off financially in a variety of ways (Porteus, Patel, Fleisch & Ruth 2001; Van der Berg 2001). These schools' higher personnel costs (a function of more experienced and qualified educators) were accompanied by higher school income through private contributions and user fees. Teacher qualifications are still the main driver of personnel expenditure and this historical inequity is not dealt with adequately in policy or in the Department's Finance Review (DoE 2003).

Since 1998 there have been indications that SGBs perceived their main responsibility as raising funds for the school. McPherson and Dlamini (1998) found principals reporting that budgeting and fund-raising topped the list as the most frequent issue discussed by SGBs. This was also the case in Gauteng (Motala et al. 2002). Some SGB members admit that they felt pressured to deal with financial matters in order to increase the school's competitive edge or simply to survive. Karlsson also concludes that the apartheid legacy of inequality 'corresponds to the governing body's capacity to raise funds and make improvements to the tuck shop' (2002: 333).

What comment do we have to make about decentralisation and in particular, financing and its outcomes in South Africa? Decentralisation, as in a number of international experiences, has not led to greater social equity in South Africa. To the extent that private resources are relatively more plentiful for schools that serve higher income families, there is a conflict which could be mitigated if increased private funding was combined with increased government spending on poorer communities to strengthen basic education programmes targeted at disadvantaged groups (Whitty, Power & Halpin 1998; see also Fiske & Ladd in this volume).

Promoting democratic participation

The existing school-based empirical work indicates differential experiences across types of schools. We draw three conclusions with regard to SASA success to date in promoting democratic participation.

- In part as a result of the technocratic, apolitical policy approach, which privileges form over function, conflict has been diffused to the local level. This has important implications for the exercise of democratic process.
- The centralising/decentralising tension in school governance and financing policy is evident in recent legislative amendments. The tightening of central control is effectively reducing the discretion and authority of SGBs.
- The decentralisation of authority for governance and financing to the school has been accompanied by a strengthening of the principal's authority in many types of schools, but not in former Model C schools. While authority is being diffused to the school, it is not necessarily being shared with all interest groups (or 'stakeholders') represented on SGBs.

Argument 1: Conflict is ignored centrally and displaced to local settings

Sayed (2002) argues that conflict is being diffused to the periphery, the school level. The policy documents, SASA and NNSSF, are conspicuously silent on class, race and gender conflict, but ignoring conflict will not make it go away. This ignoring of conflict extends to the inaccurate conception of representative democracy as a benign collaboration of local actors as partners rather than competitors for power.

There are varying views on why policy ignores conflict. Lauglo (1995) argues that the government could decentralise to silence dissenters by transferring some power to those who are in agreement with the central government. The national Department of Education's (DoE) decision to allocate to SGBs the power to sue parents who do not pay school fees is a way of diverting parents' anger from its source, the Department, to local levels. For the most part, the central government has thus far succeeded in confining tensions to local levels.

School-level studies provide insight into two areas in which conflict is evident: representation on the SGB and the dominance of the fund-raising function of SGBs.

Representation.[5] Problems of representativeness of SGB members to the community served have been documented with regard to race, class and gender. A study of SGBs in former House of Delegates (HoD), House of Assembly (HoA) and House of Representatives (HoR) schools in Durban South showed that although they had almost 40 per cent black enrolment they had no black parent, learner or educator representatives, (McPherson & Dlamini 1998: 35). SGB membership in racially mixed schools also remained dominated by the formerly dominant racial group while black members tended to be co-opted. Progress on this front was seen in the 2000 fieldwork (Kgobe 2001).

The educational backgrounds of parent representatives in former HoD and HoA schools were found to differ significantly from those in ex-DET and ex-KDEC schools in Durban South, where the majority had only a primary school education. With rare exceptions, however, parents elected representatives with literacy skills (McPherson & Dlamini 1998: 14, 36). Among non-educator SGB members, social class rules, with females in secretarial positions rather than custodians or gardeners representing this constituency. Most former DET and KDEC schools had no non-educator representative, a reflection of the lack of support staff at these schools (McPherson & Dlamini 1998: 36). Election processes often disadvantaged working parents. In rural schools in particular, the distance between schools and homes made full parental participation in the election impossible (McPherson & Dlamini 1998).

The third dimension found to be significant in SGB representation is gender. Males were found to be over-represented among parent and learner representatives. In a sample of 15 schools in Durban South, only 20 per cent of the learner representatives were female. Among educators, males dominated regardless of whether it was a secondary school, where males tend to make up the majority of educators, or a primary school, where there are greater numbers of female educators. By 2000 female representation had increased, in part because the researchers had pointed out the disparity and encouraged schools to rectify the situation.

Dominance of the fund-raising function for SGBs. It is important to highlight how the dominance of the fund-raising function results in conflict between SGB parent representatives and the parent population that elected them. The main source of funding for SGBs is school fees. The situation with regard to fee exemptions is fraught with conflict. Under SASA, SGBs have responsibility for determining who qualifies for exemptions. In a situation in which a parent representative's success is measured by the ability to raise funds and balance the budget, there is little incentive to promote fee exemptions. It is important to note that it is the SGB, not the provincial department, that has authority to sue parents that are believed to be able to afford to pay school fees but who fail to do so.

Argument 2: The centralising state is using legislation to reduce SGB discretion and authority

We turn now to examine the numerous legislative amendments between 1998 and 2002 that have affected the discretion and authority of SGBs. Sayed (2002: 36, 39) has argued that the central state in South Africa struggles to control decentralised sites while at the same time promoting citizen participation. A significant tension exists in attempting to balance state control and citizen participation. The central state employs a process of juridification, by which it attempts to control both provincial governments and institutions (SGBs) by legislating norms and standards.

With the 1999 amendment of Section 5 of the *National Education Policy Act* of 1996, parents no longer have a separate consultative process. Consultation with 'such national organisations representing parents as the Minister may recognise for this purpose' was replaced with 'such national organisations representing governing bodies of schools as the Minister may recognise for this purpose' (RSA 1999).

SGBs' authority also appears to be eroded with regard to personnel appointments. Limits were placed on the SGB power and authority to recommend appointments to teaching and non-teaching posts (RSA 1996a: Section 20). The 1999 amendment to the *Employment of Educators Act* of 1998 placed a time limit of two months for SGBs to respond to a request for a recommendation for an appointment. After that time, the provincial education department head could make a decision without SGB input. In addition, the Head of Department may temporarily transfer an educator without recommendation (RSA 1999). The *Education Laws Amendment Act* of 2002 specifies that in the case of first-time appointments and for educators re-entering the system after a break of more than one year, an appointment can be made after consultation with the governing body but that no SGB recommendation is required. Previously, the provincial Department of Education had the final say in an appointment but the process required interviews and recommendations by SGB members (RSA 2002: Section 10).

In 2001, SASA was amended to limit the functions and obligations of the SGBs to only those prescribed by the Act (RSA 2001). We may be seeing greater attention by central government to accountability mechanisms. In 2001, Heads of Department were given greater power to intervene when a governing body fails to meets its responsibilities, while at the same time their responsibility to correct the situation through capacity building was increased (RSA 2001). The same Act puts in place mechanisms to better ensure responsible financial accountability. Governing bodies can no longer take out a loan or overdraft without approval of the Education MEC (Member of Executive Council). The establishment of trusts with school funds is also restricted; any existing trust funds must be returned to the school. A mandatory code of conduct for governing bodies will be developed by the provincial departments (RSA 2002: Section 6).

Further limits on SGB discretion were placed with regard to budgets. Budget guidelines were changed to budget prescriptions (RSA 2001).

One noteworthy amendment was made to improve parent input on budgets. SGBs must now 'inform the parents that the budget will be available for inspection at the school at least 14 days prior to the meeting' (RSA 2002: Section 7). This strengthens the rights of parents to be fully consulted on financial matters affecting them.

Several of the legislative amendments are double-edged, bringing to light conflicts between the goals of promoting democratic participation and equity. The official explanation for reducing the authority of SGBs to recommend all educator appointments is an equity one, to 'ensure a fair distribution of well-qualified educators' (RSA 2001: 26). The national Department claims it needs the freedom to deploy teachers as needed across the system, especially to rural schools that have difficulty in recruiting teachers. Similarly, the imposition of a prescribed budget format may prove helpful for inexperienced SGBs, but at the same time the structure may be more sophisticated than needed and set SGBs up for failure.

On the whole, the legislative amendments of 1998 to 2002 indicate the central state's attempt to tighten the coupling between central and provincial governments and to place limits on the exercise of power by SGBs. These amendments are further evidence of what Sayed (2002: 39) refers to as the 'legalisation of challenge', after-the-fact legislation that strengthens central control, often in response to court challenges.

Argument 3: Decentralisation is accompanied at the school level by strengthening the authority of the principal

At the same time that authority has been devolved by SASA to the school level, it has strengthened the hand of the principal. While this may be positive for some spheres of activity, this is not sufficient to fulfil SASA's promise of democratic participation of role-players or stakeholders. This observed increase in professional power and authority can increase the risk of local capture of democracy (Bardham & Mookherjee 1999). We must recognise that 'local officials are no more immune to elite capture than officials in central government. Indeed, far from strengthening local democracy, decentralisation can actually reinforce the power and influence of local elites' (UNDP 2002: 67).

This centralisation of authority at the school level is not experienced in all types of schools. Bischoff and Sayed (1999: 313) found that principals of former Model C schools reported that there was no general change in the way that financial management of schools was being carried out, while principals from other types of schools stated that they had experienced a shift with regard to the principal's role. Given the limited role parents played historically in black schools, Karlsson (2002) concludes that by 2001 there had been no significant change in power relations at schools.

In all but the more affluent schools, field studies found parents playing a very limited role in school decisions. In a Wits Education Policy Unit (EPU) and Community Agency for Social Change (CASE) study, parents complained that principals at their schools imposed their views on other members of the SGB (Motala et al. 2002: 6). McPherson and Dlamini (1998: 17) found 42 per cent of principals in their study agreed with the statement that SGBs are expected to rubber-stamp decisions of the principal. Bischoff and Sayed (1999: 313) found that, paralleling research findings in England and Wales, the principal sees his or her role as 'one of being accountable and responsible in the final analysis' even though the financial management function of the school is not solely in his or her hands.

Parent representatives, comprising the majority plus one on SGBs, were found to have limited involvement in carrying out functions legislated for the SGB, because decisions were taken by the principal or school management team. These functions included the development of admissions policy, development of a school code of conduct, design of budgets, and the determination of school fees (GDE 2001: 19–21; Motala et al. 2002: 10).

Parents were also found to be disadvantaged by the language (English) of materials guiding the operations of SGBs, which contributed to their confusion or limited understanding of their roles (McPherson & Dlamini 1998: 17). Thus, the increased autonomy of the school is not a sharing of authority across stakeholders but rather a privilege granted by principals.

Learners are playing a limited role in SGBs. Initially there was tension between the prefect system, by which learners are selected by teachers based on teacher-set criteria, and the learner representative council structures, where learners elect their own representatives. This issue was resolved by the *Education Laws Amendment Act* of 2001, which stipulated that a representative council of learners 'is the only recognised and legitimate body at the school' (RSA 2001: Section 1). While this change strengthens the democratic participation of learners by ensuring that only learner-elected representatives serve on the SGB, there are still significant issues in their degree of participation. In the Education 2000 Plus study (Kgobe 2001), learner representatives at 80 per cent of the schools sampled indicated having no input in the development of their Code of Conduct. Bischoff and Phakoa (1999) found dissatisfaction with the Act for its restrictions on learners with regard to financial decisions. They found the focus of learner participation limited to fund-raising, discipline of learners and sports.

There has been very little interrogation of the multiple meanings of 'democratic practice'. In the Wits EPU and CASE study, parents and principals had different understandings of democratic practice, with parents complaining that principals unfairly caucused with educators and learners to rally support for their views. At times principals were reported to reverse decisions taken by the SGB. Principals defended their canvassing and persuasion tactics as legitimate and argued that it was important to be responsive to changing conditions (GDE 2001: 17–18).

In summary, while the rhetoric of reform in South Africa has been couched in terms of devolution of power and community and parent participation in school decision-making (Troyna 1994), in practice, decentralisation has not necessarily led to this. Tightening of central control appears effectively to be reducing the discretion and authority of SGBs.

Improving quality

From the limited empirical research which focuses directly on the relationship between equity and quality we are able to draw the following conclusions:
- There is no evidence that SGBs have allocated resources to improve quality because there is little research on expenditure of SGB budgets and even less which focuses on how SGB budgets have contributed to curriculum development concerns.
- There is evidence that SGBs in Section 21 schools have hired additional teachers. The main aim of this has been to reduce pupil-teacher ratios in an attempt to provide a better-quality learning environment.
- There is little evidence that SGBs have managed to improve the learning environment by improving the physical conditions of schools. The School Register of Needs survey of 2000 suggests that overall there was a decline in infrastructure expenditure.

The evidence seems to suggest that SASA has had little direct impact on quality in poor schools. As recently as March 2003, the government concluded that:

> The problem is that the quality of the education that the enrolled youth receive, is, on average, quite low, and worse, very unequally distributed. We now know that the distribution of knowledge wealth in our youth is at best a little better, but maybe worse, than the distribution of their parents' income. (DoE 2003: 12)

The inadequacy of redress resources combined with the difficulties faced by SGBs in capturing new funds makes quality improvements unlikely. This impacts on the attention given to school curriculum and teaching methodologies. Teacher quality is a critical aspect of overall school quality, but depends on the number that the school manages to recruit which, in turn, depends on resources (see Fiske & Ladd, in this volume). In addition, the increased emphasis on the managerial and efficiency aspects of leadership has led in some instances to a lessening of the principal's pedagogical function (Bischoff & Sayed 1999). Also troubling is the limited role that SGBs tend to play in curriculum matters (Kgobe 1999; McPherson & Naiker 2002; Motala et al. 2002).

Central responsibility for quality improvement was passed on to SGBs through SASA. This responsibility spans issues of general school promotion as well as issues of budgeting and resourcing the expenditure gap between government subsidies and basic needs. While school equity is not a manifestation of resources alone, there are profound relationships between resources, inequities and stakeholder – particularly teacher – morale. Thus, the tension of managing quality improvement in the context of limited resources is woven into the fabric of SGBs – particularly for SGBs in poorer neighbourhoods (Christie & Potterton 1997; Motala & Mngudi 1999: 19).

Significantly, most of the earlier policy documents speak explicitly of decentralisation and, as Sayed (2002) notes, the success and efficacy of decentralisation is measured according to different perspectives. A persuasive view in the South African context is that the process of decentralisation should not be seen as an end in itself but should rather promote improvements in the quality of learning (Kgobe 1999; Motala et al. 2002). It is only when learners experience improvements in the quality of schooling that one could argue that the policy of decentralisation has effected significant social transformation.

Towards a deeper understanding of the policies in practice

Perhaps due to its infancy, assessment of the 'success' of governance has been largely relegated to the consideration of form. The questions that are asked of school governance have generally been structural: How many SGBs have been formally constituted? Have they been constituted on the basis of SASA prescriptions? Do they understand their functions? Do they perform their function according to legislation?

Following on the work of Hanson (1997), Gilmour (2001) suggests that the structuralist approach to change – getting structures right, developing mechanisms and formulas to support government educational goals, and encouraging practices to conform with them – makes the gap between policy and implementation a bureaucratic problem. Educational reform is not fundamentally a bureaucratic endeavour but a political one, laden with wide-reaching values. If there is to be any hope of using decentralisation to promote South Africa's transformation into a democratic, participatory society, we must move away from the structuralist perspective of decentralisation. It is therefore disappointing that the recent *Review of the Financing, Resourcing and Costs of Education in Public Schools* (DoE 2003) should define implementation problems as due to having:

> ... been misunderstood by managers at the various levels of the departments, or at the school, perhaps because of insufficient explanation and socialisation from the DoE and the Provincial Education Departments. The remedy may then be awareness campaigns, or a rewording, though not a redesign, of the policy.

We argue for greater attention to process and values: the nature of parents' participation, the ways in which women are being excluded from elections of SGB representatives, the interpersonal interactions in SGB meetings, the substantive nature of SGB discussions and decision-making, and the impact of those decisions on the quality of schooling.

We must disentangle different actors and interests. Principals and teachers are likely to espouse and put into action theories different from those of parents or community members (McGinn 2002: 20). So too must we escape racial homogenising, by which we assume there is no conflict because the parents are all black or the teachers are all white.

Most importantly, progress will require moving towards an understanding of local theories in use. A considerable amount of analysis on SASA has focused on central government 'theories of action', that is, central government understandings of how the devolution of authority to schools will work (Weiss 1995; Angula & Grant Lewis 1997). These analyses have assisted us in looking critically at the central government's espoused theories. However, continued focus on central government understandings is very limiting and keeps us ensnared in an assessment of policy *intents*. Such a focus promotes implementation research that seeks to identify the policy-practice gap by determining whether the policy is implemented as intended. The guidance for practice that comes from such research tends to be rationalist: get conditions 'right', improve communication across levels, clarify roles, provide more and better training, increase the funding for redress (GDE 2001; Sayed 2002).

While these may all be good things to do, we believe that doing them will not prove to be 'the answer'. Rather, we need to understand the different meanings the policy has for diverse actors at various levels, by understanding the multiple understandings of how it works ('espoused theories') and the practices that reveal different 'theories in use'. If the South African government is to promote democratic participation, then local meanings of what it means to 'represent' a larger group need to be understood. Is it a symbolic role or does it entail being accountable to a constituency, voicing the views of that constituency and reporting back? How are local conceptualisations finding expression in practice? What can be done to eliminate obstacles identified by local actors? Respect for the diversity of perspectives of those trying to engage in democratic practice must be the basis for sustainable social change in South Africa.

Notes

1. The Ministerial Committee to Conduct a Review of School Governance was announced in late February 2003 with Professor Crain Soudien as chair. It is expected to 'define good and poor practice, as well as some of the variables which contribute to each of these' and to 'make recommendations for strengthening the model of democratic school governance'. The report was submitted to the Minister in December 2003. At the time of writing, it had yet to be released.

2. Authors have used various typologies for rationales for decentralisation. Lauglo (1995) refers to politically legitimate dispersal of authority, efficient use of resources, and quality of services rendered. Bray (1999) identified the motives as political, administrative or a combination of both. Welsh and McGinn (1999) use three categories of objectives: political, level of funding, and efficiency. Our adaptation of Welsh and McGinn's categories to political, economic and pedagogical draws from work by Riddell (1999) and others in educational planning. We consider efficiency concerns to be subsumed under the economic rationale, since they generally deal with cost-effectiveness.

3. McPherson and Dlamini (1998) describe the racial variations in school governance structures across five separate education departments under apartheid. The former Department of Education and Training (DET) schools had management councils comprised of parents, with the principal as an *ex-officio* member. These councils were 'largely advisory and consultative, which created an impression of parental participation in the control of education but did not give parents power outside their jurisdiction' (McPherson & Dlamini 1998: 4). In farm schools, management councils

existed at the pleasure of the farm owner. The HoR school committees and the HoD Parent Teacher Associations (PTAs) were similarly advisory.
4. Definitions of 'community' vary. It may mean the community surrounding the school or the community served by the school. The data demands for either definition are considerable.
5. The term is being used here in its simplest form, to refer to SGB members reflecting certain characteristics of the population that elected them. We are not implying a notion or practice of accountability.

References

Angula, N & Grant Lewis, S (1997) Promoting Democratic Processes in Educational Decision Making: Reflections from Namibia's First 5 Years, *International Journal of Education Development*, 17(3): 222–249

Badat, S (1997) Educational Politics in the Transition Period. In Kallaway, P; Kruss, G; Fataar, A & Donn, G *Education After Apartheid: South African Education in Transition*. Cape Town: University of Cape Town Press

Bardham, P & Mookherjee, D (1999) Relative Capture of Local and Central Governments. An Essay in the Political Economy of Decentralisation. Unpublished manuscript

Benhabib, S (ed) (1996) *Democracy and Difference. Contesting the Boundaries of the Political*. Princeton: Princeton University Press

Bischoff, T & Phakoa, TS (1999) The Status of Minors in Governing Bodies in Public Secondary Schools, *South African Journal of Education*, 19(2): 89–93

Bischoff, T & Sayed, MK (1999) The Changing Role of the Principal of a Public Primary School: A Financial School Management Perspective, *South African Journal of Education*, 19(4): 310–314

Bray, M (1999) Control of Education. Issues and Tensions in Centralization and Decentralisation. In Arnove, R & Torres, C *Comparative Education: The Dialectic of the Global and the Local*. Lanham, MD: Rowman and Littlefield

Carnoy, M (1998) Higher Education in a Global Innovation Economy. Paper delivered at a seminar co-hosted by the Centre for Higher Education Transformation and the HSRC, Pretoria, 31 July

Carrim, N & Tshoane, M (2000) The 'Holy' State? Values, Legitimation and Ideological Closure in South African Education, In Chisholm, L; Motala, S & Vally, S (eds) (2003) *South African Education Policy Review 1993–2000*. Johannesburg: Heinemann

Chakane, M (2002) *The Implementation of the School Funding Norms.* Research report prepared for the Education Foundation

Chisholm, L (1997) The Restructuring of South African Education and Training in Comparative Context. In Kallaway, P; Kruss, G; Fataar, A & Donn, G (eds) *Education After Apartheid: South African Education in Transition.* Cape Town: University of Cape Town Press

Chisholm, L & Fuller, B (1996) Remember People's Education? Shifting Alliances, State-Building and South Africa's Narrowing Policy Agenda, *Journal of Education Policy*, 6(6): 693–716

Chisholm, L; Motala, S & Vally, S (1999) Review of South African Education, 1996–1998. Paper presented to the CEPD Education 2000 Plus Conference, Johannesburg, August

Christie, P & Potterton, M (1997) *School Development in South Africa: A Research Project to Investigate Strategic Interventions for Quality Improvement in South African Schools.* Johannesburg: CIE

Chubb, J & Moe, T (1990) *Politics, Markets and America's Schools.* Washington, DC: The Brookings Institute

Crouch, L (2002) Information Systems in South Africa. Paper presented to International Conference on Decentralisation, Johannesburg

De Clercq, F (1997) Effective Policies and the Reform Process: An Evaluation of South Africa's New Development and Education Macro Policies. In Kallaway, P; Kruss, G; Fataar, A & Donn, G (eds) *Education After Apartheid: South African Education in Transition.* Cape Town: University of Cape Town Press

Department of Education (1995) *Report of the Committee to Review the Organisation, Governance and Funding of Schools* (Hunter Commission). Pretoria: DoE

Department of Education (1998) National Norms and Standards for School Funding. *Government Gazette*, Notice No. 19347 of 1998. Pretoria: Government Printers

Department of Education (2003) *Review of Financing, Resourcing and Costs of Education in Public Schools.* Pretoria: DoE

Elmore, R (1993) School Decentralisation? Who Gains? Who Loses? In Hannaway, J & Carnoy, M *Decentralisation and School Improvement.* San Francisco: Jossey-Bass

Fiske, E (1996) *Decentralisation of Education: Politics and Consensus.* Washington, DC: World Bank

Fiske, E & Ladd, H (2002) School Finance Equity in South Africa. Paper presented to the International Conference on Decentralisation and Governance, Johannesburg, June

Fullan, M (1998) The Meaning of Educational Change: A Quarter of a Century of Learning. In Hargreaves, A et al. (eds) *International Handbook of Educational Change*. Dordrecht: Kluwer

Fuller, B & Clarke, P (1994) Raising School Effects While Ignoring Culture? Local Conditions and the Influence of Classroom Tools, Rules and Pedagogy. *Harvard Educational Review*, 4 (1): 119–157

Gauteng Department of Education (GDE) (2001) *School Governance Policy*. Report prepared for the GDE by CASE and the Wits EPU, Johannesburg

Gilmour, J (2001) Intention or in Tension? Recent Education Reforms in South Africa. *International Journal of Education Development*, 21 (1): 5–20

Grant Lewis, S; Naidoo, T & Weber, E (2002) The Problematic Notion of Participation in Educational Decentralisation: The Case of South Africa. Paper presented at Africa in an Age of Globalisation Conference, Teachers' College, April

Hanson, M (1997) Educational Reform and the Transition from Authoritarian Democratic Governments: The Cases of Argentina, Columbia, Venezuela and Spain, *International Journal of Education Development*, 17 (4): 439–448

Hyslop, J (1999) *The Classroom Struggle: Policy and Resistance in South Africa 1940–1990*. Pietermaritzburg: University of Natal Press

Karlsson, J (2002) The Role of Democratic Governing Bodies in South African Schools, *Comparative Education*, 38 (3): 327–336

Karlsson, J; McPherson, G & Pampallis, J (1999) A Critical Examination of the Development of School Governance Policy and its Implications for Achieving Equity. Paper presented at Kenton Conference, 1999, Salt Rock, Durban

Kgobe, P (1999) School Level Change in South Africa. Paper prepared for the CEPD Education 2000 Plus Report. Johannesburg: CEPD

Kgobe, P (2001) School Level Change in South Africa. Paper prepared for the CEPD Education 2000 Plus Report. Johannesburg: CEPD

Kgobe, P (2002) School Level Change in South Africa. Paper prepared for the CEPD Education 2000 Plus Report. Johannesburg: CEPD

Khulisa Management Services and Lifelong Learning Services (1999) *Final Impact Study: School Governance Programme – Gauteng Department of Education*. Johannesburg: GDE

Lauglo, J (1995) Forms of Decentralisation and Their Implications for Education, *Comparative Education*, 31 (1): 35–67

Mashele, A & Grobler, B (1999) The Influence of Interest Group Organisational Structures on Educational Management/Governance in Kathorus, *South African Journal of Education*, 19(4): 295–304

McGinn, N (2002) *International and National Trends in Local Governance of Education*. Educational Studies and Documents Series, No. 70. Paris: Unesco

McLennan, A (2000) The Challenge of Tirisano. Paper prepared for SAELP and EMASA Conference, 8–10 March, Port Elizabeth

McPherson, G & Dlamini, M (1998) *Democratic School Governing Bodies in the Province of KwaZulu-Natal, The First Elections*. Durban: University of Natal EPU

McPherson, G & Naicker, S (2002) Governing Schools in an Era of Democracy. Paper prepared for the CEPD Education 2000 Plus project, Johannesburg

Motala, S (2003) Review of the Financing, Resourcing and Cost of Education in Public Schools: A Commentary. In Motala, S et al. *Education Transformation 2003: From Systemic Reform to Policy Review, Quarterly Review of Education and Training in South Africa*, 10(1): 2–12

Motala, S & Mngudi, R (1999) From Policy to Practice: Achieving Quality in Post-Apartheid South Africa. In Weeks, S (ed) *Southern African Review of Education* with *Education in Production* Vol 6. Gaborone: SARE

Motala, S; Porteus, K & Tshoane, M (2002) The South African Schools Act: Implications for Redressing Equity. Paper presented to the Decentralisation and Education Conference, Johannesburg, 13 June

Naidoo, J (2001) Education Decentralisation in Sub-Saharan Africa. A Review of the Literature. Unpublished qualifying paper for the Harvard Graduate School of Education

National Education Policy Investigation (1992) *Governance and Administration: Report of the NEPI Governance and Administration Research Group*. Cape Town: Oxford University Press/NECC

Osborne, D & Gaebler, T (1992) *Reinventing Government*. Reading, Mass.: Addison Wesley

Patel, F (2002) A Review of School Funding, *Edusource Data News* 36: 10–23

Porteus, K (2001) The Evolution of School Governing Bodies in South African Schooling. Paper prepared for the Comparative International Education Conference, Washington, DC, March

Porteus, K; Patel, F; Fleisch, B & Ruth, T (2001) *Budget Analysis for the Education Portfolio Committee of the Gauteng Provincial Legislature – Budget Statement 2001/02: Vote 5 Budget*. Paper prepared for the Gauteng Department of Education

Rahnema, M (1992) Participation. In Sachs, W (ed) *The Development Dictionary: A Guide to Knowledge as Power*. London: Zed Books

Republic of South Africa (1995) *White Paper on Education and Training in a Democratic South Africa: First Steps to Develop a New System*. Pretoria: Government Printers

Republic of South Africa (1996a) *White Paper on The Organisation, Governance and Funding of Schools*. Pretoria: Government Printers

Republic of South Africa (1996b) *National Education Policy Act*. No. 27 of 1996

Republic of South Africa (1996c) *South African Schools Act*. No. 84 of 1996

Republic of South Africa (1998) *Employment of Educators Act*. No. 76 of 1998

Republic of South Africa (1999) *National Education Policy (Amendment) Act*

Republic of South Africa (2001) *Education Laws Amendment Act*. No. 57 of 2001

Republic of South Africa (2002) *Education Laws Amendment Act*. No. 50 of 2002

Riddell, A (1999) The Need for a Multidisciplinary Framework for Analysing Educational Reform in Developing Countries, *International Journal of Educational Development*, 19: 203–217

Sayed, Y (1999) Discourses of the Policy of Educational Decentralisation in South Africa since 1994: An Examination of the *South African Schools Act*, *Compare*, 29(2): 141–152

Sayed, Y (2002) Democratising Education in a Decentralised System: South African Policy and Practice, *Compare*, 32 (1): 35–46

Sayed, Y & Carrim, N (1997a) Democracy, Participation and Equity in Educational Governance, *South African Journal of Education*, 17 (3): 91–100

Sayed, Y & Carrim, N (1997b) Inclusiveness and Participation in Discourses of Educational Governance in South Africa, *International Journal of Inclusive Education*, 2(1): 29–43

Simkins, C (2002) Human Capital Approaches in South Africa. Unpublished manuscript

Stoker, G (1996) *Governance as Theory: Five Propositions*, Enjeux des Debates sur la Governance, Universite de Lausanne, 29–30 November

Troyna, B (1994) Reforms, Research, and Being Reflexive About Being Reflective. In Halpin, D & Troyna, B (eds) *Researching Education Policy: Ethical and Methodological Issues*. London: Falmer

United Nations Development Programme (2002) *Human Development Report*. New York: UNDP

Universal Declaration on Democracy (1997). [Online]. Available <http://www.unesco.org/cpp/uk/declarations/democracy.pdf>

Vally, S (1999) Teachers in South Africa: Between Fiscal Austerity and Getting Learning Right. In Chisholm, L; Motala, S & Vally, S (eds) (2003) *South African Education Policy Review 1993–2000*. Johannesburg: Heinemann

Vally, S (2000) Researching Policy and Implementation. A Maligned or Misaligned system. In Chisholm, L; Motala, S & Vally, S (eds) (2003) *South African Education Policy Review 1993–2000*. Johannesburg: Heinemann

Van der Berg, S (2001) Resource Shifts in South African Schools after the Political Transition, *Development Southern Africa*, September: 309–325

Weber, E (2002) Shifting to the Right: The Evolution of Equity in the South African Government's Development and Education Policies, 1990–1999, *Comparative Education Review*, 46 (3): 261–290

Weiss, C (1995) Nothing as Practical as Good Theory: Exploring the Theory-based Evaluation for Comparative Community Initiatives for Children and Families. In Connell, JP; Kubisch, AC; Schorr LB & Weiss, CH (eds) *New Approaches to Evaluating Community Initiatives: Concepts, Methods and Contexts*. New York: Aspen Institute

Welsh, T & McGinn, N (1998) *Decentralisation of Education: What and How*. Fundamentals of Educational Planning series, No. 64. Paris: IIEP

West, M & Hopkins, D (1996) Reconceptualising School Effectiveness and School Improvement. Paper presented to the American Education Research Association Conference, New York

Whitty, G; Power, S & Halpin, D (1998) *Devolution and Choice in Education: The School, the State and the Market*. Buckingham: Open University Press

Wildeman, R (2000a) Redistribution of School Funding, *Budget Brief*, No. 48

Wildeman, R (2000b) Equity in Education: How Far Are We? *Budget Brief*, No. 44

Wildeman, R (2002a) *A Progress Report on the Implementation of the Norms and Standards for School Funding 2000* [Online]. Available <http://www.idasa.org.za.bis>

Wildeman, R (2002b) School Funding Norms 2001: Are More Poor Learners Benefiting? Budget Brief No. 79 [Online]. Available <http://www.idasa.org.za.bis>

5 The new face of private schooling

Jane Hofmeyr and Simon Lee

Dramatic change

The size, diversity and socio-economic spread of the private (independent) schooling sector have changed significantly in the last decade. The dominant public perception of independent schools is 'white, affluent and exclusive'. In 1990, this perception was largely true: most of the learners were white and found in traditional, high-fee, religious schools. However, there was a significant black enrolment in traditionally white independent schools, as well as a number of average- to low-fee black independent schools.

Over a decade later this public perception persists, but it is far from the current reality. The majority of learners at independent schools are now black, while the majority of schools are new (established since 1990), charge average to low fees and are religious or community-based.

By contrast, the traditional schools charging high fees initially became 'paler' with an exodus of black learners due to the opening of public schools to all racial groups. Only recently have many been able to surpass their 1990 black enrolment levels.

In 2002, the sector was almost three times the size of what it was in 1990 and more diverse, with a wide range of different religions, philosophies and educational approaches available to the full socio-economic spectrum of communities. While the sector is still predominantly non-profit, there has also been a significant growth in for-profit schools. Although only 2.1 per cent of learners overall are enrolled in this sector, the changes over the last decade merit some discussion.

This chapter will explore the changing size and shape of the independent school sector between 1990 and 2002 to better understand what has occurred. It will also attempt to examine why the change has occurred by identifying a variety of educational and societal forces as possible causes. The main argument that the authors will advance is that differentiated demand in black communities for better and different schooling has been the primary driver of this change. Finally, the paper will outline key issues and challenges for the sector as it continues to evolve.

Definition

Before discussing the sector it is necessary to deal with a few definitional issues. Internationally, both narrow and broad definitions for private schools are used. One of the broadest definitions for developing countries is that provided by Kitaev (1999):

> 'private schools' includes all formal schools that are not public and may be founded, owned, managed and financed by actors other than the state, even in cases where the state provides most of the funding and has considerable control over these schools.

By contrast, the current definition of private schools used in South Africa is a narrow one and does not include certain types of non-public education, especially what are referred to as 'public schools on private property'. These comprise state-aided schools owned by religious bodies, farmers, mining and forestry, where the vast majority are Catholic or farm schools. In most other countries these schools would be considered private, but in South Africa they are considered public schools, governed by Section 14 of the *South African Schools Act* (SASA) of 1996.

The term 'independent' school has come to replace 'private' in many parts of the world. Many associations of non-public schools worldwide have chosen the term 'independent' to categorise their members. The SASA also uses 'independent' in preference to 'private' when referring to non-public schools.

An ongoing problem is that generally the public in South Africa do not know what the term 'independent' signifies and it is usually necessary to add the term 'private' to ensure understanding. Moreover, both potential customers and opponents of private schooling commonly believe that the well-resourced, ex-white public schools in suburban areas are private schools, thus increasing the confusion about which schools are 'independent' or 'private'.

International context

Private education has grown rapidly on a worldwide scale over the past ten years (Tooley 2001). The growth of private schooling has been particularly dramatic in developing countries. Commenting on that growth, James Tooley dispels some preconceptions:

> Far from finding that the private education sector in developing countries was relatively small and catering predominately only for the élite, I found a sector which was rather large at all levels – primary, secondary and tertiary – which was expanding rapidly, and which featured remarkable examples of innovation. In countries such as Russia and Romania, which had until recently banned private education, the sector is burgeoning – in Moscow, the same proportion of students attend private school as they do in the UK (about 7 per cent). In countries such as Colombia, 28 per cent of total enrolment in kindergarten and primary education is in the private sector, increasing to 40 per cent at secondary school level; in Argentina and Côte d'Ivoire 30 per cent and 57 per cent respectively of secondary school enrolment is in the private sector; Indonesia has 23 per cent private primary and secondary school students. (Tooley 2001: 27–28)

China, previously a bastion of centralised state education, is now encouraging private education, which has grown dramatically. In 2001, 54 per cent of tertiary institutions, 20 per cent of pre-schools, 9 per cent of vocational high schools, 3 per cent of middle schools and 0.4 per cent of elementary schools were in the private sector (Tooley 2001).

In Africa the same trend is obvious: by the late 1990s in Zimbabwe, 88 per cent of primary and 85 per cent of secondary school learners were in non-public schools, while in Tanzania, 53 per cent of secondary school learners, and in Botswana, 74 per cent of secondary school learners were in non-public schools (Tooley 2001).

Many of these schools were started by communities, but currently receive significant state funding and support. As community schools, they would satisfy Kitaev's broad definition as private, but not the one in SASA. Nonetheless, the trend remains strongly towards private (with varying degrees of independence) rather than public education in the developing world.

Research

Until recently there was very little research on the whole independent school sector in South Africa. While there have been a few important studies, they are qualitative and either very dated (Randall 1982) or partial (Christie 1990), and do not meet the needs of this chapter which requires a view of changes in the sector over the last decade.

Randall's analysis (1982) pointed to the fact that many of the traditional independent schools in South Africa were modelled on the British public school system, such that they constituted 'a little England in the veld'. He argued that this history, and the influence of the English church and big business, meant that the schools tended to reproduce a white, elitist, conservative, capitalist system. Christie's research (1990) in a sample of Catholic schools pointed to the centrality of the ethos at private schools. She argued that although most private schools had 'opened' their admissions to black learners, this was done in accordance with a logic of assimilation to white, Western and largely capitalist dominant values. Only when the number of black students reached a critical mass of 35 per cent, would a different set of racial dynamics come into play. She predicted that schools would at this junction become ideological battlefields of ideas and responses. Muller's research in the Johannesburg area in the late 1980s presents a useful picture of the private schooling sector at the end of the apartheid era. A second 'snapshot' was provided by the Human Sciences Research Council (HSRC), which surveyed the whole sector in 2001. We have used the qualitative and quantitative data from the two latter studies, as well as a variety of analytical frameworks derived from international literature, local experience and non-educational sources of information, to suggest why the changes have taken place.

Data problems

As the independent sector has become larger and has featured more prominently in education debates in the last decade, both government agencies and research bodies have seen the need to quantify and understand the nature of schools within it.

Provincial databases cannot be accepted as accurate or reliable (Kane-Berman 2002). They suffer from problems common in developing countries, as well as some specific problems resulting from inadequate annual returns of independent schools to the provincial education departments. The main cause of the latter was the introduction of the National Norms and Standards for the Funding of Schools for state subsidies in 2000. The Funding Norms, which regulate state subsidies, require provincial education departments to rank independent schools from the highest to the lowest fees they charge, and allocate subsidies to eligible schools on a sliding scale. Schools with the lowest fees receive 60 per cent of the average expenditure by the province on a public school learner. Schools with fees that are more than 2.5 times the provincial average *per capita* expenditure on a public school learner receive no subsidy at all.

Since 2000, officials in provincial education departments have tended to omit non-subsidised schools from their databases. The fact that their financial accountability in terms of the *Public Finance Management Act* applies only to subsidised schools, compounds this problem.

In addition, when many schools no longer received subsidies, they did not send in annual returns – not surprisingly in provinces that continued to use forms headed 'Application for Subsidy' to collect registration information. Thus unsubsidised schools were not recorded on the provincial databases.

The confusion regarding registration and subsidisation has also led to problems in the administration of subsidies. The Gauteng Department of Education (GDE), for example, has admitted to serious database problems in its recording of independent schools.[1]

As the national database in the Department of Education (DoE) is compiled from the provincial figures, it suffers from all the same weaknesses (Perry 2002).

The fact that government databases are inaccurate has led a number of organisations to commission the HSRC to research the independent school sector. In 2001, a study by the HSRC for the Education, Training and Development Practices Sector Education and Training Authority (ETDP SETA) revealed that the independent school sector is the SETA's largest private sector constituency. With approximately 51 467 employees, it employs more teaching, administrative and general staff than universities and technikons (Erasmus 2002).

More recently, the HSRC assessed the extent of private education provision in the General Education and Training (GET) band. Using the 2000 database compiled by the HSRC for the SETA, and a telephonic and postal survey from 410 schools, the HSRC verified a database of 1 287 registered independent schools (Du Toit 2003). This is the most comprehensive quantitative research to date. Its purpose, however, was to produce a broad national survey and thus did not go into detail on demographic issues, such as learner characteristics, parental education or family income.

If the primary (Grades 0–7) and secondary (Grades 8–12) phases of schools are counted separately (as is required by the Funding Norms to determine if the school qualifies for a government subsidy), the 1 287 schools identified in the HSRC 2001 survey as a minimum of registered independent schools, is closer to 1 950. This is a dramatic increase from the 517 registered schools in 1994 and more than twice the size of the sector according to the 2001 database of the DoE (Du Toit 2003).

In the light of all these problems with independent school data, it is difficult to compare different sets of data, and outside the figures of the HSRC and those of some of the independent schools associations, most other figures over the period in review should be treated with caution. In this chapter, therefore, the authors have tended to use data as indicative rather than absolute.

Analytical frameworks

As a result of the lack of substantial research on the South African independent school sector, the main conceptual frameworks available for understanding the recent growth derive from international literature.

James (1991) argues that two main demand factors are responsible for the growth of private education in most countries: excess demand for education above what the state can provide and differentiated demand for alternative types and quality of education to that provided by the state. Typically, excess demand is found in developing countries and differentiated demand is a feature of developed countries.

Outside of this analytical construct, descriptive typologies are common. Three typologies can be used to describe the types of independent schools in South

Africa. A recent typology is Kitaev's (1999) qualitative classification of five types of private schools in sub-Saharan Africa, on the basis of their origins and purpose: community, religious, profit-making, spontaneous and expatriate schools. The second typology, developed by the Independent Schools Association of Southern Africa (ISASA), categorises independent schools according to their legal status and membership of associations. It distinguishes between legally registered schools, both affiliated and unaffiliated, and unregistered 'fly-by-night' schools (Hofmeyr & Lee 2002). The final quantitative typology classifies schools according to their socio-economic level. In the absence of more comprehensive socio-economic data, the best proxy for this is the fee level charged by each school. The HSRC research (Du Toit 2003) used this typology to good effect.

Examination of independent schools in 1990

The origins of independent schooling throw light on developments in the sector. The roots of independent schooling in South Africa are strongly religious and go back to the earliest mission or church schools (Malherbe 1977). The oldest schools today are St George's Grammar School and Diocesan College, both Anglican church schools, founded in Cape Town in 1848 and 1849 respectively. By the end of the nineteenth century, a fair number of similar schools had been established in Johannesburg and Natal.

Long after the state had already taken over responsibility for the education of white children in South Africa, private mission schools with state subsidies were the 'mainstay' of education for black children by the mid-twentieth century (Malherbe 1977: 550). When the National Party came to power in 1948 and imposed its policy of apartheid education on the country, most mission schools were forced to close. The *Bantu Education Act* of 1953 phased out state subsidies for mission schools, required them to apply for registration as private schools and follow departmental syllabuses. As a result very few were able or prepared to continue (Malherbe 1977).

In white South Africa, by contrast, there was a surge of interest in establishing private schools that would be free of government control. By 1948, at least 86 independent schools had been established. In the 42 years between 1948 and 1990, at least an additional 103 were founded (ISASA 2003b).

Government data on registered independent (then private) schools shows that in 1990, independent school enrolment consisted of 103 854 learners, of which 50.8 per cent were white. Interestingly, 37 284 learners – or 36 per cent – were black, a high percentage for pre-democratic South Africa (Muller 1992: 343).

Muller (1992) divides independent schools into three broad categories: traditional private, 'new' private and 'others'. In order to provide a consistency of approach across the last 12 years, the authors have attempted to rework Muller's three broad categories, using the Kitaev typology, governance and socio-economic perspectives so that the changes from 1990 to 2002 can be more easily tracked.

According to Muller (1992: 340), the defining characteristics of the traditional private schools were 'that they were predominantly white, predominantly church-affiliated, and – the Catholic and Jewish schools aside – they self-consciously promoted a certain Anglocentric ethos'. Thus, using Kitaev's typology, it is clear that in 1990, the vast majority of traditional schools could be classified as 'religious' in origin and function.

Muller indicates that the divide between traditional and 'new' independent schools was reflected in their affiliation to particular associations: many of the traditional schools were members of the Independent Schools Council (ISC), the forerunner of ISASA, with 77 schools in 1989, while the majority of the organised 'new' privates belonged to the more progressive South African Association of Independent Schools (SAAIS), with 36 schools in 1989.

After the Soweto uprisings, the first of the 'new' private schools began to emerge. These schools were created principally for black learners and were established as a direct response to apartheid.

Despite their common purpose, there was significant heterogeneity among the new private schools. Some of the more prestigious were established to educate the 'black cream', or black middle class that was beginning to emerge at this time (Muller 1992: 342). The Leadership Education and Advancement (LEAF) and New Era Schools Trust (NEST) schools are examples of this trend. Another group was religious, sometimes established on church property or using church facilities to reduce costs. Many of these schools, such as St Barnabas and St Mark's, had a high profile as anti-apartheid schools, both in South Africa and abroad, and thus benefited from significant foreign donations. The religious category also included more than 60 schools established by the Accelerated Christian Education (ACE) charismatic movement.

The third and perhaps most widespread type of new private school was what Muller refers to as 'street academies', with some 6 000 to 8 000 students in Johannesburg in 1988. These were commercially-run schools established in urban areas specifically to educate black students who were unable or unwilling to access education through the Bantu education system (Muller 1992: 342).

Some of these schools were exploitative and 'fly-by-night', very much in keeping with Kitaev's 'spontaneous' category of school, but others were well-managed and financially sound. Well-known and successful street academies included St Ansgar's and St Enda's, which are still operating as registered schools in Johannesburg.

The catch-all, 'other' category of private school included schools with specific educational approaches (for example, Waldorf and Montessori), schools established to serve a specific ethnic community (Greek and German schools), and the well-established, commercially-run schools, such as Damelin and Cape Tutorial College (Muller 1992: 343). The last two types of school fall quite neatly into Kitaev's typology as expatriate and profit-making respectively. The schools with alternative educational approaches were (and remain) very unusual in the rest of sub-Saharan Africa and are not catered for in Kitaev's typology.

In terms of the governance typology, private schools were required to register with their appropriate apartheid education department and a state subsidy was dependent on them doing so. Many of the new private schools did not register, either because of moral opposition to apartheid education, or because they were 'fly-by-night' operations that would never meet the criteria for registration (Muller 1992: 342). Consequently, as is the case today, government databases of the time are unlikely to be accurate indicators of the number of independent schools.

Those schools that belonged to associations were members either of a faith-based organisation, ISC or SAAIS. Overlapping membership (for example, faith-based and SAAIS) was fairly common (Muller 1992).

The state's attitude towards independent schools changed significantly between the 1940s and 1990s. After forcing the closure of most church or mission schools for black learners in the 1950s, the National Party did its best to ignore the white independent schools until the late 1970s, when the schools' defiance of segregation policies through the admission of black learners created much animosity between themselves and the government of the day. This open defiance was initiated by the Catholic schools which included some 75 independent schools in 1989 (Muller 1992: 342).

The reformist De Lange Committee Report (1981) on the state of education shifted government's attitude on independent schools towards one of grudging acceptance, especially as these schools were seen as useful 'pressure valves' to cater for and marginalise troublesome learners and non-racial tendencies (Muller 1992: 344). In keeping with this utilitarian attitude, the *Private Schools Act* of 1986 introduced compulsory registration for private schools, as well as a subsidy for many schools at a 15 or 45 per cent level.

In summary, most of Kitaev's categories of independent schools could be found in the sector at the beginning of the 1990s, as well as alternative schools not catered for in the typology. Although community schools are not identified as a category in Muller's analysis, many of the schools of the time would undoubtedly have arisen through community self-help projects. The dominance of religious schools in the early 1990s was in keeping with the religious origins of the sector.

In terms of a governance perspective, most schools were registered, but there were already a growing number of unregistered schools. In socio-economic terms, the evidence indicates that the majority of schools charged high fees, but there would have been a substantial number – typically religious, but also profit-making – that charged average fees. To cater for the growing needs of black learners, there were also a number of low-fee schools. However, owing to inadequate data, it is impossible to quantify the exact number of schools in each fee category – only the broad trends are clear.

Examination of independent schools in 2003

The independent school sector in 2003 was notably different from that in 1990 in terms of size and socio-economic diversity. Du Toit (2003) points to very strong growth in the 1990s, with 61 per cent of all independent schools having been registered between 1990 and 2001. There have been two peaks in registration: 1994/95 and 1998/99. After 1999, the growth declined sharply but since 2001 appears to be on the rise again. However, the sector remains very small in international terms. According to official statistics, only 2.1 per cent

THE NEW FACE OF PRIVATE SCHOOLING

of students were enrolled in this sector in 2000 (see Fiske & Ladd, this volume). Even at more recent estimates of 3.2 per cent (Du Toit 2003), the sector accounts for a tiny portion of the whole system.

Classifying schools according to a governance perspective shows that while there has been a growth in the number of affiliated independent schools, the majority belong to no association. Of the 1 951 independent schools in 2001 (counting primary and secondary schools separately), approximately 880 were members of an association. The major national associations are ISASA, the largest association, the Catholic Institute for Education (CIE), the South African Board of Jewish Education (SABJE), the Muslim Schools' Association, and several Christian associations such as the School of Tomorrow (ACE schools) and the Association of Christian Schools International (ACSI). At the provincial levels, there are joint liaison committees (JLCs) or provincial associations and at the national level, associations are jointly represented by the National Alliance of Independent School Associations (NAISA).

Figure 5.1 Independent schools in South Africa, 2003

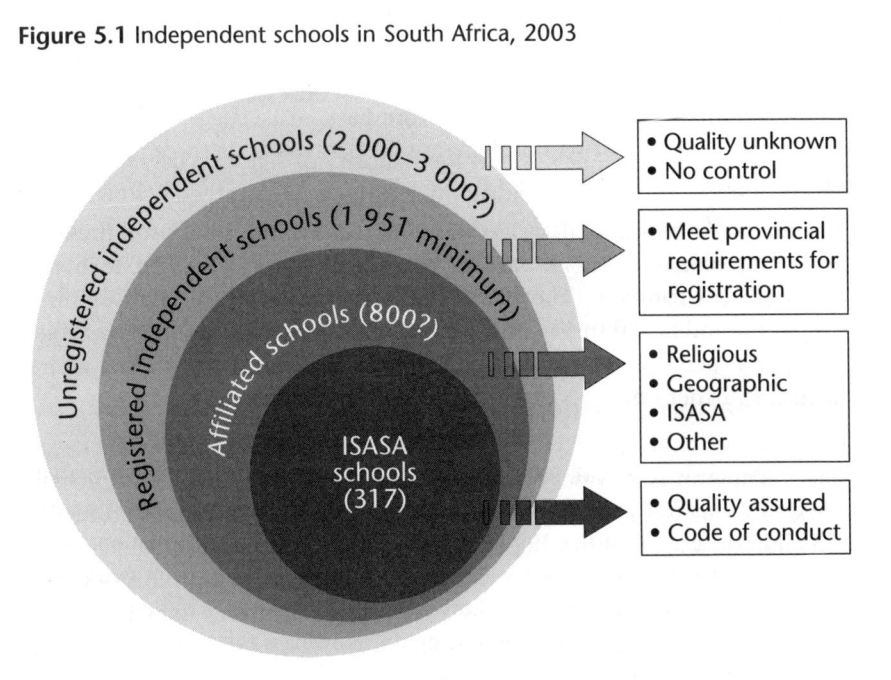

- Unregistered independent schools (2 000–3 000?)
  - Quality unknown
  - No control
- Registered independent schools (1 951 minimum)
  - Meet provincial requirements for registration
- Affiliated schools (800?)
  - Religious
  - Geographic
  - ISASA
  - Other
- ISASA schools (317)
  - Quality assured
  - Code of conduct

The independent school sector has always had its share of internal politics. The late 1980s battle of the 'new privates' (the schools associated with the SAAIS) and the 'traditional privates' (those belonging to the ISC) over largely racial issues has, to a limited extent, carried through to the present day, although the SAAIS no longer exists. There have been some tensions between school associations that regard themselves as the 'true' representatives of black independent education, like the Alliance of Independent Schools for Black Children in Gauteng, and those that they perceive as serving a traditional white, wealthy clientele, such as ISASA – even though 53 per cent of its members lie below the high-fee category (ISASA 2003b). However, the force for co-operation against common threats has proven stronger than divisiveness within the sector, as the many joint submissions of the provincial JLCs and NAISA to government demonstrate.

A limitation of the governance view is that as one moves outside the ISASA database, the size of the categories becomes less exact. Many of the other associations have only rudimentary databases and some count primary and secondary schools on a campus as one school, whereas others count them as two schools. Most worryingly, the number of unregistered schools remains impossible to determine, as most are operating illegally and are never recorded on any official database. Evidence from East Africa suggests that for every registered independent school there are probably at least three unregistered, 'fly-by-night' schools in operation (Kitaev 1999).

The categories of school described in the Kitaev typology were still present in 2002, but have undergone various changes in order to adapt to a post-apartheid environment. The HSRC used a variation of this typology in its telephonic and postal survey of a sample of schools, and from this was able to extrapolate percentages of the main categories of schools in 2001 that we have included further on.

Religious schools have experienced continuing popularity in the last decade. There is now an even wider range of different religious schools, encompassing Christian, especially of the fundamentalist variety, Jewish and considerably more Hindu and Muslim schools. According to the HSRC, over 46 per cent of all independent schools can be classified as religious. Within ISASA's membership, the database also shows that 44 per cent of its schools were faith-based in 2001 (Simmonds 2001).

At the same time, there is a trend of religious (mainly Catholic and Anglican) schools converting to public schools on private property, owing to cost considerations. In 2001, 269 of the 362 Catholic schools in South Africa were public schools on private property (Swedish Development Advisers 2001).

Community schools have grown steadily in number since 1990. In many cases these schools are still meeting unmet demand in deep rural areas, inner cities and informal settlements where there are no state schools. However, some community schools are also established to meet differentiated demand in areas that are plagued by dysfunctional public schools. HSRC research indicates that some 28 per cent of independent schools classify themselves as community schools.

Profit-making schools have continued to evolve, and now serve all rungs of the socio-economic ladder – despite being ineligible for any government subsidy. Schools like Crawford and Reddam market their ability to produce high academic results and are competitive in their approach to education. The lower-income 'street academies' continue to cater for black learners (adults or children) in the inner cities. Profit-making schools comprise five per cent of all independent schools (Du Toit 2003).

Spontaneous schools come and go in the inner cities and informal settlements on the outskirts of cities. While experience of the sector leads the authors to believe that the 'fly-by-night' schools have increased substantially in number since 1990, HSRC self-reported research puts the number at under one per cent. However, the point must be made that it is unlikely that such schools would identify themselves as such to any researchers.

The number of **expatriate schools**, serving primarily the children of expatriate and diplomatic communities in South Africa, has not grown significantly since 1990.

In short, there has been continued demand for religious education, as well as a strong growth in community-based schooling. The South African sector in this respect accords with those in the rest of sub-Saharan Africa as Kitaev found:

> At present, the majority of registered private schools in sub-Saharan Africa are still non-profit-making community and religious schools, rather than profit-making and other types of private schools. (Kitaev 1999: 51–52)

A weakness in the Kitaev typology is that it does not cater for the full range of private schools in a country like South Africa, where features of both the developed and developing worlds co-exist. The following categories of independent school lie outside Kitaev's framework and some seem to be unique to South Africa (Hofmeyr & Lee 2002):

Non-profit schools specifically to counteract the apartheid legacy. Muller (1992) noted a particular type of independent school that developed in South Africa as a response to apartheid. It served relatively poor, black communities and was found in both rural and urban settings. Some, like St Barnabas and St Mark's, had to become public schools on private property because they could no longer source the previous level of foreign donations in a post-apartheid South Africa.

Alternative schools. Another variant of secular and non-profit independent schools arose largely as the result of differentiated demand in white communities. These are typically the Montessori or Waldorf schools, which offer alternative philosophies or approaches to education to white and, increasingly, black learners. The HSRC found that schools based on an alternative education philosophy or value system comprise 5.5 per cent of all independent schools.

Virtual schools. Although these are not classified as independent schools in SASA, home education or 'micro-schools' (a small, family-based unit, usually with a single mentor or teacher) are increasingly making use of virtual material to educate learners. Brainline Junior University [2] is an example of a virtual schooling environment that offers tutorial lessons that can be accessed online or via a CD-ROM.

Most of the different types of independent schools were already present in 1990, with the exception of virtual schooling. However, today the range within each category has expanded and access to each category is available to a wider socio-economic spectrum, as the HSRC research (Du Toit 2003) indicates.

The socio-economic analysis of this research provides the most startling evidence of the changing face of independent schooling since 1990. It shows that the majority of independent schools now charge fees below R6 000 per annum. Across South Africa, only 14 per cent of independent schools charge fees greater than R18 000 per annum (Du Toit 2003).

THE NEW FACE OF PRIVATE SCHOOLING

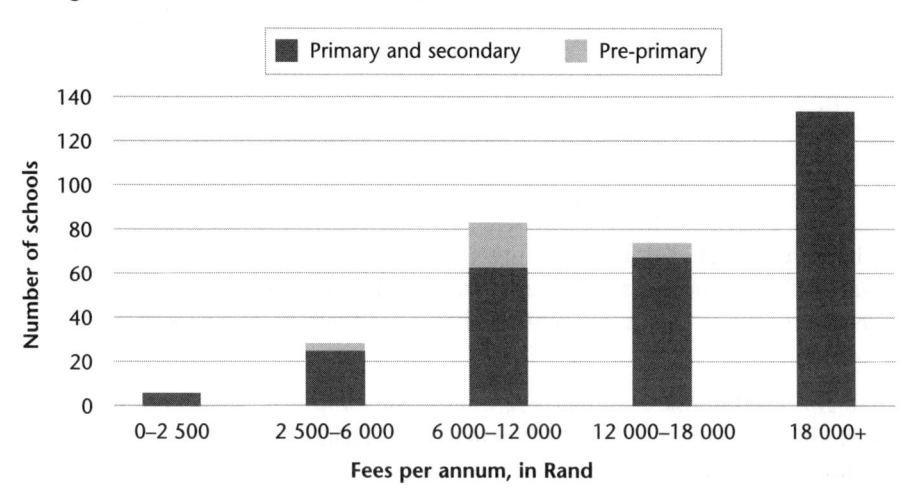

Figure 5.2 ISASA's member schools, December 2002

[Bar chart showing Number of schools vs Fees per annum, in Rand, with categories Primary and secondary, and Pre-primary]

Fees per annum (Rand)	Number of schools (approx.)
0–2 500	~5
2 500–6 000	~25
6 000–12 000	~85
12 000–18 000	~75
18 000+	~135

The nature of ISASA's members in the lowest fee category, suggests that a further division can be made between schools that rely both on their fee income and subsidies to survive, and those for which fees are not a primary source of income (ISASA 2003b). The former category is generally made up of schools that charge fees of between R2 000 and R6 000 per annum, which seems to be a minimum amount that a school can charge if it relies on fees as an important income stream (ISASA 2003b).

The latter category charges fees of less than R2 000 per annum and comprises very poor schools typically in informal settlements or black communities that are largely subsidy-funded, as well as those that receive a portion (or all) of their funds from other sources, such as religious or charitable organisations. Several orthodox Jewish and fundamentalist Muslim and Christian schools fall into this category. Unfortunately no hard data exists on the exact number of schools in each of these sub-categories, but recent research has shown that the number of independent schools charging fees of less than R1 000 per annum is small (Wits EPU 2003).

As a whole, the independent school sector in South Africa is rapidly approaching racial equity. In 2001, 58 per cent of learners in independent schools were African and 70 per cent were black (African, coloured and Indian) (Du Toit 2003).

Table 5.1 Enrolment in independent schools by racial group

Race	1990 (percentage)	2002 (percentage)
African	35.9	58.3
Coloured	7.6	4.8
Indian	5.7	7.5
White	50.8	29.4

Sources: Du Toit (2003); Muller (1992)

The influence of class is clear: a significantly larger percentage of black than white schools charge low to average fees, whereas a significantly larger percentage of white than black schools charge high fees. Race has been replaced by economic class as the determinant of who goes where (Du Toit 2003).

Du Toit (2003) also examined the interrelationship between school size and fees charged, and found that the current landscape appears to have a segmented profile characterised by smaller, low- to average-fee black schools and larger, high-fee white schools.

In 1988 the total number of black learners in predominantly white schools was 14 540 or 13 per cent of their total enrolment (Muller 1992: 338). This percentage can be compared to the finding that in 2001 in white independent schools, on average 18.6 per cent of learners were black (11.5 per cent African, 3.1 per cent coloured and 4 per cent Indian) (Du Toit 2003). When he compared racial integration in public and independent schools in 2001, Du Toit found that African and coloured independent schools are more integrated than the equivalent public schools, while white and Indian independent schools are less integrated than the equivalent public schools.

The average of 18.6 per cent black enrolment would be true for all predominantly white independent schools across all the fee categories. The independent schools in the high-fee range above R18 000 per year became 'paler' in the mid-1990s. The drop in black enrolment was partly due to a loss of black learners to good-quality public schools when apartheid policies were dismantled, and partly because of the limited financial aid made available by the schools from their annual fee income. The ISASA Benchmarking Survey (conducted by PricewaterhouseCoopers in 2001 and Learning Strategies in 2003) shows that on average ISASA schools allocated eight per cent of their income to financial aid in 2003. Now that public schools are open to all races, very few independent schools benefit from external scholarships and bursaries for disadvantaged black learners, as they did during the apartheid era.

The trend, however, is in the direction of increasing integration. When Muller's (1990: 32) enrolment data for seven well-known, high-fee schools in 1990 is compared with enrolment data for the same schools from the ISASA database of 2003, the ratio of black to white learners has surpassed the 1990 figures – in some cases by more than 50 per cent.

If Christie's (1990) analysis is applied, it would seem that many of these schools are still a long way from the critical mass of 35 per cent black learners and so the dominant school culture is likely to still be white and assimilationist. Many schools with this enrolment pattern are aware of the problem, however, and are making efforts to change their cultures to become more affirming of the heterogeneity of South African society. In many cases they have identified themselves as 'proudly South African' schools, in line with the campaign to promote South African companies, products and services.

Female enrolment of 54 per cent in independent schools is in line with the 52 per cent female enrolment in public schools (Du Toit 2003). South Africa is among very few developing countries that has achieved gender parity in its schooling system. Despite popular perception, the number of single-sex independent schools is limited. The growth of the sector has been overwhelmingly among co-educational schools (ISASA 2003b).

An important final point is the low cost of independent schools to the state. In 2002/03 provincial expenditure on independent schools was 0.4 per cent of their combined education budgets (Education Foundation 2003). As these schools educate approximately 3.2 per cent of learners in South Africa, they represent a significant cost saving to the state. Based on *per capita* expenditure in each province, the authors estimate that if every learner in an independent school were to enrol at a public school, the additional cost to the state would be around R2 billion per annum.

Why the change?

A number of issues can be suggested to explain the growth in the sector. These include:

- Demand factors: Unmet demand has historically been a feature in black communities, whereas differentiated demand has been a factor in white communities. In recent years, differentiated demand has increased significantly in black communities. 'Pull' factors could include smaller class sizes, and the perception of greater accountability and better quality of schooling in these schools.
- Supply factors: The South African government's voluntary supply severance packages and redeployment strategies for teachers in the mid-1990s created a large number of excess experienced teachers with substantial capital from pension payouts, who could be approached to establish independent schools, or did so on their own initiative. There are also many entrepreneurial individuals and corporations interested in making a profit by tapping into the strong quantitative and qualitative demand for education in South Africa.

While these are some of the most obvious factors that stimulated demand for independent schooling, it is important to examine in greater depth the variety of conditions that would have played a role in bringing about the changes in the sector. These are addressed below.

Constitutional protection

The South African Constitution of 1996 section 29(3) guarantees the existence of independent schools. This explicit protection of independent schools is unusual compared to the constitutions of other democracies (Marcus 2003). Their protection now may be linked to the strict prohibition of private schools under apartheid, as evidenced in a recent Constitutional Court ruling in the case of a challenge to the Gauteng School Education Bill of 1995. It noted that:

> ... section 32(c) is neither superfluous nor tautologous. It preserves an important freedom. The constitutional entrenchment of that freedom is particularly important because of our special history initiated during the 50s, in terms of the system of Bantu education. From that period the State actively discouraged and effectively prohibited private educational institutions from establishing or continuing private schools and insisted that such schools had to be established and administered subject to the

control of the State. (Ex Parte Gauteng Provincial Legislature: In re: Dispute concerning the constitutionality of certain provisions of the Gauteng School Education Bill of 1995/1996 (3) SA 165 (CC))

According to the Constitution, any person may establish and maintain an independent school at his or her own cost. However, a school may not operate without being registered by the head of the provincial Department of Education. An independent school's standards may also not be inferior to standards at comparable public schools, and it must not discriminate on the grounds of race (RSA 1996: Section 29(3)).

Legislation

A key piece of legislation that can be singled out for its effect on the growth of independent schools is the *National Norms and Standards for School Funding* (1998).

The Funding Norms have encouraged the growth of lower-fee independent schools able to serve black communities by awarding higher subsides to lower-fee schools. They also promoted the growth of not-for-profit schools by denying for-profit schools a subsidy. At five per cent, for-profit independent schools in South Africa are a small proportion of the sector by international standards – in complete contrast to the private higher-education sector, where the vast majority of institutions are for-profit (Hofmeyr & Lee 2002).

Changing market

New clients have come from both low- and high-income black communities. Whereas in the mid-1990s, the high-income sector (R10 000 or more per month income) was 83 per cent white, this figure had dropped to 72 per cent by 2000. The black representation in this sector grew from 8 per cent to 18 per cent during the same period (Van Wyk 2001). These figures point to the negative effect of emigration, but they also confirm the rise of the black middle and upper classes. In the longer term these groups will be the main clients of traditional independent schools. At the same time, the increase in differentiated demand among lower-middle-class, working-class black families and informal sector entrepreneurs is fuelling the growth of new independent schools at the low-fee level.

The growth of 'modern', high-fee, for-profit schools, especially in the mid-to-late 1990s, is evidence of another affluent local market. The influence of the Crawford and Reddam schools at the top end of the market has been particularly marked in recent years. The ISASA Benchmarking Survey (Learning Strategies 2003) shows that competition with for-profit schools has accounted for between 12 and 19 per cent of withdrawals from non-profit ISASA schools.

The development of Afrikaans independent schools also represents a new market. Afrikaans families have become increasingly worried that their language will die out under pressure from English-medium instruction and have started independent Afrikaans-medium schools. Some of these are highly conservative, while others are open to global influences, introduce English as another medium of instruction and write international examinations. The total number of Afrikaans independent schools is not known, but it is probably still very small (ISASA 2003b).

While the market has been growing internally, South African independent schools – particularly boarding schools – are also attracting increasing numbers of international learners (Price & Lightfoot 2002). The latest ISASA Benchmarking Survey indicates that the 5.2 per cent of learners in ISASA schools are international, and come from a wide range of countries in the rest of Africa, Europe, Asia, America and Australasia (Learning Strategies 2003: 10). Their parents are drawn to the high quality of education, the option of international examinations and the sound work ethic and discipline that are not often found at such affordable fee levels in other English-speaking countries.

Influence of key individuals

Two people can be regarded as exerting a strong influence on the nature of the independent school sector. The first is Luis Crouch, a consultant to the DoE during the drafting of the key education legislation in 1995/96. Crouch strongly advocated that the state preserve quality in public education by allowing decentralised management of public schools and permitting public schools to assume considerable control over their own budgets, including the right to charge fees (Crouch 1998). Government's adoption of this recommendation has created public schools that provide strong competition for the independent sector, and this in turn has forced many high- and average-fee independent schools to examine closely the value for money that they offer.

ISASA schools regularly testify to the fact that their strongest competition comes from the Section 21 self-governing public schools. The major movement in and out of independent schools is caused by competition with public schools: some 33 per cent of all withdrawals in 2002 at the secondary school phase, where the highest fee levels are found (Learning Strategies 2003).

Since his appointment in 1999, Education Minister Kader Asmal has had a significant impact on the future of independent schools. The Minister made no secret of his desire for greater centralised control over the independent and public sectors in the name of nation-building. This desire culminated in the *Education Laws Amendment Act* of 2002, which grants the Minister regulatory power over a wide range of areas such as admission age, discipline, curriculum, and examinations for public and independent schools.

Key issues for independent schools

A number of key issues can be identified that will profoundly affect the future of the independent schools sector.

The 'policy vice'

Independent schools are increasingly exposed to legislation on three fronts: education, labour and taxation. The volume and extent of this has grown exponentially in the last 12 years.

The cumulative effect of this legislation is to squeeze ever more time and resources out of school management and administration. Independent schools are particularly vulnerable to this kind of 'policy vice' as they are both education institutions and small/medium enterprises. Much of this burden is not felt in the same way by public schools, because the majority are not private employers.

Erosion of independence

The *Education Laws Amendment Act* of 2002 brought to the fore the issue of how much control the state has (and how much the state should have) over independent schools. The Act sought to determine the core business of independent schools: what and how they teach and the means they use to assess learners. Independent schools require a clear indication, probably only available from the Constitutional Court, of where regulation of private education is justified, and where such intervention becomes an infringement on the right of schools to exist and retain sufficient independence to fulfil their distinctive missions. Critical to this discussion would be the difference between non-subsidised and subsidised independent schools, which are accountable for the use of public money.

Access

In specific areas where the state has been unable or unwilling to establish public schools, low-fee independent schools can – and do – arise in response to unmet demand and to improve the life chances of such learners.

An interesting finding from the HSRC research (Du Toit 2003) is that a significant proportion (22.4 per cent) of low-fee schools are 'white schools'. These are probably largely faith-based schools.

Governance

Good governance is essential to the smooth functioning of a school, independent or public. SASA and the *Education Laws Amendment Act* of 2002 contain detailed conditions for the establishment of a school governing body (SGB) at every public school. These conditions do not apply to independent schools; instead, they are well regulated by a number of other statutes, such as the *Companies Act*, and common law.

More recently, independent schools have been required to register as public benefit organisations (PBOs) and, in most cases, non-profit organisations (NPOs) in order to retain their income tax exempt status and the tax benefits associated with donations. These new statutes impose more rigorous governance requirements on schools.

The level of parental involvement in governance is a critical issue for both public and independent schools. SASA stipulates that current parents must constitute a majority of any governing body, whereas in independent schools this is regarded as dangerous practice (ISASA 2002). Effective governance of an independent school requires that decisions are taken by boards that are not dominated by current parents who 'vote from their children's desks', but rather ensure that the school continues into the future for the current children's children. Continuity is not as much of a concern for public schools, as the state typically ensures the continued existence of the school.

This is not to suggest that governance problems are not found in independent schools. The mere fact that most national associations of independent schools in the English-speaking world have seen fit to develop governance manuals for their member schools points to the pervasiveness of such problems, largely as a result of 'boundary crossing' by boards and heads (ISASA 2002).

Another problem arises when the school is run by an owner-principal and there is no representative governance structure at all. This is an undesirable situation that can lead to problems including labour disputes, poor management and conflict with parents and, most importantly, no provision for the continuation of the school in the event of the owner's death. Fortunately the new PBO and NPO requirements will address this problem among not-for-profit schools.

Schools and their communities

A critical issue in education is the relationship between schools and their communities. The key underlying assumption of SASA is a neighbourhood school where there is a strong link between the school and its local community. However, freedom of parental choice and significant pupil migration have undermined this.

The largest study on pupil migration in South Africa was undertaken in 1999 by the HSRC, which sampled racially-integrated secondary schools in five provinces. This research (Sekete 2000) concluded that the large-scale movement of learners from one area to another was becoming a norm in most parts of the country and affected both the public and independent sectors. The influence of apartheid policies was clear in the spatial and demographic character of learner migration. Black and coloured learners were migrating to former Indian and white schools, which had been better resourced during the apartheid years than those in the areas designated for blacks and coloureds (see also Soudien, in this volume).

Contrary to Muller's predictions in 1992, there is evidence that most of the pupil movement was between poor and better-resourced public schools rather than between public and independent schools (Sekete 2000). Given the small (3.2) percentage of learners in independent education, there is a limit on how much these schools can affect the other 96.8 per cent of schooling. Thus, while pupil movement to independent education is real, it is exaggerated. It also flows in the reverse direction, as we have shown.

While social capital has undoubtedly been depleted in poorly-performing public schools, independent schools are not the primary cause. Most of the movement of social capital has been between public schools of varying quality, as Sekete's research (2000) shows.

Most independent schools have forged strong links with disadvantaged communities: 64 per cent of independent schools have partnership and development programmes with more under-resourced independent or public schools, even in the lowest fee category (Du Toit 2003). Some 80 schools and many hundreds of programmes are featured in a recent book on community development initiatives in independent schools (Henning 2003). As a notable example, Penryn College in Mpumalanga, itself originally a development initiative of St Stithians College in Johannesburg, reaches 725 partner schools and over 200 000 learners through its *Penreach* programme.[3]

Cost-effectiveness

Muller argues that what is 'indubitably the case is that private schooling costs a great deal more than public schooling' (Muller 1992: 351). He cites evidence at the end of the 1980s which shows that, while private schools achieve excellent results, these are not achieved at a good price-to-performance ratio. Taking only fees into account, private schools produce respectable results only with investments between six and seven times as great as those in black public sector schools (Muller 1992).

Research undertaken by the CIE in 1998 established that a sample of 13 non-public Catholic schools in black townships around Johannesburg had lower unit costs than the neighbouring public schools. The average unit cost in the 13 Catholic schools was R2 295, compared to R4 654 in provincial high and R3 173 in provincial primary schools. Although the report did not compare examination results, enrolment at the majority of the Catholic schools was increasing while that at neighbouring public schools was decreasing – which in the view of the researchers reflected a 'quality choice' on the part of parents

(Palmer Development Group 1998). A comparison of pass rates in public and independent schools shows that the total pass rate and the total pass with endorsement rate in low- to average-fee independent schools was higher than in public schools (66.5 per cent average pass rate compared to 61.7 per cent; and 27.1 per cent average pass with endorsement rate compared to 15.1 per cent). The pass rates were even higher for high-fee independent schools (72.8 per cent pass, 51.7 per cent endorsement) (Du Toit 2003). This finding clearly underscores a quality choice on the part of parents. More research is needed to ascertain whether this is a general trend or not.

HIV/AIDS

The effect of HIV/AIDS on education is a much-debated issue. Common and media perception suggests that teachers are a particularly high-risk group for HIV/AIDS infection. However, a recent study by Bennell (2003) found that teachers are probably not a high-risk group in most of sub-Saharan Africa. HIV infection there is now parallel to socio-economic class, with the poorest being most likely to contract the disease. Bennell does concede that HIV infection rates among teachers are still increasing in several southern African countries – including South Africa – while they have peaked or are declining in countries further north, such as Uganda and Zambia.

The particular problem in South Africa is confirmed by Badcock-Walters (2003). He shows that in KwaZulu-Natal, educators are dying at three times the rate of the equivalently-aged general population without AIDS. He argues that rather than a 'doomsday scenario', the prevalence of AIDS among the teaching force is likely to result in an 'incremental erosion of the capacity of the system, and will inevitably have dramatic repercussions for educator recruitment and training' (2003: 18).

Bennell's, Badcock-Walters's and other studies clearly indicate that the quality of teaching and learning at schools with HIV-positive teachers and learners will inevitably be compromised. Even among educators who are not infected, morale is likely to fall significantly. Most educators will have to take on additional teaching duties as a result of absenteeism, as well as functions for which they were not formally trained, notably counselling and grief management. Non-payment of fees will increase as well – resulting in an additional financial and human resources burden on all schools.

In the case of independent schools, they will not have access to state-sponsored HIV/AIDS support programmes or any additional resources the state makes available to combat the spread of HIV/AIDS in public schools. Some funding from the Education, Training and Development Practices SETA for HIV/AIDS programmes, however, has been accessible.

A severe teacher shortage

Current teacher supply levels are very low by historical standards, when some 15 per cent of matriculants chose to study teaching at higher education level. By 2001 this figure had dropped to 3 to 5 per cent. Crouch (2001) estimated that the combination of the existing teacher shortage and the HIV/AIDS pandemic would create a yearly deficit of 12 000 teachers between 2011 and 2015. In order to prevent this deficit the annual teacher output would have to increase to 57 000 by 2006/07. Independent schools are already reporting that it is difficult to recruit sufficient good teachers and this will increase competition between public and independent schools for quality staff and lead to increased salary costs, which will be very difficult for low- to average-fee schools to afford.

A popular misconception is that, in general, independent schools pay higher salaries than public schools. While this may be true in the high-fee schools, it is not the case in the average-fee schools, which generally pay similar salaries to the state. Figures from ISASA's Salary Survey (2003a) show that the average cash salary for a teacher at an average-fee-level independent school is R86 000 per annum. This is not significantly more than the R80 808 paid to a range 7, notch 4 teacher at a state school (a teacher with four years' training and four years' experience), and is in fact less, once benefits such as housing subsidy, medical aid and 13th cheque are considered – roughly a R115 000 total package for a public school teacher versus R112 000 for an independent school teacher.

Most low-fee schools, now the majority in the country, only survive because they pay lower salaries than public schools. Swedish Development Advisers (2001) found that, of the 79 average- to low-fee independent schools they surveyed, only 25 paid salaries equal to or above the average for public schools. Teachers in these schools are there for the love of teaching, the greater curricular freedom and the desire to make a difference, rather than for any financial reward. In many cases they are married women who can depend on their husbands' medical aid and pension benefits, and often obtain significant fee discounts for their children.

There is no regulation of salaries across the sector, but ISASA does undertake an annual salary survey for its member schools. Independent schools are not represented on the Education Labour Relations Council and most teachers in independent schools are not unionised, nor is there any clear trend in that direction. In discussion with the NAPTOSA federation, the authors were able to ascertain that some 1 500 independent school teachers belong to professional associations, primarily the National Union of Educators (NUE) and the Association of Professional Educators of KwaZulu-Natal (APEK).

A continuum of schooling

The greater degree of state regulation of independent schools, especially those that receive state subsidies, coupled with greater decentralisation of key management and financial functions to Section 21 public schools, has resulted in a blurring of the traditional differences between public and independent schools (Hofmeyr & Lee 2002). No schools in South Africa are immune from the structural problems in the society, such as HIV/AIDS, teacher shortages, the limited discretionary income of families, and moral decay.

Instead of a neat dichotomy between public and independent, there is now a continuum of degrees of independence. Some well-established, ex-white, self-governing public schools are more like high-fee independent schools than under-resourced public schools serving disadvantaged black learners. The ex-white, suburban, public schools that charge high fees and still get at least half of their staff paid for by the province, arguably have the most discretionary income of any school. If one examines which schools in South Africa were the first to install Astroturf pitches, in almost every case they were the well-established, suburban public schools! As competitors for learners, independent schools complain, with justification, that the playing fields are not level (Hofmeyr 2003).

Similarly, the poorest independent schools in informal settlements and deep rural areas share all the problems of poor public schools, as the Funding Norms limit their maximum state subsidy to 60 per cent of an equivalent public school. As many of these schools rely almost entirely on the subsidy to survive, their financial position is always precarious.

New questions for research

There are several aspects of the independent school sector that warrant further investigation by researchers. Although recent research has made great strides in describing the sector as a whole, further quantitative and qualitative analysis of the registered and unregistered independent schools is necessary. It is important to quantify the extent of this 'grey' market and determine why the schools have not registered and the nature of education they provide.

In-depth research among a sample of low- to average-fee schools to find out more about the learners and their families will be valuable. Anecdotal evidence tells us that the parents are typically salaried civil servants. If this is so, why are they not supporting the public schools?

It would also be worth considering the future of high-fee independent schools in relation to the emerging black middle and upper class. How and to what extent will such schools have to change the way they operate in order to attract significant numbers of black middle- and upper-class learners? Christie's (1990) analysis suggests that sooner or later significant cultural challenges and changes will come about, because the presence of black learners will demand a new school culture. Market research among black South Africans, undertaken for some of the high-fee ISASA schools in KwaZulu-Natal, suggests that there is a clear generation gap in black demands of independent schools. While parents may want affirmation of their African culture, learners appear to be mainly interested in accessing the global, consumer culture. Case study research of a sample of high-fee schools and their clients at different stages of integration would provide further valuable insights for such schools as they attempt to increase and embrace diversity.

More research on the cost-effectiveness of independent schools would be useful. A study by Pollard (2002) in the United Kingdom suggests that independent schools can deliver more education per unit cost than state schools, especially if the hidden costs in state education are factored into the equation. A pound spent in a private school buys more teacher for each pupil than a pound spent in a state school. Would the same hold true here?

Although public-private partnerships are explicit government policy, independent school associations have found it very difficult to get government buy-in for formal national partnership programmes, such as the ISASA

Mathematics and Science Partnership Programme. Why this should be so in the case of independent schools and not in the case of the rest of the private sector, poses another question for research.

Conclusion

The independent school sector grew rapidly between 1990 and 2003. It also changed from a set of schools serving predominantly wealthy, white learners to a more diverse sector, catering for all races and socio-economic categories, with the majority of learners now being drawn from black middle- and working-class and informal sector families. This pattern of demand accords with the main findings of Tooley (2001) with regard to private education in other developing countries.

The predominance of black learners of all socio-economic classes in the independent school sector, and the very diverse nature of educational provision, points conclusively to black differentiated demand as the main driver of the growth in the sector. While unmet demand and some supply factors have also played a role, this has been far less significant.

Independent schools face equally significant challenges. They must exercise vigilance with regard to their independence, so that they can continue to provide a wide choice to parents. At the same time they must embrace diversity within their cultures and continue to demonstrate their value to society as a complementary partner of the public education sector.

Notes

1. See Mboyane, S (2002) Millions paid to 'ghost schools' in scam, *City Press*, 24 March.
2. To see this website, go to <www.brainline.com>
3. Interview with Mr Gregory Theron, Headmaster of Penryn College, 18 December 2003.

References

Badcock-Walters, P et al. (2003) *Educator Mortality In-Service in KwaZulu-Natal: A Consolidated Study of HIV/AIDS Impact and Trends.* Durban: University of Natal, HEARD

Bennell, P (2003) The Impact of the AIDS Epidemic on Schooling in Sub-Saharan Africa. Background Paper for the Biennial Meeting of the Association for Development of Education in Africa

Christie, P (1990) *Open schools: Racially Mixed Catholic Schools in South Africa 1976–1986.* Johannesburg: Ravan

Crouch, L (1998) Why South Africa Needs a Healthy Public Education System. In *Education Africa Forum*, 2nd edition. Johannesburg: Education Africa

Crouch, L (2001) *Turbulence or Orderly Change? Teacher Supply and Demand for South Africa, Future Needs and the Impact of HIV/AIDS.* Pretoria: Research Triangle Institute and DoE

Du Toit, J (2003) *Independent Schooling: Assessing its Size and Shape.* Pretoria: HSRC, Research Programme on Human Resources Development

Education Foundation (2003) *EduSource Data News*, 40: 1–36

Erasmus, J (2002) *Sector Profile: Education, Training and Development Practices.* Johannesburg: ETDP SETA

Gender Equity Task Team (1997) *Report of the Gender Equity Task Team.* Pretoria: DoE

Henning, M (ed) (2003) *Growing Together: A Story of Schools Reaching Out.* Johannesburg: Malnor

Hofmeyr, J (2003) Myths, the Devil and the Deep Blue Sea, *Independent Education* 6 (3)

Hofmeyr, J & Lee, S (2002) Demand for Private Education in South Africa: Schooling and Higher Education, *Perspectives in Education*, 20(4): 77–89

Independent Schools Association of Southern Africa (2002) International Best Practice: Guidelines for School Governance. Unpublished paper

Independent Schools Association of Southern Africa (2003a) ISASA Salary Survey 2003. Unpublished paper

Independent Schools Association of Southern Africa (2003b) Membership database of ISASA. (Accessed 4 September 2003)

James, E (1991) *Private Finance and Management of Education in Developing Countries: Major Policy and Research Issues.* Paris: Unesco/IIEP

Kane-Berman, J (ed) (2002) *South Africa Survey 2001/2002.* Johannesburg: South African Institute for Race Relations

Kitaev, I (1999) *Private Education in Sub-Saharan Africa: An Examination of Theories and Concepts Related to its Development and Finance.* Paris: Unesco/IIEP

Learning Strategies (2003) Independent Schools Association of Southern Africa. Benchmarking Survey 2003. Unpublished study

Malherbe, EG (1977) *Education in South Africa, Volume 2 (1923–1975)* Johannesburg: Juta

Marcus, G (2003) The Constitutional Meaning of Independence. Paper presented at the ISASA Independence Workshop, St Andrew's School for Girls, Johannesburg, 2 August

Muller, J (1992) Private and Alternative schools – Are They Part of the Solution? In McGregor, R & McGregor, A (eds) *McGregor's Education Alternatives.* Cape: Juta

Palmer Development Group and Catholic Institute of Education (1998) *Scenario Planning with 13 Diocesan Schools in Johannesburg.* Final Report to the Catholic Diocese of Johannesburg. 25 August 1998

Perry, H (2002) Comment on 'Survey of the Non-Public School Sector in South Africa' by Swedish Development Advisers. Unpublished document

Pollard, S (2002) *Customers not Bureaucrats: Identifying and Getting Real Value for Money in State Education.* London: Adam Smith Institute

Price, E & Lightfoot, L (2002) Public School Values at a Fraction of the Price, *Daily Telegraph*, 27 August 2002

PricewaterhouseCoopers (2001) Independent Schools Association of Southern Africa. Benchmarking Survey 2001. Unpublished study

Randall, P (1982) *Little England on the Veld: A Study of the Private Protestant Schools in South Africa.* Johannesburg: Ravan

Republic of South Africa (1996) *The Constitution of the Republic of South Africa*, No. 108 of 1996. Cape Town

Sekete, P (2000) Learner Migration and the Impact on the Quality of Schooling. In *Education Africa Forum*, 4th edition. Johannesburg: Education Africa

Simmonds, F (2001) *Schools Directory 2001.* Johannesburg: ISASA

Swedish Development Advisers (2001) Survey of the Non-Public School Sector in South Africa. Unpublished report

Tooley, J (2001) *The Global Education Industry*. Second edition. London: Institute for Economic Affairs

Van Wyk, H de J (2001) *Personal Disposable Income in South Africa by Population Group and District*. Pretoria: UNISA Bureau of Market Research

Wits Education Policy Unit (2003) Private Sector Education and Development Study. Unpublished report. University of Sussex, Centre for International Education

Interviews

1. Mr Gregory Theron, Headmaster of Penryn College, 18 December 2003
2. David Woodhead, Director: Independent Schools Information Service, England. London, March 2003

Section 2
Changing landscapes

Chapter 6: Multilingualism and education — 177
Thobeka Mda

Chapter 7: Political change, curriculum change and social formation, 1990 to 2002 — 195
Ken Harley and Volker Wedekind

Chapter 8: Assessment, qualifications and the NQF in South African schooling — 221
Johan Muller

Chapter 9: The case of teacher education in post-apartheid South Africa: politics and priorities — 247
Yusuf Sayed

Chapter 10: Teacher unions, policy struggles and educational change, 1994 to 2004 — 267
Logan Govender

Chapter 11: Changes and continuities in South Africa's higher education system, 1994 to 2004 — 293
Jonathan D Jansen

CHANGING CLASS

6 Multilingualism and education

Thobeka Mda

Introduction

This chapter[1] recognises language as key to learning, and language rights as key to fundamental human rights. In South Africa, the issue of language in education has always been an extremely political one. Language has been used as a basis for classifying and dividing people, and as the cornerstone of segregationist education policies. During the colonial and apartheid eras, Afrikaans and English were defined as 'languages', while indigenous African languages were viewed as 'tongues' or 'vernaculars'. While the term 'language' carried esteem, rights, recognition and privilege, the reverse was true for 'tongue' and 'vernacular'. African languages were marginalised as languages of learning and were not usually used as such beyond the primary school. Through legislation and other means, South African languages did not enjoy equal status.

Despite the introduction of new policies and legislation by South Africa's first democratically-elected government to redress the imbalances of the past – especially in terms of promoting African languages, and recognising language diversity, variety and choice – the status and use of African languages in education has not improved greatly. Examining this issue forms an important focus in this chapter.

The chapter begins by outlining how South Africa's new Constitution and Language in Education Policy (LiEP) have redefined the status of South African languages, entrenched language rights and choice, and created opportunities for promoting language diversity and multilingualism in education and in society. This is followed by a discussion of the factors and constraints that militate against the realisation of the LiEP (for schools) and Language Policy for Higher Education (LPHE). An overview of language in education models, and strategies that could be used to implement language policies in education and promote multilingualism in education settings, is then proposed. The chapter concludes with the view that broader social reconstruction, teacher training and deployment, shifts in language attitudes, and incentives for the wider recognition and use of African languages, are required for the effective implementation of the language policies in education and the promotion of multilingualism.

Legacy on the eve of 1994

On the eve of 1994, the official and dominant languages in South Africa were English and Afrikaans, even though South Africans spoke approximately 24 languages (Squelch 1993) and neither English nor Afrikaans was spoken by the majority of South Africans. The effects of the official bilingual policy were felt most strongly in black schools in the mid-1970s, when the attempt to impose Afrikaans as the medium of instruction sparked a nationwide revolt amongst students that subsequently burgeoned out beyond language issues. This was symbolic of the way in which language and power have been intertwined. No significant steps were taken before 1994 to change this policy.

Legislation on languages and language in education after 1994

The new multilingual sentiment in South African education has been significantly influenced by the principles and values propagated and upheld in the Constitution of the first democratic government elected in 1994. Many of these principles were contained in the *Interim Constitution of the Republic of South Africa* (Act 200 of 1993), which paved the way for the final 1996 Constitution of the Republic of South Africa. The Constitution has redefined the status of African languages and has had a direct impact on education, and language in education policy and legislation.

The Constitution has several key clauses relating to language use and practice in South Africa. It adds the nine local African languages to the previous two official languages to make 11 official languages in South Africa (Chapter 1, Section 6). Chapter 2, Section 29 (2) gives 'everyone the right to receive education in the official language or languages of their choice' in public educational institutions where this is reasonably practicable. In order to ensure the effective access to, and implementation, of this right the state must consider all reasonable educational alternatives, including single-medium institutions, taking into account a) equity b) practicability and c) the need to redress the results of past racially discriminatory laws and practices. Chapter 2, Section 30 provides '... the right to use the language and participate in the cultural life of one's choice ...' and Chapter 2, Section 31 ensures that 'persons belonging to a cultural, religious or linguistic community may not be denied the right, with other members of that community a) to enjoy their culture, practise their religion and use their language; and b) to form, join and maintain cultural, religious and linguistic associations and other organs of civil society'.

The massive changes and newly-attained rights brought about by the first democratic elections, the adoption of the Constitution, and the integration of previously segregated education departments, under a majority government, led to expectations (from the previously disadvantaged) and fears (from the previously privileged). These fears and expectations will be explored later in this chapter.

The most important documents that subsequently guided the formulation of a new language in education policy were the Interim Constitution (RSA 1993) and the final Constitution (RSA 1996b), the *White Paper on Education and Training* of March 1995 (RSA 1995) and the *South African Schools Act* (SASA) of 1996 (RSA 1996a). These carried over the principles from the Constitution into educational institutions and emphasised, amongst other things, the equal treatment and use of 11 official languages. They provided measures to promote African languages to ensure redress in the light of historical discrimination; and the recognition of and respect for language diversity, language variety and language choice. Language rights were seen as key to fundamental human rights and multilingualism as a resource with concomitant proposals for additive bilingual and multilingual models in educational institutions. As the key to learning, language policy goals were required to be pursued in all educational institutions.

The LiEP was formally announced by the Minister of Education on 14 July 1997. This was the culmination of the work of the Language Policy in Education Committee, consisting of representatives from the Co-ordinating Committee for School Curricula, teacher organisations, provincial language groups and the national Department of Education (DoE) (School Programmes Section). The group had been constituted by the Director-General, in response to a request by the Minister of Education to look into the question of inherited language requirements in education (DoE 1995: Preface).

The national language policy of the country was entrusted to the Language Plan Task Group (LANGTAG) under the Department of Arts, Culture, Science and Technology (DACST). LANGTAG set up different language interest committees: language equity, language development in South Africa, language as an economic resource, literacy, language in the public service, heritage languages, sign language and augmentative and alternative communication, equitable and widespread language services, and language in education. The DoE, looking specifically at language in education, worked with LANGTAG under DACST.

The LiEP intends to promote multilingualism, development of official languages, and respect for all languages, including sign language, in recognition of the culturally-diverse nature of the country. It also intends to improve access of learners to education and success within education by doing away with the racially and linguistically discriminatory language in education policy of the past. It further intends to facilitate communication across the colour, language and regional barriers, towards building a non-racial nation, maintaining home language(s) while providing access to, and effective acquisition of, additional language(s). It also grants the right to choose the language of learning within the framework of the obligation on the education system to promote multilingualism (DoE 1997: Preamble).

The policy has implications for curriculum development, provision or redeployment of human as well as material resources, democratic governance, and access to education, which provides for full participation in society and the economy. The facilitation of the LiEP proposals requires initiatives, activities and changes in a number of areas of education, including qualification routes, teacher training, syllabus design, and classroom practice. It also carries a number of significant rights and obligations as far as learners, schools and education departments are concerned. Learners have the right to choose the language of teaching upon admission to a school and to request the provincial education department to make provision for instruction in the chosen language where no school in the school district offers the chosen language as the language of learning and teaching. It is the duty of the provincial education department to provide education in a particular language of learning and teaching if there are at least 40 learners in Grades 1 to 6, or 35 in Grades 7 to 12, requesting the language. The provincial education department is also required to explore ways and means of providing alternative language maintenance programmes in schools and/or school districts where additional languages of teaching in the home language(s) of learners cannot be provided or offered.

School governing bodies (SGBs) are also given a pivotal role. It is the duty of the SGB to stipulate how the school will promote multilingualism through using more than one language of learning and teaching, offering additional languages as fully-fledged subjects, and/or applying special immersion or language maintenance programmes. The SGB determines the language policy of the school in accordance with regulations in the SASA, 1996. Each learner or SGB has the right to appeal to the Member of the Executive Council (MEC) against the decision of the head of the provincial department of education and to appeal to the Pan South African Language Board (PANSALB) against the decision of a MEC (DoE 1997: 4–6).

In the years immediately after 1994, the language policy in South Africa and how it was envisaged for implementation in schools changed radically from its earlier conception under apartheid. The post-1994 policy is essentially a multilingual one, recognising 11 local languages as official languages in South Africa and according none priority over the other. Policy has not translated directly into practice, however.

To support and to facilitate implementation of the new policies, new structures have been established. They include PANSALB, the Working Group on Values in Education (2000), and the South African Language Practitioners Council (2000). The DACST has also been given the task of coming up with a national language policy '[t]o provide for an enabling framework for promoting South Africa's linguistic diversity and encouraging respect for language rights within the framework of building a united, democratic South African nation ...' (RSA 2000a).

The LPHE provides the policy framework for language in higher education (universities and technikons). It addresses languages of instruction; the future of South African languages as fields of academic study and research; the study of foreign languages; and the promotion of multilingualism in institutional policies and practices of institutions of higher education (DoE 2002: 13).

In higher education, language has continued to be a barrier to access and success for second- and third-language English and Afrikaans speakers as the majority of them are not fully proficient in these two languages, which have remained the languages of learning in higher education. African languages have not yet been developed as academic, scientific, and technical languages (DoE 2002: 8–9). It is to this that this chapter now turns.

Factors and tensions inhibiting the effective implementation of LiEP and LPHE

The language policies in education are admirable, ambitious policies whose philosophy and principles include equity, democracy and access, and subscription to the notion that learning through the home language is best. The policies and the principles behind them are aimed at the development and empowerment of languages that were formerly disadvantaged. However, there are many factors that inhibit the realisation of these principles and goals.

The most important of these are teacher training and socio-political factors that impact on language status and encourage the negation of African languages and a preference for English.

Socio-political factors, language status and inequalities

One of the principal factors militating against the success of the policy is a lack of political will. On paper, all languages are equal and are to be treated equally. In real life, the two former official languages, English and Afrikaans, are still held in high esteem by all who aspire to be successful socially and economically. The continuing state of inequality between the languages points to the difficulty of achieving 'respect for all languages', 'counter[ing] ... ethnic chauvinism or separatism through mutual understanding ...' and 'building a non-racial nation' (DoE 1997: Preamble).

Haugen (1985: 14) explains how lack of political will thwarts the success of bilingual education programmes, which appear relevant to multilingual education in South Africa:

> If bilingual education raises problems in the school, these must not be sought primarily in the classroom. If it fails to produce the desired effects, we must look back at the ultimate policies, overt and covert, public or private, of the society in which education is taking place. If the language of the home is also dominant in the

life of the nation and is supported by the prestige of an elite then the introduction into the school of another language can become a valuable supplement to one's native competence [...] But if the language of the home is looked down upon and is not supported by the prestige of an elite, then the acquisition of a second language which does have prestige may be disastrous to the pride and cohesion of the pupil's ethnic group.

Lemmer (1996: 20), having studied the establishment of language policies in Namibia and Zimbabwe, cautions:

... language in education policies designed to redress former racial inequality may unintentionally create new class stratifications. Moreover, the proposed equal treatment of the indigenous African languages embodied in Constitutional documents often means their decline in practice in the light of their impotency to compete with the popularity of and perceived advantages associated with English.

In the South African context, apartheid policies contributed to this situation since the 'African languages [were] deliberately underdeveloped and neglected' (Alexander 1998: 4). On the other hand, as Spencer (1985: 392) correctly observes:

... the apparatus of political apartheid increased the use of African ... languages in African education, thus reducing in effect the African child's access to the two [former official] languages: English and Afrikaans.

Spencer also explains the danger of 'making ... people linguistically self-sufficient through the sole use of their mother tongue' as it leads them 'towards a linguistic and cultural ghetto, with all the economic and political disadvantage [that this] entails' (1985: 392).

Since the two former official languages are still very powerful and continue to enjoy privileges as favoured languages, there are few incentives for non-African-language speakers to learn African languages and for African learners to exercise their rights pertaining to their languages.

The inequality among the languages is also demonstrated by the fact that black people are usually expected to communicate with white, Indian or coloured people in English or Afrikaans. The black person knows s/he has to switch to the other's language. Fanon (1967: 17), discussing the situation of the languages of black people all over the world, points out that communicating in a language requires not only a knowledge of the structure of the language, but a propagation of the culture and values embedded in the language. To speak means to be in a position to use a certain syntax, to grasp the morphology of this or that language, but it means above all to assume a culture, to support the weight of a civilisation.

While LiEP aims to recognise and develop all South African languages equally, in practice this does not happen as most black people still have to speak the language(s) of the dominant (white) culture. The fears of many English and Afrikaans-speaking parents about the future of their languages and the implications that integration and multilingualism in schools may have for their children, play a major role in the marginalisation of African languages and their use as languages of learning. In addition, many black parents fear that their children could lack socio-economic access and mobility if they are taught in their home languages. Many white (and sometimes Indian and coloured) parents fear the loss of privilege (usually articulated as a fear of lowering of academic standards). Afrikaans parents fear the extinction of their language and culture and black parents fear polarisation and non-access to the perceived economic benefits attached to English and Afrikaans (Mda 1997a). These fears pose a real threat to the redress and democratisation process in South Africa.

Negation of African languages and preference for English

Many African-language speakers – and other South Africans – perceive English as offering greater socio-economic and educational opportunities and as potentially 'unifying' a linguistically diverse nation. English is therefore preferred as a *lingua franca* and language of learning. In the background to the LPHE it is reported that '... no requests have been received from [universities and technikons who have voluntarily adopted flexible language policies] for additional resources to support their language strategies'. Also, instead of a growth in this area, '... enrolments in language programmes have declined in recent years resulting in the closure of several language departments' (DoE 2002: 12).

The recognition of all languages is seen to bring conflict, to be divisive, and to lead to inequities. Most people also fear the cost implications of recognising 11 languages and argue that recognising only English would be cheaper and more sensible since English is a 'world'/'international' language.

Pattanayak, cited in Skutnabb-Kangas and Garcia (1995: 221), however, responds to negative attitudes towards language diversity in multilingual countries in these words:

> The dominant monolingual orientation is cultivated in the developed world and consequently two languages are considered a nuisance, three languages uneconomic and many languages absurd. In multilingual countries, many languages are facts of life; any restriction in the choice of language is not only uneconomic, it is absurd.

Choosing one language, English, may also be a way for African-language speakers to ensure that their language is not dominated by another African language. Moorehouse (cited in Mazrui, 1974: 102), commenting on this contradiction, notes that:

> ... [t]he remarkable thing is that English has not been rejected as a symbol of colonialism; it has rather been adopted as a politically neutral language beyond the reproaches of tribalism.

However, while English is an international language, and a means to economic benefits, it is not without its problems, and is definitely not neutral.[2] An investigation into the integration experiences of African-language speakers in English-medium schools in South Africa revealed that studying through English was frustrating, demoralising and even traumatic for many learners.[3] While the populations of schools and higher learning institutions are linguistically diverse, the institutions remain monocultural, ethnocentric and monolingual (English or Afrikaans). Other cultures are either not acknowledged, or suppressed. The minority learners experience 'othering' (Soudien 1997: 18) or 'become invisible' (Vally & Dalamba 1999: 22).

As Squelch (1993: 45) reports, the tendency to 'respond to the languages of minority children by rejecting them and attempting to replace them with the language of the dominant culture' is one mechanism that contributes to the negation of some languages. In many situations this tendency is encouraged by the parents of learners whose languages have minority status. Skutnabb-Kangas (1995: 7) concurs with Squelch, and argues for linguistic rights as human rights, in these terms:

> Respecting linguistic human rights (LHRs) implies at an individual level that everyone can identify positively with their mother tongue, and have that identification accepted and respected by others, irrespective of whether their mother tongue is a minority language or a majority language.

The various African languages are either non-developed or underdeveloped as academic/scientific languages. This happened because African languages were only taught as subjects and not used as languages of learning across the curriculum – especially beyond the Foundation Phase – and were not developed to have more functions and roles. English and Afrikaans, on the other hand, were developed for specialised purposes and have, for instance, 'Business English' and 'Sake Afrikaans' applications. The limitations of African languages just mentioned are seen by many as permanent limitations, and African languages are perceived as characteristically (by nature) unable to cope with scientific, technical and technological subjects (PRAESA 1998: 3). Investment in developing these languages for wider roles and functions is seen as a waste of time and money. However, most of the arguments against the use of African languages for such purposes, especially when propagated by African-language speakers, are evidence of self-deprecation and dependence, resulting from years of colonialism and oppression (Mda 1997b).

Another sign of the self-deprecation and denigration of African languages is the reference to African languages as 'black' languages. This construction of the apartheid government has been internalised by some African-language speakers. They do not see the situation of Africans as similar to that of other people all over the world; that people in Europe are Europeans, and speak European languages, or that those in Asia are Asians speaking Asian languages (Mda 1997b). Even the use of the words 'vernacular' and 'mother tongue', which have become almost synonymous with, and substitutions for, 'African language', is not problematised.

In South Africa, black children in multicultural schools speak English to one another and with their parents. They adopt English and forget, or prefer not to speak, their own languages in favour of English and, in so doing, reject

African languages and 'Africanness'. Of course, there is the desire to 'fit' into, and not to be different from, the norm. Surveys of language preference and attitudes in institutions of higher learning show that most (first language) African-language students prefer English. This is understandable since their education (at least the first 12 years) has been through the English medium. They either cannot envisage African languages as media of instruction, or they feel they have almost mastered the language needed in the South African economic sphere to change at that later stage to one that will not be useful in that sphere. This unfortunately reproduces power imbalances between language groups and maintains the status quo. In view of this tendency, the principle of choice as contained in the Constitution, the *Schools Act*, and the LiEP, may contradict and defeat affirmative action measures for African languages, as there is no guarantee that African-language speakers will choose their languages as the language of learning.

The principle of choosing the language of learning is also constrained by pragmatic requirements such as the availability of resources. In racially, culturally and ethnically integrated schools, teachers are not usually multilingual. Hence the right of the learner or parents to request a particular language of learning from the provincial education department may not be easy to grant and implement, as it calls for effective resource deployment and redeployment.

Teacher training

There are limitations in teacher training institutions as regards multilingual education. The colleges of education which trained most South African teachers were mainly ethnically-based. Until the publication of the 2002 *Revised National Curriculum Statement*, even in institutions where teachers of all races and ethnic groups were trained together, the methodologies for teaching different languages were separate, so that there was, for example, an Afrikaans method, an isiXhosa method and a Xitsonga method. The above-mentioned policy distinguishes between 'Home', 'First' and 'Second additional language' and provides frameworks for each in all 11 official languages. This will have implications for teacher training as well. It is also reported that 'few institutions include an African language as a training requirement for undergraduate and postgraduate study, or offer short courses in African languages as in-service learning opportunities for professionals in practice' (DoE 2002: 12). Another weakness in language-teacher training is that very few language-across-the-curriculum programmes have been established and few are widely practised. Where they do exist, they have been treated as just another subject, and regarded as a 'frill'.

Most programmes on multilingual and multicultural teaching are developed and facilitated by non-governmental organisations (NGOs) and not by the DoE. In higher education, some multilingualism programmes, such as the University of Cape Town's Postgraduate Diploma and Masters in Education: Multilingual Education, have been developed. The educators who attend these courses or programmes may be doing so as individuals, for personal, academic and professional development. However, since there is no incentive of credit or remuneration from the DoE or higher learning institutions, there is no motivation for the majority of educators to take these courses.

Addressing constraints: priority areas

In recognition of these tensions and inhibiting factors, the LANGTAG language in education interest group identified a number of steps that needed to be taken to strengthen the LiEP (DACST 1996: 129–131). These included, amongst others, language awareness campaigns at the broad public and at institutional levels; establishing standard-setting mechanisms and processes in line with National Qualifications Framework (NQF) principles, especially in regard to the qualification and certification of teachers who have to operate in multilingual classrooms; promoting the status, corpus and acquisition of the African languages through the education system by means of newsletters, journals, magazines, and so on; streamlining information flows between institutions and state organs that have an influence on the formulation and implementation of language policy in education; facilitating the establishment of community or commercially-driven service centres at local level for language maintenance programmes in non-official South African and foreign languages; exploring the most appropriate language policy for tertiary education; exploring language issues in early childhood development (ECD); and exploring more appropriate and equitable language assessment models, so that due weight is given to the real language competence of learners in a multilingual society.

In the LPHE the Ministry of Education recommends:
- The development of all South African languages for use in instruction.
- Establishment of a task team to advise on the development of an appropriate

framework and implementation plan, including costing and time frames, development of dictionaries and other teaching and learning materials, in close collaboration with DACST.
- Injection of substantial financial resources over a period of time.
- Encouragement of all higher education institutions to develop strategies for promoting proficiency in designated language(s) of tuition, including provision of language and academic literacy development programmes.
- Curriculum development in South African languages and literature.
- Amending funding grids for teaching inputs and outputs for specially selected languages.
- Providing earmarked institutional development funds for research, and facilitating offering of scholarships to students.
- Offering these studies on a more cost-effective regional/national platform.
- Requiring proficiency in an African language as a requisite for a range of academic fields of study and offering short courses in African languages.
- Requiring higher education institutions to indicate in their three-year rolling plans strategies for how they will promote multilingualism, including progress in this regard.
- Requiring all higher education institutions to develop their own language policies and submit them to the Minister of Education by 31 March 2003.

Strategies for the effective implementation of multilingualism and the LiEP in the classroom

Despite the difficulties and negatives experienced with the promotion of language diversity, there are organisations (mainly non-governmental), scholars, groups and schools from all over the world that have come up with positive strategies. In South Africa, one of the most important groups to do so is the University of Cape Town-based Project for the Study of Alternative Education in South Africa (PRAESA, 1998: 4–5). Some strategies include the suggestions that where some learners speak languages not spoken by the class teachers (a common situation in multicultural classrooms in South Africa), they should use parents and volunteers from the community, including unemployed or retired teachers; other learners in the same class or other classes; and staff members who speak the language(s) of the learners as language resources. They also propose involving parents in education tasks by, for example, letting parents direct the school's educational and language policy, thereby allowing parents to bring their history, culture and values into the classroom. They suggest collecting and creating parallel texts, books, alphabets, numbers, scripts, posters and story tapes in various languages; producing two-way dictionaries; using pictures from magazines showing diversity, and so on. Assessment practices can include the use of varying techniques and items to include written and oral tests, short and long answer questions, observation strategies, and being sensitive to the language of tests, and bias in examinations (Ohio Department of Education 1985: 35–37; PRAESA 1998: 4–5; Skutnabb-Kangas 1995: 12–17; Squelch 1993: 29–58).

Some guidelines and principles for multilingualism at school level, such as those suggested by Skutnabb-Kangas (1995: 12–17), Skutnabb-Kangas and Garcia (1995), and Heugh (1998), would be difficult to implement – even though the latter are specifically suggested for South African schools. They presuppose a multilingual or at least bilingual administration and staff. Although the so-called 'immersion', 'two-way dual language', 'maintenance', 'plural multilingual' and 'dual language school' models are all relevant in different ways for multilingual South Africa, political, social, and economic factors and language attitudes may make them difficult to implement. The greatest obstacles are monolingual teachers in the integrated suburban and city schools. Bilingual and multilingual programmes and models cannot succeed where teachers belong to one racial, ethnic and, especially, one linguistic group. It will take some form of social reconstruction to address the issue. There might have to be busing of bilingual and multilingual teachers to the monolingual suburban and city schools. Training of bilingual and multilingual teachers would have to be prioritised.

The publication *The Power of Babel: Support for teachers in multilingual classrooms* (PRAESA 1998) also offers a selection of South African resources, mostly multilingual materials and materials in African languages, and a list of organisations, national and provincial, that give support or provide resources for teachers in multilingual classrooms. The PRAESA publication gives hope that multilingualism is not only desirable but also 'do-able'. It is heartening to find in this publication a long list of organisations devoted to this cause.

There are also indications that the national DoE is aware of, and wanting to take action on, the perceived non-implementability of the LiEP. The action envisaged is outlining for schools and SGBs clear strategies of implementation in an 'Implementation Plan' document. Such a process also takes time. It is hoped that in outlining the strategies the DoE recognises the realities of choices being made and plans to strengthen choices for African languages, as well as pay serious attention to how English is taught in schools. These are far-reaching changes that will not be made quickly. The point of view of this paper is that this is a worthwhile project and investment in this process will pay off handsomely.

Conclusion

There is a need to concretise and implement the multicultural ethos expressed in the Constitution, the SASA, the LiEP, and LPHE in our wider society. Stricter monitoring of implementation of the language policies needs to be done, to ensure access and success of learners in education, which was the primary intention of these policies.

Since there are presently few opportunities for, and benefits in, using African languages in higher education and in the economic world, it can be argued that it is a waste of the resources of the DoE to develop and promote African languages. It does seem to be an unnecessary complication to suggest multilingualism, instead of adhering to the former government's Afrikaans and English (bilingual) policy, if the two languages are all that South Africa needs. However, given past imbalances, the neglect of African languages, and major learning challenges in rural schools related to language use, the promotion of multilingualism is essential within the context of redress, equity and democracy in South Africa.

Like Haugen, this author believes that while the LiEP and LPHE are education policies, their success lies outside the education arena, in politics (through legislation) and in the economy (through practical, visible and empowering policies). Public awareness of language rights is also very important and efforts like the DoE's 1998 LiEP awareness campaign should be supported by, and involve, all sectors of South African society.

We need to see African languages functioning in many spheres. Creating a language-friendly environment through signs, pictures and posters (described earlier in strategy for implementation) should not be limited to classroom walls or school notice boards. There should be signs in African languages in private companies and suburban complexes, including shopping malls, rather than limiting these languages to railway stations, police stations, hospitals and other public buildings, generally associated with semi-literate, African-language speakers.

It is hoped that accreditation of multilingualism through the NQF will soon be a reality. It is also hoped that parents and teacher unions/associations, the key participants in the process of implementation, will own the process and ensure its success. Finally, as the Values in Education Working Group recommended, '[a] language in education policy must ... be supported by initiative[s] in wider society ... multilingual proficiency must be rewarded' (DoE 2000: 8). Effective and meaningful rewarding of multilingual practices and promotion thereof, is long overdue.

Notes

1. This chapter is an updated and reworked version of an earlier chapter: Mda, TV (2000) Language in education. In Mda, TV & Mothata, MS (eds) *Critical Issues in South African Education – After 1994*. Kenwyn: Juta
2. See Mda's article 'Learning best in home language', *The Teacher*, 2 (9): 6.
3. The Ntshakala's article 'Integrated schools must face issues', *The Teacher*, 2 (9): 5.

References

Alexander, N (1998) Multilingualism and the New Curriculum, *PRAESA News*, (4): 6–7

Department of Arts, Culture, Science and Technology (1996) *Towards a National Language Plan for South Africa: Final Report of the Language Plan Task Group*. August 1996. Pretoria: DACST LANGTAG

Department of Education (1995) *Towards a Language Policy in Education: Discussion document*. Pretoria: DoE

Department of Education (1997) *Language in Education Policy*. Pretoria: DoE

Department of Education (2000) *Values, Education and Democracy: Report of the Working Group on Values in Education*. Pretoria: DoE

Department of Education (2002) *Language Policy for Higher Education*. Cape Town: Government Printers

Fanon, F (1967) *Black Skin, White Masks*. New York: Grove Press

Haugen, E (1985) The Language of Imperialism: Unity or Pluralism? In Wolfson, N & Manes, J (eds) *Language of Inequality*. Berlin: Mouton Publishers

Heugh, K (1998) The New Language in Education Policy: South African Perspectives on Implementation. Paper presented at the National Conference on the Implementation of the Language in Education Policy, Pretoria, 13–15 May

Lemmer, E (1996) Issues in Language in Education Policy with Specific Reference to Namibia and Zimbabwe, *South African Journal of Education*, 16 (1): 15–21

Mazrui, A (1974) *World Culture and the Black Experience*. The John Danz Lectures. Seattle: University of Washington Press

Mda, T (1997a) The Making of the Language-in-Education Policy in South Africa. Paper presented at the Southern African Comparative and History of Education Society (SACHES) Annual Conference at Livingstone, Zambia, 10–12 January

Mda, T (1997b) The Impact of English and Afrikaans Languages on the Identity of South African, African Languages-speakers. Paper presented at the South African Society of Education (SASE) Conference, UNISA, Pretoria, 4–6 September

Ohio Department of Education (1985) *Citizenship, Multicultural, and Human Relations Education*. Columbus, Ohio: The Ohio Department of Education Division of Elementary and Secondary Education

PRAESA (1998) *The Power of Babel: Support for Teachers in Multilingual Classrooms*. Cape Town: University of Cape Town School of Education

Republic of South Africa (1993) *The Interim Constitution of the Republic of South Africa*. No. 200 of 1993. Pretoria: Government Printers

Republic of South Africa (1996a) *The South African Schools Act*. No. 84 of 1996. Cape Town: Government Printers

Republic of South Africa (1996b) *The Constitution of the Republic of South Africa*, No. 108 of 1996. Cape Town

Republic of South Africa (2000a) *South African Languages Act*. Pretoria: Government Printers

Republic of South Africa (2000b) *South African Language Practitioners Council Act*. Pretoria: Government Printers

Skutnabb-Kangas, T (1995) Introduction. In Skutnabb-Kangas, T (ed) *Multilingualism for All*. Lisse, Netherlands: Swets and Zeitlinger

Skutnabb-Kangas, T & Garcia, O (1995) Multilingualism for All – General Principles? In Skutnabb-Kangas, T (ed) *Multilingualism for All*. Lisse, Netherlands: Swets and Zeitlinger

Soudien, C (1997) 'We know why we're here': The Experience of African Children in a Coloured School in Cape Town, South Africa. Paper presented at the Annual Congress of the Southern African Comparative and History of Education Society. Livingstone, Zambia, 10–12 January

Spencer, J (1985) Language and Development in Africa: The Unequal Equation. In Wolfson, N & Manes, J (eds) *Language of Inequality*. Berlin: Mouton Publishers

Squelch, J (1993) Equality in Education. In Lemmer, E & Dekker, E (eds) *Critical Issues in Modern Education*. Durban: Butterworths

Vally, S & Dalamba, Y (1999) *Racism, 'Racial Integration' and Desegregation in South African Public Secondary Schools*. Report on a study by the South African Human Rights Commission (SAHRC). Pretoria, February

7 Political change, curriculum change and social formation, 1990 to 2002

Ken Harley and Volker Wedekind

Introduction

Writers of differing theoretical orientation are agreed that there is generally a close relationship between national political visions and national curricula.

Nowhere is this relationship illustrated more starkly than in the case of South Africa. Strikingly close alignment of curriculum policy to political vision is evident through periods of political change characterised by dramatically different political visions.

The story of South Africa's successful passage to democracy and 1994 elections does not need to be retold here. Even before the demise of the apartheid state, however, it was obvious to all that the future school curriculum would be serving a new and radically different purpose. Simply put, if the curriculum had been used to divide races (as well as men and women within their 'own' racial groups), and to prepare different groups for dominant and subordinate positions in social, political and economic life, its new mission would be that of uniting all citizens as equals in a democratic and prosperous South Africa. With the release of key figures such as Nelson Mandela in the watershed year of 1990, and with the collapse of apartheid now inevitable, there was a critical turning point in curriculum debates (Jansen 1999). In unprecedented co-operation, progressive academics and the democratic movement began discussing curriculum reconstruction in anticipation of a new democratic state (Nzimande 1997).

When the new democratic government assembled, one of its key strategic and symbolic challenges was the rapid transformation of the school curriculum. The ensuing change in the form of Curriculum 2005 (C2005) was of a scale arguably unparalleled in the history of curriculum change.

We begin this chapter with an account of the process of national curriculum construction and the development of C2005 after the dawn of democracy in 1994. In the light of a persuasive literature arguing that schools do not always function in accordance with the demands of the state (Wong & Apple 2002), we assess the impact of C2005. This impact on practice is then analysed in terms of continuities and discontinuities with previous practices. Finally, we move towards an explanation of the conclusion that C2005 contributes to social reproduction in unintended ways.

Curriculum reform in the 'new' South Africa

The new curriculum was, as in the past, intended to serve as an instrument for the new political vision. This point is central to the argument that develops as this chapter unfolds. The only thing that was entirely new was the curriculum vision itself.

New curriculum values

Since the Soweto student uprising of 1976, there had been ongoing conflict about the position and role of teachers in the apartheid education system. In the mid-1980s resistance to apartheid education was co-ordinated by the National Education Crisis (later Co-ordinating) Committee (NECC). This broad front of educational, student and community organisations developed a campaign for People's Education based on a Freirean model. While this was a powerful mobilising tool, very little substance was developed to mount a serious challenge to the dominant curriculum. Thus, when the African National Congress (ANC) and other liberation movements were unbanned in 1990, the schooling system was in crisis, but alternative models were not readily available. The NECC launched a mammoth National Education Policy Investigation (NEPI) to provide a systematically-researched set of policy alternatives for the ANC (NEPI 1993). Principles underpinning policy alternatives for curriculum were non-racism, non-sexism, democracy, equality and redress.

The democratically-elected government that was installed in 1994 inherited a complex education system with 18 education departments catering for different provinces, homelands and population groups. The adoption of the new Constitution reconstituted the educational landscape, bringing together the different teachers and their different classroom practices under one administrative body in each province. It also allocated different levels of responsibility for curriculum matters within the new educational system. While norms and standards were the domain of the national department, implementation was a provincial competence. This arrangement reflected a structural representation of the classic divide between policy and practice.

Curriculum reform

Curriculum reform followed a number of clear steps. The first, immediately after the 1994 elections, was the ironing out of variations in the curriculum used by the different education departments. The second step – presented as an emergency intervention while new curriculum policy was being developed – purged the existing curriculum (i.e. syllabi) of racially offensive, sexist and outdated content. The third wave of reform shifted the focus away from content and onto assessment, with the introduction of continuous assessment (CASS) in schools in 1996.

The master plan, C2005, was launched in March 1997, with implementation in Grade 1 scheduled for 1998, and Grade 7 in 1999. C2005 was thus to be phased in progressively so that it would cover all sectors of schooling by 2005.

The new curriculum had three design features. Firstly, it was *outcomes-based*, and this feature was positioned so centrally that outcomes-based education (OBE) became synonymous with C2005.[1] An *integrated knowledge* system was the second design feature. School 'subjects' were jettisoned, and eight 'learning areas' introduced for Grades 1 to 9. The third dimension of curriculum reform was the promotion of *learner-centred pedagogy*.

We do not have the opportunity here of entering into the interesting question of precisely how these features came to be promoted and accepted. The concept of 'figurations of interdependent individuals' (Elias 1978) alerts us to many possibilities. While at times individual personalities directly influence the process, this takes place in the context of wider national and international discourses. We suspect that here there is a story that the literature has not yet told. Suffice it to note that influences on the curriculum were both local and global (Christie 1997). In the substantial literature examining influences on the development of C2005, there is broad agreement that one of the central C2005 tenets, OBE, originated in debates about training that had been conducted within the labour movement and between labour, government and industry.[2]

Learner-centredness has been linked with OBE. However, emphasis on learner-centred pedagogy had its roots in a particular history of educational contestation that was relatively independent of OBE. The progressive discourse underpinning the pedagogy can be linked more closely to the general discourse on human rights, including children's rights, and specifically to the Freirean-inspired People's Education movement of the 1980s that had linked democracy in society with notions of democracy in the classroom. Potential tensions between goals (such as economic development, on the one hand, and equity and redress on the other) appear to have been elided by the cumulative contribution of the three design features to the transformation agenda. Thus, even while focused firmly on the desired future, the curriculum inescapably also carried within it a strong dimension of the past: it was the key instrument. The past was influential in a different kind of sense too. If the new curriculum were to fulfil its key symbolic function, it would have to be seen to be dichotomous to the 'old' curriculum in every possible respect.

Within the picture of political vision, curriculum specification and social change, two interrelated points emerge from our discussion. Firstly, as 'a direct statement of what a society believes schooling is about', C2005 displayed an unusually overt political agenda. This was evident in the Minister of Education's foreword in an early promotional document:

> The curriculum will begin to integrate education and training – incorporating a view of learning which rejects rigid division between academic and applied knowledge, theory and practice, and knowledge and skills. It will also foster learning which encompasses a culture of human rights, multilingualism and multi-culturalism and a sensitivity to the values of reconciliation and nation building. (DoE 1997)

Much other documentation could be cited to illustrate the correspondence of political and curriculum values. For example, William Spady's[3] advocacy of OBE offers three typologies: traditional, transitional and transformational. In his foreword to a series of four (undated) booklets explaining OBE to educators, the Director-General of Education stated: 'The Ministry of Education is committed to transformational OBE ...' Indeed, what makes C2005 distinctive in aligning itself to political values is the explicit way in which it does this.

Secondly, following the first point, C2005 emerged as a *political and not a pedagogical* project. Reference has already been made to the origins of OBE as a central tenet of C2005. Jansen, one of the leading figures in the NEPI policy option work in the curriculum field, notes that there was 'no reference whatsoever to OBE' in the NEPI documents (Jansen 1999). The new curriculum did not emerge from debates within the education sector about the most appropriate forms of pedagogy to bring about the new political vision, or about what was feasible in the profoundly diverse and unequal range of schools. In the parlance of curriculum studies, C2005 did not arise from a 'situation analysis' of existing realities. Teachers, and probably most teacher educators, simply found themselves in a new curriculum world.[4]

C2005 in practice

> The announcement of Curriculum 2005 in 1997 was greeted with excitement and welcomed by the overwhelming majority of people. National and provincial evaluations of the implementation of C2005 confirmed this 'symbolic' break with the past. (National Centre for Curriculum Research and Development 2000)

This judgement captures the embrace of C2005 as a political instrument. However, it is C2005 as a pedagogical project that concerns us in this section of the chapter as we deal with evidence on the extent to which the 'symbolic' became substantive. That evidence suggests that schools have responded to C2005 in very uneven ways. The argument we develop is that while the literature on schooling abounds with accounts of a disjunction between policy and practice, disjunction in the case of C2005 is more intractable. It is a case of practice *undermining* policy, the very instrument of political vision.

In presenting this account, we draw on our own research and that of our students in KwaZulu-Natal, in addition to insights from a review of well over a hundred publications, including a sample of 20 higher degree dissertations. However, it is necessary to acknowledge a major limitation. As the project of 'transforming' an education system is one of 'changing the vast webs of practices which constitute it' (Morrow 2001), an account of C2005 would ideally be based on vast webs of research. Unfortunately, there is very little classroom-based research, and the design features of C2005 are barely probed. Implementation studies and generalised debates on OBE (but not learners' attainment of outcomes) are dominant. Perhaps this is because academic forces mobilised themselves around the battle lines drawn by Jansen's 'Why OBE will fail' (Jansen 1997).[5]

We commence our view of C2005 practice with a brief overview of its introduction.

'OBE training' and implementation

What became known as 'OBE training' for teachers was clearly problematic. Given the very short time between finalisation of the curriculum and its implementation, the national Department of Education (DoE) and its various provincial counterparts had no choice but to provide crash-course training for teachers. The model adopted was one that sought to cascade the training down through the system. Because of lack of capacity, aspects of this training were sub-contracted to a range of consultants and NGOs. Quality of training was uneven. The cascade model itself was problematic since many of the teachers trained at the top of the cascade were not sufficiently equipped to replicate the training within their districts and schools. Thus the complex new curriculum quickly became associated with a few obvious dimensions that provided teachers with a simple hanger on which to peg their understanding. Complex issues of pedagogy with major implications for teachers' personal and professional identity were reduced to simplistic dichotomies such as 'teacher-centred' (an 'old', undesirable practice) and 'learner-centred' (a 'new', esteemed practice). Similarly, 'content' was replaced by 'outcomes'. Amidst much confusion amongst teachers about the implications for their practice (Jansen & Christie 1999), learner-centredness quickly became one of the teachers' defining features of the new curriculum. Groupwork became the major symbolic identifier of the new curriculum, and for many teachers, implementing groupwork was the core pedagogical shift required of them by C2005.

Implementation problems have been so well reported that a detailed account is inappropriate here. One succinct summary of implementation weaknesses includes:
- A complex curriculum policy;
- Inadequate co-ordination and management;
- Insufficient capacity in terms of personnel and finance;
- Inadequate teacher development; and
- Limited curriculum development. (CEPD 2000a [first draft])

CASS had provided early warning signals to policy planners that curriculum reform would not be a simple implementation matter. Early indications during initial C2005 implementation were of a similar kind: half of the primary schools in rural and under-serviced areas failed to implement the new curriculum (Vally & Spreen 1998).

In the research void on practice, attempts to generalise are hazardous. But there is evidence supporting the contention that where teachers have engaged C2005, there are disturbingly 'superficial trappings of the new curriculum' (Govender 1999). The C2005 Review refers to widespread evidence that teachers have 'a rather shallow understanding of the principles of C2005/OBE' (DoE 2000), linking this with a 'false clarity' around a mismatch between what teachers claim to know and their practice. In a context in which there is inadequate understanding of C2005, combined with evidence of shortcomings in the subject knowledge of many teachers (Taylor & Vinjevold 1999), 'false clarity' and symbolic displays of C2005 practice may well be widespread. There are reports of schools 'doing their own thing', and of a situation in which 'anything goes' in schools (Mahomed 2002). Certainly, studies such as Brodie (2000), Ensor (2001), Graven (2002) and Hoadley (2002) provide valuable insights into the difficulties posed by learner-centredness in schools that are typical of the majority of South African schools. Teachers' difficulties in making the necessary 'paradigm shift' in assessment are reported in Siebörger and Nakabugo's (2001) case study. We await research evidence on learners' levels of achievement in the higher grades.[6]

From this generalised background, we move to a finer-grained view of responses to C2005 in the very differing and unequal school contexts characteristic of South African schools.

Cameos of C2005 practices

The school, as an institution, is more likely to change the incoming message than the message the institution (Eisner 2000). This judgement is even more likely to be valid in a context in which there is widespread uncertainty about what the message is (in this case, C2005).

1. C2005 accommodation and compromise: a twin-stream Grade 9 policy[7]

A well-known independent school for girls runs an 'OBE' programme alongside traditional subject lessons. In this programme, Grade 9 girls are given an option of topics to research in small groups. While topics are rooted in a traditional school subject, the nature of the task requires learners to integrate both everyday and subject knowledge from across traditional subject boundaries. Effective guidance and support are provided, and groups work independently using the excellent resources – including Internet access – available in the school. It is a sophisticated programme embodying the key principles of C2005. In this way, the school runs an exemplary programme in line with national policy. But here there is another imperative no less powerful than in all other secondary schools: the Senior Certificate exit qualification known as 'matric'. Accordingly, the OBE programme has a time allocation of only three periods a week, and responsibility for the programme rests with the school librarian. For over 90 per cent of the available time, learners are engaged in traditional subject lessons. Classification and framing (Bernstein 1971) are strong. Teacher identities are strongly rooted in their disciplines and what is unique in their disciplines. There is a high degree of insulation between the subjects, as well as between the 'academic' and the 'OBE' programmes. The only concession to everyday knowledge is that it is occasionally recruited to illustrate a disciplinary point. While there is real sensitivity to learners' individual difficulties, the progression and sequencing of topics is drawn from the structure of the discipline.

Meeting different kinds of imperatives has been possible for the school because of its high level of resources (physical and human capital), but crucially also because of the high degree of consensus within the school community regarding definition of what 'school' and the curriculum are about. There is a common definition of the situation, and all are comfortable in their roles.

2. 'OBE is a good policy – but it's not for us'[8]
This was how a senior teacher in a rural secondary school summed up the position of his school *vis-à-vis* C2005. Timetabling and teaching followed traditional subject divisions, with the only concession being the grouped seating arrangements in some classes. Whatever the seating arrangement, pedagogy was formal. Although most teachers appeared kindly, the teaching did not approximate learner-centredness. The teacher poses a question (which has, as all know, an unambiguously correct answer); learners chant responses once the answer has been approved; and key knowledge of this kind is frequently consecrated by the teacher writing it on the chalkboard.

Reasons for the traditional approach included, predictably, a lack of resources. But the limited number of available textbooks were not being used. Apart from those, the only available resource was the chalkboard. Teachers' definitions of the situation were crucial: C2005 was seen to require learners with a high level of communicative skills. Consequently, learners were cast in a deficit mould because their communication skills were not yet fully developed. Hence the formal teaching approach. It was argued that learners would acquire the requisite communication skills if they were taught English language.

This, too, appeared to be a happy school in which all were comfortable in their assigned roles. If those roles led to situations in which learners were bewildered, it was a situation to be expected. In an English lesson, for example, learners volunteered sentences which were written on the chalkboard. They were then required to translate what were all active voice sentences into the passive voice. In some cases this was impossible, as it was in the sentence: 'We go to school.' Learners struggled valiantly to produce a passive voice form that satisfied the teacher. 'You see …,' sighed the teacher, 'they don't have the skills of communication.'

Minimal help was reported being received from 'the department' – in fact, it was reported that the advice of the official in whose sphere of responsibility the school lay was: 'Retain the old system in the interim' (Sineke, forthcoming).

3. C2005 deferment[9]

In contrast with the school with the 'twin-stream' policy, this ex-Model C school was characterised by a high degree of diversity. A former boys-only school for whites, it is now a co-ed school, with a staff and student body that reflects the demographic diversity of the 'rainbow nation'. With respect to transformation from gendered, racial privilege to representivity and inclusivity, it could serve as a model school. In this strength lies its weakness. School management is favourably disposed to change, and well informed on curriculum policy and school governance. The will to change is evident, but the different constituents within the school have yet to develop a common culture serving as a core of agreed and shared cultural understandings. Common understandings are doubtless being formed (or perhaps winners and losers are emerging) as diverse understandings rub up against each other. In this vibrant atmosphere, teachers believe that control (which they referred to as 'discipline') is problematic. When teachers perceive control to be problematic, curriculum restructuring, always a process requiring sustained attention and perhaps even leisurely reflection, becomes a casualty.

There is very little evidence of the integration of knowledge in Grade 9. Where learner-centred pedagogy is evident, it is generally a strategic concession in exchange for what teachers define as acceptable learners' conduct. The implication of teacher perspectives is that a common school culture or consensus has to be built before the curriculum can be developed.

4. Serious engagement with C2005[10]

Representing an affluent socio-economic community, this preparatory school is one of the leading independent institutions in the country. A scholarship entrance route specifically for previously disadvantaged students allows access to those who are most able. This independent primary school was positive about curriculum change and engaged C2005 in a comprehensive way, beginning with constructivist theory. The school set about clarifying constructivism and its implications for their own school. At the same time, the existing curriculum was analysed along the lines of a situation analysis. Foundation skills important in a globalised world were identified, such as entrepreneurial skills, technology, and lateral thinking skills. Drawing mainly on Vygotsky and de Bono, the school's curriculum was developed to facilitate learners' ability to construct knowledge. As a model designed to suit this particular school, it was regarded as an 'alternative curriculum to OBE' (Workman 2002). However, its architects also felt their curriculum was compatible with at least one of the many possible interpretations of C2005.

Regular curriculum development meetings were held, and action research monitoring set in place. The initiative went to scale with the Independent Schools Association of Southern Africa (ISASA) establishing task teams to develop core curricula with constructivist underpinning in Maths and English.

Both curriculum development and teacher development were served through the process of action research cycles of planning, implementing, evaluating, and modification.

5. Symbolic display of C2005 principles

Two related studies (Mattson 2000; Mattson & Harley 1999) are useful in illuminating pedagogy in historically disadvantaged schools where teachers had been given additional support in implementing new policy.[11] Teachers appropriated and displayed key C2005 precepts in ways that did not promote conceptual learning. 'Groupwork' and 'learner activity' were most notable in this regard, as illustrated in the following quote:

> In every classroom we visited, learners were seated in groups rather than rows, but the purpose of group formation was not always clear and whole class teaching was still the norm ... 'learner activity' has seemingly become an orthodoxy, but, according to our observations in the classroom, it is frequently more muscular than cognitive, involving hours of cutting, sorting, pasting and other forms of occupational therapy, rather than the active processing of information. In all of the lessons we observed, there was remarkably little reading and writing. (1999: 13)

At the same time, teachers were enthusiastic about C2005 and enthusiastic about their role in implementing it. Their knowledge of policy reassured them that they were 'on track'.

A similar case is reported in Dlamini and Harley (2003). Teachers who had been trained in the use of provided learner support materials upheld groupwork and learner activity with enthusiasm and vigour. However, with means towards ends becoming ends in themselves, learners' responses were simply accepted as valid knowledge irrespective of their accuracy or relevance to the learning programme.

C2005 and the political project: expectations and reality

The cameos suggest that although C2005 might have been embraced as a political project, schools and individual teachers have responded to its pedagogical design features in very different ways. No South African reader will miss the pattern of success and failure suggested by the cameos: schools most historically advantaged were flourishing with C2005; those most disadvantaged appeared to be floundering.

The cameo schools do not represent a 'scientific' sample. But in the light of broader evidence, we nevertheless believe that the emerging picture is indeed broadly representative. Citing a range of studies, Christie suggests that the sophistication of new policies has actually widened the gap between the historically advantaged and disadvantaged schools (Christie 1999). Christie is not alone in this conclusion (Harber 2001; Harley, Barasa, Bertram, Mattson, and Pillay 2000; Singh and Manser 2000; Vally and Spreen 1998; Vally 1999; Williams 1999). Indeed: 'Former Model C schools appear to have been able to implement Curriculum 2005 with greater ease than the majority of schools largely because of being better resourced' (DoE 2000).

Lack of resources, cited in a host of case studies (Hlalele 2000), is certainly the most obvious difficulty for historically disadvantaged schools. However, this intractable problem is also related to current financial issues. On the one hand, economic structural adjustment has led to reduced social spending; on the other, redress of past inequalities and the attainment of equity depends on increased spending (Czerniewicz, Murray, and Probyn 2000). This occurs in a context in which 52 per cent of schools are inadequately supplied with textbooks and where 83 per cent of schools do not have libraries. Although public libraries are being used as sites of support, their funding base is diminishing, and rural areas are poorly endowed with libraries.

The issue of resources is a multidimensional problem. It is difficult, for example, for teachers to work together because physical space is not available (Abrahams 1997). Learner-centredness is difficult to realise where there are large classes, as Reeves showed in the teaching of natural science (Reeves 1999). Settled conditions are a prerequisite to enable curriculum development (Harber & Muthukrishna 2000). Basic problems around safety, non-violence, and operational efficiency are yet again difficulties most prevalent in historically-disadvantaged schools.

Inherited disadvantage may be compounded by shortcomings in teachers' and learners' command of English. What has always been a problem for second-language speakers of English has been exacerbated by the complex terminology in which C2005 was introduced (Harvey 1999; Le Grange & Reddy 2000; Reeves 1999).

The 'deferment' school cameo reported earlier provides an example of a school receiving inadequate departmental support. Other studies suggest that C2005 is least well supported in schools most in need of support. An extensive survey showed that state support was rated as inadequate by 41 per cent of teachers in the Western Cape (Schlebusch 1999). Teachers in ex-DET (Department of Education and Training) schools (63 per cent) felt most strongly that departmental support had been inadequate. Practical difficulties multiply with the distance of schools from regional headquarters. Township and rural teachers, who are most in need of support, find it difficult to attend training sessions (Johnson, Monk & Hodges 2000).

The picture of difficulties with respect to a 'resource hungry' curriculum like C2005 in historically under-resourced schools seems to be straightforward and predictable, but the picture with respect to teachers is both complex and anomalous. Following Gross, Giacquinta and Bernstein (1971), we know that uncertainty amongst teachers is a prime reason for implementation failures, and C2005 certainly took teachers into a new and unfamiliar curriculum world. Yet despite the widely-acknowledged inadequacy of the 'OBE training', research has consistently pointed to the favourable reception of C2005 (DoE 1997; Kgobe & Mbele 2001; Vally 1999). The C2005 Review refers to 'overwhelming support for the principles of C2005' (DoE 2000: 79). This apparent anomaly is compounded by the complexity of C2005 terminology; which drew from a foremost curriculum expert an early 'confession' that he found it difficult to understand (Jansen 1997). Evidence in early research through to the Review Committee identifies complex and turgid terminology as a major obstacle to understanding of C2005. Nevertheless, teachers perceived OBE as valuable even though they were uncertain of what it actually was (Govender 1999). In another case '... respondents indicated they would support OBE and yet they do not fully understand that which they are supporting' (Williams 1999) ... [and across schools] '(m)ost of the teachers did not hold a good understanding of OBE and yet many indicated their support for it' (361).

How do we explain this intriguing anomaly? We argued earlier that C2005 was primarily a political, not a pedagogical development. From the outset, teachers expressed hope for the vision of C2005, believing it would achieve equity and redress (Vally & Spreen 1998). Available evidence suggests that teacher support for C2005 pivots on support for its *political* project. Such support is, however, uneven. With characteristic acuity and directness, Jansen points out the 'racialised' nature of C2005 in schools (Jansen 2001). Simply put, black teachers are more enthusiastic about 'OBE'. Like Hiralaal (2000), a study by Khulisa (Khulisa Management Services 1999) found that teachers in ex-DET schools were more positive than those from other ex-Departments (the ex-Transvaal Education Department [TED] in this case). This pattern is suggested circumstantially in the earlier cameos, but 'harder' evidence is provided by a 1999 GICD report observing that: 'actual practice is more readily seen in ex-TED schools, despite enthusiasm for OBE being greater in ex-DET schools' (Czerniewicz et al. 2000).

Curriculum continuity and discontinuity

How does one explain this ironic situation in which historically disadvantaged schools struggle with C2005 in a way that undermines the political project the curriculum was designed to promote? We try to do so with reference to curriculum continuity and discontinuity.

Curriculum continuity in the historically advantaged sector

We have already noted that political imperatives required C2005 to be presented as being different in every respect to the 'apartheid' curriculum. Booklets on C2005 accordingly compared the 'new' curriculum with a caricatured version of the 'old', described as being exam-driven and teacher-centred, with passive learners and rote learning (while the 'new' had facilitators rather than teachers, active learners taking responsibility for their own learning, and so on).

In the case of at least some historically advantaged schools, reality was otherwise: the new curriculum merely formalised long-standing practices that had been the norm, the formal 'apartheid' curriculum notwithstanding. Indeed, new policy is a script for modernity (Baxen & Soudien 1999). In more specific terms, a summary of the longitudinal *Education 2000+* study concludes that: 'The research also suggested that the design of the new curriculum seemed to have a particular educator and school in mind, mainly the kind found in former Model C schools' (Kgobe & Mbele 2001).[12] Some of the few available classroom studies provide evidence of this. Hoadley, for example, points out that C2005 learner-centredness means that the pacing of lessons should be sensitive to learner progress. In the ex-DET school she studied, this was translated into waiting until all learners had finished; in the ex-Model C school, there was 'strong differentiating pacing', with steps taken to get all learners to achieve outcomes in individualised ways. In linking these differential practices with broader social relations, this study supports arguments that the new pedagogy is most readily compatible with the norms of historically advantaged schools. Like Govender (1999) and Oakes (2001), Jansen notes that white teachers saw OBE as having continuity with past practices in the sense that 'it's what we've been doing all along' (Jansen 2001). Black teachers, on the other hand, saw OBE as something worth striving for. Significantly, the C2005 Review found that ex-Model C schools were having less difficulty in implementing C2005.

There is significant documentary evidence of continuity between past practices and C2005 in some former white 'own affairs' departments. The erstwhile Natal Education Department (NED) illustrates the point. The NED incorporated continuous assessment (conducted by subject teachers) into the matriculation examination in the early 1980s. A sophisticated system of continuous assessment with appropriate statistical controls had been developed with the assistance of a prominent overseas expert, Henry MacIntosh. A detailed 'Bulletin on Assessment' (NED 1989) was distributed, and supported by workshops. In the matter of content knowledge, an integrated curriculum was strongly promoted by NED primary school advisers. In the area of pedagogy, connections between NED policy and C2005 are equally clear. The following statements are from the NED 'Curriculum Policy and Model' publication:

2.1 Effective learning takes place when:
- Pupils are actively involved in learning, either inside or outside the classroom;
- Pupils discover things for themselves by asking questions, investigating and solving problems, experimenting, using references;
- Pupils are involved in differentiated learning experiences that are appropriate to their interests, experience, needs, and level of cognitive development; and
- The learning environment is stimulating and non-threatening ...

2.2 Learning how to learn and learning the processes of a subject are at least as important as the acquisition of factual content. Pupils should be encouraged to be independent, original and creative thinkers.

2.3 Pupils are individuals who have different needs and learning styles, and the curriculum must make provision for this. (NED 1991)

These statements were a summation of principles drawn from earlier guides issued to teachers. Moreover, the NED guarded its 'ethos' zealously. In a guide to its representatives on national curriculum committees, it pointed out that national core syllabuses should not outline evaluation and time allocations. Significantly, also: 'No didactical prescriptions may appear in a core syllabus' (NED undated [circa 1986]). Pedagogy was a protected provincial competence, partly delegated to teachers.

Bourdieu and Passeron (1977) argue that social reproduction occurs because students belonging to the dominant culture have the 'cultural capital', meaning the appropriate cultural attributes and norms, for success in the system. In South Africa, historically advantaged schools thus continue to be advantaged with respect to a measure of cultural capital and pedagogic continuity, as well as material resources.

Curriculum discontinuity in the historically disadvantaged sector

In reviewing research on teacher identity, Jansen (2001) argues that despite their commitment to C2005 as a political project, teachers and their pedagogy have been displaced. He refers to the 'disappearing' teacher in policy images as teachers become facilitators, with teaching and content displaced by learning and competencies. 'The miscalculation was to think that a teacher lacking professional confidence and falling short of the required subject competence could be shifted to the margins of the classroom' (243). Teachers are required to give up space, the instrument of control (corporal punishment), content, and the textbook, hence: '... the facilitator as imagined in policy lost ground in terms of symbolic space, physical control, and textual authority' (243–244).

We believe that Jansen's account of realities overlooked by policy has closest reference to the historically disadvantaged schools. For instance, child-centredness, with its encouragement to learners to question authority:

> ... presents pupil-centred education as the ultimate form of good education in line with the individualistic Western culture. In fact, this may not necessarily be the best teaching strategy in all cultures ... there are cultures in South Africa that value rhetoric, and there are teachers who excel at it. It is a means of teaching that makes sense in schools with large classes and with meagre resources. (Rogan 2000)

In a forthright formulation before the advent of C2005, French put it this way:

> The proponents of progressive education tend to have a highly-developed sense of individual autonomy, and also to have had the privilege of being steeped in a culture which gives special value to self-criticism and self-awareness. The belief that everyone else is basically like they are and is yearning to be liberated (if only they knew what was good for them) is a fond illusion of many idealistic educators. (French 1989)

More research is needed in this difficult and sensitive area of curriculum and cultural discontinuity in the disadvantaged schools. In the meantime, we take the argument we have developed to its conclusion with respect to curriculum and social change.

Social class production in the South African context

Notwithstanding support for C2005 as a political project, there is strong evidence that C2005 as a pedagogical project is working counter to its transformatory social aims. It is widening, not narrowing, the gap between the former historically advantaged and disadvantaged schools. Social class reproduction (with some reconstitution in terms of its composition) is clearly taking place. However, it is taking place in a way that differs from standard explanations premised on a more or less functional fit between curriculum and middle-class culture (Bourdieu & Passeron 1977), or between curriculum and capitalist economy (Althusser 1971; Bowles & Gintis 1976). In South Africa, the 'fit' between policy intention and curriculum effect is anything but functional. Despite admirable policy intentions and the goodwill of teachers, C2005 is reproducing class inequalities and reconstituting social class, as greater opportunities are opened up to previously disadvantaged black learners. How does one account for this ironical outcome?

We suggest that social reproduction may be explained in terms of the consequences of meliorism, the belief that the world tends to become better, and that humans can aid its betterment. Desire for improvement is, of course, an admirable feature of human activity, and it assumes a particular intensity at times of social dislocation and crisis. Such a time was the early years of the Great Depression in the USA, for example, when economic collapse, mass unemployment, and concerns about social injustice led to a powerful movement that sought to redirect the curriculum towards 'correcting social and economic ills' (Kliebard 1987). In Kliebard's account, the problem with such admirable social intentions, and what made them 'meliorist', was their very intensity. With policy focusing so intensely on the desired effects of curriculum proposals, constraining realities with respect to curriculum implementation were simply overlooked. The reconstructionist curriculum project in the USA floundered because there were 'just too many speeches on the subject and not enough grass roots efforts to work with the teachers themselves' (Kliebard 1987).

We find parallels between Kliebard's account and the C2005 story that has unfolded. As Westbury (1973) and Goodson (1994) point out, commitment to a vision of *what should be* clouds the ability to seriously consider *what is*, so that the good intentions of social reconstructionism have more influence on the policy agenda than social and school realities. In its guise of social vision and idealised practice that overlooks the reality of schools, meliorism helps us understand how social commitment to a vision has had deleterious consequences for the C2005 curriculum plan, for the administrators implementing it, for the teachers who have to carry it out, and even for the way in which issues and debates are researched. Meliorism explains how it was possible for policy-makers to overlook the profound inequalities in South African schools and to despatch teachers on what Malcolm (1999) described as a voyage of faith that they could meet the challenge in an under-resourced system and with inadequate support.

Meliorism leads to a further bind. Morrow argues persuasively that C2005 has become scriptural. He illustrates the pressures for orthodoxy arising out of the simplistic dichotomies between the 'new' and the 'old' which marked promotion of the new OBE 'paradigm':

> If we are opposed to Apartheid Education then we must be in favour of OBE. We might be a bit unsure of what OBE is, but we must find ways to 'make it work' because it is the path we have chosen to 'transform' education in South Africa, it is our New Scripture ... Commitment to the national effort requires that we should all now promote OBE. (Morrow 2001)

Scriptural interpretation of OBE is underpinned by faith. Faith is necessarily a matter of belief rather than of rationality, and the faithful do not easily tolerate heresy. As Rogan notes, 'there is already a disturbing trend to act as if Curriculum 2005 cannot even be debated, let alone modified' (Rogan 2000).[13] In a document issued shortly after his appointment, Education Minister Kader Asmal wrote: 'Curriculum 2005 represents our best hope of transforming the retrograde inheritance of Apartheid era learning theories and obsolete teaching practices' (Asmal 1999: 12). Into the office of the second Minister of Education in the new South Africa, C2005 remains sacred.

Conclusion

We began by arguing that an enduring characteristic of curriculum is its relay of an overt political vision. Historically, South Africa has exemplified this. However, while political vision clearly affects the curriculum, there is little evidence that the curriculum in practice is generating its desired social effects in bringing about the vision. On the contrary, it appears to be reproducing social class divisions. This unintended effect, we have argued, comes about because C2005 has been embraced as a political project that has been successful in the ideological domain. But as a pedagogical project, it has not been successful.

Ironically and unintentionally, the intensity and single-mindedness of the very pursuit of the social vision has undermined itself. A commitment to a vision of *what should be* has undermined the ability of policy to consider seriously *what is*. In short, the harsh inequalities and contextual realities of South African schools have been overlooked. In a meliorist stance that positioned itself against the benchmark of past practice, C2005 promotion drew crude dichotomies between 'old' and 'new' practice in a way that obscured a measure of curriculum continuity for previously advantaged schools, as well as discontinuity for the previously disadvantaged.

The prospects of turning this situation around are muted by C2005 having become an article of faith by virtue of its political values. It has become synonymous with transformation. However, even while many teachers may continue to believe with Minister Asmal that C2005 is the best means of achieving transformation, its continuing failure as a pedagogical project must have consequences. Perhaps there is a 'proximal zone of credibility' beyond which support cannot be sustained. At the end of the day, it is probably only rigorous and sustained research that has the legitimacy to serve as a basis for critical review. A promising start was made by the impressive C2005 Review's re-insertion of curriculum to its position of centrality in the education system. However, the Review was constrained by its brief 'to review Curriculum 2005 and not outcomes-based education' (DoE 2000: 5). As C2005 has been so powerful symbolically, the state may have invested too much to countenance the loss of face that would accompany fundamental rethinking and revision. This leaves the research community with a massive responsibility. However, much research up to this point has itself been meliorist in the sense that it takes C2005 as a 'given' and focuses on identifying ways of achieving more effective implementation. As Kliebard has noted:

> In the curriculum field ... the urge to do good is so immediate, so direct and so overwhelming that there has been virtually no toleration of the kind of long-range research that has little immediate value to practitioners in the field, but which may in the long run contribute significantly to our basic knowledge and understanding. (Kliebard 1975 cited in Goodson 1994: 28)

Curriculum is now a public issue. But without serious knowledge and understanding of the way in which C2005 is being enacted in schools, there can surely be little hope for the political project it was intended to serve.

Appendix to Chapter 7: Notes on the C2005 research base

There are many studies from policy critique to C2005 implementation up to the point of teacher training for C2005 implementation. Although prolific in quantity, 'professional' research publications and student dissertations leave major gaps in our knowledge of C2005 in practice. Of the three C2005 dimensions – outcomes-based, integrated knowledge, learner-centredness – there is a striking imbalance. Even given the fact that OBE has become shorthand for C2005, research privileges the outcomes-based dimension to the virtual exclusion of all else. With few exceptions, there is a dearth of research into the knowledge integration domain, while pedagogy is virtually invisible. There is almost no focus, in the literature on C2005, on the fabric of daily life in schools and classrooms.[14] Dissertations, representing the work of practising teachers and departmental officials, come closest to pedagogy. However, rather than focusing directly on practice, there is reliance on proxy measures from which implications for practice might be drawn. Interviews and questionnaires were accordingly the favoured research approaches, with observation erratically providing a supplementary perspective. In 16 of the 20 dissertations we reviewed, the focus was on teacher capacity to 'do' C2005, with 'OBE training' enjoying much attention. Unsurprisingly, as a sub-category of pedagogy, learner-centredness is neglected. The student perspective is entirely invisible in the whole research enterprise.[15] This is surprising in a system intended to be learner-centred.

POLITICAL CHANGE, CURRICULUM CHANGE AND SOCIAL FORMATION

Like C2005 implementation itself, evaluations were conducted within time frames that were 'extremely constraining' (CEPD 2000a: 9). Although evaluations invariably include 'visits' to schools, methodology falls back on self-report measures rendered even more suspect when teachers' practices are reported by bureaucratic superiors. Moreover, it is by no means easy to identify 'evaluations'. A 97-page publication entitled *Curriculum 2005: The Story of the Grade 1 Pilot Project* is in fact a commemorative exercise that looks beguilingly like, and could easily be mistaken for, an evaluation.

Notes

1. Indeed, this conflation of the curriculum as a whole with one of its design features is evident even amongst the analysts and critics (see Jansen 1998; Mason 1999).
2. Through powerful lobbying by the trade union movement, South Africa adopted a National Qualifications Framework (NQF) that interlinked adult education and training with the schooling system. In part this was recognition by the trade unions that their members' best interests would be served if they were more skilled, and had opportunity to re-enter the education system at various points. For the NQF to work, specific competencies needed to be identified at every level, hence an outcomes-based model. This development necessitated an overhaul of the entire structure of the schooling system, including the curriculum within it.
3. Arguably the most influential visitor informing curriculum design.
4. As a somewhat ironic consequence, OBE was presented to teachers as the 'new paradigm'. While this sounded suitably impressive, it severely tested the formulation of Kuhn (1970), the author of the concept 'paradigm'. C2005 was unique among paradigms in having to be announced and explained to its practitioners.
5. A more detailed comment on the research base appears in the appendix to this chapter on page 214.
6. One piece of evidence from one of the few current in-depth studies, *Education 2000+*, is that: '... Grade 9 learners are now noted as semi-illiterate – there is a huge gap between Grades 8 and 9 who have been OBE educated and 10, 11 and 12 who haven't' (Personal interview with researcher from CEPD).
7. This account is drawn from the fieldwork of Naidoo (forthcoming).
8. This account is drawn from the fieldwork of Sineke (forthcoming).
9. This account is drawn from the fieldwork of Naidoo (forthcoming).
10. We are grateful to Mike Workman for making his study available.

11. In the form of post-graduate level study of policy on teacher roles in relation to C2005.
12. This echoes an almost identical statement in Harley et al. (2000: 302).
13. In an interview with senior KZNDE officials, one of the authors was told that support for a major funded project had been withheld because its approach was not strictly in line with C2005, 'our Bible'. The same project had earlier run into difficulties with a major teacher union because its approach was insufficiently fundamentalist.
14. The position here endorses the judgement that there is a lack of extensive classroom-based research in SA (Czerniewicz et al. 2000).
15. An extensive bibliography contained not a single study dealing with the student perspective.

References

Abrahams, R (1997) Collaborative Space in South African Schools: A Comparative Perspective. *Journal of Negro Education*, 66(4): 409–422

Althusser, L (1971) *Lenin and Philosophy and Other Essays*. New York: Monthly Review Press

Asmal, K (1999) *Call to Action: Mobilising Citizens to Build a South African Education and Training system for the 21st century*. Pretoria: Government Printers

Baxen, J & Soudien, C (1999) Outcomes-Based Education: Teacher Identity and the Politics of Participation. In Jansen, J & Christie, P (eds) *Changing Curriculum: Studies on Outcomes-Based Education in South Africa*. Kenwyn: Juta

Bernstein, B (1971) On the Classification and Framing of Educational Knowledge. In Young, M (ed) *Knowledge and Control: New Directions for the Sociology of Education*. London: Collier MacMillan

Bourdieu, P & Passeron, J (1977) *Reproduction, Education, Society, Culture*. London: Sage

Bowles, S & Gintis, H (1976) *Schooling in Capitalist America*. London: Routledge and Kegan Paul

Brodie, K (2000) Constraints in Learner-Centred Teaching, *Journal of Education*, (25): 131–160

Centre for Education Policy Development (2000a [first draft]) *The Implementation of C2005 at National and Provincial Levels*

Christie, J (1997) Global and Local Contexts: A South African Perspective on Competence Debates, *Discourse: Studies in the Cultural Politics of Education*, 18 (1): 55–69

Christie, P (1999) OBE and Unfolding Policy Trajectories: Lessons to be Learned. In Jansen, J & Christie, P (eds) *Changing Curriculum: Studies on Outcomes-Based Education in South Africa*. Kenwyn: Juta

Czerniewicz, L; Murray, S & Probyn, M (2000) *Learning Support Materials (LSMs) and Curriculum 2005*. Report produced for the NCCRD

Department of Education (1997) *Curriculum 2005: Lifelong Learning for the Twenty-First Century*. Pretoria: Government Printers

Department of Education (DoE) (1997) *National Evaluation and Monitoring of the Trial of Curriculum 2005 and OBE in Provincial Pilot Schools in South Africa*. Pretoria: Government Printers

Department of Education (2000). *A South African Curriculum for the Twenty-First Century: Report of the Review Committee on Curriculum 2005*. Pretoria: DoE

Dlamini, T & Harley, K (2003) Towards Improving Project Evaluation: Reflections on the Zikhulise Project Evaluation. In *DDSP: Improving the Quality of Primary Education: Good Practices and Emerging Models of District Development*. Pretoria: RTI/USAID

Eisner, E (2000) Those Who Ignore the Past... 12 'Easy' Lessons for the Next Millennium, *Journal of Curriculum Studies*, 32 (2): 343–357

Elias, N (1978) *What is Sociology?* New York: Columbia University Press

Ensor, P (2001) From Preservice Mathematics Teacher Education to Beginning Teaching: A Study in Recontextualising, *Journal for Research in Mathematics Education*, 32 (3): 296–320

French, E (1989) Empowering Teachers to be Empowering Teachers: Slogans or Slow Steps. Paper presented at the ASSA Conference, University of the Witwatersrand, Johannesburg

Goodson, I (1994) *Studying Curriculum*. Buckingham: Open University

Govender, D (1999) *The Perceptions and Experiences of Some Grade One Teachers Implementing Curriculum 2005*. Pietermaritzburg: University of Natal School of Education

Graven, M (2002) In-Service Teacher Education: Dilemmas Confronted in a Mathematics INSET Project. Paper presented at the Kenton Conference in Muldersdrift

Gross, N; Giacquinta, JB & Bernstein, M (1971) *Implementing Organizational Innovations: A Sociological Analysis of Planned Change*. New York: Harper and Row

Harber, C (2001) *State of Transition: Post-Apartheid Educational Reform in South Africa*. Oxford: Symposium Books

Harber, C & Muthukrishna, N (2000) School Effectiveness and School Improvement in Context: The Case of South Africa, *School Effectiveness and School Improvement*, 11 (4): 421–434

Harley, K; Barasa, F; Bertram, C; Mattson, E & Pillay, K (2000) 'The Real and the Ideal': Teacher Roles and Competencies in South African Policy and Practice, *International Journal of Educational Development*, 20 (4): 287–304

Harvey, S (1999) Phasing Science INSET in Developing Countries: Reflections on the Experience of the Primary Science Programme in South Africa, *International Journal of Science Education*, 21 (6): 595–609

Hiralaal, A (2000) *The Attitudes of Grade One Teachers in Pietermaritzburg to the Training They Have Received on Outcomes-Based Education (OBE)*. Post-graduate research project for the Department of Educational Psychology, University of Natal, Pietermaritzburg

Hlalele, L (2000) *Attitudes of Township Educators Towards Curriculum 2005: Implications for School Management*. Johannesburg: Rand Afrikaans University Faculty of Education and Nursing

Hoadley, U (2002) *Time to Learn: Pacing and the External Framing of Teachers' work*. Paper presented at the Kenton Conference in Muldersdrift

Jansen, J (1997) Why OBE Will Fail. Perspectives on Outcomes-Based Education (OBE), University of Durban-Westville, unpublished mimeo

Jansen, J (1998) Curriculum Reform in South Africa: A Critical Analysis of Outcomes-Based Education, *Cambridge Journal of Education*, 28(3) 321–331

Jansen, J (1999) Setting the Scene: Historiographies of Curriculum Policy in South Africa. In Jansen, J & Christie, P (eds) *Changing Curriculum: Studies on Outcomes-Based Education in South Africa*. Kenwyn: Juta

Jansen, J (2001) Image-ining Teachers: Policy Images and Teacher Identity in South African Classrooms, *South African Journal of Education*, 21 (4): 242–246

Jansen, J & Christie, P (eds) (1999) *Changing Curriculum: Studies on Outcomes-Based Education in South Africa*. Kenwyn: Juta

Johnson, S; Monk, M & Hodges, M (2000) Teacher Development and Change in South Africa: A Critique of Transfer of Northern/Western Practice, *Compare*, 30 (2): 179–192

Kgobe, M & Mbele, N (2001) *A Report of the Case Studies: Transformation of the South African Schooling System*. Braamfontein: CEPD: 87–153

Khulisa Management Services (1999) *Evaluation of Curriculum 2005 (C2005) and Outcomes-Based Education (OBE) in Gauteng Province*. Report commissioned by Gauteng Institute for Curriculum Development

Kliebard, H (1987) *The Struggle for the American Curriculum 1893–1958*. New York: Routledge and Kegan Paul

Le Grange, L & Reddy, C (2000) Introducing Teachers to OBE and EE: A Western Cape Study, *South African Journal of Education*, 20 (1): 21–25

Mahomed, H (2002) Currents and Cross-Currents in the Present GET and FET Education and Training Curriculum Scene in South Africa: Some Challenges Facing Implementation, Conceptually and Practically. Paper presented at the Kenton Conference in Muldersdrift

Malcolm, C (1999) Outcomes-based education has Different Forms. In Jansen, J & Christie, P (eds) *Changing Curriculum: Studies on Outcomes-Based Education in South Africa*. Kenwyn: Juta

Mason, M (1999) Outcomes-Based Education in South African Reform: A Response to Jonathan Jansen, *Cambridge Journal of Education*, 29 (1): 137–143

Mattson, E & Harley, K (1999) That's How we Teach them: Teacher Roles and Competences in a Globalising South Africa. Paper presented at the Kenton Conference at Salt Rock, Durban

Mattson, L (2000) *Teacher Identities in Policy and Practice*. Pietermaritzburg: University of Natal School of Education

Morrow, W (2001) Scripture and Practices, *Perspectives in Education*, 19 (1): 87–106

Naidoo, D (forthcoming) *Case Studies of the Implications of the Integrated Knowledge Code of C2005 for the Professional Identities and Practices of Grade 9 Teachers*. Pietermaritzburg: University of Natal School of Education

Natal Education Department (1989) *Assessment: Bulletin 48*. Pietermaritzburg: NED

Natal Education Department (1991) *Curriculum Policy and Model*. Pietermaritzburg: NED

Natal Education Department (undated circa 1986) *Syllabus Revision, Provincialisation of Syllabuses and Curriculum Development: Guidelines for Officials of the NED*

National Centre for Curriculum Research and Development (2000) *Synthesis of Documents on C2005*. Pretoria: DoE

NEPI (1993) *National Educational Policy Investigation: The Framework Report*. Cape Town: Oxford University Press

Nzimande, B (1997) Foreword. In Kallaway, P; Kruss, G; Fataar, A & Donn, G *Education After Apartheid: South African Education in Transition*. Cape Town: University of Cape Town Press

Oakes, I (2001) *Difficulties Experienced by Educators Implementing Curriculum 2005*. Pietermaritzburg: University of Natal School of Education

Reeves, C (1999) Are Teachers Likely to Achieve the Natural Science Outcomes for Curriculum 2005? *Journal of Education*, (24): 45–64

Rogan, J (2000) Strawberries, Cream and the Implementation of Curriculum 2005: Towards a Research Agenda, *South African Journal of Education*, 20 (2): 118–125

Schlebusch, A (1999) C2005: Out there in Choppy Waters: A 1999 C2005 look at WCED Grades 1 and 2 Through the Lenses of Learning, Assessment, Attitude and Practice. Paper presented at Western Cape Education Department Conference, Making OBE Work, 13–15 December 1999

Siebörger, R & Nakabugo, M (2001) Curriculum Reform and Teaching in South Africa: Making a 'Paradigm Shift'? *International Journal of Education Development*, 21(1): 53–60

Sineke, GM (forthcoming) *An Investigation into the Implementation of Curriculum 2005 in Grade 9: A Case Study of Two Schools*. Pietermaritzburg: University of Natal School of Education

Singh, P & Manser, P (2000) Effects of a Shared Vision on the Attitudes of Teachers Towards Outcomes-Based Education, *South African Journal of Education*, 20 (2): 108–114

Taylor, N & Vinjevold, P (1999) *Getting Learning Right: Report of the President's Education Initiative Research Project*. Johannesburg: Joint Education Trust

Vally, S (1999) Teachers in South Africa: Between Fiscal Austerity and 'Getting Learning Right', *Quarterly Review of Education and Training in South Africa*, 16 (2): 1–24

Vally, S & Spreen, C-A (1998) Educational Policy and Implementation Developments, February to May 1998, In Chisholm, L; Motala, S & Vally, S (eds) *South African Education Policy Review 1993–2000*. Johannesburg: Heinemann

Westbury, I (1973) Conventional Classrooms, 'Open' Classrooms and the Technology of Teaching, *Journal of Curriculum Studies*, 5 (2)

Williams, M (1999) *Outcomes-Based Education: How Have Selected Teachers Responded to Curriculum 2005?* Johannesburg: Wits Faculty of Education

Wong, T-H & Apple, M (2002) Rethinking the Education/State Formation Connection: Pedagogic Reform in Singapore, 1945–1965, *Comparative Education Review*, 46 (2): 182–212

Workman, M (2002) Issues related to the Implementation of Outcomes-Based Education: Single School and Local District Curriculum Initiatives and their Relevance for Large-Scale Educational Reform Within the Broader South African Context. Mimeo

8 Assessment, qualifications and the National Qualifications Framework in South African schooling

Johan Muller

Introduction and overview

Assessment and qualifications as a compound instrument regulating learner movement through the education system is one of the most important policy levers in any education system. Together, assessment and qualifications determine the level of inclusivity or exclusivity of the system, and the degree of 'fit' with the labour market (Young 2002). Assessment is also the most important system for signalling systemic efficiency and accountability. Unsurprisingly, it is frequently bitterly contested. There are two principal axes of contestation in assessment and qualifications thinking. The first is between those who distinguish between different modes of knowledge, learning and qualification, and those who don't. For ease of reference I will call the former dualists and the latter monists. The second is between those for whom assessment in the classroom for pedagogic purposes is primary (decentralisers), and those for whom assessment as a signalling system for systemic performance is primary (centralisers). The first has mainly an individualising purpose, the latter an aggregating purpose. When the pendulum swings too far in either direction on either axis, the system becomes deformed and produces aberrations. The politics of assessment policy can be examined by asking whether it is the dualists or the monists, the centralisers or decentralisers, who control the policy agenda (see also Chisholm 2001 for related policy cycles in curriculum policy).

This chapter will explore the vicissitudes of assessment and qualifications policy in South Africa. It will not attempt to tell a comprehensive history of the shifts in policy; the appendix to this chapter on page 241 provides a list of some of the key legislative and policy documents. Rather, it will attempt to convey educational movement and change by examining shifts in the terrain of debate and contestation generative of the change. By way of introduction, these can usefully be considered in terms of three broad phases:

Phase 1: 1980s to 1994; relative policy stasis

Assessment during the apartheid era was solely norm-referenced, summative and aggregative in all but a tiny minority of white and private schools where the individualising thrust of a progressive pedagogy had found a receptive clientele amongst the children of the old and emergent new middle class. While it might be thought that the system was driven by systemic means ('apartheid' is routinely regarded as having been 'top-down'), in fact the only systemic assessment instrument during this time was the matriculation examination. This was a phase of relatively low tension. This was less an achievement of policy design than it was a consequence of benign neglect. It is fair to say that, up until political transition, the various Departments responsible for education under apartheid had a divided curricular format, were matriculation-oriented and hence centralised, and had a low-key underspecified position on school-based assessment. Not unnaturally, this entire ensemble became associated with the evils of apartheid and thus regarded as intrinsically and irredeemably flawed.

Phase 2: 1994 to 2000; policy reform and increased tension

One of the principal aims, perhaps the principal aim of the policy reform in the years immediately after transition, was to unite the divided strands of the education and training curriculum and certification system into an *integrated* system. The development of this aim can be traced from the National Education Policy Investigation (NEPI) working group on Human Resources Development (HRD) in 1992 (NEPI 1992), through debates in the reconstituted National Training Board (NTB), to early policy formulation in the ANC Policy Framework Document and the Reconstruction and Development (RDP) base document (see Jansen 1999). The goal was partly muted in the 1995 White Paper, for reasons to be discussed later on. It emerged strongly again with the passing of the *South African Qualifications Authority* (SAQA) *Act*, No. 58 of 1995, and the establishment of a National Qualifications Framework (NQF).

The 'integration agenda', as Christie (1997: 117) calls it, had an understandable desire to unify the separate qualification opportunities offered by formal and non-formal provision that were widely seen as the cause of unequal work opportunity in the workplace. Following what was taken to be international best practice in the United Kingdom (UK) and New Zealand, the aim was to eliminate artificial divisions between mental and manual labour by means of a centralised qualifications grid, the NQF. The aim became to 'link the full spectrum of qualifications in an integrated framework' by a deliberate attempt to 'blur the distinction' between 'discipline based' and 'practice based' learning and qualifications (DoE/DoL 2003: 6, 7). This distinction was premised on a single reductive 'conceptual vocabulary for all modes of learning' (DoL/DoE 2003: 13), as the joint departmental Consultation Document forthrightly put it. Here was a strongly monist position espousing a centralising qualifications-driven reform, with the vocationally-oriented learner at the centre of the policy stage. One might say that the philosophy driving the NQF was one of 'administrative learner-centredness' or administrative progressivism (see Muller 2002; Pak 2002; Tyack 1974). What was manifest from the outset was 'an implicit tension' (Muller 2002: 6) between the centralising monists of the NQF, and the decentralisers and dualists of every stripe, which served very soon to 'polarise viewpoints and exasperate relations' all round (Muller 2002: 7).

In debates around school curriculum policy at the time, a decentralising philosophy of progressive pedagogy had emerged from its refuge in the private and Model C schools, a philosophy that might be called 'pedagogical learner centredness' or pedagogical progressivism to distinguish it from administrative progressivism. With its roots in Deweyanism imported into South Africa in the 1930s by the New Education Fellowship (see Malherbe 1937), and bolstered by the progressivism of the English Plowden Report in the 1960s (Sharp & Green 1975), pedagogical progressivism survived apartheid in the faculties of education of the liberal universities and in the private and later Model C schools, to be given a new lease on life as the canonised alternative to apartheid education in People's Education (Kraak 1998) and finally Curriculum 2005 (C2005) (DoE 2000).[1] The view underlying pedagogical progressivism was one of a decentralised and individualised libertarianism, where all forms of systemic assessment are seen as summative, unfairly comparative and hence discriminatory. Consequently, ideas of continuous assessment (CASS), borrowed largely from the UK, entered policy discourse as early as 1995 (Jansen 1999: 7), and the matriculation examination as a systemic centralising tool came under fire as unfair and exclusionary (see Jonathan Jansen and Penny Vinjevold in *The Teacher*, February 1999, for a representative example of the issues in dispute). During this phase, 'systemic' was thus conjoined with 'discriminatory' in post-transition policy discourse.

In this phase then, assessment and qualifications are given dramatic policy attention by a new set of policies with different roots and philosophical heritages, hence bringing with them tensions that were quite invisible in this early phase of 'symbolic policy' (Jansen 2002). The NQF was systemically-driven, with a centralised qualifications framework and a monist 'one size fits all' epistemology; C2005 (see Harley & Wedekind in this volume) was teacher- and learner-driven, with highly particularised and individualised assessment procedures, as enshrined first in the CASS policy and later in the learner assessment proposals in the Revised National Curriculum Statement (RNCS) (DoE 2002) and the Common Tasks of Assessment (CTAs). With two such divergent assessment policy orientations impelling them, centralising for the former and individualising for the latter, the NQF and C2005 were bound to come into tension, which the DoE dealt with by simply ignoring the NQF and refraining from registering any qualifications on it, as it was bound to do in terms of the *SAQA Act* of 1995 (see NAPTOSA 2003).[2]

Phase 3: 2000 to 2002; the advent of 'systemic reform' and 'quality assurance'

In common with the systemic reform movement in the United States (see Fuhrman 1993) and spurred on by international testing comparisons, notably the Third International Mathematics and Science Study (TIMSS) and the Monitoring Learner Assessment (MLA) Study, assessment outcomes as an instrument of managerial accountability and as an indicator of systemic efficiency began by the late 1990s to enter the policy discourse in South Africa. The bellwether of government thinking in this regard was the 1997 Medium Term Expenditure Framework from the Department of Finance (DoF). Nevertheless, enthusiasm for the new assessment was very slow to take hold in schooling circles, though donors and the international community were quick to latch onto the new notion. Indeed, the new enthusiasm for assessment was sometimes recklessly driven by the donor community, and the take-up of assessment-driven evaluations was rapid by the end of the decade: compare the evaluations commissioned in the mid-1990s with those at the end of it and in the new millennium, which were increasingly assessment/outcomes-based (see Taylor, Muller & Vinjevold 2003). In this phase, the potential of systemic assessment as an instrument for determining the extent of inequitable learning opportunities began to be asserted (see the Seekings 2001 Report commissioned by the Standing Committee on Public Accounts (SCOPA)), and made its way albeit cautiously into DoE policy (Grades 3, 6 and 9 Systemic Evaluation) (see Mseleku 2002; Taylor 2002). In addition, a number of large-scale studies were undertaken that show the accountability and diagnostic potential of systemic assessment – Mahlahle, the District Development and Support Project (DDSP), the Quality Learning Project, and the Western Cape comprehensive Grade 3 study, amongst others (Taylor, Muller & Vinjevold 2003). In the Conclusion to this paper, I reflect on the negligible policy take-up of this informational potential.

A discourse of systemic reform could be discerned in schooling policy documents of the DoE early in the new millennium, but it was a very particular kind of appropriation, one that would not be readily recognisable to American proponents of 'systemic reform', for instance. Embedded in this appropriation can be seen the project of conjoining systemic reform (so far in the weak sense of sample-based rather than comprehensive performance assessment only) with individualising process evaluation, an attempt in other words to reconcile centralisation and accountability on the one hand, with self-evaluation and support on the other. The main instruments for this are:
- Whole school evaluation;
- Systemic evaluation; and
- Quality management systems, including examinations. (Taylor et al. 2003)

The DoE was set to develop an 'integrated quality management system' in 2003 (DoE 2003b), a further sign of some resolve to proceed towards systemic assessment proper, but without any apparent recognition of the dualist/monist oppositional tensions that, as the inter-departmental Consultation Document on the NQF has recognised (DoE/DoL 2003; see below), have to be addressed before progress can be effected. It is likely that the DoE will have to grapple too with the centralising/decentralising tension, in other words, with the divergent policy ends of systemic reform proper and the particularising trajectories of process evaluation, CASS, portfolios, and the performance-based CTAs.

If the DoE's omnibus construal of systemic reform rhetorically minimises the conflicting senses of assessment that constitute it, a dramatic version of the tension between the dualists and the monists, between discipline-based and practice-based learning and assessment in the NQF was, in this phase, coming to a head. It was clearly apparent in the 'broad malaise of discontent with the

NQF and SAQA' (Departmental officials as quoted in DoE/DoL [2002: 3]). The NQF had been established in 1995 to unify and integrate qualifications in South Africa, as discussed, but its parent body SAQA had, by the turn of the century, become mired in in-fighting and stalled progress. A reviewing 'Study Team' was appointed in 2001 to pinpoint the problem. Of the 'two priorities of NQF implementation that must claim the most serious attention', concluded the Study Team in their report (DoL/DoE 2002: 132), the first and arguably most important was 'the development of a plan for assessment reform'. To see why, we have to delve beyond the circumlocutions of the report.

There are two rather different meanings borne by the term 'integration' in SAQA-speak. For the administrative progressives in the NQF (broadly, the representatives of labour), integration meant the *administrative* integration of the DoE and DoL, the flattening of qualificational distinctions between education and training, both symbolising to the proponents the bridging of mental and manual, head and hand. This qualifications-driven effort at social engineering embodied a centralising agenda in the interests of the aspirational working and lower middle classes.

This agenda and the interests its protagonists serve was dealt a first blow when the two Ministries were kept separate in 1994, and 'integration' gave way to 'an integrated approach' in the 1995 education White Paper. It was dealt a second blow in the inter-departmental Consultation Document (DoE/DoL 2003), which proposes three Quality Councils to regulate three distinct learning pathways and their distinct qualification requirements, one for higher education (HI ED QC); one for general and general vocational schooling (GENFET QC); and one for work-based and non-formal training (TOP QC). The first two report solely to the Minister of Education, the third solely to the Minister of Labour. No wonder then that scholars loyal to the first sense of integration have been left with a pervasive sense of policy betrayal (or euphemistically 'slippage'; see for example Kraak 2002). 'Integration' in the strong sense promoted by the administrative progressives has not prevailed. The analysis above and the Consultation Document suggest that this is because of the implementational confusion caused by their unexamined monist assumptions (DoE/DoL 2003).

'Integration' in a second sense favoured by the pedagogical progressives in the DoL denotes *curricular* integration, that is, the replacement of discipline-driven progression by thematic (sometimes called 'problem') based learning. The result for disadvantaged learners of maths and science has been the opposite of that intended (see Taylor, Muller & Vinjevold 2003). This sense of integration, incidentally antithetical to curricula designed for the trades[3], would make the primary aim of the NQF – qualification and occupational mobility – well nigh impossible for the working class. It not only makes systemic reform in its orthodox sense impossible, but is in fact designed to do so. This is presumably what the Study Team meant when they said: 'Much of the present complexity and uncertainty stems from the government and SAQA's commitment to an integrated approach to education and training' (DoL/DoE 2002). To state the matter simply, the administrative progressives in the DoL and the pedagogic progressives in the DoE meant quite different things by integration. If the first sense has thus waned over the period under review, the second sense has not.

When it came to school-based assessment, the pedagogical progressives practised a determined denigration of grading for which the Study Team chided them (DoL/DoE 2002: 80, 81); and inclined to a set of measures for qualitative or 'integrated assessment' that are proving to be unwieldy and burdensome, likewise deprecated by the Study Team. The most radical form of this assessment so far proposed by the DoE, comes in the form of the *Guidelines for Continuous Assessment for Grades 10–12; Curriculum 2005 Assessment Guidelines Senior Phase;* and the CTAs due to be written by all Grade 9 learners as a capstone to the General Education and Training (GET) band.

In the rest of this chapter I will focus in greater detail on developments in qualifications and certification, on the one hand, and assessment and systemic reform on the other, as well as speculate on the effects these policy instruments will have on the agenda of systemic reform and quality assurance.

Qualifications and certification

The Senior Certificate

Up until the end of 1995, the old ethnic departments of education administered the Senior Certificate Examination. 1996 was the first year that all students in the same province wrote the same provincial exam, 'a major step forward' in Hartshorne's (1999: 115) view. The administrative problems in shifting to a national system should not be underestimated. In 1996 there was widespread leakage and sale of the examination papers, cases of cheating, and administrative failures in publishing the results, all symptoms of high-stakes testing in a system with inadequate checks and balances. Over the next six years measures were put in place to reduce the administrative breaches, and in December 2002 the newly-formed UMALUSI publicly recorded that the process of the national Senior Certificate Examinations could be considered satisfactory.

Up until the advent of UMALUSI, standards maintenance for the Senior Certificate, or 'quality assurance' (QA), a term first used in official policy discourse in 2001, was the province of the Joint Matriculation Board (JMB). The JMB was instituted by the *Act on Universities*, No. 61 of 1955, at the same time as the establishment of the Committee of University Principals (CUP). The purpose of the JMB was to lay down requirements for exemption from the matriculation examination, and to monitor their implementation. The official intention was that the body would function as an assurer of quality for the schooling system as a whole, presumably on the grounds that universities are the universal custodians of knowledge for society. Critics of apartheid education were convinced that the JMB acted as a quality assurer for 'white' schools only, a criticism the then-Department of Education and Training (DET) was wont to deny, as in this statement in 1981:

> The same standards apply in black schools as in the schools of other education departments with regard to syllabuses and examinations. The same core syllabuses are used and the Joint Matriculation Board requires the same standards from black pupils for university entrance as from any other pupil in South Africa. (quoted Christie 1987: 145)

While this was undoubtedly technically true, it was widely and popularly regarded as substantively false.

Therein lay the rub, however. In addition to being the universal custodian of knowledge, universities also had a sectoral interest in university entrance quality, and it was this interest that the JMB served, to mounting criticism not only from employers and human resource managers, but increasingly also from the unions. In other words, the JMB was effectively a higher education sectoral QA body which, in the absence of any other QA body for the schooling system and in the absence of any other systemic assessment mechanism, effectively became the horse that simultaneously pulled both the assessment and QA cart of the schooling system. The result was a closely monitored matriculation exemption standard, and very little else. The resultant credibility gap between matriculation and the non-exemption Senior Certificate was probably at least one reason for the establishment in 1986 of the South African Certification Council. Another was undoubtedly the need to exercise some measure of control over the rest of the certificatory landscape, both formal and informal, as well.

The South African Certification Council, initially Board (Safcert), was set up 'to ensure that certificates issued by the Board at an exit point from the system represent the same standard of education and examining' (Van Schalkwyk 1988). Its main purposes were to:
- Provide for control over the norms and standards of subject matter and examinations.
- Issue certificates at exit points from school, technical college and non-formal education.
- Provide for the conducting of common examinations.

This expanded brief of Safcert effectively 'downgraded' the JMB to a sub-committee of the CUP, advising on university admission requirements to the CUP. The CUP was enabled to advise Safcert, but it was Safcert, not the JMB, that then endorsed the Senior Certificates. This was a significant development, because for the first time there was now a national body which judged school certification, and thus quality assured qualifications, on a basis broader than just whether they prepared learners for university or not. Safcert thus became a certification-driven, effectively schooling-driven, QA body. This role was always going to be limited by the general lack of assessment policy in South Africa, and the qualifications most meagrely served were the vocational and non-formal ones. The default driver of a norm-referenced Senior Certificate school exit qualification thus continued into the 1990s and into the new dispensation without major revision or, indeed, much major thought at all, again with the singular exception of the pedagogical progressives in the liberal universities, and in the private and ex-Model C schools, for whom a progressive diagnostic assessment practice went to the very heart of a transformational pedagogic strategy.

After the establishment of the SAQA and NQF with its various bands in education and training, Safcert began to orient its vision and functions from externally validating examinations and issuing certificates to a more comprehensive quality assurance role. This 'transformatory trajectory' was aimed at fulfilling new roles of quality assurance for the GET and Further Education and Training (FET) on the NQF.

However, before Safcert could assume these new responsibilities, legislation had to be passed to enable the establishment of a General and Further Education and Training Quality Assurance body (GENFET QA). *The General and Further Education and Training Quality Assurance Act*, No. 58 of 2001, provided the legislative framework for the establishment of UMALUSI. In June 2002, UMALUSI, formally the Council for Quality Assurance in General and Further Education and Training, a fully-fledged education and training quality assurer, took up the quality assurance and certification responsibilities of Safcert together with much wider responsibilities. UMALUSI would not only award qualifications, certificates or credits towards NQF qualifications in the GET and FET bands, but also approve provider accreditation, qualifications and programmes.

Table 8.1 Senior Certificate Examination results, 1994 to 2002

	Candidates	Total passes	%	University exemptions	%	Total failures	%
1994	495 408	287 343	58	88 497	18	208 065	42
1995	531 453	283 742	53	78 821	15	247 711	47
1996	518 032	278 958	54	79 768	15	239 074	46
1997	555 267	261 400	47	69 007	12	293 867	53
1998	552 384	272 488	49	69 856	13	279 954	51
1999	511 159	249 831	49	63 725	12	261 328	51
2000	489 941	283 294	58	68 626	14	206 004	42
2001	449 371	277 206	62	67 707	15	172 126	38
2002	471 309	324 752	69	75 048	16	146 557	31

Source: Schindler (2002), except figures for 2002, which are unconfirmed; see Taylor, Muller & Vinjevold 2003.

As the figures in Table 8.1 graphically show (to date the only comprehensive time-series chart of systemic performance in South African schooling available), UMALUSI has inherited a mammoth task of QA for a system that worsened steadily for six years until 1999, only to affect a remarkable and statistically near-impossible recovery. To what could the recovery be attributed? Sceptics have advanced various possibilities: conversion of registration from higher grade to standard grade; the 'cooling out' of marginal performers in Grade 11; mark adjustments upwards for second-language speakers; the implementation of CASS (see Fleisch 2003: 16). All of these have some plausibility to a greater or lesser extent, although the CASS marks were moderated to within five per cent of the examination mark, and will thus not have had a major effect (Taylor 2002: 15). By the same token, however, little had changed in the system itself to which the recovery could be attributed.

In any event, Safcert as a QA system for schooling without an assessment policy limped along into the 1990s and beyond. UMALUSI, as a provider assessor as well as qualification or learner assessor, has inherited this unequal task, and has had to establish its mission and operating criteria largely in a vacuum, without systemic benchmarks with which to set reasonable or educationally justified targets. The body has thus understandably not got off to a flying start, largely because, as the analysis above suggests, it was not able to differentiate between different kinds of qualification (that is, it was unable to resolve the dualist/monist tension). The inter-departmental Consultative Document (DoE/DoL 2003: 26) has recommended that UMALUSI become the 'main organisational base' for the GENFET QA. Together with the recommendation that the 'operational centre of gravity would shift from SAQA to the QCs' (DoL/DoE 2003), this reconfiguration may allow quality assurance for schooling a better chance in future.

Assessment

In the apartheid era, assessment policy for learners other than those in the exit Grade 12 was not specified. In practice, for the vast majority of learners, assessment was norm-referenced, summative and aggregative by default. C2005 policy documents and the *Assessment Policy for General Education and Training* (DoE 1998) make much of the need to shift from this 'authoritarian' approach to assessment to one which is formative, standards-based and continuous. In the period since 1998 the DoE has taken steps to prescribe exactly what the continuous assessment should consist of in each learning area in the Senior Phase of the GET (Grades 7 to 9) and in each subject examined for the Senior Certificate. Although the documents for both are called guidelines, the continuous assessment requirements set out in these documents are

'compulsory' and all full-time learners must have CASS marks 'otherwise their results will be declared incomplete'. Not only is the number of assessment tasks prescribed but also the weighting of the various forms of assessment to be used. For example, in the Natural Sciences learning area for Grades 7 to 9 the following forms of assessment are prescribed:
- Investigations and projects (40 per cent) – two full investigations, one short investigation and one research project per year;
- Assignments (15 per cent) – minimum of three per month;
- Tests and examinations (15 per cent) – five per year;
- Presentations and performance (15 per cent) – three per year; and
- Translation tasks (15 per cent) – three per year.

I have commented that external or systemic assessment has been poorly served in the schooling system at grades below Grade 12. Since 1998 there has been an explosion of external assessment activity at various grades of the system. The majority of this activity has been initiated, funded and implemented outside of the DoE. This section of the chapter will examine both government and private external assessment initiatives in the period 1998 to 2002.

Government-initiated external assessment activities

The *Assessment Policy for General Education and Training* (DoE 1998) makes provision for systemic evaluation to be conducted at the Grades 3, 6 and 9 levels 'on a nationally representative sample of learners and learning sites in order to evaluate all aspects of the school system and learning programmes' (DoE 2002: 2). The four objectives of the systemic evaluation are to:
- Determine the context in which learning and teaching takes place;
- Obtain information on learner achievement;
- Identify factors that affect learner achievement; and
- Make conclusions about appropriate education interventions. (DoE 2002: 3)

The aim was thus both to aggregate and diagnose systemic gaps and shortcomings.

Planning for Grade 3 systemic assessment began in 1998. Although this was a national DoE initiative, the Grade 3 systemic assessment was conducted 'in partnership with the provincial education departments and a consortium of service providers managed by the Centre for Education Policy Development,

ASSESSMENT, QUALIFICATIONS AND THE NQF

Evaluation and Management (CEPD)' (DoE 2002: 6). A pilot study was conducted in 2000 and the main study in September 2001. After a few false starts, the report, its draft dated July 2002, finally appeared in mid-year 2003 (DoE 2003a). The analysis which follows is based on the draft report. A sample of 5 per cent of all Grade 3 learners was to participate in the study. In the event 51 307 of 1 079 252 or 4.8 per cent of all Grade 3 learners participated in the study.

Table 8.2 Number of Grade 3 learners that participated in the Grade 3 systemic assessment mainstream study, 2001

Province	Total no. of learners in Grade 3	Number of learners who participated	Percentage of total
Eastern Cape	213 915	9 456	4.4
Free State	57 699	2 889	5.0
Gauteng	126 321	6 220	4.9
KwaZulu-Natal	245 038	11 115	4.5
Mpumalanga	84 725	4 048	4.8
Northern Cape	16 397	913	5.6
Limpopo	164 577	8 062	4.9
North-West	88 979	4 524	5.1
Western Cape	81 601	4 080	5.0
Total	1 079 252	51 307	4.8

The results of the learner assessment component by learning programme and by province are set out in Figure 8.1 on the next page.

While the results suggest poor performance, the report provides little information on the nature of the poor performance, hence not fulfilling a main aim of the exercise. In learner assessment studies this is usually achieved first by making explicit the curriculum on which the test is based, so that attainment can be compared with what should have been attained. The Grade 3 systemic assessment offers no indication of the curriculum on which the assessment instruments were based. The test development process is dispensed with in two paragraphs in the report and indicates that the assessment instruments 'were based on frameworks drafted by members of the consortium together with the DoE and provincial Foundation Phase specialists for the three Learning Programmes covered by this study, Literacy, Numeracy and

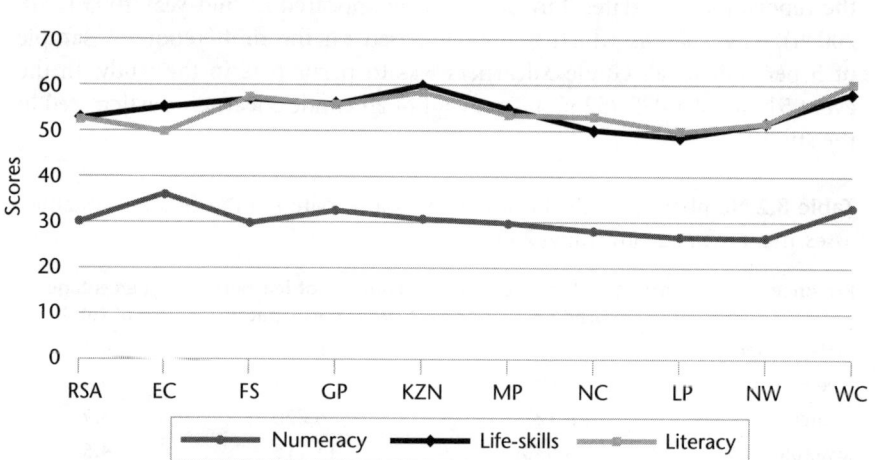

Figure 8.1 Mean scores for Numeracy, Literacy and Life-skills by province in the Grade 3 systemic assessment, 2001

Life-skills' (DoE 2003a: 7). According to the report, assessment tasks for the instruments were developed by Foundation Phase specialists but the primary responsibility for the Life-skills task was taken by the department since members of the consortium did not have the capacity to undertake this task. The pilot study for Grade 6 systemic assessment took place in 2002 and the full study was planned for the end of 2003.

Part of this tardiness in fulfilling government policy is undoubtedly due to the contentiousness of testing. Pedagogical progressives have long argued that the pressures created by testing for accountability are counter-productive to learning: for example, teaching to the test; distortion through particular curriculum emphasis; and diminution of intrinsic motivation to learn. Proponents argue that the negative effects can be minimised, and that high-stakes testing usually leads to enhanced performance, especially where curriculum, assessment, and professional development are appropriately aligned (Schoenfeld 2002). That of course depends on the tests being reliable and valid. This debate, though, has hardly started in South Africa, and progressive distaste of testing still marks governmental initiatives in this regard.

A second external assessment initiative of government in the period was the CTAs at Grade 9 level. According to the assessment policy (DoE 1998), 25 per cent of the Grade 9 promotion mark should consist of external assessment. In February 2002 the DoE proposed that this external assessment would take the form of CTAs, a form of performance assessment favoured by pedagogical progressives and very difficult to use for comparative and systemic purposes (Garden 1999: 237). These would be administered in all eight learning areas in the last school term of 2002. The CTAs were developed at national level in consultation with provincial departments of education. Problems predictably arose in the development of the instruments as the under-specification of C2005 provided no common content on which to base the tasks (see Chisholm et al. 2000). The test development teams went to enormous lengths to ensure that all learners had equal access to the content of the tasks and this resulted in the tasks being over-elaborate and extremely long – over 100 pages in one instance, and hence user-unfriendly. Problems were also experienced with translation, distribution and training of teachers in the CTAs. An investigation by one of the teacher unions in October 2002 indicated that there were many schools that had not received the CTAs, that there was little likelihood that they would be received in some provinces, and that the tasks were riddled with errors.

As a result, in late October 2002, two weeks before the CTAs were scheduled to be written, the Minister of Education announced that the CTAs would not be compulsory for 2002. It is unclear how many schools across the country wrote the CTAs but in any event, it is hard to see the upshot as anything but an abortive attempt at external assessment by the state. At the time of writing, the shape of the General Education and Training Certificate (GETC) examination, the exit examination for the compulsory phase of public schooling, has not been made known. There are indications that there will be no external assessment for the GETC at all. Were this to be the case, systemic assessment and public accountability would once again be poorly served.

A third external assessment involvement of government was the MLA Study. This study was commissioned by the national DoE, which participated for the first time in 1995 in the Joint International Unesco-Unicef Monitoring Learning Achievement Project (Chinapah et al. 2000). South Africa also participated in the 2000 study but the final report has, at the time of writing, not yet been released. In 1995 more than 10 000 Grade 4 learners participated in the South African study, and they scored an average of 30 per cent for Numeracy, coming last of the 12 African countries. A large proportion of learners scored below 25 per cent, while only about two per cent obtained scores in the 75 to 100 per cent range. In Life-skills, South African learners came second last, and in Literacy, they came eighth.

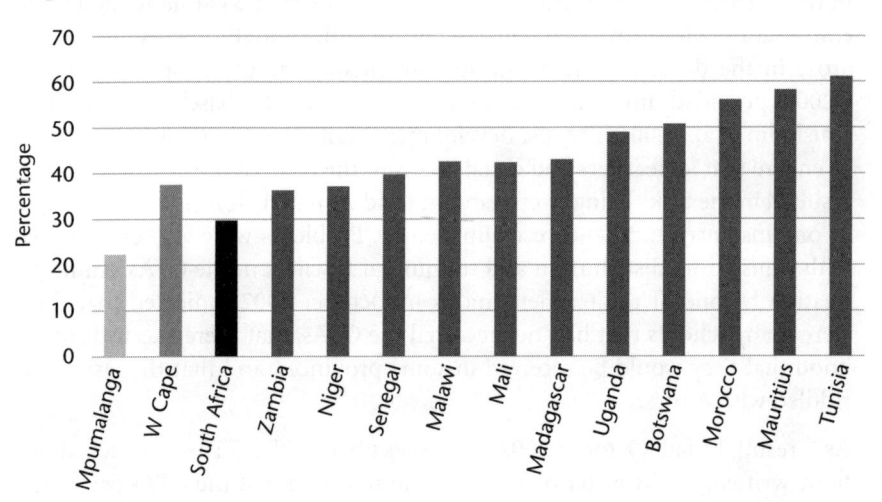

Figure 8.2 South Africa's performance on the Grade 4 MLA Numeracy test, 1995

Reviewing government progress towards external systemic assessment since political transition, we would be justified in concluding, protestations about commitment to 'systemic reform' notwithstanding (Mseleku 2002), that:
- Government moves towards external assessment have been marked by footdragging and unaccountable delays.
- The systemic data that we do have to date depicts a system that is inefficient and in extremely poor health.

It is not clear whether the dilatoriness is due to political fears that this dismal picture should become widely known, either by the DoF or the public, or both; or whether it is simply the continuing antipathy of the pedagogical progressives to systemic testing that is retarding progress towards systemic accountability. Either way, the planners in the DoE and DoF are left without crucial information about exactly who is learning and who is not, or what they are learning and what not. The planners are consequently left without the data they need to plan for rational targeted intervention. The review of financing, resourcing and costs that appeared in mid-2003 (DoE 2003b) makes a firm case for strengthening the accountability of government and schools to communities and parents: 'A public empowered with more comprehensive information about the schooling system would almost certainly exert positive pressure on institutions and leaders to account for educational performance' (DoE 2003b: 103; see also NAPTOSA 2003: 8). According to this review, the DoE will provide its first comprehensive report in 2005. In the meanwhile, it is small wonder that the private sector has begun to fill the informational vacuum left by government.

Private sector external assessment initiatives

In the period 1998 to 2002 a number of evaluation studies included learner assessment (see Taylor, Muller and Vinjevold 2003, for a review). These studies were mostly commissioned and funded by donors wishing to understand the impact of funded interventions. In these studies, tests were administered to all schools or samples of schools involved in an intervention or project. For example, the JET Mahlahle Grade 3 tests have been administered in nine different studies to Grade 3, 4 and 5 learners in over 800 schools in five provinces. In the majority of cases the learners were from disadvantaged schools, that is, former DET schools or, to a much lesser extent, former House of Representatives (HoR) schools in the Western Cape and Northern Cape.

Eric Schollar and Associates administered mathematics and reading and writing tests in the many evaluation studies they conducted in South Africa in the period 1998 to 2002. These evaluation studies included the Imbewu evaluation, the Business Trust 1000 School study, and various evaluations of the READ project, the Mpumalanga Primary Science Initiative and many others (see Schollar 2001a and b). One set of tests was administered to 5 000 Grade 3, 4 and 5 learners in nine provinces and another set to 5 000 Grade 6 and 7 learners in nine provinces (Schollar 2001a and b).

Both government and the private sector external assessment initiatives in the period 1998 to 2002 were bedevilled by the under-specification of the curriculum content in C2005. The Specific Outcomes (SOs) and Expected Levels of Performance (ELPs) of this curriculum do not provide the level of specificity required for the development of systemic assessment instruments. In response to this under-specification, assessors developed alternative curriculum frameworks within which to locate their assessment instruments.

The most ambitious of these constructions were the JET Mahlahle Grade 3 and Grade 6 tests in which international benchmarks were superimposed on the South African curriculum outcomes (see JET 1999, 2000). In the case of the numeracy instruments, Dutch numeracy outcomes were used and in the case of the reading test, the International Association for Educational Achievement (IEA) framework for nine-year-olds was used. National and provincial DoE officials and teachers familiar with the context of a wide variety of schools commented on the alignment of these frameworks with the South African curriculum and therefore their suitability for the South African situation. The process of establishing the correct 'fit' was time-consuming and laborious. The RNCS (DoE 2002) will greatly expedite the construction of tests, as in the case of the Western Cape Education Department (WCED) system-wide testing at Grade 3 level conducted in October/November 2002.

All the studies conducted in South Africa between 1998 and 2003 suggest that learner achievement scores are far below what is expected at all levels of the schooling system, both in relation to other countries including other developing countries and to the expectations of the new South African curriculum.

The Grade 8 Mathematics and Science Study, TIMSS-R, was administered in 38 countries across the world in 1998. South African learners performed well below their counterparts.

The South African mean scores of 275 for maths and 243 for science are well below the international means (487 and 488 from 38 countries) and below the mean scores of all participating countries including two African countries, Morocco and Tunisia (Martin, Mullis, Gonzales, Gregory, Smith, Chrostowski, Garden & O' Connor 2000; Howie 2001). Other studies show that South African learners not only perform below learners from other countries but also in relation to the expectations of the South African curriculum (Kanjee, Patterson, Prinsloo, Kivulu & Pheiffer 2001).

These private assessment initiatives begin to indicate the importance of systemic assessment data for taking informed educational decisions. But for all the invaluable detailed information that this privately-generated systemic data provides, what is most striking is how little of it has so far been used by the government, national or provincial. The main impact on assessment policy so far has been indirect, and though it seems to have helped shift the policy discourse somewhat, there is very little evidence of a real sea change in departmental attitudes to performance data. Above all, whether this information will be used to make targeted resource allocatory decisions remains an open question.

Conclusion

The main conclusion to be drawn from this overview of qualifications and assessment in South Africa is that qualifications and assessment policy was, and remains, the Cinderella of all the policies of public schooling. This does not mean that no changes at all are detectable. On the contrary, we can see a discernable move since 1994 away from an underdeveloped systemic policy (Grade 12 external assessment only) towards a marked progressive preference for formative, process and integrative kinds of assessment with little real progress towards comprehensive systemic assessment. The visible consequences of this are rising public concern about the lack of clarity regarding the GETC written in 2003, and efforts from the private sector to fill some of the gaps. None of this has, so far, had any direct impact on government.

As far as the monist/dualist axis of contestation is concerned, the interdepartmental Consultative Report on the NQF (DoE/DoL 2003) has established the importance of learning path and qualifications differentiation. This redresses the unrelieved emphasis on integration in the NQF with a more balanced stress on 'integration and *progression*' as two equally important principles for a national qualifications framework (DoE/DoL 2003: 22, my emphasis). One might conclude from this that learning path and qualifications dualism will begin to prevail and that this will shift some of the pressure felt by the discipline-based pedagogues in the schools and universities back onto the progressives.

As far as the centralised/decentralised axis of contestation is concerned, one might conclude that the balance between systemic and formative assessment is presently weighted against systemic assessment centralism. Whether this is due to progressive preference only, or also reflects a serious technical capacity problem in the department, is hard to say. In either case, without the data provided by systemic assessment, the learning gaps in the system can't be known, so it is not possible to make the informed decisions to allocate the kinds of targeted grants that Fiske and Ladd in their chapter in this volume propose in the form of additional grants. Until we get the data from the promised 'integrated performance monitoring system' in 2005 (DoE/DoL 2003: 104), which, with the exception of Grades 9 and 12, will be sample-based and not comprehensive data, the only data available to implement such evidence-based measures would be that made available by the large sample-based international assessments like MLA, TIMSS[4] and by private external assessments. This certainly gives the provinces a better map of their current learning geography than they had before, and it will be interesting to see whether provinces begin to use this information in order to decide where to target their interventions. Nonetheless, until there are comprehensive performance outcomes data for the early grades, effective accountability to the public and the community will be unattainable.

While the balance of power in the DoE continues to favour the pedagogical progressives, one might speculate that the DoE will probably be able to continue to resist public pressures for assessment reform, although whether they will be able to resist political pressure from the DoF for greater demonstrable efficiency remains to be seen. The recent Finance Review is forthright in this regard, as we saw above (DoE 2003). It is likely that, with the present direction in place, there will be increased class differentiation of outcomes and hence an exacerbation of disadvantage, progressive rhetoric notwithstanding, although this disadvantage will be kept more invisible than it should be by the continued lack of performance data that only comprehensive systemic assessment can provide.

Appendix to Chapter 8: Some key documents relating to qualifications and assessment

Legislation
- South African Qualifications Authority (SAQA) Act, (Act No. 58 of 1995)
- National Education Policy Act (Act No. 27 of 1996)
- Skills Development Act (Act No. 97 of 1998)
- General and Further Education and Training Quality Assurance (GENFETQA) Act (Act No. 58 of 2001)

National DoE policy documents
- Revised National Curriculum Statement: Grades R–9. Pretoria 2002
- Introducing Outcomes-based Education in Grades 10–12. Pretoria 2003
- Qualifications and Assessment Policy Framework: Grades 10–12
- Qualifications and Assessment Policy Framework: Grades R–9
- National Policy on the Conduct of Examination: ABET
- Draft Policy on the General Education and Training Certificate : ABET (Not available yet)
- Assessment Policy in the General Education and Training Band: Grades R–9 and ABET
- Policy Document on ABET

SAQA policy documents
- FETC Policy
- General Education and Training Certificate
- Recognition of Prior Learning in the context of the South African NQF
- Criteria and Guidelines for Assessment of NQF Registered Unit Standards and Qualifications

Other SAQA documents
- The National Qualifications Framework and Quality Assurance
- The National Qualifications Framework: An Overview
- Criteria for the Generation and Evaluation of Qualifications and Standards within the National Qualifications Framework
- Criteria and Guidelines for Short Courses and Skills Programmes
- Criteria and Guidelines for the Implementation of Recognition of Prior Learning: Discussion Document for Public Comment

UMALUSI documents
- UMALUSI: Organisation of Qualifications in the Further Education and Training Band: Current Thinking

- UMALUSI: *Framework for Institutional Accreditation: Draft Document for Discussion.* April 2003.

Notes

1. This is a highly compressed account. For a more considered account see Harley & Wedekind 2003, and this volume.
2. The dualist/monist tension was most clearly apparent in the response of the universities to the NQF (see the report prepared for the Council of Higher Education by Ensor & Ogude 2001; Ensor 2003). This analysis has been adopted by the recent inter-departmental Consultation Document (DoE/DoL 2003).
3. In Bernstein's (2000) terms: the pedagogical progressives with C2005 favoured a radical form of competence pedagogy; the pedagogical administratives with the NQF favoured a market-driven form of performance pedagogy. The assessment and qualification forms appropriate to each are simply incommensurable.
4. DoE/DoL 2003: 101 mentions a Southern African Consortium for Monitoring Educational Quality (SACMEQ) sample survey of Grade 6 learners conducted in 2000, a study not known to the author.

References

Bernstein, B (2000) *Pedagogy, Symbolic Control and Identity.* Oxford: Rowman and Littlefield Publishers

Black, P (1998) *Testing: Friend or Foe? Theory and Practice of Assessment and Testing.* London: Falmer Press

Chinapah, V (2000) *With Africa for Africa; Quality Education for All.* Pretoria: HSRC

Chisholm, L (2001) History and Contemporary Politics of Curriculum Construction and Development in South Africa. Unpublished mimeo

Christie, P (1987) *The Right to Learn.* Johannesburg: Ravan Press

Christie, P (1997) Globalisation and the Curriculum: Proposals for the Integration of Education and Training. In Kallaway, P; Kruss, G; Fataar, A & Donn, G (eds) *Education After Apartheid: South African Education in Transition.* Cape Town: University of Cape Town Press

Department of Education (DoE) (1998) *Assessment Policy for General Education and Training.* Pretoria: Government Printers

Department of Education (2000) *A South African Curriculum for the Twenty First Century: Report of the Review Committee on Curriculum 2005.* Pretoria: DoE

Department of Education (2002) Overview and Chapter 6: Learner Assessment in the Learning Area Statements. In *Revised National Curriculum Statement Grades R–9.* Pretoria: Government Printers

Department of Education (2003a) *The Foundation Phase (Grade 3) Systemic Evaluation (2000/2001) Report.* Pretoria: Government Printers

Department of Education (2003b) *Review of Financing, Resourcing and Costs of Education in Public Schools.* Pretoria: Government Printers

Department of Education/Department of Labour (2002) *Report of the Study Team on the Implementation of the National Qualifications Framework.* Pretoria: Government Printers

Department of Education/Department of Labour (2003) *An Interdependent NQF System: Consultative Document.* Pretoria: Government Printers

Ensor, P & Ogude, N (2001) The Development of the National Qualifications Framework (NQF) and its Implementation in Relation to Education and Training. Report prepared for the Council on Higher Education.

Ensor, P (2003) The National Qualifications Framework and Higher Education in South Africa: Some Epistemological Issues, *Journal of Education and Work,* 16 (3): 325–346

Fleisch, B (2003) The SCE: Accounting for Improvement, *Quarterly Review of Education and Training in South Africa,* 10 (1): 16

Fuhrman, S (ed) (1993) *Designing Coherent Policy: Improving the System.* San Francisco: Jossey Bass

Garden, R (1999) Development of TIMSS Performance Assessment Tasks, *Studies in Educational Evaluation,* 25: 217–241

Harley, K & Wedekind, V (2003) *A Time for Discipline: Disciplinary Displacement and Mythological Truths.* Mimeo

Hartshorne, K (1999) *The Making of Education Policy in South Africa.* Cape Town: Oxford University Press

Howie, S (2001) *Mathematics and Science Performance in Grade 8 in South Africa 1998/1999: TIMSS-R 1999 South Africa.* Pretoria: HSRC

Jansen, J (1999) Setting the Scene: Historiographies of Curriculum Policy in South Africa. In Jansen, J & Christie, P (eds) *Changing Curriculum: Studies on Outcomes-based Education in South Africa.* Kenwyn: Juta

Jansen, J (2002) Rethinking Education Policy Making in South Africa: Symbols of Change, Signals of Conflict. In Kraak, A & Young, M (eds) *Education in Retrospect: Policy and Implementation since 1990*. Pretoria: HSRC

Joint Education Trust (1999) Mahlahle: Report on the Phase One Baseline Study. Unpublished mimeo

Joint Education Trust (2000) Mahlahle: Report on the Phase Two Baseline Study. Unpublished mimeo

Kanjee, A; Patterson, A; Prinsloo, C; Kivulu, K & Pheiffer, C (2001) *Improving Learning in South African Schools: The Quality Learning Project Baseline Evaluation*. Pretoria: HSRC

Kraak, A (1998) *Competing Education and Training Policies: A 'Systemic' versus 'Unit Standards' Approach*. Occasional Paper. Pretoria: HSRC

Kraak, A (2002) Policy Ambiguity and Slippage: Higher Education Under the New State, 1994–2001. In Kraak, A & Young, M (eds) *Education in Retrospect: Policy and Implementation since 1990*. Pretoria: HSRC

Kraak, A & Young, M (eds) (2002) *Education in Retrospect: Policy and Implementation since 1990*. Pretoria: HSRC

Malherbe, EG (1937) *Educational Adaptations in a Changing Society*. Johannesburg: Juta

Martin, M; Mullis, I; Gonzales, E; Gregory, K; Smith, T; Chrostowski, S; Garden, R & O' Connor, K (2000) *TIMSS 1999 International Science Report: Findings from IEA's Repeat of the Third International Maths and Science Study at the 8th Grade*. Chestnut Hill: Boston College

Mseleku, T (2002) Department of Education Efforts to Secure School Effectiveness. In Roberts, J and Muller, J (eds) *Balancing Support and Accountability to Improve School Performance*. Johannesburg: JET

Muller, J (2002) Progressivism Redux: Ethos, Policy, Pathos. In Kraak, A & Young, M (eds) *Education in Retrospect: Policy and Implementation since 1990*. Pretoria: HSRC

Mullis, I; Martin, M; Gonzales, E; Gregory, K; Smith, T; Chrostowski, S; Garden, R & O' Connor, K (2000) *TIMSS 1999 International Mathematics Report: Findings from IEA's Repeat of the Third International Maths and Science Study at the 8th Grade*. Chestnut Hill: Boston College

National Professional Teachers' Organisation of South Africa (NAPTOSA) (2003) *Update: First Semester 2003*. Mimeo, July

National Education Policy Investigation (1992) *Human Resources Development*. Cape Town: Oxford University Press/NECC

Pak, Y (2002) Progressive Education and the Limits of Racial Recognition Revisited. *Educational Theory*, 51 (4): 487 – 497

Schollar, E (2001a) A Review of Two Evaluations of the Application of the READ Primary Schools Programme in the Eastern Cape Province of South Africa, *International Journal of Education Research*, 35: 205–216

Schollar, E (2001b) *The Final Report of the Evaluation of the Imbewu project*. Mimeo

Seekings, J (2001) *Making an Informed Investment: Improving the value of Public Expenditure in Primary and Secondary Schooling in South Africa*. Report to the Parliament of South Africa, commissioned by the Standing Committee on Public Accounts

Sharp, R & Green, A (1975) *Education and Social Control: A Study in Progressive Primary Education*. London: Routledge & Kegan Paul

Schoenfeld, A (2002) Making Mathematics Work for All Children: Issues of Standards, Testing and Equity, *Educational Researcher*, 31 (1): 13–25

Taylor, N (2002) Accountability and Support: Improving Public Schooling in South Africa: A Systematic Framework. In Roberts, J & Muller, J (eds) *Balancing support and accountability to improve school performance*. Johannesburg: JET

Taylor, N; Muller, J & Vinjevold, P (2003) *Getting Schools Working: Research and Systemic School Reform in South Africa*. Cape Town: Pearson Education

Tyack, DB (1974) *The One Best System*. Cambridge: Harvard University Press

Van Schalkwyk, O (1988) *The Education System: Theory and Practice*. Pretoria: Alkanto Publishers

Young, M (2002) Educational Reform in South Africa (1990–2000): An International Perspective. In Kraak, A & Young, M (eds) *Education in Retrospect: Policy and Implementation since 1990*. Pretoria: HSRC

9 The case of teacher education in post-apartheid South Africa: politics and priorities

Yusuf Sayed

Introduction

The emergence of the South African system of teacher education is rooted in the country's scheme of apartheid. As a consequence of the 1910 Constitution, white teacher training was located under the control of the then four provinces. The introduction of the *Bantu Education Act* in 1953 necessitated a system for training black teachers. A racially-stratified teacher education system emerged, with separate teacher education colleges for coloureds, Indians, and black people. As the 'homelands' policy took root in the early 1960s, each 'self-governing' and later 'independent' black homeland took control of teacher education in its own area. By the 1960s, teacher education colleges were segregated along the lines of race and ethnicity, creating partial, multiple, and separate pathways to teacher education.

By the early 1970s, teachers were trained in racially and ethnically separate colleges and universities. This was coupled with a system of posting which allocated trained teachers to different racially- and ethnically-segregated schools. In other words, each type of college and university trained teachers for specific schools.

The physical location of teacher education training institutions was based on the fragmented racial geography which socially engineered the 'life spaces' of South Africans. Training provision was driven by the needs of the system as a whole and, as such, was motivated by the specific political and ideological rationale of the apartheid system. It would be fair to characterise the teacher education system under apartheid as a 'system of systems', with different teacher education systems for different racial and ethnic groups. The fragmentation of the teacher education system determined whether individuals were trained, how they were trained, and where they were posted. The supply and demand of teachers was consequently conditioned by the need to maintain racial and ethnic segregation and was not related to an overall national plan.

By 1994 there were 18 education departments responsible for teacher education, with 32 'autonomous' universities and technikons, and about 105 colleges of education scattered throughout the apartheid/homelands system. This resulted in a very expensive system of teacher training (NTEA 1995) with marked differences in costs between and within colleges and universities.

For the black population, educational opportunities were extremely limited, with very few students successfully completing basic education, and even fewer successfully completing secondary schooling. Not only were there limited higher education opportunities, but the curriculum within the secondary school system was usually limited to humanities subjects such as history and religious studies. In this context, the logic of the system resulted in many students enrolling in teacher education training programmes in order to acquire higher educational opportunities. Under apartheid, the black population's higher education options were effectively limited to 'teaching or preaching'. Teacher education was thus a strategic response to the lack of higher educational opportunities for the black population.

With its fragmented and discrepant nature, the 'system' of teacher education was a costly model with wasteful duplication and overlap. Its rationale can only be understood in the context of the social and political logic of apartheid education. It is a legacy which the post-apartheid government has sought to address through its educational policy. Its initial response was to engage in a substantive process of reconfiguring teacher education at the curriculum and governance levels. These changes were concerned with ending the fragmentation that characterised apartheid teacher education. Teacher education policy is thus an attempt to ensure uniform norms and standards among all providers. It also seeks to ensure that all teachers work within the framework of the National System of Teacher Education (NSTE). Furthermore, education policy has simultaneously effected quality assurance (see Parker 2003).

This chapter examines two key policy changes that have occurred in teacher education since 1994. The first concerns the governance of the teacher education systems which resulted in the structural integration of all teacher education colleges into higher education institutions. This has shifted teacher education from a provincial to a national competency. The second key shift has occurred at the level of the curriculum with changes made to types of qualification, the system of accreditation, and new norms for educators.

These two changes are examined with a view to understanding the particular rationality that has underpinned teacher education change in South Africa. The paper argues that this rationality was a reflection of changing priorities and political contestations regarding the trajectory of educational reform in South Africa. The two changes were also affected by changing debates around, for example, the impact of HIV/AIDS on teacher supply and demand. The chapter argues that teacher education policy in post-apartheid South Africa is not simply a pragmatic and default policy response, but one that reflects a particular evolving logic of reform.

While HIV/AIDS is not central to this paper, it should be noted that the epidemic is expected to have a significant impact on the school sector in sub-Saharan Africa. A recent study notes that 'the AIDS epidemic is expected to have a highly adverse impact on the overall staffing in the education sector ... Unless appropriate measures are taken, the morale, motivation, and overall performance of all teachers and support personnel could be adversely affected' (Bennell 2003: Executive Summary). While no statistics exist as yet as to the actual impact of AIDS on absenteeism among teachers, there is growing awareness that this will be a problem for the sector.

This chapter draws on earlier research which provides a detailed empirical and analytical account of the nature of teacher education (Lewin, Samuel & Sayed 2003; see also Jansen 1998). It begins by unpacking four policy approaches to teacher education in South Africa. These provide a backdrop against which the changes in teacher education can be viewed. Although this chapter does not provide a comprehensive critique, it highlights some of their shortcomings through a discussion of the substantive changes achieved over the past decade in the areas of governance and curriculum in teacher education. It concludes by considering the politics of teacher education change in South Africa and the logic of post-apartheid educational transformation.

Different policy rationales for reconfiguring teacher education

Four different rationales are often provided to explain the character and nature of teacher education change in South Africa since 1994. These can be described as the loss of innocence approach, the efficiency and cost approach, the deficit approach, and that of symbolic rhetoric. Each of these is briefly discussed in turn. The remainder of the chapter provides an implicit critique, which is explicitly drawn out at the end.

Change as loss of innocence

The first approach sees the unfolding of teacher education policy as the 'loss of innocence'. In this view, previously radical ideas and commitments have been diluted and modified under the weight of pragmatic concerns. This position implies that the post-apartheid government's educational policies are a betrayal of the ideals and goals that underpinned the anti-apartheid struggle. Specific concerns are that equity has been compromised in the governance and financing of education after apartheid, that privilege is maintained, albeit in different ways, and that the forces of conservatism and self-interest have reasserted their ascendancy over more democratic dispensations.

'Loss' is depicted in a number of ways: in the incorporation of colleges into the higher education sector, thus losing the 'special character' of such institutions; in the failure to effectively overcome the inequities in teacher deployment, recruitment, and conditions of service within the broad goal of achieving equity and redress; and in the failure to prevent the 'triumph' of 'white' institutions over those that service the black communities. All these losses are subject to political and factual counter-argument but, in essence, reflect a belief that changes have not occurred in the desired direction. Teacher education post-apartheid is thus positioned as 'victim' of the pragmatic orientations of a new bureaucracy that has betrayed the 'true ideal' of a new South Africa.

Change as necessary cost-saving

The second approach sees the transformation of teacher education as one which overvalues efficiency and effectiveness in the system, and undervalues other social goals, processes and content. It finds its genesis in the adoption by the post-apartheid government of policies and procedures that emphasise cost-containment through central control and regulation. Teacher training is one such instance: the incorporation of colleges into the higher education system was driven by cost considerations. A number of analyses indicated that dedicated mono-function institutions were more costly than multifunction institutions. The argument was advanced that it was four times more expensive to educate teachers in colleges of education than in universities, due mainly to lower lecturer-student ratios in colleges of education. Critical to this approach was the view that training teachers at universities would reduce unit costs (Crouch 2001; Parker 2003). The case was thus made that universities would be more efficient providers of teacher education.

The rationalisation and right-sizing policy initiated in 1995 with the new teacher-to-pupil norms could be seen as another instance of this approach. The argument advanced is that, particularly in ex-House of Representatives (HoR), House of Delegates (HoD), and House of Assembly (HoA) schools, the lower teacher-to-pupil ratios were costly. This argument also had equity overtones as the main beneficiaries of new teacher-pupil norms would be ex-Department of Education and Training (DET) schools. This example reflects how, in South African teacher education, efficiency imperatives overlap with equity concerns.

These two instances illustrate concerns that teacher education be efficiently managed, and that costs per student should be 'managed down' (DoE 1996). This emphasis on efficiency in teacher education can be seen as driven by the desire to reduce costs in the education system in general.

Change as correcting teacher deficit

The third approach is grounded in a deficit-model of teachers. The assumption is that teachers are found lacking in a number of areas, including skills. This perspective presents teachers and college staff as undisciplined, failing to spend enough time on tasks, and as regularly absent. 'Teacher bashing' has become a familiar activity within the public media, which seldom reports on the stresses of coping with the numerous roles and identities that are demanded of teachers. While media reports may in part be true, it engenders a negative image of teachers.

The negative image of teachers feeds into a particular policy modality for teacher education which calls for greater surveillance and regulation of teachers' work. Examples of such policy levers are Codes of Professional Conduct, specification of the number of hours a teaching year involves, and inspection.

Policy change as symbolic rhetoric

The fourth approach is wedded to the idea of policy as complex and contradictory. This view highlights the messiness of the policy process and projects policy as often comprising symbolic gestures. Researchers working with this perspective would see policy as a government-led political process which they would argue ignores the 'realities on the ground'. Another variant of this is the view that policies are never intended to be implemented because they are focused on short-term political considerations such as ensuring electoral victory for the ruling political party. Another possible position within this perspective is to see policy as a state of fragile consensus in that policy texts speak in a 'single, public, good voice' which is sufficiently generalised to accommodate a diverse set of interest groups or 'stakeholders'. As part of this politics of compromise, policy becomes 'anything to everyone'.

These four approaches highlight different reasons for the reconfiguration of teacher education in post-apartheid South Africa. In a sense, teacher education policy is a hybrid of different rationales. What emerges is a series of tensions in the construction of teacher education policy. These are:
- Tension between equity and redress and economic growth and development;
- Tension between greater surveillance of the work of teachers and greater autonomy; and
- Tension between system maintenance and radical restructuring.

These tensions reflect the strategy of educational change and transformation in post-apartheid South Africa. They raise issues about the balance between centralisation and decentralisation, the nature of the state, and the national and international significance of the reconfiguration of teacher education. They are addressed in the following section with particular reference to governance and curriculum changes.

Reconfiguring teacher education: governance and curriculum changes

Governance

Teacher education was reconfigured in the mid-1990s in the context of a reshaped national education policy. The structural reconfiguration of teacher education has affected the way in which the system is governed and quality assured.

This reconfiguration of teacher education is arguably one of the most significant policy changes in post-apartheid education. On the one hand, one of the effects of the reconfiguration has been to end, in a relatively short space of time, the existence of separate teacher education institutions. This step marks a contrast to many other countries. South Africa is one of the few Anglophone countries on the African continent which in 2003 did not have a separate and dedicated system of teacher education colleges.

On the other hand, the move has effectively sited teacher education firmly within the higher education sphere. This also runs counter to the international trend, which increasingly places teacher education at the school level. The Malawian approach is, for example, essentially a school-based teacher education training system. In England and Wales, a significant proportion of the time trainees spend in a teacher education programme occurs at the school level. These examples reflect a move toward making teacher education more school-based and to reducing training time spent at universities and colleges.

In short, the effect of the structural reconfiguration has been to end the existence of a separate sphere of teacher education, and to make it part of the higher education system. Many commentators have expressed surprise, claiming that this is the action of a controlling state or that it reflects a lack of interest in teacher education. Others have interpreted it as the loss of policy idealism when compared to the work of the National Education Policy Investigation (NEPI), which emphasised the separate existence of a teacher education college sector. At the time of the NEPI process, this outcome was not envisaged (see Lewin, Samuel & Sayed 2003; Jansen 1998).

What needs to be unpacked in the above claims is the nature of change in post-apartheid society. The change to teacher education is not surprising, as the trajectory of state-led change was evident from 1994. Specifically, the lead has come from the national Department of Education (DoE) as the structural reconfiguration of teacher education was already in place in 1996 with White Paper 1 and the *National Education Policy Act* (NEPA) (RSA 1996). The NEPA empowers the Minister of Education to set the guidelines for the education and accreditation of educators and to determine matters such as the curriculum framework and the certification of qualifications. The national policy framework is an enabling piece of legislation giving the Minister the right to shape the trajectory of educational change. The policy architecture for decisive intervention in many areas of education policy, including teacher education, was thus put in place during the first period of democratic rule. Such a trajectory continued when it came to the contentious issue of the emergence of private higher education institutions in which the *Higher*

Education Amendment Act gave the Minister the right to determine which institution could carry the title of a university and under what conditions.

The specific mechanism for the structural reconfiguration of higher education is the *Higher Education Act* (RSA 1997). It enables the Minister of Education to declare the incorporation of a college of education into a national public higher education system. In 1998 the Minister and the DoE produced the *Incorporation of Colleges of Education into the Higher Education Sector Report* (1998b). This report was discussed and approved by the Heads of Education Departments and the Council of Education Ministers (CEM) and was followed by a Ministerial Declaration of Colleges of Education as subdivisions of universities and technikons.

A multiplicity of structures and committees responsible for the governance and quality assurance emerged. These included the Committee for Teacher Education Policy (COTEP), a sub-committee of the Higher Education Committee (HECOM), the Council on Higher Education (CHE), and the DoE's Branch for Higher Education (BHE) and the South African Qualifications Authority (SAQA).

The assurance of quality and accreditation, at least in policy terms, came to fall within the remit of CHE's Higher Education's Quality Assurance Committee (QC). The work of HEQC, with regards to teacher education, was shared with SAQA (RSA 1995), which was responsible for the standards of teacher education and quality assurance of the programme. The work of SAQA was initially complemented by the setting up of National Standards Bodies (NSBs) and Standards Generating Bodies (SGBs), which determined the standards for teacher education. At the time of writing, SAQA was in the process of establishing an Education and Training Quality Assurance (ETQA) structure for determining quality assurance in the teacher education programme.

In effect, the restructuring of teacher education reveals a new state coping with multiple and contradictory demands. First, it was expected to deliver a more just and humane society in a climate of rising expectations and hopeful promise. Second, it was simultaneously expected to provide the conditions for economic growth and development. It was presumed that the state would unify a divided society without threatening the white population. Restitution was therefore to take a limited form. Third, the state was expected to be responsive to the will of the people and to guarantee increased participation while extending democracy in society. In particular, the state was expected to establish a sound and vibrant relationship with organisations in and of civil society. The new South African state was therefore expected to fulfil at least three different functions, namely, ensure distributive justice, provide the conditions for capital accumulation, and ensure greater responsiveness and participation in forging unity/nationhood (the rainbow nation/state).

In negotiating these diverse and contradictory demands, a state emerged that on the one hand was internally reorganised into a national state at the centre and on the other was reorganised into dispersed, decentralised states at sites (provinces) (see Carrim & Sayed 1992 for elaboration). The semi-federalist, decentralised constitution of the state involves different activities and mechanisms of co-ordination between the centre and the sites (see Sayed 1995). The national centre for education is responsible for the funding of the sites but is not involved in the management and control of schools within the sites.

On the other hand, the state retained significant evaluative and norm-setting powers (Sayed 2000; Sayed & Jansen 2001), constituting what could be referred to as an evaluative state. This involves the central Ministry of Education setting uniform norms and standards through legislation that prevails across all sites. For the evaluative state, legislation is used as a constraining mechanism to control the actions of internal state actors. Thus, the argument advanced here is that the state is still powerful, albeit differently so.

One of the key conflicts in the constitution of the state was its semi-federal nature and, specifically for teacher education, the locus of authority. Until the time of change, teacher education was the shared function of national and provincial government. University teacher education providers fell within the remit of the national Ministry of Education (specifically the higher education branch), while colleges of education were under provincial control. The locus of authority for teacher education was the subject of much policy contestation, with some arguing for independence along the lines accorded to universities, others arguing for provincial control, and some arguing for their incorporation into universities (for further discussion see Carrim 2003; Parker 2003 and Steele 2003). The state has effected a constitutional, functional shift in which colleges of education were moved from the provincial to the national level and incorporated into universities, a process that has been underway since 2001. This move represents the first instance in post-apartheid education policy where the national ministry has been able to alter the relationships with provincial ministries, albeit with provincial consent. The importance of this act will become significant in the future when other issues are battled over. What it signals is the state's ability to use the legislative provisions at its disposal to effect changes. While many may see this in a negative way, it does hold out strong possibilities of decisive interventions for the purposes of redress and social justice. In this sense the structural reconfiguration of teacher education reflects a strong state which is able to act.

In the final instance, the policy decision has been to 'incorporate' all teacher education colleges into universities, with the provision that some could exist independently subject to being multi-site institutions with at least 2 000 FTEs (full-time equivalents). In other words, independent teacher education colleges could function as single-purpose, dedicated institutions if they were large enough. What has emerged from this process is the effective phasing out of colleges of education due to their incorporation into the university sector and, consequently, universities becoming the main providers of both primary and secondary teacher education. This reflects a direct reversal of about 90 years of apartheid teacher education policy. This shift has been motivated not only on grounds of comparative cost between universities and colleges of education, but also signals a belief that what is required in teacher education in South Africa is a strong focus on 'subject/learning area content knowledge' and a research culture which universities rather than colleges are seen to provide. It can also be construed as an attempt to inject into the university sector a longer-term commitment to teacher provision, rather than the conventional one-year diploma.

One governance question that has only now begun to be adequately addressed is that of 'private' teacher education providers. The focus on public teacher education providers has led to insufficient concern with the growth of the private education sector, which by 2000 accounted for about 40 000 students (about 37 per cent of all teacher education students). The majority of these 'private' students were enrolled in programmes that were 'partnership/franchise' arrangements with public universities, including the University of Port Elizabeth (UPE) with Azalia, and the University of Pretoria (UP) with Success College. At the same time that the state was acting decisively to restructure the college sector, there was a rival and parallel process of public institutions allying themselves with private providers to maximise income by recruiting students into 'soft' fields such as teacher education. In a sense this process has been fed by the discourse of derision which has made teaching an unattractive option and thus many have used this as a route out of teaching (Heystek, Smit & Sayed 2003).

While the changing landscape of teacher education has been a centrally directed strategy it is important to note that what it has in effect done is to decentralise teacher education. In becoming a national competency, teacher education is no longer faced with the strong centralisation it experienced under provincial control which, for example, includes the vetting of papers and moderation of marking. Thus teacher education has secured the same degree of autonomy that universities enjoy, including curriculum autonomy (discussed below). This shift frees the national and provincial education departments from micro-managing colleges. This in effect disperses conflicts from the centre and frees the state from management responsibility. In this respect the changes are consistent with the creation of an oversight and evaluative state as explained earlier.

More crucially, these governance changes re-site college lecturers as employees of autonomous institutions rather than public service authorities. This means that the state (centre and province) is able to free itself in the long-term from the financial obligation to provide salaries. More importantly the basis of college lecturer salaries will now be dependent on student numbers (as is the case of universities) rather than being a standard public civil service contract (as was the case under provincial control).

Curriculum

With the change to the structural landscape comes significant alteration to curriculum issues in teacher education. The change to teacher education curriculum takes its lead from school curriculum changes. Curriculum 2005 (C2005) and the work of the Review Committee (DoE 2000a) which produced the *Revised National Curriculum Statement* (RNCS) have committed the education system to an outcomes-based education system, with the emphasis on learning areas rather than on discrete and separate subjects. The key epistemological shift in this framework has been a focus on learner-centred approaches, identifying different types of competencies that learners are expected to achieve, and the different roles that educators are expected to play. The new curriculum sets up different expectations of teachers from those held under apartheid, which expected very little of teachers. Teacher education providers are accordingly also expected to provide newly qualified teachers with the skills to operate in an outcomes-based framework, to train them to work in a learner-focused, critical and problem-solving environment, and to work on the basis of learning areas. In many senses, this is a welcome shift away from a rote and transmission-oriented learning approach. But there is a risk that providers might focus only on teaching methods, and ignore the need to provide trainee teachers with the content knowledge they also require.

These curricular changes are underpinned by a key shift in what it means to be an educator in post-apartheid South Africa. In 1997, the DoE outlined Norms and Standards for Teacher Education (NSTE) (DoE 1997, 2000b and 2000c). It provides a detailed account of what a competent educator is expected to be. This policy identifies seven roles for teachers/educators in South Africa. They are meant to be learning mediators, interpreters and designers of learning programmes, leaders, administrators and managers, scholars, researchers and lifelong learners, play a community, citizenship and pastoral role and be learning area specialists (see Christie and Jansen 1999 for a critical analysis of the underlying epistemology of this shift). What it means to be a teacher/educator has also been affected by the South African Council for Educators (SACE) set up in 1996, which is responsible for teacher registration, discipline and conduct, and professional development. The conditions of service under which teachers labour is determined by the *Employment of Educators Act* (RSA 1998) and the statutory Education Labour Relations Council (ELRC). A further policy document that will affect teacher work is the proposed regulations for teacher professional development and career pathing and grading under consideration by the national DoE.

The implication of C2005 and the RNCS is that teacher education providers are expected to reorientate their own as well as school-based staff. This occurs at the same time as they have to induct new entrants into the new framework as well as provide in-service support to those they had trained under the previous system.

The crucial shift is that teacher education colleges, as part of the higher education system, now have more curriculum autonomy than they did under provincial control. They are now freed from direct control including determination of curriculum, examination, and marking that characterised their location under provincial control. This is a positive shift which is not sufficiently recognised in the debate about teacher education in South Africa. On the one hand it frees colleges from the restrictive practice under provincial control, which in many senses reflected a school-type management style. It would be fair to say that most provinces simply saw colleges as 'beyond secondary' schools and most staff recruited saw colleges as a 'step up' from school teaching. The integration within the higher education sector offers a stronger possibility for a different approach to curriculum renewal. On the other hand, the integration 'forces' universities and technikons to engage with teacher training in ways they have not done before. For example, they need now to consider more clearly who they are training and at what level. But this does not apply equally to all universities and technikons. Those who are not integrated with colleges now are likely to project themselves as 'post-graduate' elite training institutions. In essence the key curriculum shift that has been brought about is the decentralisation of teacher education curricula.

Decentralising curriculum in this way, as noted earlier, creates a more evaluative state. Thus, what it increases is the transaction cost of monitoring and assuring quality, given the panoply of structures involved. The complexity and high transaction cost of the quality assurance system is reflective of the approach to governance in education more generally. The policy approach of the new government has been to create broad-based participatory structures that are meant to be inclusive and representative. The success of this approach hinges on the extent to which such fora are able to secure 'sufficient consensus' and agree on binding behaviours. In the absence of such conditions, decision-making and co-ordinated action may be difficult to achieve (Sayed & Jansen 2001).

The dispersal of quality assurance reflects, in more general terms, a particular paradox of the post-apartheid state's change strategy for education. On the one hand the narrative that unfolds is a change strategy which utilises the centralising thrust of legislation to effect change. It is important to note, though, that this centralising thrust is highly individualised as it centres on individuals with incumbency. Thus it is the Minister of Education as an individual who is empowered to act decisively. On the other hand, the key effect of the change is to disperse authority and controls which will reduce central responsibility and make it more difficult to intervene directly. But one real effect of this is that the system becomes opaque and is mainly navigable by those within and close to the core.

The decentralisation of teacher education through incorporation raises a number of curriculum problems at the institutional level. One way in which this is manifest is the theory/practice divide: colleges have argued that 'special' kinds of providers are more intimately connected with the realities of schooling. It has also been argued that universities might inject into colleges a stronger research base for their work. In a sense, at the curriculum level, the structural changes have surfaced the theory/practice divide debate. The structural changes also require a merging of two institutions with different understandings and approaches to curriculum development.

The change to the curriculum has a crucial effect on teachers and their work. In this regard the teacher education change has brought about a significant rethink (though there are serious doubts about the extent to which it can be implemented). The seven roles that teachers are expected to play represent a significant advance from the very narrow notion of teacher as subject specialist/content transmitter. In an international development context, it reflects recognition of the many roles that teachers play in schools and the multitasked nature of the profession. However, as Jessop and Penny (1998) and others point out, there is a gap between the seven professional roles identified in policy, and the practices in classrooms. They point out that, in practice, teachers are unable to fulfil the requirements for all seven roles adequately. This poses a challenge to teacher education institutions regarding their training methods.

Learning areas are closely tied to the seven new roles of teachers. Learning areas reflect an attempt to project a modernising government in concert with global developments. They also represent a radical break from the past and encourage (or expect) teachers to operate in flexible and multitasked ways. It should be noted that for primary education, learning areas are hardly new; in many senses they codify practices already in existence.

Much of the discussion of teacher education curricula has taken place largely at the macro-level, focusing on issues such as expectations of an ideal educator or the types of programmes that should be recognised. Where curriculum issues have been addressed, these have been in response to the curriculum changes in schooling. As such, the specific content and pedagogies of initial and continuing teacher education have not been sufficiently discussed and problematised.

In the new policy framework, teaching has been conceptually recast as education. This is a significant policy change, based on the grounds that teaching is an activity akin to other aspects of professional education work, such as working with adult learners. This significantly alters the professional context in that it breaks with the traditional tight coupling of institutional forms such as schooling and teaching. In other words, it potentially allows those trained to function in diverse contexts. This point is significant in the developing world context as it becomes obvious that low participation rates in schools are related to the fact that what government offers to those who are marginalised, are traditional schools run in traditional ways. In his analysis of teacher identity, Carrim (2003) notes how this thrust is broadly progressive, but tends to diffuse the specific occupational activity of teaching and, potentially, implies interchangeability between different educational activities. Carrim (2003) foregrounds the loss of agency in this redefinition, noting the significance of the shift with respect to the changing nature of professional practices, an issue that has not been adequately debated and theorised.

Conclusion

This chapter has mapped the changes to teacher education in post-apartheid South Africa. It has argued that teacher education changes in South Africa are more than the loss of innocence or policy symbolism. It has argued that what has occurred can be described as substantive and fundamental change albeit for reasons with widely discrepant reactions.

In essence the chapter argues that much of the criticism of the policy changes reflects an ideal image of what teaching and teacher education is about. However, none of the critics really spells this out in precise terms. At the same time, many of the progressive critics of policy have based their analysis on some measure of 'deviation' between what they feel should have occurred in post-apartheid South Africa and what did in reality happen. Many efforts have been made to explain this deviation in terms of gaps (Sayed 2002), failure to pay attention to implementation (Sayed & Jansen 2001), betrayal of the poor and a middle-class settlement. In a sense, there is an overwhelming feeling that not much has changed; a sense of loss.

While there is merit in the claims made by critics, there have, by all accounts, been significant shifts in teacher education. What needs to be acknowledged is the fact that in South Africa, unlike in many other countries, teacher education has been relocated (back) into the higher education sphere, a move that bucks much of the international trend. At the same time, this move, coupled with policies such as those in the norms and standards document, radically alters the work of teachers and teacher education providers. In this shift the state has effected a complex balance between decentralisation and centralisation, a consensus which is likely to rupture and in some cases already has.

One of the more significant changes has been related to the state's ability to act in a decisive fashion to restructure the educational landscape of post-apartheid South Africa. If there is one major difference between the first two phases of democratic rule in South Africa, it is the fact that what is emerging is more decisive action. This is not to imply that not much happened before. In fact, the earlier phase laid the legislative framework for decisive transformation action. In this sense the state needs to be continually challenged to act and that crucially depends on the existence of civil society. This is already beginning to happen with the Education Rights Project which, if it realises its potential, may force the state to utilise the arsenal at its disposal. In this regard, the wide political significance of the reconfiguration of teacher education is that it is the precursor to the restructuring of higher education in general. This small structural reconfiguration thus allows the state to test reactions to more wide-scale changes should it choose or be compelled to do so.

This chapter has sought to show that the particular form of the post-apartheid South African state that has come into being is, in many senses, and this is not sufficiently acknowledged, one that has removed itself from direct and day-to-day intervention – a state that is less intrusive in all spheres and domains. But it is nonetheless a strong state securing this strength from its ability to monitor, evaluate, and set norms and standards. In other words, it is a state that could be argued to be more powerful in that is has secured for itself greater surveillance power, and its effects are more insidious in that they operate through capillaries and indirectly. But it is also a state constrained by its commitment to co-operative governance, which has generated a Byzantine web of structures and procedures. It could be argued that this makes it even more powerful and its web reduces the efficacy of participation.

Related to the idea of the state is the change strategy that emerges in post-apartheid South Africa. The chapter has argued that the strategy has been to use the 'evaluative powers' of the state to intervene decisively in teacher education, resulting in a greater degree of decentralisation. In short the modality of change has been largely legislative and in some sense top-down, given a very clear focus on national norms and standards.

The changes to teacher education in post-apartheid South Africa have, as the chapter notes, been responsive to the specific legacy of apartheid education. At the same time the changes reflect a wider strategy of educational change which can be said to be based on the power of the state to set norms and standards. The change strategy has not, surprisingly, reflected a centralising approach with strong decentralising impulses. And unlike many of the earlier analyses, the chapter argues that there have been important changes. Moreover, the changes to teacher education set the scene for other transformations that may occur in relation to politics, priorities, and approaches.

References

Bennell, P (2003) The Impact of the AIDS Epidemic on Schooling in Sub-Saharan Africa. Background paper for the Biennial Meeting of the Association for the Development of Education in Africa, December 2003

Carrim, N (2003) Teacher Identities: Tensions between Roles. In Lewin, K; Samuel, M & Sayed, Y (eds) (2003) *Changing Patterns of Teacher Education in South Africa: Policy, Practice and Prospects.* Johannesburg: Heinemann

Carrim, N & Sayed, Y (1992) Civil Society, Social Movements and the National Education Co-ordinating Committee (NECC), *Perspectives in Education,* 14 (1): 21–34

Christie, P & Jansen, J (eds) (1999) *Changing Curriculum: Studies on Outcomes-Based Education in South Africa.* Cape Town: Juta

Crouch, L (2001) *Turbulence or Orderly Change? Teacher Supply and Demand in South Africa – Current Status, Future Needs and The Impact of HIV/AIDS.* Discussion Paper 26. Multi-Site Teacher Education Research Project, Centre for International Education, University of Sussex

Department of Education (DoE) (1996) *Medium Term Expenditure Framework.* Pretoria: Government Printers

Department of Education (1997) *Draft Norms and Standards for School Funding in Terms of the South African Schools Act* (No. 84 of 1996), Government Gazette, Vol 388, No. 18349. Pretoria: Government Printers

Department of Education (1998) *The Incorporation of Colleges of Education into the Higher Education Sector: A Framework for Implementation.* Pretoria: Government Printers

Department of Education (2000a) *A South African Curriculum for the Twenty-First Century: Report of the Review Committee on Curriculum 2005*. Pretoria: DoE

Department of Education (2000b) *Norms and Standards for Educators*. Government Gazette, Vol 415, No. 20844. Pretoria: Government Printers

Department of Education (2000c) *Criteria for the Recognition and Evaluation of Qualifications for Employment in Education Based on the Norms and Standards for Educators*. Government Gazette, Vol 423, No. 21565. Pretoria: Government Printers

Heysteck, J; Smit, B & Sayed, Y (2003) The Case of University of Pretoria: Franchising Option. In Lewin, K; Samuel, M & Sayed, Y (eds) *Changing Patterns of Teacher Education in South Africa: Policy, Practice and Prospects*. Johannesburg: Heinemann

Hofmeyr, J & Hall, G (1995) National Teacher Education Audit: Synthesis Report. Johannesburg: Edupol

Jansen, J (1998) Curriculum Reform in South Africa: A Critical Analysis of Outcomes-Based Education, *Cambridge Journal of Education*. 28(3): 321–331

Jessop, T & Penny, A (1998) A Study of Teacher Voice and Vision in the Narratives of Rural South African and Gambian School Teachers, *International Journal of Educational Development*, 18 (5): 393–403

Lewin, K; Samuel, M & Sayed, Y (eds) (2003) *Changing Patterns of Teacher Education in South Africa: Policy, Practice and Prospects*. Johannesburg: Heinemann

Parker, B (2003) Roles and Responsibilities, Institutional Landscapes and Curriculum Mindscapes: A Partial View of Teacher Education Policy in South Africa: 1990 to 2000. In Lewin, K; Samuel, M & Sayed, Y (eds) *Changing Patterns of Teacher Education in South Africa: Policy, Practice and Prospects*. Johannesburg: Heinemann

Republic of South Africa (1995) *South African Qualifications Authority Act*. No. 58 of 1998. Pretoria: Government Printers

Republic of South Africa (1996) *National Education Policy Act*. No. 697 of 1996. Pretoria: Government Printers

Republic of South Africa (1997) *Higher Education Act*. No. 101 of 1997. Pretoria: Government Printers

Republic of South Africa (1998) *Employment of Educators Act*. No. 76 of 1998. Pretoria: Government Printers

Sayed, Y (1995) Educational Policy Developments in South Africa, 1990–1994: A Critical Examination of the Policy of Educational Decentralisation. Unpublished PhD dissertation

Sayed, Y with Akyeampong, K & Ampiah, JG (2000) Partnership and Participation in whole school development in Ghana, *Education Through Partnership*, 4(2): 40–51

Sayed, Y & Jansen, J (2001) *Implementing Education Reform: The Case of South Africa*. Cape Town: UCT Press

Sayed, Y (2002) Changing Forms of Teacher Education in South Africa: A Case Study of Policy Change, *International Journal of Educational Development*, 22 (3–4): 381–395

Steele, M (2003) Teacher Education in KZN: The Case of the Incorporation of Colleges. In Lewin, K; Samuel, M & Sayed, Y (eds) *Changing Patterns of Teacher Education in South Africa: Policy, Practice and Prospects*. Johannesburg: Heinemann

10 Teacher unions, policy struggles and educational change, 1994 to 2004

Logan Govender

> We need a unionism that not only restricts itself to traditional union concerns, such as wage bargaining and conditions of employment, but to also address broader issues, such as ownership and the role of the state and what is our role within that state.
> (SADTU National Executive Committee meeting,
> 13 to 14 August 1998: 21)

Introduction

South Africa has a long history of teacher unionism. At an organisational level, the face of teacher unions has changed considerably, reflecting the changed socio-political landscape of South Africa in the 1990s. More importantly, given the changed nature of the state, teacher-state relations have changed. Overall, South African teacher unions currently enjoy a much closer relationship with government than they did before 1994. They are represented in joint policy-making forums such as the Education Labour Relations Council (ELRC), the South African Council for Educators (SACE) and the Public Service Co-ordinating Bargaining Council (PSCBC). They also have two representatives each in the Department of Education (DoE) who are employed to ensure collaboration and sharing of ideas, specifically with regard to curriculum and its implementation.

The experience of teacher unions in South Africa is not unique. Prior to the 1960s, members of the National Education Association in the United States were viewed as 'handmaidens' of the state, and functioned as agents for the preservation of the status quo. The national teachers' unions in Korea (KFTA) and in Mexico were seen by many as serving to legitimate the decisions of state elites and not the interests of educators (Ginsburg, Kamat, Raghu & Weaver 1995 and Murillo 1999). In Mexico, the National Union of Education Workers (SNTE) was established with strong backing from the Institutional Revolutionary Party (PRI) and later served as a political machine for the party at elections. In return for their close relationship with the governing party, union leaders were rewarded with management positions in the educational bureaucracy and appointed to key positions at the legislative and executive levels (Murillo 1999: 40). This narrative bears a striking resemblance to the rise of the South African Democratic Teachers' Union (SADTU) in South Africa, especially its close political association with the African National Congress (ANC) from the 1980s to the present. This is part of the story, but not the whole story of teacher unionism in South Africa. The full story deserves closer investigation, which this chapter endeavours to accomplish.

Whereas there was a small amount of literature dealing with teacher unions and the relationship with the state in South Africa in the 1980s and early 1990s, there is nothing that charts and attempts to explain changes in the more recent period. This chapter will try to provide such an analysis. The chapter will argue that the relationship of teacher unions to government in South Africa since 1994 has been mediated by the fractured nature of the union movement, a consequence of political, ideological and cultural factors. It will begin with a historical overview, examine teacher unions' growth after 1994 in the context of a favourable labour relations environment, and then highlight unions' role in the development of policy. The chapter will demonstrate that the status of teacher unions in South Africa since 1990 has improved significantly, leading to a powerful teacher union presence in the policy domain, partly due to a new-found unity among teacher unions. Associated with this trend is a more flexible approach to teacher unionism and professionalism by government and teacher unions alike. Teacher unions' agency has highlighted particular strategies in negotiating the difficult terrain of 'policy politics', especially where contestation over ownership and control of policy is concerned. Central to teacher unions' ability to negotiate the policy terrain are organisational challenges, notably the perennial struggle over membership recruitment, union growth and gender politics, challenges compounded by the threat of HIV/AIDS.

The chapter uses a conceptual framework founded on an understanding of the political nature of teacher union-government relations that are shaped by shared partisan identities and union fragmentation (Murillo 1999). Teacher unions have influenced education policy and social change throughout their history. Conversely, the development and history of teacher unions are closely related to their political relationship with the government of the day. Because of their role in policy implementation, teacher unions are able not only to sabotage or promote reforms but also to influence citizens' views about government performance (Murillo 1999). There is, therefore, an inherently 'political' edge to the work of teacher unions, which also have the potential for effecting social change (Ginsburg et al. 1995).

An important factor in understanding teacher-state relations is teachers' conceptions of the ideologies of professionalism and unionism.[1] The traditional view, which juxtaposes these ideologies, has been the subject of much criticism, particularly since the early 1980s (Ginsburg, Meyenn & Miller 1980; Ozga & Lawn 1981). More recently, an approach emphasising collaboration rather than confrontation, and advocating the complementarity of both professionalism and unionism, has emerged. Notions of 'new realism' and 'professional unionism' exemplify this approach (Torres, Cho, Kachur, Loyo, Mollis, Nagao & Thompson 2000).[2] The notion of 'new realism' emphasises improving services to members, regaining professional status and leadership in the educational debate and developing a long-term vision on educational reform. In like vein, professional unionism, while retaining the traditional features of unionism and professionalism, goes further and recognises the need for teacher unions to address issues of school productivity and efficiency as well as mechanisms for performance management, discipline and dealing with incompetence (Torres et al. 2000: 12–13). In this chapter, it will be argued that while teacher unions in South Africa were constrained by the professionalism-unionism dichotomy in the early 1990s, there is an increasing trend towards professional unionism that has underpinned the nature of teacher union-state relations in recent times.

The evidence for the chapter is based on my current research relating to teachers' participation in policy development.[3] Interview material and documentary sources, both primary and secondary, have been used.

Teacher unions and the transition to democracy

For teacher unions, the political and social transformation of the 1990s, and the impact of neo-liberal agendas,[4] have presented new challenges, not only with regard to workplace relations, but also in relation to questions of education policy and social justice. The decision to embark on a negotiated political settlement in South Africa was crucial. The political compromises in the transition to democracy allowed actors spawned by the apartheid regime to wage their own struggle for the protection of privileges accumulated during apartheid.

Teacher unions were not immune to the contested nature of South Africa's transition. This became apparent during the formulation of new policies for school governance and funding, as teachers continued to be divided along political and racial lines. The nature of civil society changed. It was no longer confined to the oppressed black majority, as small but powerful interest groups, notably middle-class – especially white – parents, business groups and 'policy experts' entered the fray (Govender 2001). At the same time, mass-based constituencies within civil society, including teacher unions and women's movements, found their agency power somewhat constrained because of their loyalty to the new ANC government. Many of their leaders had become part of the new establishment. SADTU's president, Shepherd Mdladlana, and general secretary, Randall van den Heever, became ANC Members of Parliament (MPs). Conversely, white teacher unions struggled to find an identity, some aligning themselves with the new, non-racial order while others sought comfort in existing racial structures.

In due course, the government's adoption of neo-liberal economic policies (exemplified by the Growth, Employment and Redistribution Programme [GEAR] in 1996), such as privatisation schemes and cost-cutting measures, gave rise to tensions with the labour movement and other civil society constituencies. The government's social transformation agenda had moved national policy sharply to the right, thereby subjecting the goals of equity and democratisation in education to the rationale of market-led fiscal and governance policies (Motala & Singh 2001). Simultaneously, there has been a revival of human capital theory in which teachers' roles are narrowly conceived as producers of human capital for economic growth; and the introduction of new policies promoting new forms of management, teacher accountability and outcomes-based curricula (Chisholm 1999).

It is within this backdrop of political compromise, the realignment of political coalitions, issues of identity and loyalty and the modern hegemony of neo-liberalism, that the role of teacher unions in educational change will be located. First, though, it is necessary to reflect on the historical trajectory of teacher union development in South Africa, and how that trajectory found expression during South Africa's transition to democracy.

Historical overview

Teacher unions' engagement with government and policy in South Africa was mediated by the racial policies of the apartheid government. In the main, white teachers enjoyed substantial representation in policy-making at the state level, while black[5] teachers were deliberately excluded from participating in education policy processes (Chisholm 1999). The latter worked under a bureaucratic and authoritarian system, in which decisions and policies were formulated for them by mainly white government officials. This was the prevailing pattern until the early 1990s.

Historically, the development of teacher unions in South Africa has come to mirror the broader context of socio-political change, an integral part of which is the ideological tension between professionalism and unionism. During the 60s and 70s, teacher unions were divided along racial lines, in keeping with the apartheid system of separate education departments. Thus, separate teacher organisations for whites, coloureds, Indians and Africans had established themselves by the 1960s. These organisations espoused a traditional 'professional' approach in dealing with the education authorities, relying primarily on strategies of consultation and persuasion, while eschewing militant and 'political' action (Hyslop 1990). In the 1980s, with the intensification of the political struggle for liberation, several progressive teacher unions emerged. These unions adopted a strong unionist approach in dealing with educational change and policy. From the outset, the progressive unions had a combined political and educational agenda. They constituted themselves as non-racial[6] and allied themselves to the vanguard organisations of the liberation struggle, notably the ANC, the Congress of South African Trade Unions (Cosatu) and the South African Communist Party (SACP). They attacked the 'professional' associations for their conservatism and apolitical stance. A serious schism resulted – pitting the new generation of progressive unions against the older, professional associations. The latter were labelled conservative and prioritised their commitment to the interests of the 'child' over those of 'politics'; while the former were labelled radical and regarded themselves as 'workers' and would not balk at taking strike action (Chisholm 1999; Govender 1996). The discourse around whether teachers were 'workers' or 'professionals' became 'symbolic markers of political difference' (Chisholm 1999: 114).

However, towards the latter half of the 1980s, a serious attempt was made to unify the teaching profession on the basis of a single, non-racial union with the objective of contributing to the establishment of a non-racial, democratic education system. The National Teachers' Unity Forum (NTUF) failed in its objective, resulting in the establishment of two broad formations in the early 1990s, namely the National Professional Teachers' Organisation of South Africa (NAPTOSA) and SADTU (Govender 1996). Three key factors led to the demise of the unity initiative: failure to reach consensus on the question of political alignment, of which a strong undercurrent was differences over the 'political' role of teachers, both within and outside the classroom; disagreement on whether a unified body should be based on unionism or professionalism, encapsulated by SADTU's insistence on the teacher's right to strike as opposed to NAPTOSA's emphasis on the learner's entitlement to uninterrupted learning; and, whether a united organisation should be a federal or a unitary structure.[7]

Teacher organisations, therefore, had fragmented along political, ideological and organisational lines. The legacy of this history was to carry over, albeit somewhat differently, into the transition. An interesting dynamic of the 1990s is the further splintering of teacher organisations, an effect that can be explained in both historical and contemporary political terms.

The changing face and strength of teacher unions

The shape of teacher unions in the 1990s was to be influenced quite decisively by new education and labour legislation. The *National Education Policy Act* of 1996 provided for the management of education along national and provincial lines, which compelled teacher unions to restructure to ensure a presence in the nine provinces; moreover, government was required to consult with the organised teaching profession and other role-players (or 'stakeholders') in the area of policy development. Ground-breaking labour legislation was introduced. Besides recognition of workers' rights in the new Constitution, teachers' rights to collective bargaining and strike action were guaranteed in the *Labour Relations Act* of 1995. With the passing of the *Education Labour Relations Act* in 1993, a formal mechanism for collective bargaining and determination of labour policies, the ELRC, had been instituted. This marked the institutionalisation of teacher trade unionism in South Africa. It was also the period when the idea of a 'dialectical unity' between unionism and professionalism was mooted (Hindle & Simpson 1993). In time, even the older, 'professional' teacher organisations would come to accept and even embrace tenets of unionism.

With the dawning of a new, democratic government in South Africa, SADTU experienced phenomenal growth as more teachers joined its ranks, especially the younger generation of black teachers. This was particularly the case from 1993 to 1995 when about 80 000 teachers joined SADTU on the back of a massive recruitment drive and the fervour around South Africa's new democracy, taking its membership to close to 100 000 (SADTU 1995: 17). The impetus for SADTU's meteoric rise in this period was, therefore, largely political. SADTU would continue to sustain its membership growth over the next four years. But before delving into these statistics, it is necessary to evaluate the changes within the rest of the organised teaching sector.

NAPTOSA and its affiliates were confronted with challenges of their own as new legislation, cultural tensions and the politics of non-racialism caused them to fragment and restructure. When NAPTOSA was formed in 1991, most of its 16 affiliates were from the African Teachers' Association (ATASA) and the white Teachers' Federal Council (TFC); by November 1994, the United Teachers' Associations of South Africa (UTASA), representing coloured teachers, joined them. A major blow to NAPTOSA's unity initiative was the withdrawal of its white, Afrikaans-speaking teacher organisations in June 1996. Among the reasons cited for their withdrawal were the treatment of Afrikaans and its mother-tongue status, the inclination of some NAPTOSA affiliates to engage in resistance politics and reservations concerning affirmative action (NAPTOSA: 6). As a result, a third teachers' union, the Suid-Afrikaanse Onderwysersunie (SAOU), was established and duly recognised by the ELRC.[8]

Between 1994 and 1998, several of the founding members of NAPTOSA merged with others to form new unions, under new names, or disbanded so that their members could join other affiliates. For example, the establishment of the National Union of Educators (NUE) in 1997 was a culmination of a merger process that started in 1995, involving the white Transvaal Teachers' Association (TTA), the coloured Transvaal Association of Teachers (TAT), and the white South African Teachers' Association (SATA). This union brought together teachers from the provinces of Gauteng and the Eastern and Western Cape. Today, the NUE has extended its membership to include African and Indian teachers, with branches established in Alexandra, Lenasia, Mamelodi and Soweto in Gauteng province. It also has members in most other provinces and remains an influential affiliate within NAPTOSA.[9] In terms of a labour ruling that all references to racial groups be removed, a number of NAPTOSA's affiliates were unable to register as trade unions. Subsequently, these organisations registered under new names, for example, the Natal African Teachers' Union (NATU) registered as the National Teachers' Union (NATU) and the Transvaal United African Teachers' Association (TUATA) became the Professional Educators' Union (PEU), both in 1998.

These developments are symptomatic of how the broader political and legislative dynamics of the transition have shaped the responses of teacher unions in different and contradictory ways. On the one hand, the formation of the NUE symbolised the willingness of some constituencies to embrace the new, non-racial democracy in South Africa, and thus leave behind the baggage of their racialised history; on the other, the concerns of Afrikaans teachers over the erosion of their 'cultural' heritage, meant that some aspects of South Africa's political history would be perpetuated in the transition. At an ideological level, however, these organisations were still bound by their commitment to professionalism and, for the most part, were trade unions in name only.

SADTU's membership continued to show enormous growth, jumping from 106 000 members to about 200 000, a growth of 88.3 per cent, between 1996 and 1999. It was only towards the latter part of 1999 that its membership peaked, and then experienced a slight decline. During this period, NAPTOSA's membership grew marginally, while SAOU experienced a similar decline to SADTU (see Table 10.1). Available statistics reveal that the majority of teachers employed in mainstream schools, that is, both public and independent schools, belong to unions. In 2001, of the 354 201 teachers in the system,[10] approximately 97 per cent (or 344 437) were members of unions.

Table 10.1 Union membership

	1999	2000	2001	2002
SADTU	218 878	214 247	211 480	210 235
NAPTOSA	84 841	91 375	90 157	95 988
SAOU	46 920	43 878	42 800	41 315

Sources: ELRC 2002 and SADTU Congress Report, 2002

SADTU's assessment of its decline over this period includes a failure to offer better quality service and the application by the state of the 'No Work, No Pay' principle after strike actions. Traditionally, NAPTOSA has excelled in the provision of members' benefits and may well have gained from SADTU's loss. The ability of unions to maintain their custodial role, including the provision of 'professional' benefits, depends very much on their financial stability. Here membership subscriptions are paramount. However, while members' contributions remain the main source of union funding, income from other sources is also fairly significant. For example, SADTU's income for 2001 comprised membership subscriptions (60.5 per cent); ELRC levies (15.6 per cent); insurance commissions (9.5 per cent) and grants, sponsorships and advertising (14.4 per cent).[11] Based on rough calculations at the time of writing, SADTU's annual budget for 2003 stood at about R100 million.

The financial power and stability of unions, therefore, is an important aspect of their overall status in the education sector, enabling them to expand the quality of service to members and, more importantly, the quality of their influence in the education policy arena. For example, SADTU's growth and improved financial autonomy since 1993 allowed it to develop its policy and research capacity; on the other hand, its reticence in providing better quality services to its members contributed to a loss of membership and income. This has led the union to consider recruitment of members from sectors other than public schools, such as private schools and universities, and to increase its subscription fees with effect from 1 January 2003 for the first time in years. The union also took a significant step in improving its services to members by jointly establishing a new trade union-owned, independent consumer services company, Lesaka Holdings, in 2002. The company provides a range of assurance and financial services and products, including healthcare, property, funeral benefits and asset management.[12] Whether these initiatives will halt the recent downward trend in the membership of South Africa's largest teachers' union remains to be seen.

Any perceived loss of political influence will ensure that membership competition remains high on the agenda of teacher unions. Equally significant is SADTU's embrace of the material dimension of professionalism and NAPTOSA and SAOU's tacit acceptance of unionism.

The gender and HIV/AIDS challenges

A critical challenge for teacher unions, both in terms of membership strength and unions' commitment to educational and social change, is the question of gender politics. Arguably, gender concerns continue to be marginalised (Parker 1993 and Unterhalter 1998). Teacher unions can be criticised for having laudable policies but little to show for it. At 66 per cent, women teachers constitute the larger proportion of the general teaching force. They comprise 64 per cent of the members of both SADTU and NAPTOSA and 70 per cent of SAOU's members. Yet their numbers in leadership positions within the unions remain small. In SADTU, women hardly feature in leadership positions at the national level (1 woman out of 8 serves on the National Working Committee and 1 out of 26 on the National Executive Committee); at the provincial level, the picture is somewhat better (19 out of 72 being women); and, at local branch level, the situation is more representative of the demographics. The picture is similar within SAOU and NAPTOSA, where women occupy about 25 per cent of leadership positions overall, again with proportionally greater representation at branch level.[13] Thus, while women do serve in leadership roles in teacher organisations, they are often under-represented in senior positions.

Table 10.2 Total number of teachers in mainstream schools by gender in 2001

	Combined male/female	Female	Male
Teachers	354 201	233 058	121 143

Source: DoE, preliminary data from the 2001 Snap Survey[14]

SADTU, arguably, has been the most active union in addressing the challenge of gender subordination and patriarchal relations in education. Soon after its establishment, the union held a conference in Durban in 1991 to raise awareness around women's oppression and formulate a progamme of action for women teachers. This led to the launch of a Gender Committee in 1993 (SADTU 1995). A year later the Gender Committee still identified gender awareness as an area of concern, together with the marginalisation of women in SADTU structures.[15]

SADTU and the other unions, however, were not inactive in taking up concerns of the majority of their membership. In the period 1993 to 1998, teacher unions made several gains, notably salary parity between women and men; maternity leave for single and divorced women and extended maternity leave to four months; equal pension benefits and housing subsidies extended to all women (SADTU 1998). Since then, according to SADTU, it has been difficult to negotiate additional gains or even consolidate what has already been achieved, primarily because of government's adoption of a neo-liberal economic framework (GEAR), leading to cuts in public spending. The union is currently embarking on a Childcare Campaign, calling for childcare facilities in the workplace or state subsidies for childcare. Given their numerical significance alone, addressing gender concerns is a critical organisational issue for teacher unions because of its impact on membership competition and unions' political power.

A huge challenge that faces teacher unions at present is how best to respond to the HIV/AIDS pandemic in South Africa, especially its implications for teacher supply and the provision of quality education. Government employees (including teachers) are second only to mining employees (and a close second at that) in terms of registered infection rates. SADTU's own research, focusing on the period August 1999 to May 2000, suggests that up to two SADTU members could be lost to HIV/AIDS on a *daily* basis, a chilling statistic even if it was one a day.[16] The union identifies several related issues that could impact on the supply and quality of education in South Africa, including high mortality and infection rates of teachers, pupils and administrators, and an exacerbation of geographic inequities as infected teachers leave rural schools to be closer to medical facilities or families.

SADTU's approach to this challenge is to link the promotion of attitudes and practices for minimising HIV transmission with its campaigns for greater gender equality and the empowering of women. These range from struggles for women to be free to choose their preferred contraceptive methods to persuading male teachers to participate in HIV/AIDS education programmes – a task usually passed on to women teachers (SADTU 1998). Both SADTU and NAPTOSA have initiated awareness programmes and are busy developing workplace policies on HIV/AIDS. A related problem, in which male teachers have been implicated, is the sexual abuse of girls at schools. Although SADTU acknowledges that it has been slow to react to this scourge within its own constituency, it has started to deal with transgressors in the recent past invoking its own code of conduct. And, at a national level, the SACE has recently adopted a hard-line approach in dealing with offenders.[17] This represents a significant embrace of professional unionism by both government and teacher unions.

In the assessment of SADTU's Gender Desk, certain fundamental problems have to be addressed if the situation of women teachers is to be alleviated and social changes in gender relations achieved. These include addressing the enormous imbalance of women in leadership and decision-making positions; the male-dominated culture of caucusing and lobbying; male teachers' patriarchal and sexist attitudes and monitoring the implementation of gender equity, childcare and sexual harassment policies. By all accounts, this situation is not different in the other unions.[18] Thus, in spite of tremendous strides having been made in material benefits for women teachers, the fundamental patriarchal and exclusionary relationship between male and female teachers within teacher unions remains. Addressing the subordinate status of women teachers, therefore, remains an ongoing struggle. Further research is needed, however, on the role of women and gender politics within teacher unions.

Towards a 'professional unionism'

As intimated earlier, the apartheid state favoured a conservative, professional form of teachers' organisation, which was challenged in the mid-1980s by the newly emergent teacher trade unions. This challenge consolidated in the early 1990s, but would gradually give way to a 'new realism' as teacher unions began to adopt a 'professional unionist' approach in confronting organisational and political challenges in the later 1990s. Teacher unions may, therefore, employ strategies of unionism and professionalism, independently or together, depending on the particular historical, political and ideological conjuncture (Ginsburg, Meyenn & Miller 1980: 206). The state also thrives on this potential: on the one hand, unions are given the space to defend members' interests; on the other hand, they are encouraged to work in partnership with government in the development of policy and to uphold standards of 'professionalism'.

With an increasingly favourable political and legal climate in the 1990s, teacher trade unionism became entrenched in South Africa, resulting in the rapid growth of SADTU. In the years following its establishment in 1990, SADTU confirmed its unionist policies as it firmed up its alliance with Cosatu. Politically, the union has remained an important part of the tripartite alliance,[19] and has maintained its commitment to the workers' struggle and the advancement of a socialist agenda in South Africa, in spite of tensions over the

ANC-led government's economic policies (SADTU 1995 and 2002). The road to achievements on the labour relations front, however, has not been easy. It was only after many years of struggle that the labour rights of teacher unions were recognised. SADTU embarked on strike action in 1993 over salary disputes and the period was marked by ongoing tensions between SADTU and NAPTOSA, with allegations of the apartheid state's favouring of the latter (SADTU 1995: 22). A year later, NAPTOSA and its affiliates had to deal, for the first time, with a pro-unionist government, and found the new labour environment somewhat intimidating:

> The ELRC and its committees such as the Bargaining Committee ... became the main battlefield where ... NAPTOSA had to adapt to the hard world of trade unionism and to operating in a hostile environment as the second largest employee party. (NAPTOSA: 17)

Indeed, NAPTOSA clashed with the new government in 1997 when the federation forced an agreement with the employer over the latter's partisan behaviour during collective bargaining (NAPTOSA: 18). This represented quite a turnaround in the fortunes of teacher organisations in South Africa, as under apartheid it was the NAPTOSA affiliates that enjoyed a cosier relationship with government. That relationship was underpinned by an anti-unionist stance and a reciprocal reliance on the ideology of professionalism. SADTU, however, determined not to be perceived as a 'handmaiden' of the state, embarked on a National Day of Action on 12 May 1994 over the restructuring of education and other issues, barely weeks after the first democratic elections.

In spite of these tensions, teacher unions have generally benefited from the new and more structured labour relations environment. The latter paved the way for increased co-operation between unions and also resulted in notable achievements around salary increases and parity, thereby addressing historical inequalities based on race and gender. Pension and other benefits, such as medical aid and housing subsidies, were brought in line with the public service at large. After a protracted struggle, including marches and rallies by teachers across the political spectrum, agreement was also reached on post provisioning and teacher retrenchment (NAPTOSA; SADTU 1995). In part, these achievements may be attributed to closer working relations between teacher unions, as they gradually set aside historical differences and united around mutual interests. The state encountered united teacher resistance, especially with regard to cutbacks in education spending and rationalisation policies (Vally & Tleane 2001). Teacher union struggles, therefore, extended beyond shop-floor concerns to embrace broader policy issues in the middle-to-later 1990s (see below).

Simultaneously, there was a gradual thawing in the attitude of NAPTOSA and SAOU to trade unionism, which culminated in affiliates within these organisations joining SADTU in strike action for the first time in August 1999.[20] The dispute, which centred on salary increases, was part of a larger public service strike organised by Cosatu. Although still bound by their commitment to 'conservative professionalism', the two unions identified with the broader grievances of the public service at large, and this marked a turning point in teacher union co-operation. Thus, teacher unions' capacity to effect change and influence policy is not just a consequence of close relations with government but also with forces within civil society, such as the labour movement. At the same time, teacher unions' ability to forge a closer working relationship among themselves in dealing with traditional union concerns and 'professional' matters signalled a new realism in teacher unions' ideological and strategic practices.

Education policy and social change

Besides engaging with government on the labour relations front, teacher unions were also active in the broader policy domain. The nature of contestation was typical of policy dynamics and social change, and brought to the fore issues of underlying power relations and control (see Bowe & Ball with Gold 1992; Taylor, Rizvi, Lingard & Henry 1997), as well as issues relating to redress, policy ownership and the privileging of 'elites'. This was certainly the case when the ANC-led government took up the challenge to transform South Africa's education system.

Teacher unions themselves were proactive. SADTU led the way in pioneering new approaches to teacher appraisal and development, with assistance from the Wits Education Policy Unit (EPU) (Chisholm 1999). Since then, all teacher unions have hotly contested the question of performance management for more than a decade, with no final resolution in sight by 2004, even though some agreements have been reached. NAPTOSA and SAOU, on the other hand, had been preparing for the looming battle on school organisation, governance and funding (discussed below). However, state-initiated policy development soon took centre stage, and unions would become sucked into a whirlpool of new policies, which would further highlight the close but ambiguous nature of their relationship with government.

As part of the government's programme of economic and social transformation, several new education policies were introduced, ranging from the National Qualifications Framework (NQF), 1995, the *South African Schools Act* (SASA), 1996, and new curriculum policies from 1997 onwards. The corresponding policy development processes would test severely the resources and expertise of teacher unions. Arguably, NAPTOSA was able to respond to the challenge of contributing to policy development far more effectively than SADTU. Here the former's historical focus on 'professional' matters held it in good stead, as it was able to draw on technical and policy expertise from within its own ranks, which included university academics. SADTU's strength, on the other hand, was its keen awareness and responsiveness to the political dynamics in education. The country's largest union, however, gradually realised that its neglect of 'professional' matters was a source of weakness, and it decided to correct this imbalance. By 1998, education and research departments had been established, and more recently, a legal department.[21]

Overall, teacher unions have had mixed success in relation to making an impact on the development and outcomes of education policy, and on the broader questions of economic and social justice. As it is beyond the scope of this chapter to deal with the various policies developed since 1990, teacher unions' engagement with two key policies will be highlighted.

The case of SASA

SASA was the new government's most important policy aimed at addressing historical inequalities in the school system. Teacher unions served on the Committee to Review the Organisation, Governance and Funding of Schools, appointed by government in 1995, which kick-started the process. Both SADTU and NAPTOSA made policy recommendations, with NAPTOSA, in particular, revelling in an area that it considered central to its professional status. Two specialist committees within NAPTOSA, the Management and Governance of Schools Working Group and the Working Group on Constitutional Implications, undertook research and prepared detailed technical submissions on matters relating to SASA (NAPTOSA: 14–15).[22] SADTU, with assistance from the Wits EPU and the Centre for Education Policy Development (CEPD), was equally responsive in making submissions.

Arguably, the main aspects of contestation centred on school financing policy and the status of Model C schools (white schools). In this regard, the political distance between SADTU and NAPTOSA was highlighted. SADTU was clearly concerned with questions of redress and redistribution to benefit especially black working-class parents, while the influential white teacher associations within NAPTOSA were intent on preserving the privileged status of white schools. This became apparent during the work of the Review Committee and in the aftermath of its recommendations, when a powerful 'white' lobby, comprising white teacher organisations and community-based education structures, became active. Together, these organisations mounted an intensive campaign to mobilise 'affected' communities to oppose any erosion of the status of their schools during the formulation and legislative phases of SASA.[23] Mobilisation of influential opinion-makers was also part of the strategy of NAPTOSA and SAOU, and included networking with the main political parties – the ANC, the National Party and the Democratic Party – and lobbying key personalities in the Parliamentary Portfolio Committee on Education and the ANC Education Study Group, especially its chairperson, Blade Nzimande. NAPTOSA enjoyed a much closer working relationship, though, with education representatives of the main opposition parties, namely, Renier Schoeman of the National Party and Mike Ellis of the Democratic Party, as evidenced by the following excerpt from correspondence on the South African Schools Bill:

> As you are aware, NAPTOSA is politically non-aligned. The following issues are nevertheless raised with you in your capacity as spokesman on education for your party, with the request that you consider raising these issues during any further debates either within the Parliamentary Portfolio Committee or in the National Assembly.[24]

Thus, although NAPTOSA and SAOU might make claims to political non-alignment, they were not short of ideas when it came to the 'politics' of policy work. A major feature of teachers' agency in the process, therefore, was its inherently political dimension, which underlined the importance of lobbying and unions' cultivation of strategic alliances in their relationship with government.

In their response to the adoption of the new funding model, known as the 'User Fee' option, SADTU maintained its criticism that user fees reflected a 'two-nation' growth strategy that would perpetuate the inequalities of the past, and concluded that education was being 'left to the mercy of market forces'.[25] The strategic thrust of the white teacher associations belonging to NAPTOSA and SAOU, on the other hand, was to stress the merits of the existing Model C school system as benchmarks for transforming all schools, especially historically disadvantaged black schools. Their arguments resonated with the position advanced by the government's foreign consultants, Luis Crouch and Christopher Colclough, who stressed the importance of retaining middle-class support for the survival of the public school system, a position that eventually gained currency within state administrative and political circles.[26] SAOU, moreover, expressed concern on behalf of the Afrikaans-speaking community about the retention of a particular school ethos regarding language, culture, and religious convictions from the outset.[27]

Teacher unions were thus split along political, economic and cultural lines in their responses to SASA, reflecting stark differences in attitudes towards broader issues of economic and social justice. Ironically, it was the conservative lobby, in which NAPTOSA and SAOU played a critical role, that emerged 'victorious', underlining the power of organised resistance to the state. SADTU, however, in spite of having the inside track to the echelons of political power, found its own influence somewhat constrained by its alliance with the ruling party, as reflected, for example, in the dynamics of the ANC Education Study Group, which debated extensively the Alliance's position on SASA (Mathieson 2001: 51).[28] These developments confirm the inherently political nature of teacher-state relations, especially with regard to issues of 'partisan identity' (recalling Murillo 1999), and policy contestation.

The curriculum development process

Teacher unions participated in the curriculum development process from the outset, beginning with the 'cleansing' of the curriculum of all racist and sexist content in 1994. But the real contestation and struggle for ownership of the curriculum process started with the launch of Curriculum 2005 (C2005), which was based on the philosophy of outcomes-based education (OBE), in April 1997. Although teachers were not party to the decision to adopt the philosophy of OBE (Jansen 2000; Kruss 1998), teacher unions soon became involved in the mechanics relating to the implementation and subsequent revision of C2005. Teacher union representatives served on the Learning Area Committees (LACs), which were the key forums deliberating on the new subject areas. NAPTOSA claims to have played an effective participatory role in these committees, which it attributed to the huge 'reservoir of persons with outstanding expertise and knowledge' from its ranks. The unions soon identified problems that were widely experienced by teachers, including unrealistic timeframes, the need for teacher training programmes and lack of basic infrastructure and resources.[29]

The concerns raised by teacher unions were echoed by several others. With public pressure mounting, the government instituted a review of the new curriculum in 2000. The Report of the Review Committee echoed many of the implementation problems identified by the unions and recommended strengthening human rights and social-justice aims. Subsequently, after further consultations and refinement, the *Revised National Curriculum Statement* was declared the new official curriculum policy in April 2002 (Chisholm forthcoming). Surprisingly, teacher unions were not officially represented on the Review Committee, which led to sharp reaction, especially from SADTU. The exclusion of teacher unions was to become symptomatic of a growing tendency within the education ministry not to engage in participatory policy processes in the latter 1990s.[30]

Nonetheless, according to Chisholm, teacher unions were probably the most influential. While NAPTOSA and SAOU were generally more sympathetic to the review process, SADTU was concerned about a perceived detraction from official OBE policy. The DoE was probably mindful about too strong an influence in the revision process by the teacher unions, given their sustained criticism prior to the review, and thus ensured that departmental officials and external stakeholders would be represented on an equal basis. In this way, the Department managed to maintain its grip on the direction and outcome of the process. The unions overall influenced the outcome by ensuring that the curriculum remained outcomes-based, was more workable, secular and responsive to poorer constituencies (Chisholm 2003). In spite of substantial involvement by teacher unions, however, the balance of power in the curriculum development process had favoured government.

Conclusion

The work of teacher unions in South Africa over the last decade has, in the main, mirrored the broader political, economic and 'cultural' dynamics of South Africa's transition. Nevertheless, teacher unions have been critical actors in shaping educational and social change. Initially, teacher unions, particularly SADTU, were concerned with securing a stable labour relations climate, which was facilitated by the new government's favourable constitutional and legislative framework. In the process, there was a significant rearrangement of the existing power relations between teacher unions and government, which played itself out in unions' struggle over membership recruitment, organisational development and ideological reappraisal, resulting in a marked improvement in the status of teacher unions and a more widespread societal acceptance of trade unionism, which had been demonised by the previous regime.

Simultaneously, there has been a perceptible trend towards 'professional unionism', with the potential for increased collaboration among unions despite the continued fragmentation of the teachers' movement. Although the prospect of a single teachers' union remains remote, the combination of SADTU's political clout and NAPTOSA and SAOU's 'professional' expertise makes for a potent force, especially when they are prepared to operate beyond traditional ideological boundaries and when the majority of teachers in South Africa are members of these unions. This is a remarkable transformation, given the acrimonious past shared by them.

A powerful teacher union presence in the policy domain, with the potential to influence issues of economic and social justice, has become a reality, giving rise to complex teacher union-state relations, both with regard to labour relations and education policy. On the one hand, as part of their professional role, teacher unions have worked in close co-operation with government, for example, in the establishment of SACE and in the development of curriculum and other policies; on the other hand, they have been critical of, and have contested, those very same policies. Thus, contestation over ownership and control remains a major source of tension between teacher unions and the state, in spite of a more co-operative era in the policy domain. Here, teacher unions have had to confront the harsh reality of the 'politics' of policy work, especially in their relations with government. Indeed, teacher unions outside the inner circle of political power, such as NAPTOSA and SAOU, have struggled for a more influential role in the policy stakes, while SADTU has come to realise that, even with partisan allies in government, the shaping and influencing of policy is an ongoing contest. Advocacy work, such as lobbying of key parliamentarians, and protest action still constitute an integral part of teacher union-government relations, as it did under apartheid. This has seen the emergence of new forms of alliances, not only between teacher unions themselves, but also among teachers, political parties and civil society organisations. Nevertheless, teacher unions' political influence has been compromised by organisational fragmentation arising from political, cultural, economic and lingering ideological differences, and their differing levels of capacity and expertise.

Teacher unions continue to be faced with their own skeletons in so far as broader issues of social justice are concerned. This applies particularly to the continuing subordination of women teachers, which has become exacerbated by the threat of HIV/AIDS. One consequence could be the further fragmentation of the union movement, as was the case in England with the creation of the National Union of Women Teachers in the early 1920s (Lawn 1995: 128), although this looks unlikely in the foreseeable future, given the dormant state of women's organisational capacity. A critical policy challenge, for both government and teacher unions in the years ahead, is the spectre of the AIDS pandemic, especially its impact on teacher supply and the quality of teaching. And, here too, as in other aspects of union-government relations, 'co-operation, matched with resistance', are likely to be the operative words.

Teacher unions in South Africa have finally come of age. It remains to be seen whether they can build on the political, ideological and organisational advances of the last decade to create a truly powerful teachers' movement.

Notes

1. The unionism-professionalism debate captures the existing tension between teachers as workers and teachers as professionals. Although its meaning is highly contested, professionalism, for many, refers to the question of standards for controlling entrance into a profession, and has thus come to be associated with certification, social status and high salary levels. It is also synonymous with strategies of persuasion and reason rather than force. While unionism is equally concerned with maximising control in work-related

areas such as remuneration and service conditions, it is also concerned with broader issues of economic and political contestation with the state, and advocates militant strategies, such as strikes (see, for example , Hindle & Simpson 1993 and Ozga & Lawn 1981).

2. The term 'new realism' is attributed to Martin Lawn and Geoff Whitty (1992) and the notion of 'professional unionism' to Charles Kerchner and Douglas Mitchell (1988) (cited in Torres et al. 2000).

3. This is the subject of the author's doctoral thesis.

4. Neo-liberal agendas and policies have come to be associated with notions of free trade, decreased state intervention in the economy, and fiscal austerity. These policies are believed to have had a pervasive influence in policy development of developing countries (for example, Morrow & Torres 1999, and Oldfield 2001).

5. The term 'black', when used on its own in the chapter, refers to racial groups designated coloured, Indian and African.

6. 'Non-racial' refers to the practice of not discriminating against individuals and organisations on the basis of racial classification.

7. In the event, SADTU constituted itself as a unitary structure, with members from all four of South Africa's main racial groups, while NAPTOSA became a federal organisation with its affiliates retaining their racial and ethnic identity.

8. NAPTOSA and SAOU entered into a working agreement on 27 August 2002, for the 'purposes of negotiation, consultation and bargaining'. A development with ramifications for the labour movement in South Africa was the establishment of the Confederation of South African Workers' Unions (CONSAWU) on 8 March 2003. One of the main reasons behind the move was the need for 'a strong platform for the combined but independent and non-aligned unions in South Africa'. NAPTOSA was a prime initiator in the process, with its executive director, Henry Hendricks, serving as chairperson of the confederation's Steering Committee (NAPTOSA *Update*, September 2002 and *Mail & Guardian*, February 7–13, 2003, p.10).

9. Similar developments unfolded in KwaZulu-Natal, where the white Natal Teachers' Society (NTS) and the coloured Society of Natal Teachers (SONAT) merged to form the Association of Professional Educators of KwaZulu-Natal (APEK) (NAPTOSA Term Report, Nov. 1994–October 1998: 6; and interview with NUE official, 26 April 2002).

10. As per the 2001 Snap Survey conducted by the DoE. A small number of NAPTOSA and SAOU members are believed to be from the pre-primary and ELSEN/special schools' sectors, which are not accounted for in the Department's survey (cf. note 14).

11. SADTU 2002: 92 and interview, R Naidoo, SADTU, 29 January 2003.

12. Lesaka Holdings newsletter, *Dialoq*, Issue 1, December, 2002.
13. The gender statistics are based on estimates provided by teacher union officials as at April 2003.
14. As per personal electronic communication with Christo Lombaard, DoE, EMIS Directorate. The 2001 Snap Survey was conducted on the 10th school day. Data excludes educators associated with stand-alone pre-primary schools/centres and ELSEN/special schools/centres.
15. NAPTOSA has a Gender Issues Working Group, which has drafted a Gender Equity Policy; with the establishment of a Human Rights Desk in 1997, the union began to focus on issues of gender, HIV/AIDS and child abuse as part of its wider social responsibility, acknowledging that its main focus until then had been on professional and labour matters. (Interview, R Veldman, 14 February 2002)
16. Wits EPU, Quarterly Review of Education and Training, April to June 2000; Internal Document, SADTU HIV/AIDS Proposal, 2001.
17. For instance, SACE has introduced new clauses to its Code of Ethics for Teachers, one aimed at eradicating 'raunchy' and 'unruly' public behaviour, and the other prohibiting teachers from 'engaging in improper physical contact with learners' (*Sunday Times*, 9 February 2003); Interview, Jon Lewis, SADTU Research Officer, 18 October, 2002.
18. Interviews: Rosaline de Wee, 29 January 2003 and Jon Lewis, 18 October 2002, both of SADTU, and P Martins, SAOU, 28 January 2003.
19. The 'tripartite alliance' refers to the coalition comprising the ANC, Cosatu and the SACP.
20. Interview, Pieter Martins, CEO, SAOU, 28 January 2003 and NAPTOSA: 12.
21. Interview, Jon Lewis, 18 October 2002; SADTU 2002.
22. Moreover, SAOU, which was still affiliated to NAPTOSA at the time, was equally well prepared, perhaps more so, as they had been warned by ex-President FW de Klerk to prepare for fundamental changes in the education system. See Govender, LV 2002. *The historical dimension in critical policy analysis: Reflecting on issues of democracy and social justice*. Paper read at Kenton at Muldersdrift, 1 to 4 November.
23. Two organisations stand out, notably the Suid-Afrikaanse Stigting vir Onderwys en Opleiding (SASOO) and a national governing body association, the South African Federation for State-Aided Schools (SAFSAS). Interview, Prof. Koos Steyn, SAOU, 11 June 2002; also see Karlsson et al. (2001) A Critical Examination of the Development of School Governance Policy and its Implications for Achieving Equity, in Motala & Pampallis (2001), for details on the emergence of governing body associations.

24. Letter dated 6 September 1996 from the desk of NAPTOSA's Executive Director, Dr EH Davies, addressed to Mr RS Schoeman MP, NP Spokesman on Education, and copied to Mr MJ Ellis, DP. This is just one example of several items of correspondence between the organisation and opposition party spokespersons covering a range of issues relating to SASA, such as the abolition of corporal punishment, the school governing body's (SGB) right to employ additional teachers and the participation of learners in SGBs.
25. Cited from SADTU's written submission to the *South African Schools Act*, 1996.
26. Interviews, Prof. Koos Steyn, SAOU, 11 June 2002 and Luis Crouch, 10 July 2002.
27. See comments made by the Transvaalse Onderwysersvereniging (TO), representing four provincial affiliates, to the Review Committee, 3 October 1995.
28. For example, SADTU was forced to submit to the Alliance's position that parents should constitute an overall majority on school governing bodies as opposed to equal representation of parents and other stakeholders.
29. See NAPTOSA p. 16, SADTU Congress Report, 2002, p. 139 for further details and union initiatives in this regard.
30. Leaders of teacher unions across the political spectrum have criticised Education Minister Kader Asmal's centralisation of decision-making, observing that this has eroded the more open and co-operative relations that were enjoyed between the previous administration of Minister Sibusiso Bengu and themselves.

References

Bowe, R; Ball, S with Gold, A (1992) *Reforming Education and Changing Schools: Case Studies in Policy Sociology*. London: Routledge

Chisholm, L (1999) The Democratisation of Schools and the Politics of Teachers' Work in South Africa, *Compare*, 29(2): 111–126

Chisholm, L (forthcoming) The Making of South Africa's National Curriculum Statement, *Journal of Curriculum Studies*

Chisholm, L (2003) The Politics of Curriculum Review and Revision in South Africa. Paper presented at the Oxford Conference on Education and Development, 10 September

Education Labour Relations Council (ELRC) (2002) *Annual Report*. Pretoria

Ginsburg, M; Kamat, S; Raghu, R & Weaver, J (1995) Educators and Politics. In Ginsburg, M (ed) *The Politics of Educators' Work and Lives*. New York: Garland

Ginsburg, M; Meyenn, R & Miller, H (1980) Teachers' Conceptions of Professionalism and Trade Unionism: An Ideological Analysis. In Woods, P (ed) *Teacher Strategies: Explorations in the Sociology of the School*. London: Croom Helm

Govender, L (1996) *When the 'Chalks are Down': A Historical, Political and Social Interpretation of Teacher Militancy in South Africa*. Pretoria: HSRC

Govender, L (2001) Participation in the Education Sector: Fallacies and Challenges of Representative Democracy in South Africa. Paper presented at the joint HSRC/CNRS/NRF conference on Democracy and Governance, Bordeaux, France

Govender, L (2002) The Historical Dimension in Critical Policy Analysis: Refelecting on Issues of Democracy and Social Justice. Paper presented at Kenton Conference in Muldersdrift

Hindle, D & Simpson, L (1993) Teachers Don't Talk in Class! A Class Analysis of Teachers and their Organization in South Africa. In Pendlebury, S et al. (eds) *Kenton-at-Broederstroom, 1992: Conference Proceedings*. Johannesburg: University of the Witwatersrand Education Department

Hyslop, J (1990) Teacher Resistance in African Education from the 1940s to the 1980s. In Nkomo, M (ed) *Pedagogy of Domination: Towards a Democratic Education in South Africa*. Trenton: Africa World Press

Kruss, G (1998) Teachers, Curriculum 2005 and the Education Policy-Making Process. In Morrow, W & King, K (eds) *Vision and Reality: Changing Education and Training in South Africa*. Cape Town: UCT Press

Lawn, M (1995) The Political Nature of Teaching: Arguments around Schoolwork. In Ginsburg, MB (ed) *The Politics of Educators' Work and Lives*. New York: Garland

Mathieson, S (2001) The Role of the ANC Education Study Group in the Legislative and Policy Process. In Sayed, Y & Jansen, J (eds) *Implementing Education Policies: The South African Experience*. Cape Town: UCT Press

Morrow, R & Torres, C (1999) The State, Social Movements and Educational Reform. In Arnove, RF & Torres, CA (eds) *Comparative Education: The Dialectic of the Global and the Local*. Lanham: Rowman & Littlefield

Motala, E & Singh, M (2001) Introduction. In Motala, E & Pampallis, J (eds) *Education and Equity: The Impact of State Policies on South African Education*. Sandown: Heinemann

Murillo, M (1999) Recovering Political Dynamics: Teachers' Unions and the Decentralization of Education in Argentina and Mexico, *Journal of InterAmerican Studies and World Affairs*, 41 (1): 31–57

National Professional Teachers' Organisation of South Africa. (NAPTOSA) *Report on the period 11 November 1994 to 28 October 1998*

Oldfield, S (2001) The South African State in Transition: A Question of Form, Function and Fragmentation. In Motala, E & Pampallis, J (eds) *Education and Equity: The Impact of State Policies on South African Education*. Sandown: Heinemann

Parker, B (1993) Intellectuals and Education System Change. *Perspectives in Education*, 14 (2): 221–228

Ozga, J & Lawn, M (1981) *Teachers, Professionalism and Class: A Study of Organised Teachers*. London: Falmer Press

South African Democratic Teachers' Union (SADTU) (1995) Secretariat Report to the Third National Biennial Congress

South African Democratic Teachers' Union (1998) Meeting of the National Executive Committee, Reports for Congress

South African Democratic Teachers' Union (2002) Secretariat Report, Book 2, 5th National Congress

Taylor, S; Rizvi, F; Lingard, B & Henry, M (1997) *Educational Policy and the Politics of Change*. London: Routledge

Torres, CA; Cho, S; Kachur, J; Loyo, A; Mollis, M; Nagao, A & Thompson, J (2000) *Political Capital, Teachers' Unions and the State: Value Conflicts and Collaborative Strategies in Educational Reform in the United States, Canada, Japan, Korea, Mexico and Argentina*. Los Angeles: University of California, Los Angeles Latin America Centre. [Online] Available <http://www.isop.ucla.educ/lac/cat/fpriart.htm> (Accessed 18 June 2003)

Unterhalter, E (1998) Economic Rationality or Social Justice? Gender, the National Qualifications Framework and Educational Reform in South Africa, 1989–1996, *Cambridge Journal of Education*, 28 (3): 351–368

Vally, S & Tleane, C (2001) The Rationalisation of Teachers and the Quest for Social Justice in Education in the Age of Fiscal Austerity. In Motala, E & Pampallis, J *Education and Equity: The impact of State Policies on South African Education*. Sandown: Heinemann

CHANGING CLASS

11 Changes and continuities in South Africa's higher education system, 1994 to 2004

Jonathan D Jansen

The purpose of this chapter is to trace and describe the major changes that have taken place in South African higher education over the past decade, to explain why these changes were introduced into the higher education system, and to examine briefly the future consequences of such changes for the sector and its constituencies. In examining changes in higher education, it will also be necessary to identify continuities in the national system, since what remains constant is as important a reflector on change and its pretensions in any social system – but especially in the case of post-apartheid education.

There is a multitude of changes that have transformed higher education in South Africa. Some of these are small and gradual changes, initiated from within institutions; others have been large-scale changes initiated from without, that is, through government and donor interventions. It is very clear that while continuities remain, the higher education system does not resemble the distortion, upheaval and fragmentation that marked the sector at the start of the 1990s. In my review of the policy, planning and political landscape, I propose that the ten most important changes in higher education have been the following:

1. The changing size and shape of higher education;
2. The changing meaning of autonomy and accountability;
3. The changing nature of higher education providers (private higher education);
4. The changing character of student distribution and characteristics in higher education;
5. The changing organisation of university management and governance (new managerialism, councils);
6. The changing roles of student politics and organisation;
7. The changing models of delivery in higher education;
8. The changing notion of higher education – between free trade and the public good;
9. The changing value of higher education programmes (the rise of the economic sciences and the decline of the humanities); and
10. The changing nature of the academic workplace.

Each of these changes is related to the other, and reasonable analysts might arrive at a slightly different list of key experiences that have transformed the sector. What cannot be denied, though, is that these ten events are at least among the most important not only in terms of immediate impact on higher education but also in relation to long-term effects on the system of higher education provision. Each deserves further description and analysis.

The changing size and shape of higher education

The founding policy document on higher education after apartheid is the report of the National Commission on Higher Education (NCHE) – *A Framework for Transformation* – that was produced by 13 commissioners whose terms of reference included advising the Minister on 'the *shape* of the higher education system ... in terms of the types of institutions' and 'what the *size* of the higher education system should be' (NCHE 1996: 266, emphases added). Little happened until July 1999, following the appointment of the second post-apartheid Minister of Education. In his *Call to Action*, the Minister announced that:

> The shape and size of the higher education system cannot be left to chance if we are to realise the vision of a rational, seamless higher education system ... The institutional landscape of higher education will be reviewed as a matter of urgency in collaboration with the Council on Higher Education. This landscape was largely dictated by the geo-political imagination of apartheid planners.
> (DoE 1999)

On 5 March 2001 the Minister released a National Plan for Higher Education that argued that '... the number of public higher education institutions in South Africa could and should be reduced' (DoE 2001: 87). In December 2001, a National Working Group appointed by the Minister released its report, *Restructuring of the Higher Education System in South Africa*, and recommended the reduction of higher education institutions (universities and technikons) from 36 to 21 through the specific mechanism of mergers, listing the specific institutions in various provinces to be targeted for merging.

A parallel process was followed for colleges of education, through a Departmental Technical Committee appointed in September 1997 and that delivered in the following year a document called *The Incorporation of Colleges of Education into the Higher Education Sector: A Framework for Implementation* (DoE 1998). It is this committee that recommended the option of incorporation or autonomy for colleges with the proviso that 'an autonomous College ... to be financially viable [it] would require a minimum enrolment of 2 000 students' (1998: 15).

The provincial reaction to the so-called Framework Document was swift as the 'rationalisation' of colleges started to take effect. The number of colleges was reduced from 120 (80 000 students) to 50 (15 000 students) by the start of 2000 (CHE 2001: 22) and to 25 'contact institutions' holding 10 000 students (and 1 000 staff) by the end of that year (2000). Another 5 000 students were registered in two distance colleges (with 500 staff): the South African College for Teacher Education (SACTE) and the South African College for Open Learning (SACOL).[1] Both these distance colleges were absorbed into the University of South Africa (Unisa).

This happened so quickly that the Minister's National Plan for Higher Education then declared quite boldly, if prematurely, '... that Colleges of education were rationalised and *successfully incorporated* into the higher education system with effect from January 2001' (DoE 2001, emphasis added).

At the start of 2003, colleges of education had all but disappeared from the higher education landscape as a result of either being closed down or, in the case of a few, being incorporated into universities and technikons. At the same time, the merger of universities and technikons had been finalised after an intensive political process, with a specified schedule for each of these events. The Cabinet approved the following mergers and incorporations:[2]

- The University of Natal and the University of Durban-Westville;
- The University of the North-West and Potchefstroom University;
- Technikon Pretoria, Technikon Northern Gauteng and Technikon North-West;
- The University of Fort Hare and the East London Campus of Rhodes University;
- The incorporation of the Vista University campuses into specified universities and technikons in the region where each campus was located, for example, the incorporation of the Mamelodi Campus of Vista University into the University of Pretoria;

- The University of Port Elizabeth and Port Elizabeth Technikon;
- The University of the North and the Medical University of South Africa;
- The University of the Transkei, Border Technikon and the Eastern Cape Technikon;
- Rand Afrikaans University and Technikon Witwatersrand; and
- Cape Technikon and Peninsula Technikon.

In a relatively short period of time, therefore, the higher (and further) education landscape in South Africa altered dramatically: 21 universities became 11 institutions; 15 technikons became five 'stand alone' technikons and six comprehensive institutions (combinations of universities and technikons); 150 technical colleges became 50 merged technical colleges. And 120 colleges of education eventually became (at the time of writing) only two colleges of education, with the rest either incorporated into universities or technikons (about 30 such incorporations) or 'disestablished'. And these two remaining colleges of education would also be incorporated into the proposed Institutes of Education for Mpumalanga and the Northern Cape. In short, **306 separate** institutions for post-school education were radically reduced to at best **72 remaining** institutions – not counting the ongoing restructuring of nursing and agricultural colleges. This dramatic alteration of the post-school institutional landscape is the single most important change in higher education (broadly defined) and requires explanation.

The changing meaning of autonomy and accountability

The concept of autonomy has always been contested in South African higher education. It was the rallying call of especially the white English institutions during the days of apartheid when their liberal credentials insisted on the right to decide on the admission of students to their universities. While autonomy was the public rallying-point for student admission on a non-racial basis, this extended to the right to decide what and how to teach in line with institutional orientations in much of the Western world. In short, much of the history of South African universities was preoccupied with asserting autonomy against the constant interventions of the apartheid state to regulate and maintain racially- and ethnically-separate universities. Occasionally, this assertion of autonomy was also made by the English universities in relation to black students who demanded that conservative academics be denied speaking rights on such campuses; the most prominent case being that of the Irish academic Conor Cruise O'Brien. And at other times, the insistence of mainly black academics that the international academic boycott of white South African universities should be honoured, met with the same assertions of autonomy by the English universities. This concept of institutional autonomy was embedded in TB Davie's classic formulation of academic freedom as 'our freedom from external interference in who shall teach, what we teach, how we teach and whom we teach' (cited in Du Toit 2001).

In the 1990s, however, the concept of autonomy was fiercely juxtaposed with the requirement for accountability, driven, this time, by the emergent post-apartheid state. Within a few years of the newly-established democracy, a range of external policies created new demands on universities which were regarded in many quarters as leading to an erosion of autonomy. Government required a reformatting of academic qualifications that were assembled along the lines of the new National Qualifications Framework (NQF). Government indicated that the subsidy formula for funding universities would privilege certain academic subjects or disciplines and, in this way, discourage others. Government required a process of quality assurance that pushed for explicit declarations of performance in academic enterprise. Government required mergers and incorporations of higher education institutions, with dramatic implications for staffing, students and programmes. Government required order in institutions which provoked new legislation – unheard of in apartheid days – in which a Minister of Education could displace an academic leader and appoint an administrator to run a university. In a short period of time, government had intervened quite directly in higher education institutions both to restore order in organisation but also to require compliance with a new regime of academic regulations. This raised muted and sometimes fierce charges against government on the basis of infringing on institutional autonomy. The response from governmental authorities was that autonomy was never meant to be absolute, and that accountability for public resources was an important part of the equation.

This interventionist position of government was not the only source of change to the meaning of autonomy in higher education. As Andre du Toit points out, the transition from academic self-rule to a new managerialism has as much to do with 'the practices and policies of the new class of professionalised university managers' (2001: 5) as it has with external intervention by the democratic state. Unfortunately, Du Toit underplays the impact of trans-national and state regimes on institutional behaviour. As Philip Altbach observes in other contexts,

> Government authorities make it clear to university officials that continued good relations, budgetary allocations, and research funds depend on the appropriate academic and political behaviour on the part of the faculty. (2000: 270)

But Du Toit is correct in pointing to institutional choices that also infringe on concepts and understandings of autonomy. This will be explored further in discussions on the changing academic workplace.

It is not the intention of this review to re-enter the debate on autonomy and accountability; rather, the goal is simply to argue that the concept of autonomy is now, more than ever, up for grabs. How institutions settle, especially after the radical altering of the institutional landscape, will determine what meanings will be assigned and challenged when (if at all) the question of autonomy is again on the agenda. To conclude, underlying all the striking physical and programmatic alterations to higher education has been the shifting meaning of autonomy; this change cannot be underestimated in terms of what it means for 'the academic estate' (Altbach 2000).

The changing nature of higher education providers

The data is suspect, but the growth in private education institutions in South Africa has been quite dramatic since the 1990s. The number of private schools increased from 518 in 1994 to around 1 500 in 2001 (Hofmeyr & Lee 2002), while more than 100 000 students are now registered in 145 private higher education institutions (Mabizela, Subotsky & Thaver 2000). This flooding of the South African market for higher education, long dominated by public institutions, compounded (and may even partially explain) the problem of completely unexpected declines in the enrolment fortunes of public universities. The judgement of private higher education is less severe than a few years ago as more reliable data suggests that:
- The private provider market is more heavily concentrated in the further rather than higher education sector;

- The private providers concentrate their efforts on a restricted curriculum (often low-level commercial and business courses) and therefore represent less of a threat to public higher education than initially thought;
- The private provider market was in fact expected to grow – at least from the perspective of the 1996 National Commission on higher education; and
- The private provider growth is completely common to development trends in other countries – without dramatic declines in public sector fortunes.

Nevertheless, this varied but successful, emergent economy of private higher education transformed the higher education landscape in South Africa. The response of the state has been somewhat ambivalent. On the one hand, several actions were taken to regulate the growth and quality of the sector by requiring registration, accreditation and quality assurance of both private providers and the programmes they offer. At the same time, foreign as well as local higher education institutions continue to be registered despite the acknowledgement of the limited interest in 'a relatively narrow range of programmes that are economically lucrative' (DoE 2001: 65). The ambivalence can in part be explained in the context of the ongoing debates on free trade as a subject that includes higher education and that forms the subject of negotiations in the WTO (World Trade Organisation) and GATS (The General Agreement on Trade in Services), all of which have strong implications for developing countries like South Africa (Sehoole 2002).

Another way in which the logic of private higher education has played itself out in the South African market is through public-private partnerships. In such cases:
- The public institution registers the students and provides materials, while the private provider pays for tuition and carries administrative costs.
- The students have limited access to the facilities of the public institution even though the state subsidy eventually accrues to the public entity.
- The private entity structures the fees and decides on the loan distribution, with limited financial exposure on the part of the public institution.

According to one study, six public institutions in 2000 claimed a total of 24 000 full-time equivalent (FTE) students whose primary registration was with a private provider (Cloete, Fehnel, Maassen, Moja, Perold & Gibbon 2002: 160). Once again, government signalled that it would institute a stronger regulatory and monitoring environment with respect to public-private partnerships, especially in the delivery of distance education programmes.

What this all means is that the dominance of a limited number of public sector institutions offering contact tuition has changed dramatically in the past ten years under review, and the future landscape with respect to private providers will depend crucially on governmental behaviour with respect to international private and national public forces on higher education as a whole.

The changing character of student distribution and characteristics in higher education

In the recent history of South Africa, a constant refrain was the problem of access to higher education by especially black students. Between 1990 and 1994, however, both the historically black and white universities and technikons experienced a sudden rush on higher education institutions. In this brief period, the historically black universities expanded by 28 000 (37 per cent) and their white counterparts by a total of 10 000 (or 8 per cent).[3] This sudden expansion masked three other realities at the time. First, the fact that gross participation rates remained low, standing at 9 per cent for black and 13 per cent for coloureds. Second, that participation rates were highly unequal by apartheid constructed 'groups', standing at 70 per cent for whites and 40 per cent for Indian South Africans. Third, that 69 per cent of enrolments were in universities with more than 50 per cent of university graduates and enrolments in the humanities. In other words, the technikons and the technological and science fields were heavily under-represented in the early 1990s.

By the end of the 1990s, however, marked shifts had taken place in student enrolments and distribution, using the period 1993 to 1999 as benchmark (DoE 2001: 36–37).
- Black student enrolments increased from 191 000 to 343 000 (80 per cent);
- Black students now constituted 59 per cent of the total headcount enrolments in higher education;
- Black student enrolments had decreased by 7 000 (9 per cent) in historically black universities;
- Black student enrolments had increased by 22 000 (138 per cent) in historically black technikons;

- Black student enrolments had increased by 10 000 (100 per cent) in historically white, English-medium universities;
- Black student enrolments had increased by 56 000 (1 120 per cent) in historically white, Afrikaans-medium universities; and
- Black student enrolments had increased by 49 000 (490 per cent) in historically white technikons.

These radical and rapid shifts in the demographic spread of students can be attributed to changes in the external environment. Such changes include the unexpected decline in the number of qualifying high school graduates eligible for especially university-level studies (see South African University Vice-Chancellors Association 2001); the unexpected competition from private higher education providers, albeit in limited fields of study; the expected compliance with national goals for equity in student (and staffing) enrolments; the need for institutional survival – especially on the part of black universities – since state subsidies were largely dependent on student enrolment (and progression); and an unexpected but logical shift in the public mind in favour of vocationally-oriented training.

These demographic shifts will be further advanced by the mergers planned for higher education in the sense that universities and technikons will be combined in some cases (such as the Rand Afrikaans University and Technikon Witwatersrand), and former white and black universities in other cases (such as the Universities of Durban-Westville and Natal).

Against this backdrop, the problem for South African higher education will not be race – at least not in a black majority state. The new problems will be the background class and regional character of students as urban institutions are strengthened and deracialised while rural universities remain marginalised in terms of institutional capacity, racial character and class status. The problem for urban institutions, on the other hand, will be the complex task of transforming institutional cultures in ways that are more inclusive and accommodating of the statistical diversity of their student populations.

The changing organisation of university management and governance

The collegial model of faculty organisation and faculty-university relations dominated the character of universities in South Africa for much of its recent history. Deans were appointed by, responsible to, and defenders of their faculties. Faculties decided on which curricula they wished to launch based principally on the intellectual merits of a particular disciplinary or subject direction. The academic department was the basic unit of scholarly life within the university – responsible for teaching, research and community outreach. The administrative functions of the university were highly centralised, enabling the dean and his or her Heads of Department to concentrate on the academic functions of the faculty. The scholar-dean, whose function was academic leadership, was never in question. Faculty members pursued co-operation with other departments or faculties on a purely voluntary basis; there was no iron requirement for co-ordination or co-operation. Students passed or failed on the basis of academic decisions within the faculty, and these decisions were seldom queried from outside of the academic world of the department. It was understood that faculties and departments worked in the interests of their students, and made such decisions on the basis of time-honoured academic standards. Professors professed; deans led; councils governed; administrators administered; and students studied.

And then things changed. By the mid-1990s, a sea change in university management and governance had taken place. Many observers have documented the elements of this change but it includes the following:

- The institutional prominence of centralised and strategic planning covering all aspects of university life. The elevated status and pervasive discourse of 'strategic planning' was in part provoked by governmental expectations of 'three-year rolling plans' and the need to monitor and attain institutional performance against planned outputs.
- The decentralisation of core administrative functions in the direction of faculty and departmental units. Such functions include finance and budgeting, planning, facilities (in multi-campus institutions), personnel management, student administration, marketing and communication, and quality assurance.
- The expansion and concentration of executive management on a centralised basis, effectively changing the roles of deans and directors from academic leaders into executive managers. A new language of affirmation accompanied these organisational changes. For example, vice-chancellors became chief executive officers and deans became executive deans. A critical shift in this environment was that deans were now appointed by 'management' rather than by their colleagues.

- The expansion of the functions of councils of universities and technikons as they became much more involved in the management of institutions, compared to their traditional governance role with respect to institutional policies. This created considerable conflict in many institutions as the line between management and governance became blurred through the activism of otherwise distant councils.

These changes in governance and administration at institutions dramatically changed the social relations on campuses between staff and students, between academics and administrators, between university managers and their external communities, between government and institutions. These changes are further explored in later discussions on the changing academic workplace.

The main point for now is to record the emergence of a new administrative and managerial architecture in higher education during the late 1990s which significantly altered not only the physical organisation but also the social character of universities.

The changing roles of student politics and organisation

One of the most distinctive features of the anti-apartheid resistance since the 1960s was the prominent role of students and student organisations at schools and universities. Many of the political leaders in government, for example, rose to prominence through their student activism after the 1970s. Students were well organised and connected to major political movements inside and outside South Africa. Students lived simple and often dangerous lives in their daily battles against the apartheid regime and its representatives on university campuses. Students played very prominent roles in institutions, with the capacity to mobilise mass resistance with relative ease and to focus the attention of 'comrades' on burning social and political issues of the day. Students worked closely with staff unions and academics as a common battlefront against government and unsympathetic administrators. In the process, students generated considerable respect within the broader community and acknowledgement from the liberation movements for their bold stance on matters of injustice and inequality.

But the emergence of a new and democratic government in 1994 threw student focus, organisation and mission into considerable disarray. For example, the focus of student organisation, especially in historically black institutions, shifted from protests against an illegitimate government to demands for unrestricted access to higher education, expanded financial aid to needy students, and relief from personal debt to the institutions.

But what followed after the election of the new government was a period of ambivalence on the part of the state, from 1994 to 1998. It was this period of ambivalence towards students and student organisations that would create considerable instability during the mid- to late 1990s. Student organisations and their leaders were fêted by their institutions with everything from personal cellphones, car allowances, impressive offices, full or partial fee remissions, representation on most if not all key committees of the institution, and a general status and wealth unheard of in the student movements of the 1970s and 1980s. It was also during this period that universities were reluctant to come down hard on students without the ability to pay; institutions dug deep into their accumulated reserves – sometimes with sound motives – not only to accommodate needy students but also to raise the remuneration of the lowest-paid administrative staff. At this point, students and unions became very powerful organisations, a key example being institutions like the University of Durban-Westville (UDW). Many institutions – like the University of the Western Cape and other HDIs (historically disadvantaged institutions) – really did expect a massive bail-out from the state on the basis of their historical disadvantage.

The consequences were disastrous. Institutions with healthy reserves (like UDW) went into massive debt. Student organisations became a major drain on institutional resources – continuing to demand the kinds of excesses institutions could no longer afford. Students insisted on 'bail-out' from debt and unlimited access to their constituencies. Unions joined the fray, insisting on better remuneration for their staffing constituencies despite this declining resource base in the institutions. These events disrupted institutions on a scale not seen since the 1970s. University vice-chancellors experienced their highest turnover in years; senior administrators lived through periods of unprecedented stress; some campuses became completely unworkable, with extremely violent acts from inside and outside these institutions. A newly-elected, democratic government stared down on a set of institutions – many of which had become completely ungovernable – and found its very authority, if not legitimacy, threatened by an unstable, volatile higher education sector.

And then things changed. Government took a strongly interventionist stance on students and student organisations and their responsible institutions. A stream of political messages required that students pay fees; that university and technikon managements were responsible for collecting such fees; that only academically-deserving students from poor backgrounds would receive funding; and that disruption would not be tolerated. But in addition to these persistent and subtle political messages, a new set of legislation was created that empowered the Minister of Education to replace vice-chancellors with 'Administrators' in the event that the institution was unable to manage itself. Institutions were held directly accountable for institutional performance in terms of indicators such as efficiency, equity and effectiveness. These were specified terms of reporting in the mandatory 'three-year rolling plans' which had to be submitted to government. This combination of politics, legislation and performance measures enforced on institutions a stronger managerial responsibility towards student organisations. This had two effects. First, it provided institutional managers with the political support they needed to require specific behaviours from their students and student organisations. Second, and as a consequence, it moderated student organisational behaviour towards greater discipline and conformity within the new managerial environment. This regulation of student organisation and behaviour is a most important shift in institutional life over the past decade.

The changing modes of delivery in higher education

Before the 1990s, higher education institutions acted according to clearly defined roles. The contact institutions offered contact instruction and the designated distance education institutions offered what was for many years a form of correspondence education. The two distance education institutions were Unisa and Technikon South Africa, the latter concentrating on vocational education programmes.

But during the 1990s a group of traditionally contact institutions started to expand their instructional programmes into various kinds of distance education. Between 1993 and 1999, distance education headcount enrolments in traditionally contact institutions grew by 492 per cent: from 14 000 to 69 000. The strongly-entrepreneurial Afrikaans universities in particular, sensing a market within the rural areas of South Africa, started to work with private entities to deliver programmes that would advance the career prospects of, especially, practising teachers and school leaders. This market niche appeared to be poorly served by institutions like Unisa. The private-public partnerships that spawned this opportunity worked with considerable success for universities like Pretoria, Port Elizabeth, Potchefstroom, the Rand Afrikaans University and the University of Natal (Pietermaritzburg). The private partners provided an efficient mechanism for registering students and collecting fee payments on site, while at the same time enabling the contact institutions to concentrate on the delivery of instruction, field support and examinations.

Another shift in delivery happened within both contact and distance education institutions as a result of the impact of technology on teaching, learning and assessment. The advances in technology enabled contact institutions to offer a range of alternative modes of delivery that included web-based programmes that students could access with or without face-to-face contact teaching. In some cases, therefore, the web-based or 'telematic' programmes were simply used to create a complex of instructional opportunities and resources that complemented the formal lectures or seminars. In other cases, such programmes served as the exclusive means for receiving instruction. Such technologies also enabled distance education institutions to make regular contact with distance students through, for example, electronic mail. This has already spawned an interest in exploring the potential of mobile phones (which appear to be owned by an overwhelming majority of rural teachers and principals, for example) for maintaining contact with distance education students, given the unreliable record of traditional mailing services in rural areas.

The consequences of these shifts in modes of delivery include the following:
- The definitional line between contact and distance education institutions became increasingly blurred, with experts in these fields beginning to talk about a continuum at which extremes sit conventional correspondence courses and pure face-to-face tuition. As it turned out, in the new century there were very few institutions that did not offer 'mixed mode' forms of delivery.
- The viability of the traditional distance education institutions started to be called into question as the common *perception* was that the decline in enrolments at these institutions paralleled the growth in enrolments in the established and traditional contact institutions.

- The policy and financial bases for government subsidisation of these historical institutional types – contact and distance – was thrown into disarray. It was increasingly clear to government that terminating funding of distance education programmes at contact institutions may create 'order' within the higher education system and bolster the fortunes of the flailing distance education institutions. But there was also a sense in government that doing so might interrupt what many experts see as an inevitable global trend towards 'mixed mode' delivery systems – in both types of institutions. Government therefore played a soft hand on the contact institutions, requiring high levels of quality, strong statements of articulation with the institutional vision and programme profile, better systems of support to distance education students, and careful decisions on 'capping' programmes deemed to be oversubscribed – such as education management.

What is clear is that the 'pure' institution types of the 1980s are a thing of the past. The combination of technological advances in teaching and learning and the entrepreneurial flair of some institutions has completely altered the traditional missions and forms of delivery in higher education. While there are still core missions that are distinguishable among former contact and distance institutions, the changing demands on institutions and the new opportunities offered by technology might eventually erode the certainties of institutional typologies in the coming decades.

The changing notion of higher education – between free trade and the public good

There is a powerful view emanating across the world that higher education should be regarded as simply another form of economic trade. At the very least, this means that private international institutions should have the liberty of accessing education markets without strict governmental regulations or trade barriers. In other words, higher education and Levi jeans would enjoy the same status as products of trade which should be transacted under the same conditions of international exchange. There are powerful bodies advancing this view, including the WTO, and this movement is being debated most strongly in Europe and North America, but with strong resonance within South Africa. A number of studies have been commissioned by the South African Universities'

Vice-Chancellors' Association, the Council on Higher Education (CHE), and the Centre for Higher Education Transformation – all with the aim of clarifying the meaning and implications for legislation, policy and practice within higher education.

Already the space provided for private higher education institutions from Europe, Australia and the United States, for example, has created niche markets that continue to alter the landscape for universities and technikons in South Africa. The most immediate, tangible consequence is competition for the best students – something which clearly impacts on weaker institutions more than on stronger ones. The rise of such institutions partly explains the growing interest of public institutions in business education, with the result that new business schools have emerged since the 1990s as prominent components of public higher education. The marketing of such programmes has also altered enrolment patterns dramatically in larger universities, with considerable interest among students in the business and commercial sciences.

This transnational trade in higher education represents a critical shift in the field and its full impact in the coming decade will depend in part on what government does and in part on how well public institutions respond to these new terms of higher education delivery in South Africa.

The changing value of higher education programmes

Not a single university in South Africa has escaped the sharp downward spiral in humanities enrolments in the past decade. For reasons that are still not well understood, humanities and social science faculties bore the brunt of the unexpected decline in matriculants from the school system. A combination of factors might explain this impact:
- The strong sense of the need for vocationally-oriented courses among the general public and the student population in particular, hence the overall shift in enrolments in the late 1990s in favour of technikons;
- The new opportunities opening up for, especially, black students in (non-humanities) fields previously limited to white graduates under apartheid;
- The growing status of the commercial sciences and allied subjects (such as actuarial science) as high-income, rewarding fields to new graduates;
- The declining status of the teaching profession – for a number of reasons including the rationalisation programme of the 1990s and the persistent

stories of chaos and disruption in schools; teacher education was the single largest field of enrolment in post-school education prior to the 1990s; and
- The declining numbers of graduates from the school system; this would impact on humanities faculties directly because the weaker students (with many exceptions, of course) tend to end in the 'soft disciplines'; with fewer students coming through, there is greater space for accommodation within non-humanities faculties.

Whatever the nature and combination of reasons, humanities went into serious decline in the last decade, leading several universities to retrench humanities academics, to restructure humanities faculties and to terminate certain humanities programmes – such as foreign languages or music, art and drama (see Ensor 2002: 287).

The plan of government to shift the balance in enrolments between the humanities; business and commerce; and science, engineering and technology from the established ratio from 49 per cent : 26 per cent : 25 per cent to 40 per cent : 30 per cent : 30 per cent is puzzling since this has already happened at great speed and without government intervention. This dilemma might explain the contradictions and tensions in the planned enrolment shifts which, on the one hand, indicate downward planning for the humanities but, on the other hand, propose increased enrolments for teacher education (DoE 2001: 31–33).

It will be difficult to resuscitate the humanities at universities in the coming decades. Senior academics have been lost, powerful intellectual traditions have been terminated, and a culture of critical and creative thought in the social sciences and humanities has been eroded. The decline of the humanities must therefore rank as one of the most important changes in South African higher education over the past decade.

The changing nature of the academic workplace

What does it mean to work in a South African university at the start of a new century? The principal changes in the academic workplace now prominent in institutional culture and organisation are the following:
- There is a much greater sense of the need to compete, both within the institution as well as with competitors outside the institution. For all the

talk about co-operation, the dominant impulse among academics is to compete for programmes, students and therefore jobs. Universities now have marketing directors to recruit students and sometimes staff, something unheard of in the 1980s. Large budgets are set aside for marketing, communication and publicity on a scale not yet seen.

- There is a much greater sense of vulnerability in the wake of the unprecedented retrenchments and restructuring in higher education during the 1990s. Job security, long an established reality in a higher education system without any strong sense of tenure, is being disrupted. The same holds true for administrative staff as 'outsourcing' becomes a preferred mode of delivering key support services. Although more psychological than real, such vulnerability is also felt among white academics as the demand for employment equity moves from a polite requirement to a punishable offence in institutions.
- There is a much greater sense of the need to perform, the result of a new regime of surveillance in the form of performance management systems, quality assurance protocols and institutional benchmarks on everything from research outputs to pass rates. Academics and administrative staff now have to account regularly and in public on personal and unit performance. And such performance determines not only promotion but also remuneration and retention as an employee.
- There is a much greater sense of the limited resource environment to support key academic and administrative tasks. With more academics and managers now part of the budgetary processes of institutions, and with the declining revenue base in many universities and technikons, there is a sharp institutional consciousness about resource limitations that did not exist in the same ways ten or more years ago.
- There is a much greater sense of responsibility towards students as clients (the language of new managerialism) and as critical resources (the result of declining enrolments) than in the previous decade. Students used to seek a place within a university; now universities seek to offer students a place against the competition, for their very survival depends on strong enrolments.

The academic workplace has changed dramatically and the meaning of such changes in the lives of students and staff is described in terms of disruption, alienation, the loss of community and shared identity, and an increase in emotional labour (Webster & Mosoetsa 2001). Whether this new culture and context of academic work will be sustainable is unclear, especially in developing countries where changes in political and economic regimes could also change the nature of the academic workplace, again.

Synthesis, reflection and conclusion

If these are the changes, what has remained constant? First, the profile of academic staff at institutions has remained constant. The recruitment and retention of especially leading and promising black scholars will remain one of the most difficult tasks facing higher education, in part because of the financial attractions of the private sector and in part because of the nature of the academic workplace (Potgieter 2002). Second, the knowledge producers in higher education remain largely white and male. As the simple but alarming statistics of the Department of Arts, Culture, Science and Technology (DACST) demonstrate, not only has research production remained low; it has remained unequal – still favouring researchers who are white, male and ageing (DACST 2002: 53). Without dramatically new modes of training and support for a new cadre of academic researchers, this situation is unlikely to change. Third, the 'institutional cultures' of higher education have remained more or less the same. Institutions still bear their racial birthmarks in terms of dominant traditions, symbols and patterns of behaviour that remain distinctive despite the broader changes sweeping the higher education landscape. These deep-rooted beliefs and behaviours will take some time to change, and compose the subject of several research investigations underway at the time of writing.

Returning to the changes described, how can these shifts be explained as a collective of events? It is impossible to account for these changes outside the global context of higher education developments. As international commentators have warned, it is too easy for South Africans to claim uniqueness when in fact much of what is happening locally has its roots in what is taking place globally. The spread of new managerialism is a reflection and outcome of a broader neo-liberal discourse that has transformed relationships between the state, civil society and universities in major ways throughout the world (Webster & Mosoetsa 2001). The emergence of international private higher education is part of a global sweep of trade in a borderless education environment (Knight 2002; Scherrer 2002). The changing meanings of accountability and autonomy are as contested in Europe and North America at the present time, as they might be in Africa and Latin America (Altbach 2000). The restructuring of higher education through mergers and other forms of realignment is by no means a South African or even an education phenomenon (Harman & Meek 2002) – even though its local manifestation might invoke apartheid's illogical development as the stimulus for such radical changes.

What, in conclusion, are the consequences of these changes for higher education and its constituencies? First, it means that *social relationships* within institutions are perhaps permanently altered – relationships between students, staff, administrators, and managers. Managerial models of relationships have effectively displaced collegial models long familiar, and comfortable, to institutions. Second, it means the *political relationship* between higher education institutions and government is also permanently altered; it is unlikely that government will withdraw its intervention-oriented disposition now that it has a firm foothold within institutions. Third, it means the *economic relationship* between universities and their competitors has changed, based as it is on a powerful logic of survival and domination. Left to the market, strong institutions will remain strong, and the weak will remain marginalised. But the primary impulse of institutions will be towards competition for standing and resources. The only difference is that the national cast of competitors will increasingly include a world market that has extended its trade liberalisation arguments to include educational services.

Notes

1. All student numbers are cited as full-time equivalent (FTE) students, that is, the subsidy value of a student determined on the basis of courses and contact time. This is typically less than a straightforward headcount enrolment of students. So, for example, SACTE and SACOL had 20 000 students in the late 1990s but this number comes to about 5 000 FTE students because of factors like the registration for single courses by individual students under flexible registration requirements.
2. Press statement by the Minister of Education, Professor Kader Asmal, on the transformation and reconstruction of the higher education system, Pretoria 9 December 2002.
3. Much of this data is drawn from the meticulous work of Ian Bunting, in Cloete et al. 2002: 149–180.

References

Altbach, P (ed) (2000) *The Changing Academic Workplace: Comparative Perspectives.* Boston: Centre for International Higher Education

Cloete, N; Fehnel, R; Maassen, P; Moja, T; Perold, H & Gibbon, T (2002) *Transformation in Higher Education: Global Pressures and Local Realities.* Cape Town: Juta

Council on Higher Education (2001) *The State of Higher Education in South Africa (2000–2001)* Annual Report. Pretoria

Department of Arts, Culture, Science and Technology (2002) *South Africa's National Research and Development Strategy.* Pretoria: Government Printers

Department of Education (1998) *The Incorporation of Colleges of Education into the Higher Education Sector: A Framework for Implementation.* Pretoria: Government Printers

Department of Education (1999) *Call to Action: Mobilising Citizens to Build a South African Education and Training System for the 21st Century.* Pretoria: Government Printers

Department of Education (2001) *National Plan for Higher Education.* Pretoria: Government Printers

Du Toit, A (2001) Revisiting Academic Freedom in Post-Apartheid South Africa: Current Issues and Challenges. Commissioned paper prepared for the Centre for Higher Education Transformation, Pretoria

Ensor, P (2002) Curriculum. In Cloete, N; Fehnel, R; Maassen, P; Moja, T; Perold, H & Gibbon, T (eds) *Transformation in Higher Education: Global Pressures and Local Realities.* Cape Town: Juta

Harman, K & Lynn Meek, V (2002) Introduction to Special Issue – Merger Revisited: International Perspectives on Mergers in Higher Education, *Higher Education,* 44 (1): 1–4

Hofmeyr, J & Lee, S (2002) Demand for Private Education in South Africa: Schooling and Higher Education, *Perspectives in Education,* 20 (4): 77–88

Knight, J (2002) *Trade in Higher Education Services: The Implications of GATS.* Report to The Observatory on Borderless Higher Education, United Kingdom

Mabizela, M; Subotsky, G & Thaver, B (2000) The Emergence of Private Higher Education in South Africa: Issues and Challenges. Discussion document presented at the CHE Annual Consultative Conference

National Commission on Higher Education (1996) *A Framework for Transformation.* Cape Town: NCHE

Potgieter, C (2002) *Black Academics on the Move.* Centre for Higher Education Transformation, Pretoria

Scherrer, C (2002) GATS: The Lock-in of Education. Paper prepared for the European Cultural and Educational Forum, Brugge, Belgium, 18–24 November

Sehoole, C (2002) The Implications of Free Trade for Higher Education in Developing Countries: A South African Case. Paper prepared for the European Cultural and Educational Forum, Brugge, Belgium, 18–24 November

South African University Vice-Chancellors Association (2001) *The Challenges of Access and Admissions*. Pretoria

Webster, E & Mosoetsa, S (2001) At the Chalkface: Managerialism and the Changing Academic Workplace 1995–2001. Commissioned paper prepared for the Centre for Higher Education Transformation, Pretoria

Section 3
Changing margins

Chapter 12: Don't bite the hand that feeds you: South African education NGOs in a period of change — 317

Seán Morrow

Chapter 13: The state of play in early childhood development — 339

Kim Porteus

Chapter 14: Youth development in transition, 1992 to 2003 — 367

Margaret Perrow

Chapter 15: Adult basic education and social change in South Africa, 1994 to 2004 — 393

Ivor Baatjes and Khulekani Mathe

Chapter 16: The education business: private contractors in public education — 421

John Pampallis

CHANGING CLASS

12 Don't bite the hand that feeds you: South African education NGOs in a period of change

Seán Morrow

This chapter outlines the history of non-governmental organisations (NGOs) in the field of education in South Africa; in particular this sector's transition from the struggle against apartheid to the period of majority rule. It outlines the relationship of education NGOs with government, seen as a funder, and with other donors. It discusses tensions between service delivery and critical advocacy, and notes the increasing expansion of South African education NGOs in other parts of Africa. It also briefly considers what directions might be available to NGOs in addition to that of collaboration with government.

Sources for the chapter are interviews with personnel from education NGOs, government and funding bodies; a survey of the current literature on NGOs in South Africa and elsewhere; and material from websites, publicity and pamphlet literature and other 'grey' material. While debates about the correct terminology for organisations of this type are noted, here there will be no attempt to define the term. Its definition will emerge from its use in the chapter.

The historical and political context

When the National Party came to power in 1949, casting aside the long history of educational provision by Christian missions in South Africa (see Bredekamp & Ross 1995; Comaroff & Comaroff 1991; Landau 1995), it forced education to serve a narrow ethnic nationalism, expanding basic education to the mass of the population under the rubric of Bantu Education, while as far as possible shifting black secondary education to the homelands (Hyslop 1999: 51–62, 102–131). Liberals and radicals viewed the takeover of education as a further attempt at state domination and an attack on already meagre services for the black population (see, for example, Abraham 1989) and from the 1970s, a new generation of education NGOs began to emerge. They channelled dissenting voices where conventional politics rarely offered opportunities for dissent, and attempted to compensate for the many failures of the state in providing education for all South Africans.

Even where overseas donors played a major role in supporting NGOs, they tended to take a less formative approach than elsewhere, probably believing that the liberation struggle and associated cultural and educational initiatives should be primarily a domestic concern. This led to a strong, politically-oriented, and generally oppositional NGO sector in South Africa before 1994 (King 1999). There was little room for 'working within the system' in the South Africa of the 1980s, as the literature on NGO educational activity at this time indicates (for example, Barnes & Haya in Kallaway 2002: 145–154; Motala & Vally in Kallaway 2002: 174–194; NECC 1993; Perrow 2002, and Perrow's chapter in this book). The most innovative educational thinking took place outside the official system. Indeed, the modern phase of the South African struggle stemmed from the revolt against the National Party's educational dispensation, mobilised in particular by the United Democratic Front (UDF), banned in 1988 but re-emerging as the Mass Democratic Movement (Seekings 2000; Van Kessel 2000; Houston 1999). In many respects it was a loose coalition of NGOs and other organisations, forced into overt politicisation and militancy by the obdurate environment. Thus important elements in the NGO sector were formed in radical opposition to government. This, subsequently, was its strength and its vulnerability: its liberation credentials were clear, but transition from opposition to co-operation was difficult.

As Kallaway notes, ideas born in the turbulent 1980s often stultified in the 1990s, 'a time when educational alternatives associated with socialism or Third World radicalism ... lost much of their political potency' (Kallaway 2002: 5). It tended to be agencies such as the World Bank that provided working models for government educational plans. Majority rule came through negotiations, with the bargaining and concessions that this involved. The new Government of National Unity (GNU) incorporated the African National Congress (ANC) and elements of the old regime suspicious of the NGO sector. The ANC, whose inheritance included state-oriented centralism from its Communist Party partners and now defunct East European supporters, was trying to assert itself in the context into which it had been thrust so rapidly. It also considered itself the embodiment of many decades of struggle against apartheid.

Thus, surprisingly at first sight, the struggle against apartheid preceded an attempt to centralise and integrate the type of activities typically carried out by NGOs in the state's Reconstruction and Development Programme (RDP).

Funders were expected, and were generally willing, to divert resources to the state's developmental priorities, and NGOs were meant to align and even subsume themselves with and in the state's programme.

The new emphasis on value-for-money, accountability and measurable outcomes did not always sit well with some NGO inheritances. As one commentator put it in 1995, South African education NGOs tended to have 'high legitimacy, but low productivity' (Ward 1995: 3). In particular, strategies for the volatile socio-political environment of the 1980s and early 1990s, amounting at extremes to the 'struggle accounting' that could be a euphemism for using donor funds for political and even personal purposes, ran counter to this increased emphasis on probity and accountability.

There was another dynamic. Many NGOs found it difficult to think themselves out of the apartheid environment against which they inevitably defined themselves, and adapt to the new world where educational theories and practices that emphasised quantifiable performance outcomes accompanied and were to some extent embedded in the rationalising, market-oriented discourse that was increasingly dominant from the early 1990s (for a contemporary example, see King and van den Berg 1993: 196). Funding tended to follow this new alignment.

In addition, as South Africa 'normalised', other issues began to impinge. Radical politics began to fracture and elide in new, loose coalitions, and the boundaries between politics and human rights, cultural movements, the environment, gender and so on, often the domain of NGOs, became increasingly blurred. Thus South African NGOs emerged from bitter political conflict, and had to start redefining themselves, just when, globally, the very basis of radical thought and action was changing in unpredictable ways.

NGOs had several alternatives: they could continue to seek non-governmental funding and attempt to survive independently, or semi-independently, from government; they could attempt to integrate themselves more closely with government initiatives, becoming implementers of official policies; they could become consultancies, losing the characteristic NGO service ethos and becoming little different from businesses; or they could close, tacitly acknowledging that the aims for which they had been striving had been achieved.

Size, shape and funding of the sector

However, the NGO sector has certainly not disappeared. The most authoritative recent study of the area attempted to estimate the size and importance of the not-for-profit sector in South Africa as it was in 1999 (Swilling & Russell 2002). Swilling and Russell estimate that there are 98 920 NGOs in South Africa, of which 53 per cent are less formalised, community-based organisations working at local level. They indicate that this is an industry that accounted for 1.2 per cent of South African gross domestic product in 1998. The sector as a whole employs the equivalent of 645 316 full-time workers, of which just over half are in paid employment, the rest being volunteers. This comprises 7.6 per cent of the total non-agricultural workforce, and 9 per cent of the formal non-agricultural workforce, and makes the sector a larger employer than, for instance, the mining industry. This makes the South African not-for-profit sector proportionally larger than the average for the 28 countries studied by the Johns Hopkins Centre for Civil Society Studies in its series of large-scale international studies, of which the study by Swilling and Russell is one (see Salomon 1999, updated in Institute for Policy Studies 2002).

In terms of funding, South Africa's domestically-generated resources are far greater than those available to other African countries. Stringent economic policies are not due to unmanageable debt and consequent external demands for structural adjustment, but are rather what government considers fiscally and financially prudent. This places the country in a stronger relationship to external donors than is often the case elsewhere. The government is confronted not so much with an absolute lack of resources as with the problem of identifying and deploying the administrative competencies to spend available money judiciously.

The relationship between donors, government and NGOs is many-sided, complex and sometimes problematic. Donors intersect with government in many spheres apart from the educational, and in education the vehicle for utilisation of donor aid is not always the NGO sector (see Ngeleza, Chabane & Dlamini 2000). Unlike in many African states, donor funding in South Africa is a small proportion of total expenditure. But, especially if it is discretionary, it tends to give leverage, and can lead to time being spent managing a relatively small amount of money rather than concentrating on spending the much larger sums which it is the obligation of government to use constructively. As the Deputy Director General (DDG), Planning and Monitoring, in the national Department of Education (DoE) said in 2002, 'We have … grants, which are unspent, of hundreds of millions of rand, and here we're scrapping over two or three million for a smaller agency, and spending an enormous amount of time talking to them, quarterly meetings, quarterly reports, all of those kind of things. Absolutely a waste of time'. He cites a large grant from a foreign governmental agency that the donors attempted to make conditional on a proportion of it going to a certain NGO. To the DoE, this was unacceptable: 'they're trying to say, we'll only fund government, but we'll tell government who they must fund, and that for us can't work'. This sort of conflict indicates how relative economic strength can give South Africa leverage to resist what some might consider unacceptable external conditions. On the other hand, it could also be seen as illustrating the degree of control that government exerts over both NGOs and donors. However, there seems to be no principled objection from government to donor funds being directed independently towards education NGOs. In fact, they are acknowledged to be in a better position than government in some contexts to spend them usefully.

Governmental grants to NGOs may be directed through parastatal funding organisations, or through ministries and departments at national or local levels. Such direct funding is through tenders for which NGOs and other appropriate organisations can apply, or longer-term partnerships between government and NGOs into which programme funding is channelled. The national and provincial DoEs are amongst the main ministries working in this way.

While government feels that the mechanisms in place do not put NGOs at any particular disadvantage, at least some education NGOs think that the tendering process disadvantages them in a fundamental way, in that criteria for black empowerment written into tender documents are oriented towards companies rather than not-for-profit institutions. While the basic criterion should be an organisation's ability to stimulate educational or other action on the ground, nevertheless, as Swilling and Russell have demonstrated, NGOs are generally far 'blacker' than commercial companies (Swilling & Russell 2002), and tender documents are habitually weighted in favour of previously disadvantaged groups. Yet because they are not structured so as to have black shareholders, this aspect is discounted in their applications. This, according to Andrew Miller, the Chief Executive Officer (CEO) of Project Literacy, reveals the contrast between the rhetoric favouring civil society and actual practice, and is a factor pushing NGOs towards a more formally commercial orientation.

There have been several phases in the direct granting of funds to NGOs from government, involving successively the Independent Development Trust (IDT), the Transitional National Development Trust (TNDT) and the National Development Agency (NDA). The national Lottery is another potential source of funds. The rate of disbursement has been slow, and there have been many accusations that it is enveloped in obscurity (see, for instance, David MacFarlane, 'National Development Agency still underperforms' *Mail & Guardian*, 19 April 2002. Though ostensibly intended to provide reliable funding for NGOs and other civil society bodies, from the NGO point of view, organisations such as the NDA and national Lottery are often seen as demonstrating continuing state gatekeeping and a narrowing of funding opportunities.

The Johns Hopkins studies reduce NGOs to 11 categories, of which 'education and research' is one. There are 5 691 in this category in South Africa, which is 5.8 per cent of all NGOs, 4 667 of them operating in elementary, primary and secondary education, none in higher education, and 1 024 in adult and continuing education. It should be noted that the methodology of this report excludes many NGOs in South Africa with a para-educational or even directly educational role. The categories of 'public health and wellness education', encompassing 1 038 organisations, and 'job training programmes' with 3 790, are examples, as are categories such as 'voter education', 'consumer education', 'health education', and 'legal and human rights education'.

The NGOs examined in this report are for the most part established and stable, having an average age of 19 years. However, those in education and research are amongst those established most recently, with an average life of 8 years. Of existing education NGOs, 142 go back to before 1976, 1 901 have their origins in the period 1976 to 1993, and 3 648 post-date 1994. They employ 23 962 full-time employees, 1 629 part-timers, and the equivalent of 5 548 volunteers.

In terms of the overall profile of the South African economy and society, NGOs tend to utilise more women, more black people, and more black women in particular, than other sectors. Black South Africans are preponderant at every level, including the managerial. The role of women is particularly marked in education NGOs. These characteristics are indicated below:

Table 12.1 Role of women in education NGOs

Percentage managerial				Percentage professional and technical				Percentage support and administration				Percentage blue collar			
M	F	B	W	M	F	B	W	M	F	B	W	M	F	B	W
15	85	88	12	14	86	88	12	12	88	100	-	6	93	42	58

Note: M = male, F = female, B = black, W = white

However, as compared to the other 28 countries in the Johns Hopkins studies, though remembering the not fully inclusive criteria utilised, at 6 per cent a considerably smaller proportion of the South African NGO workforce is employed in education than the 22 per cent over all the countries covered. South African NGOs receive a total funding of R14 billion. Of this, R815 million goes to education and research, R490 million from the private sector.

Each NGO had its own history, and NGOs should not be divided mechanically into 'radical' NGOs that failed to deal with the new circumstances, and 'liberal' ones that survived because of relative managerial, financial and administrative stability. The complexity of the options and choices are apparent in Perrow's chapter. Some radical NGOs adapted to the new circumstances, and others grounded in such a paradigm emerged while the transition to democracy was under way. For some it was not a question of possibilities, but of inevitabilities. After 1994, donors altered their funding policies, applying new and rigorous criteria; government, from being the enemy by definition, became both a rival for funding, and the major and often demanding customer for the products and services (this new vocabulary indicates the changed atmosphere) of education NGOs. With the apparent normalisation of South African society, and the decline of funding from international and local corporate sources, there was a mass-extinction of NGOs. This was the situation faced by South African education NGOs in the mid-1990s.

Government, NGOs and education: service provision

The period when government-initiated policy led to the cutting off of much funding to NGOs lasted relatively briefly, but devastated many. The extinction of many education NGOs in the 1990s probably represented the natural demise of some that had really lost their role, and which appeared not to have had the intellectual and managerial flexibility to adapt. However, it also led to the death of some that arguably could have contributed usefully in the new dispensation, such as the Science Education Project, and the PROMAT Trust, founded in 1982 to run centres offering professional development and support to black teachers in secondary and tertiary institutions.

While the situation remains fluid, some stability has now been achieved. NGOs work with government at national and provincial levels on a range of educational concerns, from early childhood education, through Adult Basic Education and Training (ABET) and literacy, to special needs and many other areas. In the core formal school system they are less prominent, though they participate in teacher and materials development and, on the periphery, work on drug abuse, school safety and the like. Though there is no overall forum for interaction between government and education NGOs, there are various committees which some in government feel that NGOs utilise insufficiently.

The role of donors is more varied. It is difficult to say precisely what donors contribute, or to exactly define a donor: funding for education NGOs comes, among others, from South African trusts and foundations, corporate social investment, multilateral and bilateral aid, and foreign foundations and trusts. To Cawthra, Kraak and Maepa, 'quantitative, and to some extent qualitative, information on South African non-profit sector income and funding is very scarce and highly contested' (2000). With commercial organisations in particular, the line between investment and donation can be a fine one. However, the South African donor landscape features a range of domestic and international donors, commercial, private and governmental. In addition, increasingly, many education NGOs generate resources through commercial or semi-commercial activities. Cawthra et al. say that:

> ... it would seem that there has been a withdrawal of foreign funds to the non-profit sector from at least 1994, and that this has not been substituted by an influx of domestic funds, either from government or from other sources. Most experts argue that this has plunged the non-profit sector into a major funding crisis, which can be divided into two phases: a foreign funding crisis mainly between 1994 and 1996, and a primarily domestic funding crisis from 1996 onwards. (2000: 67)

Seen from 2003, the situation may not be quite so bleak, at least for education NGOs that have oriented themselves towards governmental and commercial opportunities. Whether this means excessively diluting the critical and advocacy roles that many consider characteristic of and necessary for NGOs is another matter.

The government primarily engages the NGO world in the sphere of service provision. This is at the heart of the current situation of NGOs. There is no overt objection by government to the critical, advocacy role of NGOs, but this is simply not seen as the point at which NGOs and government interact. This point will be taken up later. The other side of this coin is that government does not recognise an NGO role in the making of educational policy, though they may have a considerable role, as service providers, in how policy is implemented. As the DDG, Planning and Monitoring, said: 'We have a democratic government ... we make policy here, and we don't need [NGOs] to assist us in that. For those who have read the signs right,' he said, and he was referring to the service provider role, 'I would hope there is a future.'

Nevertheless, policy-making is complex. In practice many NGOs have played a significant role in providing the data without which policy cannot be intelligently decided upon – and the compilation and presentation of data is itself never a neutral process. NGOs also sit upon committees where education policy was and is hammered out. As examples, one can take Project Literacy's contributions to ABET policy, the Independent Examinations Board (IEB's) role in assessment, and the role of the Education Foundation in providing crucial data. Nevertheless, to government, in the DDG's words, NGOs must go 'a consultancy or contractor route'. He argues that, far from this reducing the effectiveness of NGO interventions, it may actually increase it. NGOs that choose not to work with and for government are in:

> ... a very difficult position. There isn't much funding outside of government [which] has a lot of money to spend ... Where these NGOs are willing to become service providers, it enables them to grow enormously, and those who have ... made that choice, are probably the stronger ones around at the moment ... It shouldn't undermine their independence.

However, the time has passed, he said, when 'a little bit of passion and a fax machine' were a sufficient passport to educational relevance. Donors, in fact, are more problematic for government than NGOs. Government is confident that service provision, the ground on which it interacts with NGOs, is clearly defined and controlled by itself. Donors are not similarly susceptible to control.

An example of an NGO that has successfully read the signs of the times and moved in a semi-corporate direction, stressing effective service provision, is Project Literacy. The organisation was founded in 1973 and initially concentrated on teaching domestic workers to read and write. With the political transition of the early 1990s, it found itself, like many NGOs, dependent on declining donor grants and needing to redefine its role in the new dispensation. However, like other NGOs that had the ambiguous advantage of coming from a tradition of liberal commitment to improvement and advancement, it had a record of frugality, hard work and dependability. In the polarised environment of the 1980s, even this stance could and did lead to clashes with the regime, both ideological and in terms, for instance, of raids on black students studying in 'white' areas. Handled intelligently, this ethos could bridge the divide between the heroic days of the eighties and the increasingly insistent demands thereafter for financial accountability and for structures that would provide measurable 'deliverables'. Ironically, it was the 'struggle' NGOs, with radical political credentials but not always a strong record of educational delivery or bureaucratic expertise, that tended to wilt in the new atmosphere.

Project Literacy, then, transmuted into a businesslike, professional organisation, while remaining an NGO. The crucial factor was the Board, chaired by prominent lawyer and businessman Dikgang Moseneke. The organisation was already successful in terms of donor assistance, having had, in particular, grants amounting to R38 million from the Joint Education Trust (JET). However, the Board and management attempted to read future trends, and Project Literacy changed its management style, raised staff salaries and let go many who could not or did not wish to adapt to the new regime. In CEO Andrew Miller's words, the organisation 'became very action-output oriented'. The production of good-quality teaching materials, outsourced to the best authors and illustrators available, was emphasised, and the organisation ceased to produce materials directly, entering into a partnership with Maskew Miller Longman, a major publisher.

Though this activity is now less central, the organisation continues to teach, largely also by outsourcing, running classes both for the poor and underprivileged, for which donor funding is obtained, and for employees of companies that pay for the service. It is, Andrew Miller says, 'a chameleon-like game'. He cites the big United States NGOs. These are, he says, 'very good chameleons ... and they compete against private people for jobs'. In his view, given the realities of South Africa and the world, this is the way forward.

From resistance to advocacy

Internationally, 'advocacy' saturates the language of NGOs. It implies a commitment to the poor and disadvantaged, and to those who are thought to be, and perhaps are, unable to speak for themselves, or at least to whose voices those in power do not listen. A more questionable implication with which NGOs from the north that concern themselves with the south have always struggled uneasily, is that of an intrusive paternalism: why should people from another class, or nation, 'advocate for' those with whom they seem to have no organic links? Literature from northern NGOs tends to ponder their role *vis-à-vis* development, and asks anxiously whether they can truly be said to represent the interests of 'the poor'. As a recent Oxfam study puts it, metropolitan NGOs 'have a particular duty to avoid projecting their own institutional or sectoral interests as though these necessarily represent the interests of people living in poverty' (Eade & Ligteringen 2001: 17).

These debates speak only indirectly to the South African situation. The large overseas NGOs that are prominent in other African countries are much less so in South Africa. There are several reasons for this. One is that in many African countries, even quite small sums from NGOs represent a significant part of expenditure. In South Africa, however, the scale of domestic resources makes contributions by these agencies of relatively minor importance.

The South African context has given a particular twist to the question of advocacy. Advocacy implies acceptance, however critical, of existing power structures. However, the situation before 1994 meant that the stance of many NGOs was one of outright, even revolutionary, opposition. South African NGOs, in other words, were obliged to be highly political, even when this consisted of an attempt to manoeuvre around or engage with the existing power structures. Also, questions of class and race in relation to NGOs were rooted in the country, and South African NGOs, self-evidently part of the society, did not feel compelled to justify their presence or concern as international NGOs sometimes felt they must.

It has been seen that there are substantial pressures for education NGOs to become delivery agencies. Some have balked at this, and have often paid for it by marginalisation or disappearance. Many of the most successful organisations are going down the delivery agency road, generally with few qualms that their advocacy role is being compromised. Since this seems at variance with their earlier trajectory, it is worth asking what is happening.

One answer is survival. There are jobs and futures at stake in a country that cannot guarantee employment even to those with the education and skills that NGO employees tend to possess. More fundamentally, brought up with the rhetoric of revolution rather than that of advocacy, it was in fact possible, the revolution having been achieved and the government now representing the majority, for NGOs to see involvement in implementation as a continuation of the struggle rather than a deviation from it. Thus the debate that wracks northern NGOs about relevance and the nature of their role in the south has not touched South African NGOs to the same extent: as will be seen, for example, some at least move 'into Africa' without much interrogation of their role in relation to the spread of South African influence.

What, in any case, in the context of NGOs, is 'advocacy'? On one level it presumably implies an attempt to engage with and mobilise those with whom NGOs work to enable them to articulate their needs and their conceptions of how these needs might be met. On another level, it may mean an attempt at active engagement with the authorities, so that the needs of the poor are heard and are acted upon effectively by those with the power to assist them. The implication is that NGOs are well placed to act as interlocutors between elements in society assumed to have difficulties in communicating with and understanding each other. It is easy to see that this could be a sensitive issue to a government such as that of South Africa, which has emerged recently from a liberation movement founded on the conviction that it represented the poorest and most oppressed.

There is a range of approaches to advocacy. Depending on their sphere of activity, some NGOs avoid the question through immersion in the job at hand. Of course, this implies that the overall framework, in large part set by government, is sufficiently conducive to enable them to operate without obliging them to challenge it. However, policy does matter, and many NGOs in a position to do so attempt to influence its direction. Project Literacy has taken the road of 'corporatisation', as its CEO terms it. He asserts that the organisation's corporate persona has not meant the loss of 'our faith, or our identity, or our commitment to work with poor people'. However, though he argues that NGOs, and Project Literacy in particular, have had a very important role in policy development, 'if not written a lot of the stuff', the financial and psychic costs are large: there is a 'lack of understanding in government about the new world of NGOs ... [D]onors have been saying to NGOs – you've got to become self-sufficient, run like a business', while the bureaucratic mindset often appears to be that they should do things for free, or nearly so. Ironically, while the most successful NGOs have moved to a more professional approach, some in government, he argues, maintain a 'Lady Bountiful' approach to what NGOs should be and do.

Further, if NGOs depend on government tenders, it is difficult for them to remain open to being critical of government policy. Having been quoted in a Sunday newspaper as critical of some aspect of DoE policy, Andrew Miller was rung early one Monday morning by a senior official reminding him that 'you don't bite the hand that feeds you'. The difficulty, he feels, is to get the balance right between 'being a service provider to the State but also ... maintaining the ability to be critical: and that's the difference with a commercial provider, because a commercial provider would never be critical'. He argues that donor money is crucial in this context, since it gives leeway for independence. Some donors do not understand this, and try to ingratiate themselves at all costs with the DoE. Others grasp the importance of supporting an independent sector, and strengthening civil society through encouraging a multiplicity of voices and ideas.

However, it is necessary to stress complexity, in government as amongst NGOs. Whilst accusations of biting the hand that feeds you may be one, informal governmental response, there are also thoughtful voices within government that articulate the tension between delivery and critique and are by no means unsympathetic to the critical role that is key to at least some visions of the role of NGOs. As far as Bobby Soobrayan, until recently DDG for Planning and Monitoring in the national DoE, was concerned, the tension between a role defined by service delivery, and the need to maintain a critical edge is 'the issue' for NGOs. NGOs are circumscribed by the imperative need for the next project and for mere survival:

> the consistency of what we're doing now with the democratic values of our struggle ... gets lost sometimes ... in the exigencies of actual governing ... I'm saying ... that it's a confusion of mission, and at some point I think some NGOs are going to have to make a choice. They either work for government, or you decide that you've got an intellectual project, some critical thinking, and ... we find ways in which that can be resourced, because it comes down to finances basically, this thing that mitigates against peoples' independence.

He would like to see people moving easily between government, NGOs and universities. In short, 'I don't want to see an NGO that is simply the handmaiden of the state: *that* isn't going to help us, because then they might as well work in government.' However, it will always be difficult to ensure the security of this space where systematic and informed comment and, where necessary, critique, can be generated.

While many South African NGOs have had difficulties redefining themselves in relation to government, this could not be said of NGOs representing religious organisations in education. The case for religious education had to be made in the face of exceptional difficulties in the apartheid era, but its proponents believe that it is no less necessary to make that case in the contemporary context. For example, in the interactions from 1994 to 1996 leading to the new *South African Schools Act*, which set the framework for contemporary schooling in South Africa, the Catholic Institute for Education (CIE) played a key role in defining sections of the Act concerning church-run schools, and continues to promote church interests in education. As Thantshi Serote, the deputy director, says:

> We made an input, and it was taken as is ... from then onwards, we've really positioned ourselves to work in partnership with government. But the partnership I don't think compromises us. It allows us to be critical of government. Like right now, we are unhappy about the amendments to the education laws that will give lots of power to the Minister ... so we criticise the government where it is necessary; we collaborate with them and we work with them.

The organisation thus regards itself as a critical ally of government. Particularly concerned to maintain and protect the interests of the poorer

Catholic schools, its overall aim is to preserve the Catholic ethos in all kinds of church-run institutions. The intriguing aspect of such NGOs is that however allied they may be with government, they come from a perspective literally not of this world. This means that they do not have to struggle to identify or justify their separate identity or interests and that their advocacy role is clear. While they may be under pressure from donors to act in certain ways as far as their practical work is concerned, they are unlikely to compromise their basic religious interests. Existentially they contrast with secular NGOs that operate in the same moral and practical universe as the new government, who may struggle to find solid ground from which to interrogate and even criticise power.

However, are the days of advocacy amongst education NGOs largely over, except for some faith-based organisations? Do NGOs in this sphere face a future where they become ancillary to the state's conception of national problems and their possible solutions? It is too early to say, but there are indications that a new generation of NGOs may be emerging, engaged from outside established centres of power and wealth with basic problems of poverty, equality and quality. The Treatment Action Campaign (TAC), agitating for the rights and interests of those infected with HIV/AIDS, and the Landless Peoples' Movement are examples. Such organisations do not, as did many in the 1980s, defy the state on principle, but they do approach it untrammelled by financial and contractual obligations. In education, locally, unemployed teachers and others have initiated various educational schemes, often trying to persuade the state to bring these into the established system.

South African education NGOs in Africa

Power is relative to the position of those wielding or subject to it. The picture emerging from this chapter is, ironically, that of education NGOs adapting to more substantial pressures and making more substantial changes than they did in the 1980s. However, the situation looks somewhat different when they are seen from the perspective of their relations with the rest of Africa.

Successful South African education NGOs differ from the norm in other parts of Africa. They have substantial domestic sources of income; they rely less on overseas funding; they are larger and, though it would be wrong to generalise too emphatically on this, are possibly in many cases better-managed than those elsewhere; and they have often built strong and apparently enduring relationships with government.

Some analyses would have seen and possibly still see South Africa as representing a bastion of aggressive capitalism in Africa. While this is an oversimplification, the NGO sector in South Africa *does* appear to share the spirit of South African companies and entrepreneurs who are currently carving out export and investment opportunities throughout the continent (Daniel, Naidoo & Naidu 2003).[1] Many of the most vigorous South African education NGOs are expanding 'into Africa', a phrase that many still use. This expansion takes place without much apparent interrogation of their role in relation to the spread of South African influence and indeed often with a sense that South Africans *per se* are likely to have more feel for the rest of the continent and may do a better job than those working for northern organisations. This may or may not be true. However, it is intriguing that this expansion appears to be taking place with so little reference to debates elsewhere in NGO circles.

In their relationship with the rest of Africa, the NGOs interviewed for this research take a commercial view. Clients elsewhere benefit from the accumulated experience of South African organisations, but pay an economic price for this as they would for any commercial service. Some examples will add substance. Project Literacy has grasped the commercial route with both hands. As the CEO puts it, 'part of our strategic plan is to become a sub-Saharan player ... if we can sell South African Breweries to Africa, then why can't we sell Project Literacy?' The organisation has spent two-and-a-half years exploring the possibilities, making sure to work through local NGOs, 'so we wouldn't be Cecil John Rhodes, we wouldn't be Oxfam'. Wherever they went, including Mozambique, they found an insistent demand for literacy in English, and have already produced materials for Botswana, Namibia, Kenya and Mozambique. Staff have been sent to study Portuguese so as to facilitate work in Mozambique.

The Molteno Project, which works with mother-tongue literacy, is also growing, invited by countries where the reputation of the 'Breakthrough to Literacy' materials had spread. These have been introduced nationally in schools in Botswana and Lesotho, where material could easily be adapted from South Africa, but they have also been translated and adapted for use in languages in Namibia, Zambia and Uganda. There have been preliminary approaches from Mali and Ethiopia.

JET Education Services is working in the SADC region, and even in Ghana, which has a long history of first-rate education, but where recurring economic and political crises have led high-level personnel to seep away, opening opportunities for foreign organisations. The research NGO, the Education Foundation Trust, has also made a conscious decision to extend its work outside South Africa's borders, especially into the SADC region. The IEB sells its examinations in Zambia, Swaziland and Mozambique, and is looking at opportunities in Malawi. Some of the university-based Education Policy Units (EPUs), a category of educational research NGOs, carry out educational research in collaboration with organisations as far as west Africa. Even what could be called para-educational NGOs are working in other parts of Africa. For example, personnel from Soul City, a health and particularly HIV/AIDS education organisation which uses the mass media to spread its message, largely through drama and entertainment, are acting as technical advisors in countries – Zambia, Zimbabwe, Botswana, Lesotho, Swaziland 'and other sub-Saharan countries' – wishing to present television programmes similar to the popular South African models.

There are many fascinating aspects to this growing South African NGO involvement north of its borders. It is a phenomenon that has received little academic attention. Though some in the sector may feel themselves to be in a long hangover after the heroic 1980s, many South African education NGOs are advancing from their role as service providers within the country and are vigorously engaging with the rest of the continent. They are doing this with little of the angst and self-doubt that can characterise metropolitan NGOs. Whether this represents a qualitatively new factor in the African educational scene that could result in more nuanced and appropriate development models, or is simply an intervention from a regional metropole that parallels Western aid agendas is, at this stage, an open question.

Conclusion

NGOs have developed in a way in some respects not typical of the rest of the continent. They have a history of independence and assertiveness stemming from the apartheid past, and are often deeply rooted socially and financially. On the other hand, since 1994 many have struggled to clarify their roles in the context of the political and social changes that have brought a government to power, claiming to represent the very aims for which many NGOs would assert that they stand.

Compared with other African societies, South Africa is wealthy, albeit highly unequal. The independent economic base for NGOs is therefore more robust than elsewhere on the continent. While foreign donors are important in South Africa, they are not predominant. There is a large 'indigenous' donor community, mostly corporate. While such donors have their own agendas, their location does differentiate them from external funders. Nevertheless, the ironical result of the accession to power of a democratically-elected regime is that its very legitimacy has led to the diversion of funding from the NGO sector directly to government. Typically, funding now comes to education NGOs through the 'service provider' role. This is a legitimate and necessary function, but leads to direct dependence on government and a limitation of the critical 'advocacy' that is crucial to the creativity and independence of the sector.

Though there are many variations between NGOs, the paradox is in general true, and recognised by some within government, that, overall, South African education NGOs are weaker now than they were in the apartheid period. Because of the political context, donors in the apartheid and transitional periods were unusually tolerant of relatively loose financial controls and ideologically-driven agendas. They have now become more commercial and results-oriented in approach. Education NGOs have made the adjustments demanded by these changes in the funding landscape. Where they have not, they have often not survived.

In spite of these problems, a rapidly-growing and innovative aspect of many of the most successful South African education NGOs is that they increasingly operate in a regional and even continental context, though perhaps, in terms of the power relations underlying this expansion, in a somewhat unreflective manner.

Notes

1. For a view from Nigeria, see A Mohammed's article Nigerian Economy: The South African Invasion, *Weekly Trust*, 13 September 2003.

References

Abraham, G (1989) *The Catholic Church and Apartheid: The Response of the Catholic Church in South Africa to the First Decade of National Party Rule 1948–1957*. Johannesburg: Ravan Press.

Barnes, T & Haya, T (2002) Educational Resistance in Context: Zingisa Educational Project in the Eastern Cape: 1975 to 1993. In Kallaway, P (ed) *The History of Education*. Cape Town: Pearson Education

Bredekamp, H & Ross, R (eds) (1995) *Missions and Christianity in South African History*. Johannesburg: Wits University Press

Cawthra, HC with Kraak, G & Maepa, N (2000) *Working with the Non-profit Sector in South Africa*. West Malling: Charities Aid Foundation

Comaroff, J & J (1991) *Of Revelation and Revolution: Christianity, Colonialism and Consciousness in South Africa*, Vol 1. Chicago: University of Chicago Press

Daniel, J; Naidoo, V & Naidu, S (2003) The South Africans Have Arrived: Post-Apartheid Corporate Expansion into Africa. In Daniel, J; Habib, A & Southall, R (eds) *State of the Nation: South Africa 2003–2004*. Cape Town: HSRC Press

Eade, D & Ligteringen, E (eds) (2001) *Debating Development: NGOs and the Future*. Oxford: Oxfam International

Houston, GF (1999) *The National Liberation Struggle in South Africa: a Case Study of the United Democratic Front, 1983–1987*. Aldershot: Ashgate

Hyslop, J (1999) *The Classroom Struggle: Policy and Resistance in South Africa 1940–1990*. Pietermaritzburg: University of Natal Press

Institute for Policy Studies (2002) *Global Civil Society At-a-Glance: Major Findings of the Johns Hopkins Comparative Nonprofit Sector Project*. Baltimore: Johns Hopkins University, Institute for Policy Studies

Kallaway, P (ed) (2002) *The History of Education Under Apartheid 1948–1994: the Doors of Learning and Culture Shall be Opened*. Cape Town: Pearson Education

King, K (1999) Aid to South African Education: A Case of the Reluctant Recipient? In King, K & Buchert, L (eds) *Changing International Aid to Education: Global Patterns and National Contexts*. Paris: Unesco/Norrag

King, M & Van den Berg, O (1993) The Independent Examinations Board, August 1989–February 1992: A Narrative. In Taylor, N (ed) *Inventing Knowledge: Contests in Curriculum Construction*. Cape Town: Maskew Miller Longman

Landau, PS (1995) *The Realm of the Word: Language, Gender, and Christianity in a Southern African Kingdom*. Cape Town: David Philip

Motala, S & Vally, S (2002) People's Education: From People's Power to Tirisano. In Kallaway, P (ed) *The History of Education Under Apartheid 1948–1994: The Doors of Learning and Culture Shall be Opened*. Cape Town: Pearson Education

National Education Co-ordinating Committee (1993) *National Education Policy Investigation: The Framework Report and Final Report Summaries*. Cape Town: Oxford University Press

Ngeleza, B; Chabane, S & Dlamini, D (2000) *Development Co-operation Report: Evaluation of ODA to the Education Sector*. Rosebank: International Organisation Development

Perrow, ME (2002) Learning in Transition: Youth Development in Post-Apartheid South Africa. Unpublished doctoral thesis, University of California at Berkeley

Salomon, LM (ed) (1999) *Global Civil Society: Dimensions of the Nonprofit Sector*. Baltimore: Johns Hopkins University, Institute for Policy Studies

Seekings, J (2000) *The UDF: A History of the United Democratic Front in South Africa, 1983–1991*. Cape Town: David Philip

Swilling, M & Russell, B (2002) *The Size and Scope of the Non-profit Sector in South Africa*. Johannesburg and Durban: P&DM and CCS

Van Kessell, I (2000) *Beyond our Wildest Dreams: The United Democratic Front and the Transformation of South Africa*. Charlottesville: University Press of Virginia

Ward, SJ (1995) Planning for Change in Educational NGOs: Three Case Studies. Unpublished masters thesis, University of the Witwatersrand

Interviews

1. CIE. Thantsi Serote (Departmental Director) and Marlene Jardine (Developmental Officer). Johannesburg, 29 July 2002
2. DoE. Duncan Hindle (DDG for General Education and Training). Pretoria, 16 August 2002
3. DoE. Bobby Soobrayan (DDG for Planning and Monitoring). Pretoria, 25 September 2002
4. Education Foundation Trust. Lomthie Mavimbela (CEO), Lindani Mthethwa (Technical Manager), and Derrick Pavaday (Corporate Services Manager). Johannesburg, 30 July 2002
5. IEB. Lyn Scott (CEO). Johannesburg, 26 July 2002
6. JET. Hemant Waghmarae (Divisional Manager). Johannesburg, 26 July 2002
7. Mathematics Centre for Professional Development. Sharanjeet Shan (Executive Director). Johannesburg, 26 July 2002

8. Molteno Project. Patience Lekganyane (Manager: Admin and Human Resources) and Paula Gains. Johannesburg, 24 July 2002
9. Project Literacy. Andrew Miller (CEO). Pretoria, 8 August 2002
10. Soul City. Joel Sebolao (Divisional Manager). Johannesburg, 24 July 2002
11. South African Commission for Higher Education Development. Jenny Rabinowitz (CEO). Johannesburg, 25 July 2002
12. South African NGO Coalition. Lungi Mathole (Co-ordinator, Gauteng Region). Pretoria, 29 July 2002
13. United States Agency for International Development. Cashief Lombard (Workforce Development Specialist). Pretoria, 25 July 2002

13 The state of play in early childhood development

Kim Porteus

One of the central principles of the 1994 moment was an unambiguous affirmation of the rights of the child. It opened up a new conversation about the boundaries of the possible for the lives of South African children. The first decade of democracy marks a massive transition in the life of South African children. Despite progress, the gains have not yet been strong enough to work against the momentum of inequity facing the nation's young. The structure of the economy, combined with a range of global pressures, has worked to support the meta-structure of poverty facing many South African children.

Both local and international research suggests that many children born into poverty may confront their greatest and most long-lasting disadvantage during gestation and the first few years of life. While child rights have formed a central conceptual pillar for post-apartheid policy development, the processes of early childhood development (ECD) have been widely relegated to the periphery of policy attention, particularly in the education sector. Further, the policy and development choices have not been oriented to effect massive redress; the current trajectory of development carries the danger of deepening the inequities facing young children.

This chapter attempts to summarise the debates and developments in the field of ECD over the first ten years of democracy in South Africa. The chapter begins by describing the conceptual complexity of ECD in the context of South African education development. The chapter then describes the patterns of ECD provisioning in South Africa, the process of policy development, and finally postulates the relationship between the policy choices and the changing patterns of ECD provisioning into the future. Through this discussion several reasons are postulated for the peripheral placement of ECD in the first decade of policy development in South Africa – the lack of fit between the nature of ECD needs and the state apparatus, the nature of the feminised voice of ECD policy advocates, and the tensions between the proactive servicing of child rights and macro-pressures on fiscal restraint in social spending.

What is early childhood development?

The Convention on the Rights of the Child (1989), the World Summit for Children (1990), the World Convention on Education for All (1996), as well as South African policy frameworks (DoE 1996; RSA 2001; Office of the President 1996), define 'early childhood development' as strategies that meet the basic needs of young children from birth to at least nine years. In the conceptual definitions, these policies emphasise the integrated nature of service provision between the state and civil society (families, communities, non-governmental organisations [NGOs], private sector) on the one hand, and between state departments (Education, Welfare, Health and others) on the other.

The consensus begins to break down, however, when this concept is operationalised through the lens of education policy. In many respects, the implications of ECD for other sectors are less complicated, if still difficult to achieve. Strategies to enhance maternal, infant and child nutrition, to provide safe and secure accommodation, to break the back of entrenched poverty – all logically emerge from the integrated definition of early childhood development.

The operationalisation of ECD through the lens of education is more complicated. Children between at least six and nine, relegated to primary schools, are often quickly left out of ECD. With reference to children from birth to six years old, there are two related but distinct imperatives. First, what is best for a child? And second, what is best for the primary caregiver? Given that the majority of primary caregivers in South Africa are women (mothers, surrogate mothers, and grandmothers) this latter question becomes central to the pursuit of women's rights on a wider level. What forms of ECD services open up space for child development, and at the same time open up space for women to navigate their own lives (economically, socially, educationally and personally)?

While there is little disagreement that children need love, safety, stimulation, and creative play, there is no consensus of the best place for children to receive this educational care. Dominant notions of what is best for young children immediately locate 'good ECD provisioning' within ECD institutions (crèches, pre-schools, nursery schools). While it is beyond the scope of this paper to explore the derivation of this, it is arguably linked not only to greater participation of women in the workplace, but also the dichotomy that exists between the nuclear family on the one hand and institutional care on the other in more industrialised settings, where there are few social practices for group or shared care located between these two extremes.

Problematising the assumption that the best early childhood care takes place in institutional settings is important in the South African context. There are two important critiques of this notion. First, what resources have to be minimally available within this model to underpin good care? At what point does the function of an institution shift from 'care' to warehousing? While the picture of 20 children in a bright play space, with a safe space for outside play, facilitated by a well-trained caregiver may be appealing, the image of 50 children in an unventilated dark space, sitting in rows, hesitant to play for fear of frustrating an overburdened and under-trained careworker is less so. At a certain point in quality, the 'care' not only does not reach its best goals, but becomes counterproductive – undermining curiosity, stimulation and relationships of trust.

The second problem with overly focusing on a model of centre-based care is that it underestimates other models of educational care for young children in South Africa. Large numbers of South African children live in the context of extended families, wherein a range of shared childcare strategies are brought to bear. In some rural areas, the village itself is the educational centre with a range of elders, parents, and young people providing educational support and care. The form and function of the extended family and community with reference to child-rearing is wide. However, it would be unwise to suggest that children who are cared for within a village set-up – often learning from a range of relationships, self-relegated play, and chores – are by definition in a less educational environment than more institutional settings. If this is embraced, there are a range of ECD strategies that could be developed to support families and communities to provide conducive environments for their children.

The complexity of operationalising ECD reflects two conceptual shifts in thinking in the early 1990s. Rachel Bray in her examination of the contributions made by social surveys to our understanding of child well-being in South Africa (2002: 3) cites two important shifts crystallising in the early 1990s about child well-being. First, through the course of the ratification of the UN Convention on the Rights of the Child (1989) (and reflected across the human rights movement in South Africa), the rather more dependency-based approach to child development was replaced with a rights-based approach providing children, in theory, with legitimate claims to state resources and to participating in decisions that affect their daily lives. The second important conceptual shift is the greater recognition and cognisance given to the historical and cultural variation in notions of ideal childhoods, and of children's active participation in society. Taken together, these two shifts frame the complexity of the policy question: in the context of a rights-based approach that appreciates a range of ideal childhoods, what is the best form and function of early childhood provisioning with reference to so-called 'education'?

Socio-economic and health status of young children

It is beyond the scope of this chapter to summarise the state of South African children across all indices of well-being. It would be too restrictive, however, to embrace an integrated definition of ECD, and then shift to a narrow discussion of site-based ECD centres. In order to paint a picture of the reality of early childhood development in this period, this section summarises some of the most important developments in the social and economic lives of young people over the past ten years.

Poverty, employment and socio-economic security

A range of survey data has been collected to better understand the socio-economic circumstances of children in South Africa (Bray 2002). It is unclear from current data sources whether or not the number of children who are living under thresholds of poverty is stabilising or slightly increasing. What is clear is that there has been no dramatic decrease in the number of children living under poverty thresholds (Bray 2002). Children are disproportionately represented among the poor. Using different poverty lines and data sets, various studies estimate that between 58 and 75 per cent of South African children live below the poverty line.[1]

Extreme income inequalities persist. Cumulatively, 20 per cent of the households, constituting the most wealthy quintile, command approximately 66 per cent of the national household income, while the remaining 80 per cent of households account for approximately 34 per cent. The poorest 20 per cent of the population account for only 2.8 per cent of the total household income (Wildeman 2003a: 8).

Poverty is concentrated among black households – 52 per cent of black people, 17 per cent of coloureds, and less than 5 per cent of Indians and whites are poor (StatsSA 1999). Comparing household income data from 1995 and 2000 suggests that annual average household income declined in real terms for black children, while it grew for white children (Hirschowitz 2002). Female-headed households are twice as likely to be poor than male-headed households. Poverty is concentrated in the rural areas. In 2000, 40 per cent of non-urban households were in the bottom poverty quintile, and 4 per cent in the top quintile, compared to 19 per cent of urban households in the bottom quintile and 18 per cent in the top (Hirschowitz 2002).

Perhaps even more important than absolute poverty rates for South African children, is the changing structure of employment over the past decade (see also Bhorat, in this volume). Formal sector employment for households of young children is not growing. While 34 per cent of black men were officially unemployed in 1996, the figure rose to 43 per cent in 2001. Similarly, official unemployment among black women rose from 52 per cent to 58 per cent in this period. The increased unemployment over this time reflects both the lack of rapid growth in formal sector employment and the growth of the economically-active cohort. The loss of formal jobs is tempered somewhat by a rise in informal sector employment; however, the informal sector jobs are significantly less well paid and less secure, and many are described as 'survivalist' in nature (Taylor 2002: 21).

To what extent has the state been able to intervene in providing social security for children living in the poorest households? Two intervention strategies have been particularly important for young children – the provision of social infrastructure, and the provision of social security grants. With reference to social infrastructure, the 2001 Census suggests some limited but important gains with reference to the provision of housing, water, electricity and sanitation. Sixty four per cent of South African households lived in formal dwellings in 2001, up from 58 per cent in 1996. Sixty one percent of South African households used electricity for cooking, up from 47 per cent in 1996. One-third of South African households in 2001 had access to piped water in their dwelling, up slightly from 1996. Almost 52 per cent of households had access to a flush or chemical toilet facility in 2001, rising from 50.5 per cent in 1996 (StatsSA 2003: 49).

The two most important state interventions to impact on income distribution are the State Old Age Pension (SOAP) and the Child Support Grant (CSG). The SOAP is the largest social assistance programme, benefiting about 1.9 million beneficiaries in 2001. There is evidence that these resources are highly invested into child welfare (Barbarin & Richter 2001: 144). Even so, 76 per cent of children live in households with no pensioners, and are less likely to benefit significantly from this income (Barbarin & Richter 2001: 58).

The CSG is arguably the most important governmental programme with reference to the livelihood of young children. This grant was introduced in April 1998 to provide R100 per child per month for children under seven years old, within a means test. Importantly, the grant was designed to 'follow the child', making the grant independent of the child's family structure. The stated policy goal was to reach three million children within five years. In April 2001, 800 476 caregivers received grants, to a value of R120 million. Later in 2001, the number increased significantly, reaching up to 1.5 million. Several concerns remain about the CSG, relating to the reach (while the intake rate has increased there is concern that the children most in need are not targeted effectively), scope (eliminating children who are over seven), grant size (the grant does not meet the basic costs of childcare), and means testing (currently representing a barrier to suitable applicants gaining grant access) (Taylor 2002: 58).

Child health

One of the most important indicators of the well-being of the family is the profile of child health. Some of the most rapid processes of transformation for children in post-apartheid South Africa were achieved in the health sector. Through its primary health system reform process, the state extended free healthcare to children under the age of six and to pregnant mothers. Subsequently, the free healthcare programme at public primary healthcare facilities was extended to all South Africans. While the gains have been important, the quality of service provision remains a challenge. The Committee of Inquiry into a Comprehensive System of Social Security in South Africa suggests that the rights of the young child will ultimately require both a substantive upgrade in state quality of service and a system of national health insurance (Taylor 2002: 85–86). Two interrelated sets of health crises are making early childhood support services both more urgent and more complicated – poverty-related childhood illnesses and the HIV/AIDS pandemic.

The most common poverty-related illness among South African children is stunting, with 25 per cent of black children demonstrating stunting.[2] Ten per cent of black children in South Africa demonstrate signs of malnutrition. Both wasting and stunting are more prevalent in rural areas than urban areas. While definitions of food security are elusive, the National Food Consumption Survey suggests that up to one in two children in South Africa has an intake of less than half the recommended levels of important nutrients (Labadarios 1999).

The 2002 HIV prevalence study sponsored by the Nelson Mandela Foundation among others (Shisana & Simbayi 2002) suggests that the HIV prevalence rate among children between the ages of two and 14 is approximately 5.6 per cent, and increases by age through the age cohort (Shisana & Simbayi 2002: 45). Beyond the impact on children who are directly infected by HIV/AIDS, there is a massive impact on children through the effect of the disease on caregivers, neighbours and loved ones. The 2002 study suggests that 13 per cent of children between two and 14 have lost either their biological mother or father. Three per cent of households were reported as being headed by a person between the ages of 12 and 18 (Shisana & Simbayi 2002: 67–68). The full story of the physical and emotional challenges of the pandemic on the lives of children and the new types of support that children require are only just beginning to unfold.

This quick review of indicators of childhood well-being illustrates both the progress and challenges that face the integrated goal of improving the life circumstances of young children in South Africa. The global economic environment has proven a range of barriers to the massive growth of formal sector employment during this period. The structure of the economy largely works to maintain the meta-structure of poverty facing South Africa's children. While there have been important but limited gains in key areas of social service provision, these gains have not yet been strong enough to work against the tide of inequity facing the nation's young. The danger of these trends, combined with the effect patterns of the HIV/AIDS pandemic, is the continuation, even entrenchment, of 'two worlds within one nation' – a world of relative opportunity for a few privileged children, and a world of closed-down opportunities for too many. In this environment, the development of explicitly educational ECD services becomes exceedingly important. How can South Africa open up early childhood educational opportunities in a way to counteract the wider social pressures working against the healthy development of our youngest citizens?

Patterns of ECD centre provisioning

Historical process

The current pattern of *formal* ECD centre provisioning began to be established as least as far back as the 1930s, and carefully reflects segregationist and apartheid policy intent (Padayachee, Atmore, Biersteker & Evans 1994: 8–9). By 1940, the Union Department of Welfare provided *per capita* subsidies to 'day-care centres' and provincial education departments provided subsidies in support of 'nursery schools'. The divide between 'welfare' and 'education' was polarised, with welfare supporting custodial childcare, and 'education' providing 'nursery schools' that were seen to be educational. While welfare subsidies were available across the race divide to some extent, education subsidies were not available to black children. In other words, the state would provide some black children with custodial care, but not educational care.

Subsidies were originally calculated to cover half of the costs, but were not increased over time, creating an increased reliance on user fees to cover costs. The privileged position of white parents allowed them to pay more. Due to both colonial culture and the increased privatisation of services, the quality of care became increasingly differentiated along the basis of race. Support for early childhood services was dramatically decreased under the Nationalist Party and the launch of formal apartheid. The minimal state-subsidised services targeted poor white children.

At the same time, pre-primary education was taken over by the provincial education departments, as articulated in the *National Education Policy Act* of 1967, establishing the basis for the expanded provision of pre-primary services to white children. As pre-primary education expanded for white children in the 1970s and 1980s, the Department of Education and Training (DET) was forced to discontinue subsidising pre-primary centres of education for black children, relegating the responsibility of provision to parents, communities, foreign and NGO funding, and the private sector (Padayachee et al. 1994: 9). (There was some expansion of ECD programming in the former Bantustans through the 1990s.) While welfare continued to subsidise centres of childcare on a limited basis, the subsidisation model essentially eliminated support to black children (DoE 2001: 9). In the context of the state neglect of ECD provisioning in black areas, the NGO sector emerged as the dominant provider. While the NGO sector was an important site for creative and quality innovations, it remained limited and fragmented in scope.

Beyond subsidisation, perhaps the most important driver of racial polarisation in early childhood services was the race-based discrepancy in practitioner training. Training courses for black ECD practitioners were largely curtailed after 1958. Provincial training initiatives, particularly for black educators, were phased out by the end of 1990 (Padayachee et al. 1994: 9). Thus, while white ECD practitioners on a limited basis obtained credentials from formal state programmes, it was largely the non-governmental sector that was servicing black ECD practitioners.

It would be a mistake to interpret this history as simply a combination of lack of state capacity, bureaucratic neglect and under-expenditure. The treatment of children under apartheid was an important piece of the apartheid scaffolding. Beyond the *destruction* of potential good, apartheid served to actively *construct* a society based on the principles of inequity and human disgrace – the patterns of development, the differential seeding of human possibility, conceptions of power and worth. The symbolic challenge of policy developments since 1994 has not simply been to rebuild the social fabric of a nation from a neutral starting point, but to re-engineer a society that was originally designed to serve social objectives hostile to those of a democratic order.

ECD service provisioning at the launch of democracy

What was the pattern of ECD service provisioning resulting from this history? At the time of the democratic transition, there were few sources of data to describe the provisioning patterns of ECD services. The system of registration was fragmented, with public pre-primary schools registered under education, and 'educare centres' and 'crèches' registered under welfare – according to different statutes. A large number of ECD centres were not registered at all. Many ECD sites in informal settlements and rural areas were not registered because either they were marginalised from the formal bureaucracy, or they could not meet the apartheid statutes largely suitable to serviced urban sites.

A study undertaken in 1992 by the World Bank and the Centre for Education Policy Development (CEPD) (Padayachee et al. 1994) provided an initial estimate of coverage (Table 13.1). The study estimated that almost ten per cent of South African children between birth and six had access to some form of ECD site, and three per cent had access to a subsidised service. While over one-third of white children attended early childhood facilities, only six per cent of black children had such access. The differential between expenditure *per capita* on white children and black children exceeded 40.

Table 13.1 ECD provisioning: access, state subsidisation, expenditure

	Total 0–6 population	Subsidised by state	Non subsidised	Total	Percentage subsidised	Percentage of total	Expenditure by race
Black	4 838 200	108 062	226 688	334 750	2	7	R38*
Coloured	448 600	25 519	28 481	54 000	6	12	R752
Indian	119 800	15 239	1 761	17 000	13	14	R118
White	430 100	49 409	110 519	159 928	11	37	R1 684
Total	5 836 700	198 229	367 449	565 678	3	10	

Source: Extrapolated from Padayachee et al. 1994; Biersteker and Short 1994; and NEPI 1993.
Note: *State expenditure on ECD in the homelands was approximately R536 per child.

Beyond this limited coverage, there was no data on which to base a national planning exercise. In 1996, the political leadership of the Department of Education (DoE) (the Council of Education Ministers) approved a nationwide audit of ECD sites, seeking external funding to support the audit. While methodological weaknesses may have worked to under-represent services in some underprivileged communities, the audit provided the most comprehensive national data set on ECD services in South Africa. The results of the audit were finally published in 2001 (DoE 2001), providing data on 23 482 sites and over a million children between the ages of zero and seven across the nation. The audit provided information on four key aspects of early childhood provisioning – the scope and demographics of ECD access, the typology of ECD service sites, the financial basis of ECD provisioning, and a profile of ECD practitioners. The most important findings include the following:
- **Access:** One out of six children between the ages of zero and seven has access to some sort of site-based ECD services. The majority of children are five to six years old; coverage is much more limited for children under

four years old. Children in rural areas have the least access to services. Black children have access to services with lower indices for infrastructure and practitioner quality. Too few children have access to services which cater to their home languages.

- **Typologies:** There are three typologies of ECD sites nationally – school-based sites (17 per cent), community-based sites (49 per cent) and home-based sites (34 per cent). Of these, 72 per cent are located within one kilometre of a primary school. Over 80 per cent of the sites are multi-age sites providing services to children between the ages of three and five years old. Home-based sites are smaller, have more practitioners per child, and tend to be the site of the youngest children. Community- and home-based sites are more likely to be open for a greater number of hours per day, have more practitioners per child, and have greater access to electricity, water, and sewerage than school-based sites.

- **Financial basis:** Learner fees are by far the most important financial input into the ECD sector. School fees were the only source of income for 28 per cent of the sites. The user fees are less than R25 per month at one-third of the sites, between R25 and R75 at another third, and are over R75 in the final third. Fee payment rates are poor across the three site typologies. Some sites depend upon limited subsidisation from the government Departments of Welfare (20 per cent), Education (ten per cent) and Health (seven per cent). The current financial basis of most sites is tenuous.

- **Practitioner profile:** The field of ECD is highly feminised with 99 per cent of practitioners being women. A large number of practitioners either have no training (23 per cent) and/or do not have qualifications recognised by the government (88 per cent). Sixty per cent of the practitioners without any training are black; 61 per cent of practitioners with recognised qualifications are white. Low qualifications are associated with low pay. Forty-four per cent of practitioners earn less than R500 per month. The qualification and salary profile demonstrate a deep discrimination against black practitioners.

While the audit provides essential data for the purpose of policy formulation and planning, it is important to note what it does not provide. Most importantly, it does not describe the tenor of day-to-day care or educational activities, differentiate between custodial and educational care, or suggest the propensity for innovation or stagnation. Data describing the educational validity of sites transcends a survey instrument or simple methods of quantification. The authors of the audit alluded to this in their conclusion, noting that, 'not only has ECD been marginalised and fragmented, but the predominant model of provisioning has been inherited from white, Euro-centric, middle-class contexts, which may not be the most appropriate model in the current context. The *laissez-faire* replication of this model in disadvantaged communities without sufficient funding and support results in questionable provisioning' (DoE 2001: 11).

The policy process

The early 1990s: planning for democracy

The policy challenge of the early 1990s was framed by both the complexities of the ECD challenges and the highly fragmented and unequal patterns of provisioning crafted under apartheid. The key policy questions in the context of this legacy were: 1) what is the best form of ECD provisioning in South Africa, 2) how can the state best effect massive redress to ensure vulnerable children have access to ECD services, and 3) how should the state fund these services?

One of the most important pre-1994 processes for education policy articulation was the National Education Policy Investigation (NEPI). NEPI was a project of the National Education Co-ordinating Committee (NECC) conducted between December 1990 and August 1992. The objective of the process was to investigate policy options in education within the broad values of the democratic movement. One of 12 sectoral reports was dedicated to the area of ECD, culminating in NEPI recommendations for the sector. The NEPI report identified the central policy challenges facing the ECD sector as: highly inequitable and fragmented access to quality services biased against black children, rural children, and working-class children; inequitable and inadequate training and support services; poor governance (neither regulatory of quality nor promoting of community participation); and inadequate public resource allocation (NEPI 1993: 118–121). NEPI located the ECD policy questions in a rights-based approach whereby ECD provision is an extension of both children's rights 'to live and develop to their full potential' and women's rights 'to have choice and control over their own lives' (NEPI 1993: 116). The NEPI policy options affirmed both the need for comprehensive and responsive services as well as increased public investment into ECD provisioning. In terms of policy options, NEPI framed a range of policy options for five- to nine-year-olds including a range of pre-primary options, and a range of policy options for children up to six, inclusive of centre-based care, home-based care, childcare leave and allowances, part-time programming, and family educational support programmes, supplemented by feeding schemes, food aid, health support and health education.

The NEPI policy recommendations identified the privatisation of ECD services under apartheid as a primary driver of inequity, undermining access to quality services by poor children (1993: 122). While NEPI calls for a partnership in the financing of ECD services between the state, households and the private sector, it argues against an emphasis on private funding and places the central responsibility for subsidisation of ECD services on the state. NEPI criticised the expenditure on pre-primary education under apartheid as unacceptably low at less than one per cent of the budget in 1990. They advocated an increase in pre-primary expenditure to at least five per cent of the budget through redistribution of education spending, state Lottery proceeds, indirect taxation, and local government rates. They advocate subsidisation on a *per capita* basis as the best means of extending provision in a way that promotes redress and community innovation of service provisioning. To a great degree these recommendations were reflected in the *Yellow Book*, and other articulations of education policy options of the African National Congress (ANC) prior to elections (ANC 1995).

During 1993 and 1994 the ANC, the Congress of South African Trade Unions (Cosatu), the South African Communist Party (SACP), the South African National Civic Organisation (SANCO), the NECC and other mass democratic organisations engaged in a process of policy formulation culminating in the Reconstruction and Development Programme (RDP) 1994 – a policy framework and programme around which the ANC would contest the elections. While the RDP formulation for ECD policies was less specific than the NEPI recommendations, the RDP called for increased public and private funding, and assigned the democratic government 'ultimate responsibility for training, upgrading and setting of national standards' for pre-primary services.

Thus, while many of the details were still contested or unclear, the policy processes within the democratic movement leading up to the elections in 1994 began to provide a framework for answering the key policy questions facing the ECD sector. First, ECD was prioritised and articulated within a human rights approach to policy development. Second, there was a commitment to integrated and multifunctional ECD services catering to the range of needs of children and mothers of young children. Third, value was placed on the innovation and service provision provided by NGOs and community-based organisations (CBOs). While the state subsidisation of services was advocated, the state's taking over all of the provision of services was not. And finally, there was a commitment to increased governmental expenditure, with the specific goal of enacting massive redress in the sector.

The first years of democracy: 1994 to 1996

Arguably the most important policy development in the democratic era with reference to early childhood development was the ratification of the Constitution of South Africa, whereby a range of human and specifically child rights are articulated and guaranteed. All citizens are guaranteed the right to life (11), human dignity (10), freedom of religion (15), expression and association (16, 17), a basic education (29), adult education (29), health care, food, water, social security (27), and an environment which is not harmful to their wellbeing (24). Every child is guaranteed the right to basic nutrition, shelter, basic health care and social services, and to be protected from maltreatment, neglect, abuse and degradation (28[1]). While the Constitution provides a rights-based legislative framework upon which to base the mandate for equitable and quality ECD services, these services, *per se*, are not articulated as a specific right.

During the first two years following the elections there was little policy development around ECD in the education sector. The *White Paper on Education and Training* (RSA 1995: 33–34) identified ECD as a priority needing urgent attention. The White Paper committed the government to providing ten years of free and compulsory schooling per child, starting with a Reception Year for five-year-olds. It affirmed government's responsibility to curriculum frameworks, while affirming the innovation residing in non-state service providers by suggesting that the actual provision of services would be rendered by NGOs and CBOs.

The DoE's *Interim Policy on Early Childhood Development* of 1996 provided a broad policy vision for early childhood development. It suggested a 'facilitative state' working in collaboration with a range of partnerships. The interim policy emphasised the 'multi-pronged and integrated' (DoE 1996: 7) nature of ECD strategies for children from birth to nine years old and, at the same time, suggested a framework for the introduction of a Reception Year of education through a National Implementation Plan.

The 1996 moment was critical for policy and programme developments for ECD. While the pre-1994 policy discussions assumed a massive increase in state expenditure in ECD at this time, the process was instead overshadowed by macroeconomic policy choices located within the Treasury and Department of Finance (DoF). A massive investment into ECD service expansion was simply counter to the political and economic moment. Rather than articulate a programme of redress and support of integrated services, the political leadership of the DoE (Council of Education Ministers [CEM] and the Heads of Education Departments Committee [HEDCOM]) approved two research processes – a national audit of service provision mentioned earlier, and a national pilot project considering models of ECD service provisioning. While these research processes arguably served to delay decisions of investment into ECD services, they were motivated as a basis for a more informed articulation of a vision for ECD service provisioning.

Research into policy options

At the same time as the national audit, the DoE undertook a national pilot project (the Impilo Pilot Project) that would finally be used to justify the policy choices for the ECD sector announced in 2001. From the beginning of the policy process there is an unresolved tension between two models of ECD service provision: a community-based, multi-age-group model of integrated intersectoral provision on the one hand (emphasising the development of safety nets for children and families), and a school-based model emphasising the provision of Reception Year education on the other. While in reality there is a continuum of models between these poles, the two models represent profoundly different ways of conceiving of ECD services. If research were required on which to justify policy choices, the core question would have been: what is the most viable model (or combination of models) for ECD provisioning (including costs) and how can the state best facilitate the realisation of this model, with particular respect for issues of redress? If this was the key policy question, the national pilot project was in fact never designed to answer it.

The pilot design was restricted to considering Reception Year services for five-year-old children, and the viability of minimal state funding. This pilot provided a R2 subsidy per five-year-old learner in each participating site. The design did not consider alternative subsidy frameworks (R2, R3, R5, R20, R100 ...). The conclusion reached was that R2 per learner was neither 'adequate nor appropriate' (DoE 2001: 23). Given the design of the research, nothing could be said about what would constitute an 'adequate' or 'appropriate' subsidy.

There were a range of findings that transcended a sole focus on the provision of Reception Year classrooms. Findings supported the wide reach of ECD programming in order to be responsive to local needs, including parent education and mobilisation (and the conceptual link between ECD and adult basic education and training [ABET] programming), early identification and intervention for children with special needs, childhood protection, HIV/AIDS programmes, food security programmes, income-generation, toy libraries and other activities that support child development. However, recommendations concerning services that integrated across age groups and services that were less school-based were for the most part under-emphasised in the final report.

The policy choice

The *Education White Paper (5) on Early Childhood Development* (RSA, 2001) was released in 2001. At the time of policy development, policy-makers had access to the findings of the national audit, the pilot project, and a range of international research, affirming ECD as a cost-effective national investment, particularly at the earlier ages of up to to six years.

The White Paper singles out five-year-old children as the focus of provisioning. Minimal attention is given to pre-Reception Year services. While the policy provides a strong argument for these services, it provides no guidelines or concrete support toward this end. The responsibility for the nought to four-year-old cohort is largely shifted to the Department of Social Development. There is reference to collaborative programming between education, health and welfare departments, but little direction and no funding specifications are suggested. Servicing of six- to nine-year-olds is captured by suggestions of quality improvement in the Foundation Phase of primary schooling.

The policy puts forward the establishment of a national system of provisioning of a Reception Year based in public primary schools with a small community-based component. Subsidies for the Reception Year in public primary schools will take place via direct grants-in-aid from provincial departments of education to school governing bodies (SGBs). SGBs will receive subsidies for each appropriately-aged child at the rate of 70 per cent of what it costs for a child in Grade 1. The medium-term goal articulated within the White Paper is for all children entering Grade 1 to have participated in an accredited Reception Year programme by 2010. The policy does not take advantage of the possibilities of better linking early childhood and parental services. The link between ABET programming and ECD programming is conspicuous in its absence.

The diversity of the community sector is well documented in the national audit. A source of employment for women, small ECD sites of various forms have emerged and developed. Given the lack of funding, and the lack of monitoring and support networks, the large number of well-intentioned sites comes with a smaller number of more dysfunctional sites. The policy had two choices: to try to actively support the development of quality within these community initiatives (through subsidies, better networking mechanisms, better registration protocol, and realistic monitoring) or to move away from the 'informal' sector in favour of school-based development. This was not an 'either-or' choice – the critical question was one of emphasis. Over the long term, the White Paper makes a clear choice of school-based Reception Year services at the expense of community-based centres.

The policy states that it supports a limited community-based sector of ECD provision. Community- and home-based services currently represent over 80 per cent of the sector; it is envisioned in the medium term to represent 15 per cent of the sector, and in the long term to decrease even further. Community-based sites only qualify for subsidy if they are located in areas without reasonable access to primary schools, even though the vast majority of viable community sites are within one kilometre of a local school. These rates of coverage would reach less than ten per cent of the learners who are currently attending community-based sites in Gauteng. Funding for community sites is not guaranteed beyond three years of the release of the White Paper.

The policy places 85 per cent of the provision of Reception Year services into public primary schools. The policy reads 'with *some* additional investment in building rehabilitation to accommodate the learning, extra-curricular and safety requirements of the Reception Year, we believe that our 23 000 strong primary school system provides wide access and coverage to our country' (RSA 2001: 29). There is no provision stipulated within the policy for any additional capital expenditure funding for ECD upgrading.

While the policy is largely unsupportive of the community-based sector, it tries to incorporate the 'reduced costs' associated with 'using community energies and relative informality' seen in community- and home-based sites (RSA 2001: 32). The average monthly community-based practitioner's salary was only R688 compared to an average full-time teacher who earns approximately R6 700 per month. Rather than challenging the low salaries reflecting apartheid polices of neglect, the economic model tries to incorporate perhaps the most problematic aspect of community services – the systematically-underpaid practitioners. The policy does not embrace the community and school sites of less than 19 : 1. The policy says it attempts to 'get the best of both worlds', when in fact, from the point of view of a child, it appears to be picking the less desirable of 'both worlds'.

Funding patterns

The national ECD audit suggested that 75 per cent of funding for ECD services derives from private sources (DoE 2001). The audit underscores the financial vulnerability of the sector and suggests that the over-reliance on parental fees places a large number of sites on a marginal footing.

Public funding for ECD centres continues to come from three departments – health, social development and education. The national audit suggested that approximately one per cent of children between nought and five are in ECD services with food subsidies from the health sector. There has not been a significant increase in this expenditure area (Biersteker 2001: 21). The Department of Social Development spent approximately 0.6 per cent of its overall budget across the past five years, providing per child subsidies to between three and four per cent of the zero to five-year age cohort. The expenditure patterns do not reveal a significant expansion of services (Biersteker 2001: 21).

Resources for ECD services within education are reflected both within provincial education department budgets, as well as a short-term conditional grant. Before the onset of the conditional grant, provincial expenditure on ECD remained at approximately 0.3 per cent (Biersteker 2001: 19). Since the inception of the grant, ECD expenditure has climbed to approximately 0.8 per cent, and is scheduled to grow to some extent across the medium term (Wildeman 2003b: 12; also in this volume). The grant was only provided for three fiscal cycles. During this period there has been large-scale underspending due to severe administrative difficulties in establishing systems of payment to the sites in some provinces. The ECD grant will be phased out in 2003/04, leaving provincial education departments responsible for funding this area through their provincial budgets. There is some fear that other budgetary pressures will make discretionary ECD spending vulnerable in many provinces, leading to concerns about the sustainability of ECD provisioning post 2003/04 (Wildeman 2003b).

Reflection on choices

The policy choices adopted in 2001 are justified on the basis of a rational connection with empirical research – both internationally and domestically. In fact, the policy choices, focusing on 'five-year-old Reception Year programming' outside of a more integrated servicing strategy is, in fact, supported by neither the national audit, the pilot project, nor international research. While the national audit documented a range of multi-age integrated services, represented to a greater extent in community- and home-based sites, the pilot project was not designed to allow consideration of models outside of a Reception Year model. At some stage (and probably very early in the process) a decision had already been made that regardless of the viability of alternative models, the future policy would focus on Reception Year provisioning.

This analysis is not meant to suggest that Reception Year services are inappropriate in all contexts. However, the combination of the policy vision and funding strategies makes the provision of quality services questionable. As suggested earlier, at a certain point in quality, 'care' not only does not reach its intended goals, but may become counterproductive, undermining stimulation, curiosity, and relationships of trust. Further, perhaps more than any other policy area, ECD policy provided an opportunity for the public sector to embrace and financially support community initiative and local model development where it is already growing. This opportunity was not taken up; the policy choice works largely against, rather than with, the diversity of local initiatives in the area.

The current state of play

What is the current state of play of ECD services, ten years into our democracy? To what extent has the pattern of provisioning been transformed or maintained? And what is the impact of these changes on the most marginalised of South Africa's children?

At the time of writing this chapter there is no source of data describing ECD provisioning since the national audit undertaken in 2000. However, an analysis of the policy choices, combined with other environmental factors raised in this chapter, points to at least two worrying possibilities for the future – the decline of the community-based and home-based ECD sub-sector, and the relegation of five-year-old learners in poor communities to under-resourced Reception Year classrooms in public school settings.

Community- and home-based centres represented 80 per cent of the sector in 2000. The White Paper envisions community sites representing a maximum of 15 per cent in the medium term, and declining further after that. The audit described the viability of these centres as delicate, with an over-reliance on parental fees. There are several important pressures converging on this sector. The persistence of household poverty among the ECD cohort suggests that any significant increase in reliance on parental fees is ultimately unviable. Donor funds, traditionally a source of support for the NGO and CBO sector, are continuously retracting. Neither the health nor social development department appears to be in a position to significantly increase investment into the sector. Beyond the decline in funding sources, the expansion of primary-school-based Reception classrooms runs the risk of undermining community-based centres. Community-based centres are predominantly multi-age centres servicing three- to five-year-olds. The extraction of five-year-olds from this system, beyond its pedagogical consequences, runs the risk of 'crowding out' the community-based sites. This would lead to an overall decline in services for the nought to six-year-old cohort.

The most positive development on the horizon is the dramatic expansion of Reception Year classrooms. In 2001 there were 241 525 learners in Reception classrooms, a significant increase from 156 292 in 1999. There is some concern that the scale of the envisioned expansion will not happen due to budgetary pressures on provincial education departments. Perhaps the most important concern, however, is the danger that the expansion will bring particularly poor-quality services to previously disadvantaged communities. The funding of Reception Year classrooms is estimated at the rate of 70 per cent of current per learner expenditure for a Grade 1 child. There is no additional capital expenditure allocated explicitly to this programme expansion. The *School Register of Needs* (2001) makes clear the continued high levels of basic infrastructure requirements (classroom space, water, electricity, sewerage) of schools, particularly those in previously disadvantaged neighbourhoods. This needs to reach beyond capital to access of learning support materials and educator ratios. The development of adequate Reception Year classrooms in current primary schools will not require 'some additional investment' as suggested in the policy, but massive additional investment – an investment that is not going to be made available in the medium term at least.

The danger is clear – while Reception classrooms in more resourced areas may thrive, Reception classrooms in more disadvantaged areas may be better-structured to serve the function of 'warehousing' than educational play. The question becomes, 'Is this a good first step – essentially, better than nothing?' Let us imagine 40 five-year-olds sitting in rows in an overcrowded classroom, 'taught' by a teacher who is not well trained in the pedagogy of educational play. Is this image better than the opposite danger – of children being left to their own devices to play and explore in a dangerous world? The question is not easily answered. If the human brain is developed through stimulation and creative engagement, we may be further disadvantaging children, and particularly those living in the deepest of poverty, through providing environments that are not conducive to these ends.

The impact of these trends is particularly concerning for children and their caretakers living in poor households and communities. Community- and home-based sites may decline; those that remain viable will increase parental fees, further marginalising the poorest learners from their service. Thus, fewer children under five will have access to any ECD-based setting. If this fear is realised, it represents a setback for parents and caregivers, largely women, who will have fewer opportunities to navigate their own social, educational and economic lives. Five-year-olds may have increased access to Reception Year classrooms. However, the combination of state financing and parental investment may serve to reproduce the patterns of inequity inherited from the past. Disadvantages at the most important period for cognitive, emotional and physical development may not work to lighten the load of these children in the future.

What happened along the way?

How did the visions of the pre-1994 policy processes translate into the post-1994 experience? The early policy processes emphasised integrated service provision and partnerships – placing value on community-based services, NGO innovation, a wide range of sites of quality to service children facing the challenges of poverty, and significantly increased state financial support for ECD provisioning. The post-1994 experience has ultimately emphasised shifting ECD services from a diversity of typologies to school-based Reception classrooms and demonstrated limited support in the form of public expenditure. What accounts for the distance between the early policy visions rooted in the democratic movement and the post-election experience in this sector?

Perhaps the most noteworthy reason explaining the divergence is that early policy processes in education misunderstood the location of the most important debates defining the parameters of possibility for education policy, which lay not with educationists but rather with economists in the DoF and the Treasury. The adoption of policies of fiscal restraint in social spending at the moment of the democratic challenge perhaps determined policy possibilities more than research or policy processes related to specific social programming issues. From 1997, the discourse shifted from massive redress toward budgetary restraint. The *Medium Term Budget Policy Statement* concluded that the state was investing too much in education, and prioritised ways to increase efficiency in the system (DoF 1997). It was argued that addressing inefficiencies would release funds for redistribution. For a range of reasons, few funds were 'released'. The limited funds that became 'discretional' in this process were largely consumed by the investment requirements by what was considered the clearer constitutional mandate of primary and secondary schooling – at best reaching Reception Year classrooms, but falling short of integrated services that fell outside of ordinary public schooling. Simply put, the macroeconomic strategies and their consequences for social spending implied from early on that massive innovation and redress in the ECD sector would not be possible through state investment.

However, the ultimate policy choice cannot be explained in resource terms alone. There were several other factors that contributed to the problems of translating early visions into practice. Four are worthy of mention here. First, the sector is highly feminised, in the context of a society where women's voices are still relatively weak in the policy process. Second, the early childhood education sector is, by definition, less organised than other sectors of education. Unlike in the sector of ordinary schooling where organised students have a voice, children between the ages of nought and nine are usually lacking a socially-organised voice. Due to the disparate nature of the sector, even labour and parents tend not to be organised into cohesive bodies to advocate state change. Throughout the early policy process, the ECD sector for the most part was represented by practitioners. The practitioner community was widely disparate but in the early 1990s organised itself under the banner of the South African Congress for Early Childhood Development. While a critical policy voice advocating for ECD development, the Congress was inconsistent in its organisational strength, and consistently weak as a rural constituency.

Third, while there was a range of initiatives upon which to base more South Africanised models for early childhood provisioning, the Reception Year focus for ECD was enjoying international dominance during the early and mid-1990s. The World Bank, among others, pushed hard in this direction – even though it has stepped back from this position in more contemporary position papers. The World Bank study of 1992 was designed to place the policy process on the path of Reception Year provisioning. At a more subtle level, the Reception Year is an established model in industrialised countries, and had been a privilege of white children under apartheid. In a world where power and services have been polarised along race and class lines, models rooted in richer nations or within the white community have come to be viewed as 'better' or 'superior'. At first glance there is a great deal of support for the Reception Year proposal. All parents want their children to have access to the 'best', and in the shadows of our minds, the 'best' models come from privileged nations and communities.

The last factor relates to the complexity of policy development in this area, and the lack of fit between the needs of young children and the operations of the state bureaucracy. The early sections of this chapter frame the complexity of the ECD policy challenge in education. In the context of a rights-based approach that appreciates a range of ideal childhoods, what is the best form and function of early childhood provisioning with reference to so-called 'education'? An answer to this question includes the exploration of a range of innovative models, ranging from school Reception classrooms, to integrated community childcare workers at the community level. While many of the proposals for more innovative approaches focused on concepts of community organising for children, and were put forward with detailed strategic plans for implementation, they in essence transcended the structure of the state. While intersectoral programming has been an active concept in policy proclamations and in the form of a range of meetings and structures, concrete intersectoral programming has been more difficult to realise. Programmes that require community workers (community health workers, community child workers) outside of the more professionalised categories of teachers, social workers and nurses, were largely eliminated from state operations during this period due to the lack of state capacity to organise, support, and provide accountability for these categories of workers. In essence, to realise the ECD models that were based more on integrated community development models meant a radical reform of the state apparatus, which went beyond the bureaucratic transformations realised in this period. Despite a high degree of innovative thinking among political leaders in the early democratic process, the state bureaucracy has proved to be more conservative than expected in relation to both structure and tradition.

Conclusion

As was emphasised in the introduction to this chapter, one of the central principles of the 1994 moment was an unambiguous affirmation of the rights of the child. It opened up a new conversation about the boundaries of the possible for the lives of South African children. The first decade of democracy marks a massive transition in the lives of South African children. The South African Constitution is perhaps the most assertive affirmation of the rights of child citizens anywhere in the world. A range of initiatives across governmental departments has started to operationalise these rights, including free access to child and maternal healthcare, child support grants, primary school feeding schemes, and extended access to services such as water and electricity.

Despite progress, the gains have not yet been strong enough to work against the momentum of inequity facing our nation's young. The structure of the economy, combined with a range of global pressures, has worked to support the meta-structure of poverty facing too many South African children.

Closely tied to the affirmation of the rights of the child, the 1994 moment affirmed the role of education in deconstructing past inequities and injustices for young people. Once transformed, education was embraced as a decisive state instrument to steer a child's life in the direction of dignity.

This chapter has reviewed the process of change in ECD, and especially educational services. The chapter has served to highlight the potential dangers woven into the current trajectory of service development, particularly for marginalised children. It is suggested that the current strategy for ECD development may not be oriented to confront the inequities inherited from our past, and may serve to further entrench them.

It is still too early, however, to predict the ultimate form and function of ECD provisioning in South Africa. While the policy processes adopted in education suggest that an underfunded Reception Year strategy will be the centre of state developments in the sector over the coming decade, there are innovations in different areas – both inside and outside of the state – taking advantage of the policy spaces available. While it has taken a long time to gain momentum, the Early Childhood Institute in Gauteng, representing an integrated effort between the Departments of Education, Welfare and Health to address the needs of young children between birth and four, adopts many of the more innovative ideas emerging in the 1990s. Another location of innovation is local authorities, where the National Programme of Action for the Child is being decentralised to local authorities, and child rights are becoming a greater focal point for integrated local development plans.

There is a rethink occurring among many activists in the ECD sector. The lens of early childhood development, particularly as applied specifically to 'education', has been difficult to shift beyond formal classroom possibilities. More and more the challenge of building a nation where children thrive physically and in regard to human possibility, is being shifted from the challenge of ECD *per se*, to the challenge of realising the rights of children. This rights-based approach is well-located in a wider conception of social development, pioneered by Amartya Sen, placing emphasis on human agency. While sustainable agency is the engine of development, what people can positively achieve is determined both by the expansion of real freedoms (including confident education) and the removal of sources of 'unfreedoms' (entrenched poverty, non-engaging early childhood services). The challenge will be to use a rights-based discourse, committed to the expansion of agency, to mobilise the state and civil society around pro-child social development, while at the same time maintaining the mandate on education to ensure children are confident learners – a confidence that is surely rooted in the earliest period of children's lives.

Notes

1. The October Household Survey (OHS, 1998–1999) suggests that 75.8 per cent of South African children lived in poverty in 1999 as compared to 64.7 per cent in 1995 (Streak 2002: 3–4). Given different formulations and definitions of poverty, other national surveys have calculated the child poverty rate between 60 per cent (1995 Income and Expenditure Surveys [IES]) and 70 per cent (composite index of poverty indicators, 1994 PSLSD data [Haarmann 1999: 28]). Cited in Bray 2002.

2. Stunting refers to children who have not grown as tall as they should have for their age (according to international references) and is an indicator of long-term under-nutrition. Wasting refers to low weight-for-age amongst children, and is an indicator of more recent under-nutrition. Both stunting and wasting have negative implications for children's long-term well-being with respect to physical health, psychological development and social capacity.

References

African National Congress (1995) *A Policy Framework for Education and Training.* Manzini: Macmillan Boleswa

Barbarin, O & Richter, L (2001) *Mandela's Children: Growing Up in Post-Apartheid South Africa.* London: Routledge

Biersteker, L (2001) *Early Childhood Development: A Review of Public Policy and Funding.* Cape Town: Idasa, Children's Budget Unit

Biersteker, L & Short, A (1994) *Early Childhood Services for Black Children in South Africa.* Umtata: National Educator Forum

Bray, R (2002) *Missing Links? An Examination of the Contributions Made by Social Surveys to our Understanding of Child Well-Being in South Africa.* CSSR Working Paper No. 23. University of Cape Town, Centre for Social Science Research

Department of Education (1996) *Interim Policy on Early Childhood Education.* Pretoria: Government Printers

Department of Education (2001) *The Nationwide Audit of ECD Provisioning in South Africa.* Pretoria: Government Printers

Department of Finance (1997) *Medium Term Budget Policy Statement 1997*. Pretoria: DoF

Gauteng Department of Education (2002) *The Gauteng Institute for Early Childhood Development (ECD)*. Johannesburg: Monyokolo and Associates

Hirschowitz, R (2002) *Earning and Spending in South Africa: Selected Findings and Comparisons from the Income and Expenditure Surveys of October 1995 and October 2000*. Pretoria: StatsSA

Labadarios, D (ed) (1999) *The National Food Consumption Survey: Children Aged 1–9 Years*. Pretoria: Government Printers

National Education Policy Investigation (1993) *The Framework Report And Final Report Summaries*. A Project of the NECC. Cape Town: Oxford University Press

Office of the President (1996) *National Programme of Action for the Child*. Pretoria: Office of the President

Padayachee, R; Atmore, E; Biersteker, L & Evans, J (1994) *Report of the South African Study on Early Childhood Development: Recommendations for Action in Support of Young Children*. Washington DC: World Bank, Centre for Education Policy Development

Republic of South Africa (1995) *White Paper on Education and Training*. Pretoria: Government Printers

Republic of South Africa (2001) *Education White Paper 5: Early Childhood Development*. Pretoria: Government Printers

Shisana, O & Simbayi, L (2002) *Nelson Mandela/HSRC Study of HIV/AIDS: South African National HIV Prevalence, Behavioural Risks and Mass Media, Household Survey 2002*. Pretoria: HSRC and Nelson Mandela Foundation

Statistics South Africa (1999) *October Household Survey*. Pretoria: StatsSA.

Statistics South Africa (2003) *Census 2001 Compared with Census 1996: Changes in Living Conditions and Life Circumstances*. Pretoria: StatsSA

Taylor, V (2002) *Transforming the Present – Protecting the Future: Consolidated Report: Report of the Committee of Inquiry into a Comprehensive System of Social Security for South Africa*. Cape Town: Committee of Inquiry into a Comprehensive System of Social Security

United Nations (1989) *Convention on the Rights of the Child*. New York: United Nations

Wildeman, R (2003a) *The Proposed New Funding in Provincial Education: A Brave New World?* Cape Town: Idasa

Wildeman, R (2003b) Reviewing Provincial Education Budgets 2003. *Budget Brief*, No. 130

14 Youth development in transition, 1992 to 2004

Margaret Perrow

Introduction

In demographic terms, South Africa is a youthful country: the 2001 Census reported that people under the age of 35 accounted for more than two-thirds of the overall population (StatsSA 2001). More specifically, 32 per cent of the population was reported to be under 15, and an additional 29 per cent between 15 and 29; South Africans under 30 thus constituted 61 per cent of the overall population. Disaggregated by race, these figures vary significantly: 65 per cent of black South Africans, but only 41 per cent of the white population, were reported to be under 30.

Youth is not only a significant numerical category; the vulnerable status of youth presents a social challenge to the country as well. Young adults are caught in a web of intersecting social issues. Youth – especially black youth – are disproportionately affected by HIV/AIDS: 60 per cent of new infections occur in those under 25 (DoH 1998). Young adults are significantly affected by crime, poverty, and lack of formal education. They also experience a higher-than-overall official unemployment rate: in 2000, 35 per cent of those under 30 were officially unemployed, compared to 19 per cent of those aged 31 to 45 (South African Government Online 2000; see also Bhorat, this volume). This sobering situation led one recent government report to include youth among segments of the population at risk of 'social exclusion and vulnerability' as South Africa restructures in a global economy (South African Government Online 2000).

This categorisation represents a dramatic repositioning of youth historically, and a significant shift in both what it means to come of age as a young adult, and what it means to operate as a youth development organisation in South Africa today. Since the Congress Youth League was formed in 1943, 'youth' long stood for political resistance, militancy, and struggle. The 1976 student uprisings cemented in international public imagination the centrality of youth to the resistance movement, and the struggle of young people became inexorably linked to the larger 'movement' as masses of students in the1980s enacted the slogan 'liberation before education'. In this climate, the role of youth clubs and other organisations became more prominent. Youth groups, including non-governmental organisations (NGOs), proliferated, organising the energy of youth around the anti-apartheid struggle, and beginning to frame youth issues nationally. In the living memory of many young adults today, to be a 'youth' then was to feel oneself a significant agent of social transformation – and to be a youth development NGO was to play an active role in organising that transformation from the ground up. In the early 1990s, this energy resulted in concentrated national attention on youth issues, including the importance of national co-ordination of holistic, integrated youth development policies and planning.

Since 1994, however, limited literature has addressed the situation of youth, and the significance of 'youth' as a category and social force has been de-emphasised (Chisholm, Harrison & Motala 1997), beyond a narrow focus on employment and training. Significant youth organisations and youth leaders have been incorporated by government departments and parastatals, or disbanded altogether. Indeed, there is evidence that the very essence of what it means to grow up as a young person in South Africa has changed dramatically (Soudien 2003; Stevens & Lockhat 1997) in a climate of globalisation and market-orientation. Yet despite resilience and optimism on the part of youth (Leggett, Moller & Richards 1997), the material reality of most young people – especially poor, black youth – has not improved dramatically since 1992. For large numbers of young people, the post-apartheid promise clashes with deeply entrenched structural inequalities, framing the experience of what it means to succeed as a youth in South Africa today (Ramphele 2002).

The Joint Enrichment Project as a youth development lens

This chapter looks at the changing state of youth development through a close-up lens, by considering the case of a leading youth development organisation in Johannesburg – the Joint Enrichment Project (JEP), a highly significant and militant organisation before 1994 – as a microcosm of broader social changes and changes in the youth sector over time. JEP's story reveals a great deal about the path youth development has taken in South Africa over the past decade, for two reasons. Because of the longevity of its work, JEP's story reflects many of the patterns that affect the youth sector more broadly. And because of its tenacity and impact on the youth sector – largely due to its consistently dynamic and influential staff – JEP played a significant role in the evolution of the youth development sector over time, significantly influencing the work of other NGOs in the sector.

JEP is a Johannesburg-based youth development NGO. It offers a variety of life-skills and employment-preparation programmes to young adults, primarily between the ages of 18 and 30, who are out of school and unemployed. Its constituents are primarily black, from both rural and urban areas, both male and female. Between 1986 and 1992, JEP served approximately 2 000 young people in a variety of capacities. Today, it implements programmes for several hundred young people annually. JEP staff themselves are mostly young (under 35), so arguably it is a youth-run and -directed organisation. However, JEP's youth constituents do not play a direct role in shaping the curriculum or work of the organisation, beyond the community-based needs-assessments that determine the focus of their work projects.

Whereas in US parlance, the term 'non-profit' discursively positions such organisations in a politically 'neutral' way against the framework of *economic* capitalist motives, in South Africa the term 'non-governmental' has long been *political*, rather than economic: during apartheid, most NGOs were literally anti-government formations, driving the anti-apartheid struggle (see Morrow, this volume), and JEP was no exception. In the late 1990s, many South African NGOs – historically in *opposition* to government – found themselves in the paradoxical position of having to reposition themselves as potential *partners* with the government to survive under the new dispensation. This dramatic repositioning contained inherent tensions that significantly shaped JEP's programmes and the learning experience of its participants.

As society changed, so did youth development organisations, whose changing discourse and practices came to represent and further enact shifting social and economic orientations at the national level.[1] The changing discourse at JEP over the past 12 years reflects the organisation's engagement with larger social, political, and economic changes; as youth issues shifted to state auspices, the organisation's position, structure, and function (essentially, its *identity*) also shifted. This chapter argues that this engagement is – paradoxically – at once the organisation's ticket to survival, and its biggest vulnerability. It draws on research originally conducted as part of a doctoral degree in education at the University of California at Berkeley. The large-scale research project combined ethnographic, historical, and discourse analysis methods to contextualise the learning experiences of young adults from Soweto, who were participating in a job-training programme in 1997 to 1998 (Perrow 2000).

Youth policy and JEP since 1991

Two major related trends are evident in youth policy, development and JEP since 1991. First, between 1991 and 1994, JEP led youth-based structures within civil society in a movement that strongly lobbied for youth issues, bringing them to national attention. However, after 1995 – the year the National Youth Development Forum (NYDF) collapsed – youth issues began shifting to *state auspices*. There was a noticeable lack of a coherent youth-focused movement by 1995, when the civil-society NYDF was rendered ineffectual by internal discord, and the National Youth Commission (NYC) had not yet come into being. Issues pertaining to out-of-school and unemployed youth were subsumed by the National Qualifications Framework (NQF) and Adult Basic Education and Training (ABET), where they were given little explicit attention, even in the *1995 White Paper on Education and Training*. Likewise, Department of Labour (DoL) programmes under the Reconstruction and Development Programme (RDP) were focused on skills training and human capital development, not on the unique holistic needs of youth. As Chisholm et al. (1997) have argued, and this chapter suggests, youth issues remained fragmented and sidelined despite the high visibility of the Youth Commission. In contrast to the high expectations and visibility of the NYC, programme delivery based on the National Youth Policy (NYP) was exceedingly slow (and frustrating for partner NGOs, as this chapter illustrates). No major youth development policies have emerged since the 1997 NYP and the *1998 Green Paper on National Youth Service*. And 2002 policy documents circumvented out-of-school, unemployed youth by emphasising ABET, the national Grades R to 9 level curriculum, and higher education.

The second, related observation is that as this process of *centralisation* changed the landscape of youth development, JEP's role and identity shifted radically. Rather than continuing to spearhead the youth development movement, JEP took up the role of offering research findings and consultation to the NYC, and 'marketing' its programmes to government. Over a period of several years, some key JEP staff members moved into influential positions in government and parastatal agencies. And in exchange for its survival under these new conditions, JEP as an organisation slowly gave up its historical position as driver of youth policy and discourse. Centralisation carried with it this irony: youth development NGOs had brought youth issues into high relief in the first part of the 1990s, and the discourse of youth development in the late 1990s reflected the earlier efforts of JEP and the NGO sector. But youth development NGOs had in practice became more marginalised and less empowered in the latter part of the decade. For many, that meant closing shop altogether. For JEP, it meant negotiating a new identity that would allow for its survival.

The history of JEP, through a discourse lens

A 'map' of JEP's shifting identity through time can be found in documents from various periods of its history from 1986 to the present, as JEP repeatedly repositioned itself through five time periods that correspond roughly to five of its leaderships.[2] During these periods JEP's focus shifted from changing the societal structures of apartheid, to changing sectoral and organisational 'systems', to skilling individuals, to producing marketable 'products', and finally to negotiating strategic relationships. These shifts meant that the emphasis of the organisation's work moved from sanctuary for youth and antidote to a collapsed school system, to drama and cultural activities, to technical skills acquisition for both participants and the youth sector, to personal development and accountability with a high degree of self-reflexivity[3] and self-promotion in a free-market economy.

As the external political and social climate changed, JEP underwent corresponding discursive shifts in each of these periods: from a discourse of collectivity and resistance; to a discourse of systemic capacity-building and individual skill-development; to a 'development discourse' of productivity, accountability, and efficiency; to a self-reflexive discourse of individuation and strategising in a competitive free market. In the early 2000s, JEP nearly imploded under the stress of navigating a new identity in a sea of competing interests. Its discourse became tension-fraught, its staff and management fragmented, and its focus on youth development was nearly subsumed by the conflicts that raged both within it, and between it and external agencies and organisations.

This chapter now considers key changes in each period in greater depth.

1986 to 1991: the discourse of resistance

JEP was formed in 1986 as a joint creation of the South Africa Council of Churches (SACC)[4] and the South African Catholic Bishops' Council, at the height of anti-apartheid resistance. Overthrowing apartheid, not seeking education, personal development, and employment, was on the minds of most young black South Africans. The education system serving the black majority was in disarray; the media increasingly portrayed young people as a 'lost generation' of violent 'young lions'. A central aspect of the resistance movement in the 1980s was the rapid proliferation of NGOs dedicated to the anti-apartheid struggle.

The brief history of JEP in its *Human Resources Manual* sets out what one former deputy director calls 'the idealistic view [of the reasons for its existence]'.[5] The manual notes that, 'The creation of the JEP was an expression of the churches' commitment to sustaining a culture of learning despite the chaos in the schooling system caused by Bantu Education and the general rejection of this by students.' Between 1986 and 1992, JEP offered 'a wide range of cultural projects for students expelled from the school system because of their political involvement.' During this time, JEP filtered European funding to a variety of alternatives to formal schooling: local youth projects, study groups, cultural activities, and increasingly arts and cultural projects devised and implemented by JEP itself. When in 1990 the National Education Crisis Committee (NECC)[6] – with JEP director Eric Molobi at its helm – launched its 'back to school campaign' and just-released Nelson Mandela urged young people to return to their classrooms, JEP was obliged to review its *raison d'être*. If it was to survive, JEP had to look to the future and envision how to best position itself in relation to the anticipated new government.

Because evasiveness or vagueness was one of the hallmarks of the discourse of the resistance movement, there is a noticeable absence of documentation about the activities of this time period. Existing documents are often undated or untitled; even African National Congress (ANC) publications from the resistance era frequently bear no publication date. Documenting resistance activities under the apartheid regime was ill-advised as it might make those activities (or activists) traceable by the state.[7] And the sheer intensity of the movement meant that all energy and enthusiasm were devoted to resistance activities; record-keeping was relegated to a secondary activity. For these reasons, resistance discourse often does not situate activities distinctly in place or time. In the discourse of resistance, accountability – in the contemporary development sense – was discouraged. The focus of resistance was on action, not its discursive representation.

A former JEP staff member recalled some of that action:

> One time we had a cultural day in Jabulani. The school hall was packed with kids coming from all over, you know? And then [laughing] the police came. They surrounded the school, and it was so many vans of police. I just saw police, all over the room. And I was still upstairs trying to fix the mikes and all that, whilst downstairs the kids were busy with their poetry. And they wanted to just lock everybody up! Just arrest everybody! I had to talk to them, say 'no, these are kids, they are just doing their dramas and nothing political about it'. Well, they just took some names ... they couldn't find anybody.

The assertion that 'they are just doing their dramas and nothing political about it' is a good example of the way a word or a label can simultaneously disguise, reflect, and create a reality. Playing off the technical or literal definition of a word against its more metaphorical meanings in order to avoid arrest was a common tactic of resistance discourse. It was easy enough to play on the literal meaning of *political* to argue that a group of schoolchildren performing a play were 'just doing their dramas' and not engaging in anything directly related to government or politics. Double meanings and vagueness at the discursive level disguised the inherently *political* nature of acting out scenes from everyday lives characterised by oppression. And the co-ordinator's telling the police that there was 'nothing political' going on was itself a political act, leveraging the power of discourse to index, ironically, the power relations between them but leaving the police powerless to exercise their power except in a discursive way: though police couldn't take bodies in this case, 'they took some names'. On the discursive plane, speech (names) rather than bodies were 'captured' in this case. During the resistance era, the way a term like *political* was used and defined had significant implications for people's lives. Creative co-opting or inverting of terms and phrases – seizing or 'capturing speech' (de Certeau 1997) – was a key feature of the discourse of this era.

Public resistance discourse was a discourse of collective demands in an anti-authoritarian, anti-hierarchical voice to oppose, undermine, and subvert authority. JEP participated in a campaign in 1987 to assemble a list of 'demands put forward by students, teachers, workers, parents, and others concerned with education'. The preamble to the list of demands tied 'equality in education' to 'a free and democratic South Africa', and based the demands on a famous clause of the *1955 Freedom Charter*, 'The doors of learning and culture shall be opened!' That well-known document reads: 'We demand education for liberation not for slavery ... We demand that troops get out of our schools ... We cannot learn when we are being harassed by police, soldiers and security guards.' An inclusive list of backers, as well as the repetition of the first-person plural pronoun 'we', creates the effect of an authoritative collectivity acting in consensus. Summing up this era, a former JEP staff member recalls, 'those were the *real* dark days'. The urgency of the struggle taking place 'on the ground' meant that accountability was not yet a significant part of the discourse of anti-apartheid NGOs, and individuation, self-promotion, and a competitive market ethos were not at issue for either youth development organisations or their individual constituents.

1991 to 1994: challenging discursive constructions of youth with a discourse of skills

In 1991, JEP came under the leadership of Sheila Sisulu, a high-profile visionary, activist, and teacher with strong ties to the ANC. Under her direction, JEP faced several new challenges. The politics of impending transition, especially the shifting relationships between NGOs and government, presented a navigational challenge to anti-apartheid NGOs. 'Human-resource development' consequently became a focus at JEP: building social systems and resources that would be ready to deploy after the elections. The challenge of shifting from a political struggle to a developmental one was rendered especially difficult by increasingly stringent funding processes (in part a reflection of the government's desire to control social development functions) that threatened the existence of many NGOs. Concepts like 'accountability' and 'outcomes' began circulating. In the early 1990s, overseas programmes – both from the US and Europe – began to capitalise on these transitions, marketing systematic 'capacity-building' and 'organisational learning' paradigms to development practitioners in South Africa. Participating in the globalised discourse of systems-thinking and skills-building sustained the impression that eventually the economy would 'come right' and jobs would be available. Organisations that did not participate in this new 'development discourse' of accountability and productivity risked being marginalised in the 'new' South Africa of bilateral funding agreements and increased accountability. In addition to the politics of transition and the corresponding shift in funding climate, a third challenge faced JEP's new director in 1991: the media's portrayal of young people as violent and out of control – in short, as a collectively 'lost' generation.

In response to the shifting political context, increasingly stringent funding requirements, and the portrayal of young people in collectively negative and despairing terms, JEP focused its energies in two areas: coalition-building towards a youth sector that would discursively reposition young people as 'marginalised' rather than lost, and a consequent shift towards skills-based projects and a discourse of skills-building. While JEP poured time and resources into summits, national conferences, and the formation of the NYDF, it also transformed itself from an organisation offering youth arts and culture programmes, to an organisation with a focus on skills-building and personal development. Appeals to overseas funders explained unemployment as 'a youth problem', and identified 'the lack of economic growth and the contracting job market' as the 'primary factors behind a youth sub-culture of violence'. JEP's skills-projects had the explicit intent of providing youth with both saleable skills, and a coherent resume; in other words, a discursive reconstruction of their identity in anticipation of a more inviting job market.

Between 1991 and 1994, then, JEP led an explicit national move away from the discourse of a 'lost generation' to one of 'marginalised youth', thereby implicating social structures – rather than youth themselves – in the process of marginalisation, and implying the potential for 'youth development' rather than fatalistically viewing young people as irretrievably lost. This had two consequences. First, JEP was able to mobilise the beginnings of a South African 'youth sector'. To do this, it drew on a larger corresponding trend in organisations towards a systems-thinking, capacity-building, skills-oriented discourse in anticipation of South Africa's entry into the global competitive marketplace. And second, to ensure itself an influential spot in the 'new' South Africa, JEP focused on becoming a development *provider*.

Two main features characterised the discourse of this period. The first was the continued drive for consensus, derived from the anti-authoritarian, anti-apartheid discourse of the resistance movement. One former JEP administrator remembers this as 'the time of consensuational [sic] democracy at its best, with forums springing up on every single issue ... It was a mirror of the broader consensus that the country [was] trying to come to in terms of what the transition is going to look like ... so the model for the politics of seeking consensus became entrenched' though the endless discussions slowed the decision-making process (and ultimately contributed to the collapse of some organisations, like the NYDF). And second, there emerged a new discursive focus on developing skills and 'building capacity' in young people, and in the organisation itself.

1994 to 1996: redefining skills with a discourse of personal development

Between 1994 and 1996, JEP was led by Steve Mokwena, a young charismatic activist who was both 'excited about all the work', and concerned that despite the remarkable changes in South Africa, 'youth remain[ed] an afterthought in most policies and programmes'. Mokwena believed that conducting pilot projects was 'the best way to create an identity for JEP that would be distinguished from' the NYDF, an alliance of youth development providers that JEP had convened in 1993, but that had fallen apart not long afterwards. 'It was clear,' he recalls, 'that funders were a bit fatigued with the process of doing business: consultation [talking], and things like that. So the only way we were going to get ourselves any resources was to *implement* some stuff.'

Mokwena was instrumental in integrating a 'personal development' emphasis into the Skills Training Programme. Thus JEP made another discursive turn that would affect the sector at large, by redefining *skills* to include 'personal development': self-reflection, psychological support (a foreign concept to virtually all the participants), and individual cognitive development. In other words, the term *skills* came to refer to more than the acquisition of technical competencies, and skills development hence drew on a Western discourse of cognitive psychology, psychotherapy, and self-reflection. By 1996, 'personal development' was deeply ingrained in JEP's youth development philosophy, and personal development workshops went hand in hand with training in bricklaying, carpentry, and catering (this would later be formalised in terms of JEP's trademark 'Integrated Approach to Youth Development'; see next section). Although conducted in groups and focused on communication and interaction with others, 'personal development' workshops called on an individualising, psychologising discourse that – unlike the discourse of collective resistance – emphasised the individual reflecting on his or her own life trajectory, needs, desires, and beliefs.

A staff member recalls that many youth-service providers then still thought 'training was going to be the answer to unemployment' yet at the same time, 'there was some really crappy training being provided [by various training programmes]: two-week courses to be a plumber, but don't let them near the geyser 'cause they'll blow the thing sky high. It was really bad training … Escom, for example, would take a person to go to their electronic course, but they would never accept those people at Escom as workers, because they would want people with the proper N4, N5, N6 qualifications'. Furthermore, because most employment training programmes focused solely on (often poorly taught) technical training, participants were not equipped with skills to help them handle this paradox, skills that 'personal development' might provide: conflict-resolution, critical perspective, knowledge of resources, flexible communication skills, and so on. This, then, was the dilemma: how was a 'skilled' young person to be defined? JEP was attempting to shift the definition of *skills*, as a former deputy director recalls:

> We were arguing that if you're doing training for people who've been outside of school for this long, who are traumatised by apartheid, who have all kinds of problems that they bring to the training environment, *just providing training won't work*. You have to provide long-term training and supplement it with some kind of cognitive development, probably look at communication in it, psychological counseling, preferably link it into the community if you can, and come up with something more holistic.

During this time, the JEP was hard at work on its *own* development, establishing its identity in its own particular social context. The core of the organisation became its pilot projects. Beyond their immediate youth development function, the pilot projects were intended to create links both with communities and with 'institutions of society' (a term vague enough to include, when timely and appropriate, government). Pilot projects would then, it was hoped, be replicated by others, 'leaving JEP flexible to maintain other projects and respond to other needs' (JEP Mission Statement 1994). And for JEP as an organisation, the political shift to democracy intensified the discursive shift toward a language of individual rights, and organisational advantage in a competitive economy. The discourse of youth development NGOs like JEP no longer functioned primarily to organise tactics of collective resistance, but to strategise individual, organisational, and sectoral futures in 'the new dispensation'.

1996 to 2000: market discourse and reflexive, strategic planning

South Africa's 1994 transition to democracy, which afforded it an entrée into the global economy, had a number of significant impacts on NGOs, and threatened the youth sector's existence. First, many NGO leaders moved to government or the private sector. Second, funders re-routed money through the newly legitimised government, or withdrew from South Africa altogether. Third, the newly competitive funding environment called for skills like 'business planning' and financial accountability as funders suddenly 'want[ed] numbers'. Fourth, despite its rhetoric of partnership, JEP found the government in practice reluctant to engage with NGOs as true partners for systemic social change, while eager to position itself as driving the provision of youth services for the new South Africa. (The NYC, for instance, which was criticised for being ineffectual, was widely misunderstood. It was never meant to implement programmes itself, but rather to ensure that the interests of youth were made relevant in *all* other government departments. As such, it was seen by some as a government attempt to pay lip service to youth development, by bringing it under one roof. For various reasons, the NYC did not become the unifying entity it might have been.) For all of these reasons, Mokwena recalls, it became evident that JEP's original assumption – that 'by 1997 government would have recognised youth development as a key national priority and allocated resources to implementing large-scale youth programmes' that could be drawn from the existing NGOs – was just not happening. Mokwena identifies 'the error in planning' as 'thinking that the government would be prepared to take on these projects, to finance and run them. We didn't realise how hard it would be for the government just to get itself established as a government, let alone fund and administer projects. We just had the wrong predictions about the government.'

In order to survive, NGOs had to enter the realm of market-based, competitive, strategic planning. During this period, a former JEP director posed what he called 'the unaskable question'. He asked, 'Is there really such a thing as a youth development sector? Or is the youth sector a myth, and it's just a bunch of NGOs not really communicating with each other, competing for resources?' His comment exposes a tension NGOs had begun experiencing: a tension between the pressure for an emerging individual (that is, competitive) orientation and a nostalgia for the unified, collective ethos of the resistance.[8]

Looking toward the future in 1998, concerned about its internal structures and functions, and trying to position itself to exert the maximum influence on both youth policy and practice, JEP under its new director Neville Naidoo undertook a series of evaluations and 'strategic planning' sessions. This organisation-wide process encouraged institutional self-reflection, a luxury for which NGOs had not had time in the earlier era. This increasing focus on self-reflexivity in the interest of improving JEP's 'products' (often called 'deliverables') was evident in staff meetings and retreats. At these gatherings, staff were often asked to 'share objectives'. One supervisor said his goal was to 'capture all the learnings happening'. The director suggested that 'these aims be captured in diaries'. The technicist conception of 'learnings' as discrete (even concrete) items that can be recorded by individuals, internalised by others, and transported to another context for implementation is significant. In other words, there was an emphasis on formalising the learning process of the organisation and staff, thus giving it a new 'weight' and legitimacy in the currency of development discourse.

One goal of this formalisation, and a key to JEP's survival, was establishing a unique identity that would influence government policy. In 1997 JEP began formalising an Integrated Approach to Youth Development (IAYD) as a model or 'product' that could be implemented by partner organisations. IAYD entailed looking at young people as having multiple, but interrelated, needs: social, psychological, financial, *and* technical. JEP argued that such 'an integrated approach' to youth development would 'make a contribution to the country's social and economic development'. In fact, by participating in the drafting of a Youth Commission policy on National Youth Service, JEP brought a focus on personal development into those documents. A former JEP administrator recalls that 'the big conflict between the Youth Commission and the line departments [was] that the line departments don't see the point of the developmental parts of the youth service. So when you say there has to be life-skills, there has to be personal development ... they're saying "Why? We can't afford that." ' Significantly, while JEP was attempting to become a government 'partner', JEP was not willing to compromise its belief in the relevance of integrating 'life-skills' into technical training programmes for young people.

Another good example of this shift towards formalising learning and adding reflexivity to the discourse of capacity-building was a staff workshop on Monitoring and Evaluation (M&E). The workshop was facilitated by a staff member who had attended a session run by a large past funder of JEP and an important conduit of overseas funding to development agencies (clearly demonstrating the link between funding constraints and development discourse). The facilitator opened the workshop by saying that one of his objectives was 'to demystify M&E as a tool'. However, even using the acronym M&E, as he continued to do, veiled the phrase in mystery and authority.

Paradoxically, in fact, one of the main effects of this workshop seemed to be to impose a vocabulary and set of concepts from outside the organisation, and to leave intact the veil of authority. One staff member's concern for 'knowing when things should be done', for instance, was translated by the facilitator into 'monitoring the time frames', raising the question of whether the staff was appropriating the discourse, or the discourse was appropriating them. By the end of the workshop, an M&E procedure had been outlined on posters and hung on the walls. Terms and definitions had been given a great deal of attention and effort to get them 'right'. Staff who once fought the war of resistance and learned to mistrust and even invert language as part of that resistance were now being asked relatively uncritically to adopt a discourse of development.

While the origins of what this chapter refers to as 'development discourse' are diverse and multiple, the link between the objectifying discourse of war and that of NGO accountability is worth noting. During the resistance era in South Africa, terms like *target, strategy, capture,* and *mobilise* were used in a militaristic sense: NGOs and individuals were 'targeted' by government surveillance; resistance leaders were 'captured' by the police; 'strategic thinking' referred to revolutionary activities; and young people were 'mobilised' for the 1976 uprising. Today, these terms have been co-opted by the new discourse of development, metaphorically establishing parallels between the 'struggle' then and the 'struggle' today. For the NGO, the new struggle is about asserting and marketing its identity in a climate of accountability. For participants, like the organisation, the struggle is no longer about building the resistance movement, but about building themselves. 'Target' refers to the population being served by the NGO. 'Strategic thinking' applies to the paradigms with which the organisation or individuals plan their future. Learnings are 'captured'. And the staff is 'mobilised' to make the organisation more efficient and accountable. Discourses and identities have shifted together.

As 'development discourse' came into its own, so did an accompanying 'globalised' discourse of free markets, competitiveness, and individual entrepreneurship. This latter is consistent with the individualised, psychologising discourse that was beginning to emerge at JEP in the early 1990s, a discourse that was encouraged by the larger socio-political environment but around which it was necessary to tread lightly nonetheless. In a climate of fiscal tightening, 'any time you talk to [the government], they think you want money,' says a JEP administrator, describing the battle to get the government to collaborate with JEP, and the efforts that the organisation exerted in that direction – a complete reversal from the 'dark days' when the objective was to resist and defeat the government. She describes telling the Department of Safety and Security:

> We've got money, but what we want is to meet with you once a month as a reference group, to feed back the results and for you to ask key questions so we can test them out. That's all we want ... And their reply: 'I'm afraid we don't really have the human resources to engage in something like that, but if you'd send us a report at the end of your programme, we'd be interested.' Now, you feel like weeping ... They won't *say* they're not interested, but they're not interested. It's really disheartening.

Organisational identity had shifted from helping youth in an anti-apartheid context, to fighting to 'help' the government in a development context. A remarkable shift in a decade and a half, for an organisation that started out as an anti-apartheid NGO with 'no contact with the government for political reasons,' emphasises the director. Another administrator observes, 'I think JEP has manoeuvred its way out of that general position of just being a youth programme-running organisation. We're not just doing that. We're actually advocating ourselves to national departments, saying "You want effective youth development, we're the organisation that can deliver it." ' And so, the 'strategic challenge' facing JEP in 2000 was, as the director saw it, 'to position ourselves in such a way that we get *used*, that we contribute to the implementation of the National Youth Service Programme.' In other words, JEP's primary objective had become not deployment for youth, but deployment for the organisation and its projects.

In summary, this period saw a discursive shift in youth development at JEP, from institutional capacity-building as skills, to capacity-building as institutional reflexivity *about* skills. The new discourse of development, spawned and fostered by international funders, aimed for efficiency, accountability, rationality, standardisation, and monitoring and evaluation. In other words, it was no longer just about developing capacity, but also about *measuring* it, a process calling for more overt reflexivity. The technicisation of learning, reified in formalised procedures for planning and self-evaluation within the organisation, was a central part of this process. Another key part of the discursive process of self-reflexivity is the marketing and positioning of individuals and organisations. A JEP board member notes that 'for participants, it's not enough simply to acquire technical skills; they have to *sell* their product [their know-how] now ... You have to learn how to present yourself. You even have to sell *yourself.*' This was the same marketplace challenge facing JEP in the newly competitive world of development, and both participants and the organisation set to work mastering the discourse that would allow them to 'sell themselves' in a competitive marketplace. For participants, that meant increasing emphasis on 'deployment', 'personal development', and 'psychological support' components of the programme. For JEP it meant adopting the development discourse of funders offering workshops in accountability, and positioning itself as a partner to government, to whom it could market its 'learnings' in the hope of having its programmes deployed. In this respect, JEP's new position represented a 180-degree pivot from its position at its inception in 1986.

2000 to 2003: discourse of competing interests and positionality

By 2000, with former ANC Youth League leader Neville Naidoo at the helm, JEP was reaping the rewards of having marketed the organisation and its programmes to government departments. JEP had secured three major government contracts: a National Youth Service pilot programme (in which young people retrofitted buildings for people with disabilities); a DoL project (in which young people cleared non-native plants from watersheds); and a youth-entrepreneurship programme funded by Ntsika, a government agency under the Department of Trade and Industry (DTI). In each case, JEP was contracted to run the life-skills component of the project, and to oversee co-ordination of the various aspects of the programme, into an *integrated* or holistic approach. On the surface, it looked like JEP had steered a steady course, weathered the storms, and found a harbour.

While these government contracts were lucrative, however, they quickly became problematic. The goal of government 'using' JEP had been achieved, but JEP staff began to feel 'used' in a more negative sense. For example, the National Youth Service pilot programme was a joint effort on the part of the NYC, the Department of Public Works (DPW), and the South African Association of People with Disabilities. While the DPW funded the programme, they subcontracted the Independent Development Trust (IDT) to 'project-manage' it. Established in 1991 to formalise the distribution of government development monies, the IDT was itself undergoing internal transformation similar to that of JEP – learning how to systematically manage development projects – but without a clear vision of what constituted effective, holistic youth development. The most obvious instrumental goal of the Youth Service programme was to retrofit buildings, making them accessible to people with disabilities. However, there was another goal: the development of the young people who participated in the project. This was arguably the primary goal for JEP staff. And this goal, staff began to feel, was being neglected.

Thinking back on this project, staff recall the 'competing interests' that made it very difficult – some said 'impossible' – to keep the young people at the centre of the project's goals. The DoL had subcontracted the carpentry and other such work to private contractors who were not youth workers, and 'had never bought into a developmental approach'. Although – or perhaps *because* – they were responsible for paying the young people their weekly stipend, they felt no compulsion to integrate the participants into the technical aspects of the work. More often than not, recall staff, their view was that young people 'waste my tools, waste my materials, and cost me more'. Consequently, the young people found themselves 'doing all the grunt work' or 'sitting around and doing nothing'. It is not illogical that private contractors would see this as 'a profit-making opportunity'. They, like JEP, had their own interests at heart, and the role that they saw for project participants was quite different from the role JEP had had in mind originally. At the political level, the organisation was secure; on the ground, however, 'youth development' was drifting out of focus.

This conflict of interests intensified as JEP staff tried to correct the situation. Thinking back, they describe the discourse of the time as fraught with 'competing interests' and 'in-fighting'. One project director recalls, 'we were delegitimised as partners in the project, because we weren't able to fulfil our monitoring role' of ensuring that participants' development was holistic, meaningful and integrated. Life-skills workshops for young people in the project often became complaint sessions, 'fire-fighting and counselling around frustrations and anger' about conditions at the worksite. To life-skills facilitators, rather than performing an integrative function, these sessions had become 'a tacked-onto-the-end piece'. JEP staff, at this and the other two government-contract projects, felt mounting frustration at the way youth development was being played out in these situations: 'We were being put in positions where we absolutely could not do the work we'd been hired to do,' remembers one.

To their great credit, the JEP project staff refused to compromise their values and their view of youth development as an integrated, holistic process. But internally at JEP, they found less and less of a forum for airing their concerns productively. The management had 'very significantly changed the direction of our fund-raising and sustainability strategy, without anybody having brought on, or bought into it ... All of a sudden, the only work we were doing was government contracting!' Thus job security became an issue within the organisation. A tremendous amount of valuable resources – emotions, finances, time, and energy – was devoted to these internal issues; that is, to the matter of (re)configuring the identity of the organisation. A discourse of 'competing interests' and conflict management threatened to submerge JEP's youth development work.

Emerging from conflict with the board, staff and government agencies that had contracted JEP, the director began rethinking the nature of JEP's relationships with its partners. Ironically but fortuitously, this process was facilitated by the departure of two experienced staff members and their eventual re-employment in related offices. One took a position as Skills Development Manager at the Umsobomvu Youth Fund (UYF), a government fund established in 2001 from demutualisation levies. There, she began working closely with youth development organisations like JEP to help them 'design and conceptualise strategies' and 'implement programmes on behalf of Umsobomvu' (UYF brochure). JEP's newest project[9] in the North-West is a partnership with the provincial Department of Social Services, the municipality, and Umsobomvu, the project's primary funding source. However, rather than 'being used' by government, or acting as a service provider to government, this time around Naidoo emphasises that JEP 'implements the programme. It is as much their programme as it is our programme, they give certain things and we give certain things, but we *implement* it.' This discursive repositioning is significant; rather than being contracted in to provide one piece of a larger programme, JEP in fact will subcontract the technical skills components, but implement the overall programme. To that end, Naidoo refers to Umsobomvu and the government branches as 'strategic partners' which will be complemented by 'community partners' for each of the three youth development projects in the North-West programme: agriculture, counselling and outreach services, and construction.

Another experienced JEP staff member left to join the Youth Development Network (YDN), an alliance of seven influential youth development organisations[10] that were all funded by the Royal Netherlands Embassy (RNE). One original purpose of the YDN was to work toward sustainability strategies, in anticipation of the RNE withdrawing direct funding. Consequently, the YDN began, in the late 1990s, to channel RNE funding, so that its member organisations would have the best chance of survival by pooling resources, capitalising on each other's strengths, and compensating for each other's weaknesses. In addition to supporting JEP in this capacity, the YDN has been busily producing documents that grow out of and support the work that JEP has been doing for years. Two of these are especially significant to JEP and other NGOs: a training manual and brochure on 'Integrated Youth Development' and an assessment tool designed to help South African youth development organisations assess youth competencies. Because JEP's goal is to align the life-skills components of their new programmes with the NQF, this tool is of vital importance to them. Both these products, which now are available to the youth sector, have their roots largely in the pioneering work of JEP in previous eras. And both are enabling JEP to move forward in its pursuit of a sustainable position in the youth development sector.

Implications for practitioners

Fernando & Heston (1997: 11) warn of the contradictions and tensions facing NGOs as they find themselves at the intersection of the state, the increasingly powerful market, and civil society. They note that the 'ideological orientations and organisational practices of [successful] NGOs have tended to converge with those in the market economy', a practice that has become a virtual necessity for JEP's survival (see Morrow, this volume, for further discussion of this trend). Drawing on research by Brown & Covey (1987), Stewart (1997) notes that as NGOs fight for survival by 'capacity-building' internally, and 'scaling up' externally, 'their need for funding increases, and this creates organisational schizophrenia, with fund-raisers focusing on their constituency (donors), whilst field staff focus on theirs, the target group' (1997: 14). As social providers in a globalising world, contemporary South African NGOs like JEP are caught between increasingly 'naturalised' economic and free-market imperatives of globalisation, and widespread expectations of social delivery. Thus, a 'successful' education NGO might be one that reconfigured, redefined, and reoriented itself under the new dispensation in the 1990s.

Yet the contemporary NGO that is simultaneously a potential government partner, a free-market player, the voice of the historically oppressed, *and* socially conscious change-agent is burdened with a complex and potentially conflicted identity. JEP is a case in point: as South Africa underwent its momentous transition to a universal democracy, culminating in the 1994 national elections, JEP survived and even thrived. While the flotilla of NGOs that had sailed into the resistance movement in the 1980s (fuelled by what Ramphele [1995] calls the 'development gravy-train') washed aground in the early 1990s, JEP managed to turn with the tide and continued to grow. Its survival rested on its ability to navigate these multiple and potentially conflicted roles. Yet this pressure to navigate a new and complex identity consumed ever more of JEP's resources, eventually threatening to subsume the youth development work (for example, the work of attending to the identities of young adults in transition) that was the organisation's original *raison d'être*. Ultimately, the trade-off that ensured its survival also resulted in the loss of a significant amount of autonomy and power in the youth sector.

The identity of youth, youth development NGOs, and of the sector as a whole, has shifted rapidly over the past decade. Until very recently, the youth development sector itself could be said to be exuberantly 'youthful'. However, the sector has been steadily maturing over the past decade, and some sobering trends have emerged.

- The sector saw a centralisation of youth issues under government auspices, particularly after 1995.
- This centralisation, however, did not result in widespread and effective delivery of youth development programmes.
- This centralisation positioned youth development NGOs largely as implementers, rather than the social discourse-shapers and policy drivers that they once were.
- Many skilled and experienced youth workers moved from NGOs into influential positions in new areas of the youth development sector, providing support for organisations they once worked for, and bringing with them a deeper understanding of work 'on the ground'.
- As funding was more commonly filtered through parastatals like Umsobomvu and networks like the YDN, alliances and partnerships became ever more crucial to the survival of youth development NGOs.
- An 'integrated' or holistic approach – rather than a focus strictly on technical skill development – is increasingly cited in youth development literature. However, an 'integrated' approach, even when embraced conceptually by government and funding agencies, proves challenging to implement on a large scale.

These trends suggest two key implications, both for youth development NGOs and those who fund and evaluate them. First, *a view of youth development NGOs as important sites of learning* requires a broader definition of learning than the traditional cognitive/psychological one, where learning is equivalent to technical skills mastery by an individual. Learning, in the youth development sector, is increasingly viewed as a holistic process, with interrelated psychological, emotional, social, financial, and cognitive aspects. However, despite government policy pronouncements about the importance of holistic youth development, in practice this view of learning is still insufficiently understood.

And second, as the youth sector centralises, we need *a better understanding of a tacit tension in organisational focus*: a tension between marketable products, and participants' development. JEP has made the journey from an organisation that profoundly shaped the social discourse about youth, to one in the grips of dominant discourses of centralisation and implementation. There is always the danger that an NGO's creative vision, its focus on holistic learning, and its drive for social justice may be subsumed by its need to create a marketable identity and strategic positioning. Scaling up youth development in South Africa continues to require a balancing act, between developing the identities of its youth constituents in a holistic way, and developing the identity of the organisation in a socio-political context in tremendous flux. JEP's story illustrates both the necessity for, and the perils of, performing this balancing act.

Notes

1. This analysis draws on Fairclough's (1992) framework of critical discourse analysis, in which discourse functions as a mode of social action and representation, in a dialectical relationship with larger social structures. Discourse, in this view, both *reflects* and has the power to *change* relations of power and the ideologies that sustain those relations.
2. While this chapter argues that these phases are distinct and represent a general movement in discourse and identity over time, it is important to realise that they are not discrete episodes in the organisation's existence, but rather overlapping and sometimes combined ways of talking about and conducting youth work in South Africa.
3. The concept of *self-reflexivity* is based on Giddens's (1991) notion of the 'reflexive project of the self', which he argues is a key feature of modernity.
4. For an 'inside' look at the role of the SACC in the resistance movement, see Tutu (1994, part II). For a discussion of the role of churches in shaping South African politics, see Borer (1998).
5. There is an alternate view of the original function of JEP: that the United Democratic Front (UDF) activist Eric Molobi was, in a sense, 'paid by JEP to do his political work'. A former JEP director notes that 'JEP gave Molobi a very safe space' to pursue his antiapartheid activism. Molobi had spent six years in prison, along with prominent SACC leaders and anti-apartheid veterans. When he came out of prison, he was instrumental

in the formation of the UDF, and was constantly in hiding from the police. His personal connections from prison and from the UDF led him to the job as JEP's first director in 1986. In this sense, from its very inception the identity of JEP – and youth development in general – was multifaceted.

6. The National Education Crisis Committee (NECC) was later renamed the National Education Co-ordinating Committee, and thus retained the same acronym. A large part of the NECC's mission was to plan the new education department that would be implemented when the new government came to power.

7. A resistance movement pamphlet in the JEP archives called *Coping in Crisis* warned activists, 'The Emergency regulations say that you cannot say anything that the state does not like. If the state does not like something you said and they think it is "subversive" you can go to jail for up to two years.' Therefore, urged a similar publication outlining a 'Code of Conduct for Comrades', 'security-consciousness' was of the utmost importance; lack of this awareness 'can easily lead to untold harm and suffering'. Examples of security violations included 'loose talk ... for it is difficult to say where such information eventually ends up', and lax 'security at home', which meant leaving documents and records of one's activities lying around.

8. He later rephrased this dilemma: the youth sector, he said, had 'too many songs, and no music' any more. In other words, the voices of the individual organisations were not singing in concert, as Biko (1998/reprinted) metaphorically described the fundamental African philosophy of *Ubuntu*, but were instead each singing their own song. As they repositioned themselves *vis-à-vis* government and funders, they in turn wrestled with repositioning themselves in relation to *each other*. This resulted in a tension between the individual and the collective, between the need to reposition NGOs in relation to the government and the market economy.

9. At the start of 2003, JEP had three new projects in the works, of which this one was the furthest developed. The other two will take place in Gauteng and KwaZulu-Natal.

10. The YDN comprises: JEP, Junior Achievement SA, The Centre for Education and Enterprise Development, School Leavers Opportunity Training, Southern African Association of Youth Clubs, Resource Action Group, and Establishment for Comprehensive Youth Development.

References

Biko, S (1998) (Reprinted) Some African Cultural Concepts. In Coetzee, PH & Roux, APT (eds) *The African Philosophy Reader*. London: Routledge

Borer, T (1998) *Challenging the State: Churches as Political Actors in South Africa*. Notre Dame, IN: University of Notre Dame Press

Brown, D & Covey, J (1987) *Organizing and Managing Private Development Agencies: A Comparative Analysis*. New Haven, CT: Institution for Social and Policy Studies

Chisholm, L; Harrison, C & Motala, S (1997) Youth Policies, Programmes and Priorities in South Africa, 1990–1995, *International Journal of Educational Development*, 17 (2): 215–225

de Certeau, M (1997) *The Capture of Speech and other Political Writings*. Minneapolis: University of Minnesota Press

Department of Health, South Africa (1998) *Youth in South Africa Bear a Terrible Burden – HIV/AIDS*. [Online]. Available <http://www.doh.gov.za/docs/pr/1998/pr0612.html> (Accessed 8 August 2003)

Fairclough, N (1992) *Discourse and Social Change*. Cambridge: Cambridge University Press

Fernando, J & Heston, A (1997) NGOs Between States, Markets, and Civil Societies, *Annals of the American Academy of Political and Social Science*, 554: 8–21

Giddens, A (1991) *Modernity and Self-Identity: Self and Society in the Late Modern Age*. Stanford: Stanford University Press

Leggett, T; Moller, V & Richards, R (eds) (1997) *My Life in the New South Africa: A Youth Perspective*. Pretoria: HSRC

Perrow, M (2000) Learning in Transition: Youth Development in Post-Apartheid South Africa. Unpublished doctoral thesis, School of Education, University of California, Berkeley

Ramphele, M (1995) *A Life*. Cape Town: David Philip

Ramphele, M (2002) *Steering by the Stars: Being Young in South Africa*. Cape Town: Tafelberg

Soudien, C (2003) Routes to Adulthood: Becoming a Young Adult in the New South Africa, *IDS Bulletin*, 34 (1): 63–71

South African Government Online *The State of South Africa's Population Report* 2000. [Online]. Available <http://www.gov.za/reports/2000/population> (Accessed 8 August 2003)

Statistics South Africa *Census 2001*. [Online]. Available <http://www.statssa.gov.za/special-projects/census2001/census2001.htm> (Accessed 18 August 2003)

Stevens, G & Lockhat, R (1997) 'Coca-Cola Kids' – Reflections on Black Adolescent Identity Development in Post-Apartheid South Africa, *South African Journal of Psychology*, 27 (4): 250–255

Stewart, S (1997) Happy Ever After in the Marketplace: Non-Governmental Organisations and Uncivil Society, *Review of African Political Economy*, 24 (71): 11–35

Tutu, D (1994) *The Rainbow People of God: South Africa's Victory over Apartheid*. London: Doubleday

CHANGING CLASS

15 Adult basic education and social change in South Africa, 1994 to 2003

Ivor Baatjes and Khulekani Mathe

Introduction

The role of adult education as an agent for social change has been prominent for several decades and has informed the activities of civil society and government campaigns in various countries such as Cuba, Brazil, Nicaragua, Guinea Bissau, Tanzania and many others. The radical tradition, in particular, views civil society as a privileged domain of radical learning, political struggle, social movements and social change. This tradition also has a notable history and presence in South Africa. Much provision of non-formal adult basic education (ABE)[1] in South Africa by non-government organisations (NGOs) – especially in the 1970s and 1980s – was influenced by it. The basic tenet of this tradition is that the socio-economic and political system that produces and perpetuates conditions of inequality is unjust and must be changed. The victims of oppression, inequality and injustice are called upon to unite, to challenge the system and to recreate the social world in which they live. Within this tradition, non-formal ABE instruction, for instance, is not just the imparting and acquiring of knowledge by teachers and learners respectively, but is a political process of raising critical awareness of injustice, and a joint investigation and creation of measures to change oppressive and undemocratic systems. In the South African context, illiteracy amongst adults is viewed by this tradition as not only a deeply-rooted social problem, but a result of a determinate structure and dynamic of classes and a consequence of the apartheid capitalist organisation of production. Non-formal ABE is viewed as authentic, revolutionary and inclusive and a vehicle that incorporates the illiterate and under-educated into a new form of democratic citizenship that opposes the perpetuation of asymmetrical power relations.

We write this chapter from the premise that the radical tradition of adult education has great relevance to the education of under-educated and illiterate adults in South Africa – a tradition that is re-emerging as we continue to grapple with the social, economic, political and moral issues facing us in a complex, violent, unequal and rapidly-changing society. We believe in its potential to identify and use spaces where forms of counter-hegemonic learning can take place, whether these be spaces of critical awareness, the formation of social movements, spaces in which learning is free from power and domination or spaces for democratic practices that are free from the state and the economy (Murphy 2001). We focus our discussion here on the role of ABE and argue that ABE, as a vehicle of social change, has failed largely because of its perceived worthlessness to economic growth and that, as a result of this perception, the vision of ABE as a tool that can enhance active involvement in the social and political life of the nation has been lost. Our argument is supported by a discussion and reflection on a range of developments that have taken place in the ABE field between 1994 and 2003. A key focus of our discussion is the tensions between the two well-known ethics of adult education – emancipatory ABE and instrumentalist ABE. We recognise the significance of instrumentalism, which is an integral aspect of any human resource development strategy of governments, but will argue that the application of this ethic, which has emerged as the dominant ethic driving ABE provision and delivery, is failing as a vehicle of social change while the other has been effectively weakened and undermined by it.

We start with a description of instrumentalist and emancipatory ethics, highlighting their differences and implications. We argue that ABE as an emancipatory project holds greater promise and can contribute to social change. Following an overview and description of key developments we conclude that the result of ABE policy and practice over the last decade, undergirded as it has been by neo-liberalism, instrumentalism, technocratic rationality and the 'cult of efficiency', has prohibited the promise of ABE as an agent for social change, precipitated the marginalisation of ABE, and reinforced its status as the stepsister of mainstream education. ABE policy in its current form is not addressing social exclusion and fails to incorporate large numbers of adults into democratic forms of citizenship. The emancipatory project, although inherently counter-hegemonic, holds better promise in building democratic forms of citizenship and advancing the themes of justice, freedom, participation, equality, care, stability and development (Baatjes 2003a). The emancipatory tradition requires further exploration and should be reinvented to exist and flourish alongside instrumentalism in South Africa. We conclude that emancipatory ABE would be most successful if located within a social movement able to fight for ABE as an integral part of the struggle for a just society.

The two ethics

Instrumentalist ABE

One of the most striking features in the economic debate in South Africa has been the importance attached to human capital as a determining factor of economic success. Globalisation has made the issue of how nations organise their skill formations in the context of the new competition an urgent research question (Murphy 2001; Brown 1999; Burbules & Torres 2000; Dale 1999; La Belle 2000). Governments around the world invest heavily in the education of adults and adult education has clearly emerged from the margins. In the case of South Africa, the terms 'adult basic education and training' (ABET), 'further education and training' (FET), 'outcomes-based education' (OBE), 'human resource development' (HRD) and 'lifelong learning' are increasingly being used to signal new concepts of adult education, particularly to support economic productivity and economic growth. Education systems, it is argued, should concentrate on developing people's competencies, their skills, knowledge and values to enable them to move across jobs from one sector of the economy to another and even from one country to another. Curricula are redesigned along competency-based lines, enabling recognition of existing competence as well as the more effective articulation of different levels of education and training. Education is seen as one component of a comprehensive approach to workplace restructuring, one which includes changes in industrial relations, technology and workplace organisation. The aim of education is a highly skilled, mobile workforce that will help make industry more competitive in the world economy (Brown 1999; Foley 1994; Welton 1995).

Human capital theory is integral to this restructuring of education (Brown 1999; Fragoso & Lucio-Villegas 2002). The term 'human capital' refers to knowledge, skills and attitudes that are developed and valued primarily for their economically productive potential (Baptiste 2001). It refers to the productive capacities of human beings as income-producing agents in an economy and to the present value of past investment in the skills of people. 'Human capital formation' is the term given to the process by which such capital is deliberately developed. Expenditure in terms of time, money, resources and so forth, is called human capital investment. Schultz (cited in Baptiste 2001) made the unqualified declaration that human capital enhances the productivity of both labour and physical capital. People at each skill level are more productive in a high capital environment compared to one that is low in human capital (Schultz cited in Baptiste 2001). Blaug (cited in Torres 1990) and others have argued that literacy and basic education of adults, in general, contribute to economic development in distinct forms. This contribution is achieved through: 1) increasing the productivity of the newly literate; 2) increasing the productivity of those who work with the newly literate; 3) expanding the diffusion of the general knowledge of individuals through training in health and infant nutrition and generally reducing the cost of transmitting practical information; 4) stimulating the demand for technical training and vocational education; 5) acting as an instrument for selecting the most valuable elements of the population thereby enhancing occupational mobility; and 6) strengthening economic incentives through exploiting the tendency of people to respond positively to an increment of compensation for their efforts (cited in Torres 1990).

Human capital theory that reduces adult literacy to an instrument of economic productivity has spawned critique, especially from radical adult educators. Critics like Baptiste (2001) have cited the theory's overly-mechanistic, one-dimensional view of human beings, its narrow understanding of labour, its use of correlational data to establish cause, the inconclusiveness of its empirical evidence and the insurmountable methodological hurdles associated with calculating returns on educational investments. Amongst these hurdles are the difficulties of separating educational consumption from investment, of determining the stock of its educational capital and of ascertaining the marginal productivity of education.

Other critics (Foley 1994; Welton 1995) have examined the theory's ominous societal impact, for instance, its exacerbation of social inequalities, its development of underdevelopment and its blaming of the victims. Some criticism has also been levelled at the theory's negative impact on day-to-day pedagogical practices. Baptiste's analysis provides a succinct description of the implications of human capital theory for pedagogical practices. He argues that: 1) human capital theorists treat people as 'homo economica' – radically isolated pleasure-seeking materialists who are born free of social constraints or responsibilities, who possess no intrinsic sociability and who are driven largely by the desire for material happiness and bodily security; 2) it assumes that the world is an educational meritocracy in which a person's socio-economic status is limited presumably only by his or her educational investment – more educated people are always more productive than less educated people and this differential productivity is sufficient to explain all social inequities; 3) it construes social inequalities not as injustices – the result of exploitation and oppression – but rather as the natural and inevitable outcome of a competitive free market; 4) the free market is the most, if not the only, legitimate social institution – the only institution that can adequately and justly govern, regulate and explain human behaviour and achievement; 5) human capitalists believe that there is no need to appeal to non-market forces such as unequal power or structural barriers to explain human and social behaviour; and 6) they are certain that the invisible hand of the free market, the co-ordinated force of price, supply and demand is well able to account for most, if not all, of the functions assigned to structure in sociological theories.

Instrumentalism permeates government educational policy, programmes, plans and strategies. It portrays ABE as education that increases productivity and leads to more employment opportunities. There remains, however, no convincing evidence to support this claim. This ethic is perpetuating exclusion and has failed to contribute to social change in South Africa. This failure is linked to globalisation, whose implications are best captured by Hall (cited in Foley 1994). Hall points out that globalisation: 1) is *narrowing the scope* of adult education through an increase in emphasis on *training*; 2) precipitates the *withdrawal of the state* from the financing of education; 3) has led to an increase in the *centralisation* of adult basic education policy formulation; 4) has led to an increase in *crisis-orientated adult education*; and 5) has led to an *increase* in the number of people in the world who do not read and write (our own italics added).

Emancipatory ABE

The emancipatory ethic, mostly associated with education for liberation or popular education, and largely linked to the work of Paulo Freire (1970), is a collective educational activity which has as its goal social and political transformation. This tradition is driven by the belief that people living in unjust situations can change their lives through their collective actions. It argues that the aim of ABE should be to develop a critical understanding of major contemporary problems and social changes, and the ability to play an active role in the progress of society with a view to achieving social justice. It is also informed by an educational approach that places great emphasis on relating education to real issues and problems, establishing closer links with day-to-day struggles, community action and social movements, creating an alternative adult education system which stresses linking education and action.

The emancipatory ethic also opposes the social pathology approach that characterises current ABE practices in South Africa where emphasis is placed on helping adults to *adapt* to the existing deteriorating order. Under-educated and illiterate adults in South African society face multiple forms of oppression including unemployment, disease, poverty, homelessness, and many more. This liberal orientation to education, which creates a belief that education provides the means of further benefits and fulfilment, whilst at the same time promoting social justice, equality and the integration of the diverse interests of differing groups in society, is rejected because of its failure to address growing disadvantage and alienation (Lovett, Clarke & Kilmurray 1983).

Programmes informed by the emancipatory ethic are designed as mechanisms or instruments of pedagogical and political collaboration with subordinate social sectors. It is a pedagogy for social transition, and hence defines its educational activity as cultural action (Freire's term) whose central objective can be summed up in the term 'conscientisation' (Torres 1990). Torres describes it as a non-authoritarian pedagogy that emphasises the sharing of experiences in dialogue within cultural circles. A principal characteristic of this approach is its resistance to links with the state and the bureaucratic organisation of educational practice. Adult education, from this perspective, is more closely linked to the needs of communities and responds more easily to the demands of communities than does the system of formal education. It is also characterised by curricular and organisational flexibility that formal schooling lacks. The results of this form of education are usually more immediate than those of schooling. Adult education, inspired by this tradition, has proved to be of great importance as an instrument of mobilisation and the development of political consciousness in revolutionary states such as Cuba and Nicaragua (Torres 1990). This ethic plays an important role in community work, community development, community organisation and community action and highlights the failure of the formal education system to effectively address the struggle for social and political justice. Lastly, adult education is also viewed as an important vehicle in the struggle for democracy – a belief in the value and worth of people, and in their rights and freedoms; in the recognition of people's desire and right to manage their own affairs and to participate actively in decisions that affect their lives.

Given these two ethics – instrumentalism and emancipation – we would argue that the emancipatory ethic could contribute more effectively to social change in the country. We recognise the limited role of ABE in economic development, and remain sceptical of its ability to address social, political and community problems. ABE does not support economic productivity or lead to employment opportunities. The emancipatory ethic, we would argue, presents alternative routes that incorporate solutions for both the social and economic challenges. This orientation argues: 1) for adult education as a vehicle in fostering democratic social action; 2) for action based on theoretical constructs; 3) against instrumental rationality that works purely to the advantage of business, industry and large-scale organisations; and 4) for inclusion – serving the interests of the poor, oppressed, disenfranchised and exploited. We argue that this tradition needs to be reinvented to help construct a vision of a new democracy based on equality, freedom and social justice. We will show that ABE for instrumentalism is emerging as the dominant ethic and that it fails to address the illiteracy dilemma in South Africa.

Overview of developments in the adult basic education field since 1990

A connection with the past

It is important that we place our analysis within its rightful context by providing a brief outline of the legacy of apartheid with specific reference to ABE. The history and development of ABE in South Africa is well documented (Aitchison 2003; Aitchison, Houghton, Baatjies 2000; Bird 1984; French 1982; Harley, Aitchison, Lyster & Land 1995; Roux 1964). The intention here is not to reproduce these works. Instead, this chapter draws attention to developments of ABE from the period when the first official government policy for ABE was developed. It is also necessary to highlight the connection between the changes in economic policy and how these changes shape education policy formulation.

In his *A History of Inequality in South Africa 1652–2002*, Terreblanche (2002: 25) notes that the democratically-elected South African government of 1994 'inherited a contradictory legacy: the most developed economy in Africa on the one hand, and major socio-economic problems on the other. The most serious of these are high rates of unemployment; abject poverty among 50 per cent of the population; sharp inequalities in the distribution of income, property and opportunities; and high levels of crime and violence'. Unemployment is high, and adult illiteracy[2] stands at 50 per cent (see also Bhorat, in this volume).

Apartheid policy deprived black people of access to education and opportunities to work towards prosperity. This was intended to provide a regular supply of cheap and unskilled labour for the apartheid capitalist state. The ruling political class, whose power was anchored in the economic structure of apartheid capitalism, shaped the political economy of adult basic education. Illiteracy among black adults was an integral part of the concrete forms of domination and asymmetrical relations of power that functioned to actively silence blacks (Baatjes 2003a). It was only in the early 1990s that academics and institutions produced several studies and policy proposals in preparation for the new South Africa.[3] Until this point, the tradition of ABE as an agent of social change (alternatively referred to as the emancipatory ethic) was prominent among many NGOs and activists in higher education. These groupings viewed ABE as a fundamental vehicle for achieving social, political and economic power and central in providing people with knowledge and skills to enable them to live productive lives. However, during the same period, instrumentalist ABE gained prominence within the business sector and the labour movement working together on the National Training Strategy Initiative (Harley et al.1995), which championed this approach.

The changing economic policy framework

Government policy during the period 1994 to 1996 was inspired and driven largely by the Reconstruction and Development Programme (RDP). This programme was informed by the principles of social justice and adopted a strong redistributive agenda. ABE as an object of social policy was viewed as integral to other social issues such as housing, water, unemployment and health. In fact, the RDP policy recognised ABE as an integral part of all development projects (ANC 1994). As part of a redistributive policy, the RDP would play a significant role in the redistribution of life chances of the historically disenfranchised. Implementation initiatives such as the Ithuteng Campaign were informed by this redistributive agenda and took on a strong political and revolutionary passion. Ithuteng was rooted in the political and social analysis of the living conditions of the marginalised and their deepening problems (poverty, unemployment, hunger, disease and death) and attempted to engage them in collective awareness of those conditions.

Perspectives and orientations in response to the structural position of the marginalised began to change in 1996, when the RDP was abandoned in favour of the Growth, Employment and Redistribution (GEAR) strategy (Baatjes 2003a; Bond 2000, 2002). Subsequent policy and implementation plans precipitated a more formal, standardised and utilitarian adult education system. The perspective of ABE as a vehicle in the reconstruction of South African society shifted from a *political-revolutionary position* (ABE for emancipation) to a *social-gradualist position* (ABE for economic growth). Both positions are contributing to efforts to educate marginalised adults in South African society. However, these are potentially competing and contradicting ideologies with different social, economic and political interests as highlighted in the earlier sections.

The promises of the policy-making process

ABE as an agent for social change was institutionalised within the government bureaucracy in 1995 when the national government established the Directorate for Adult and Community Education, later renamed the Directorate for Adult Education and Training. The establishment of this unit within the national Department of Education (DoE) was viewed as a significant development and was well-received because it was believed that the new government had a good understanding of the socio-economic and political characteristics of the educational clientele. The ideological position of policy planning held by the policy planners and policy-makers was supportive of the plight of the excluded, subordinate and marginalised. It was also believed that policy-makers, given their strong connections with the marginalised, would ensure and secure, through rapid policy-making processes, a voice for the marginalised. From the perspective of the state, ABE policy and programmes were also viewed as mechanisms that would promote political participation in civic and governmental affairs – participatory ABE policy and programmes were perceived as meaningful developments that would provide political legitimation of the state.

A significant development in the policy process was the shift from literacy to ABE in the mid-1990s. With the growth in technological advance and transfer, the ever-changing definition of literacy and the emergence of lifelong education as an important societal concern, the state committed itself to the universalisation of basic education, which increased the commitment to education beyond simply the ability to read and write.[4] Post-literacy was recognised as necessary. ABE became enshrined in the Constitution and literacy was subsumed in the definition of ABE. ABE is defined as:

> ... the general conceptual foundation towards lifelong learning and development, comprising of knowledge, skills and attitudes required for social, economic and political participation and transformation applicable to a range of contexts. ABET is flexible, developmental and targeted at the specific needs of particular audiences and ideally, provides access to nationally recognised certificates. (DoE 1997a: 5)

This expansion of ABE to subsume literacy meant that approximately ten million people require or could benefit from ABE. The term 'adult basic education' in South Africa has taken on an extra meaning with the introduction of training as a vital element of the new education and training enterprise. South Africans – government, labour, civil society, business and industry – have adopted the term 'Adult Basic Education and Training', which supposedly reflects greater integration of education and training (the right to work and the right to be educated to work). The emphasis on training emanates from organised labour, which argues for the recognition of existing technical skills of the worker and the need for these skills to be acknowledged as part of the learning and teaching process (Baatjes 2003a).

Key policy developments

Government initially supported ABET and introduced a range of policies, programmes, projects and campaigns (see Aitchison et al. 2000). We highlight a few of the key developments that have shaped the current bureacratisation and formalisation of ABE and laid the foundation for the dominant role that the instrumentalist ABE is currently playing in South Africa:

- In 1995, two significant developments took place: *The Interim Guidelines* appeared as the first ever policy for ABET in South Africa. This policy played an important role in unifying the ABET sector. The Directorate for Adult Education and Training was established to work closely with a stakeholder-driven body, the National Stakeholders Forum for ABET.
- In 1996, sub-directorates of ABET were established in all nine provincial departments of education and the government launched the Ithuteng 'Ready to Learn' Campaign with a once-off budget of R50 million; new staff in the national department and provincial departments were also appointed.
- In 1997, the *Interim Guidelines* were replaced by the *Policy document on Adult Basic Education and Training*, operationalised through the *Multi-Year Implementation Plan* and nine Provincial Multi-Year Implementation Plans. This concluded the first phase of legislation for ABET which started in 1996 – the development of a Regulatory Framework that would transform existing sites of delivery, better known as night schools, into effective Public Adult Learning Centres (PALCs).
- Between 1998 and 1999, a range of policy developments were concluded. Examples of these are: 1) the establishment of a new stakeholder representative structure – the interim ABET Advisory Board – with sub-structures; 2) the development of Conditions of Service for Adult Educators; 3) the registration of existing adult educator qualifications for remuneration purposes; 4) the development of the first unit standards-based qualifications for adult educators; 5) the development of basic policy for ABET materials; 6) the registration of qualifications and unit standards in eight sub-fields of learning with SAQA; 7) the development of draft learning programmes for implementation in the provinces; and 8) the conceptualisation of the Ikhwelo and Rivoningo Projects[5] was completed.
- In 2000, the DoE launched the South African National Literacy Initiative (SANLI) as a literacy campaign targeting 500 000 learners (out of three million) in the first year of its implementation.
- In 2001, the DoL launched the National Skills Development Strategy (NSDS), setting a target of raising the basic education levels of workers in the workplace so that 70 per cent of all workers would have a General Education and Training Certificate (GETC)[6] by the year 2005.
- By the end of 1998, the DoE had effectively managed to complete, at great financial expense, the key elements of the ABET policy, except for the

development of an *Adult Basic Education and Training Act*, which was completed only in 2000.
- Between 1998 and 2000, the policy development process continued alongside the implementation of projects, including the Ikhwelo and Rivoningo Projects and more recently, the SANLI Campaign. During 1999, the first assessment of ABET learners through the South African Certification Council (Safcert)[7] was undertaken and the Ikhwelo and Rivoningo Projects were implemented.
- The number of NGOs in ABET started to decline in 1997. Effective partnerships between the state and ailing NGOs failed to materialise, leading to the demise of many NGOs. This demise has been linked to bilateral and multilateral agreements between the state and donor agencies which significantly reduced funds to NGOs. For instance, in a study published in 2000, only 38 of 150 ABET NGOs surveyed in 1997 were still in operation (Aitchison et al. 2000). By contrast, commercial providers of ABET that provide programmes to business and industry in line with the NSDS have flourished.
- Funding for ABET through PALCs has remained meagre while the NSDS is channelling more funds to ABET programmes in mainly big business and industry, such as in the mining and manufacturing sectors (Baatjes, Aitchison & John 2002; Baatjes 2002b). Small-scale ABET provision in support of the instrumentalist orientation has displaced mass-based ABET provision for emancipation over the last four years. This is evident in the current scale of state-centre provision versus Sector Education and Training Authorities (SETA) supported provision as well as the distribution of funding between these two kinds of sites. We will return to this point a little later.

In summary, since 1996 a range of policy developments have taken place with emphasis on the formalisation of a national ABET system placing ABET under firm control of government with the understanding that government would be the major driving force of ABET as a vehicle for social change. We discuss this in greater detail in the next section.

Discussion of ABE policy and implementation since 1994

The South African print media has been very sympathetic to ABE, especially the *Mail & Guardian*, which has constantly published articles on government provision of ABE. Various commentators (Aitchison 1999, 2000, 2003; Baatjes 2002a, 2003a and b; Mathe 2001, 2002; Rule 2002) provide detailed analyses of the failure of the implementation of government ABET policy. We draw on these analyses as part of our discussion.

The failure of the state-sponsored mass ABE campaigns

The first attempt by the state to implement an ABE campaign, which aimed at reaching 90 000 learners in the country, failed. The targeted numbers were not reached and critical success factors were not properly addressed (Baatjes 2003b). It was believed that Ithuteng would precipitate a mass ABE campaign that would mobilise communities in support of literacy education. However, it soon became clear that this would not happen given, amongst other things, the poor economic commitment to the campaign and, perhaps of greater concern, the political consequences of the emerging *reformist*, neo-liberal economic policies that perceive ABE as an *expense* rather than an *investment* in social development.

Following the failure of the campaign, the DoE, supported by an enthusiastic NGO-sector, developed a very sophisticated policy and an ambitious plan for ABET (DoE 1997a, 1997b). The development of both policy and plan started during the second year of what became a two-year Ithuteng campaign. Ithuteng was originally planned as a one-year campaign, but was extended because most provinces could not implement the campaign for a number of reasons including staffing, availability of funds, insufficient planning and tender regulations and procedures.

The state as a major ABET provider would set high targets for itself in the *National Multi-Year Implementation Plan (1997)*. This was largely based on the belief that the state would honour its commitment to ABE as stated in the RDP, and commit sufficient resources to it. The *Multi-Year Implementation Plan* (MYIP) would have required R18 billion over a period of five years. This soon proved impossible as the state continued to commit less than one per cent of the overall education budget to ABE (Aitchison et al. 2000; French 2002).

In 1999, ABE received a boost with the appointment of Kader Asmal as Minister of Education. He immediately threatened to 'break the back of illiteracy' as a priority of his *Call to Action*.[8] In the same year, he echoed his commitment to ABE on International Literacy Day, stating that: 'No adult South African should be illiterate in the 21st century ...' Beginning in 2000,

Asmal instituted various planning processes, including the establishment of SANLI and a Board of Advisors to assist with his national literacy campaign. Three years since the launch of SANLI the initiative has hardly produced any results. Various analysts attribute this inertia to the power struggle within the department over the control of SANLI and the constraints that GEAR places on funding the initiative (Mathe 2001; Baatjes 2003a; Aitchison et al. 2000; Rule 2002).

The allocation of resources by the South African government must be understood within the context of the elite compromises of the early 1990s between the liberation movement and the corporate sector and emergent GEAR policy. From this point of view, committing the resources that would be required to 'break the back of illiteracy' would increase the government deficit or require other forms of funding (such as increasing taxes) and would therefore be inconsistent with the policy commitment to which the ANC had attached itself. Government denies that GEAR dictates the South African ABET agenda (Mathe 2001). Explanations by the state for the lack of financial support for ABET are yet to be provided.

The formalisation of ABE

ABE in South Africa is currently firmly placed in the hands of government, and to some extent, a reluctant business sector. This centralisation of ABE through the National Qualifications Framework (NQF) (see Muller, this volume) has also been linked to the formalisation of ABE programmes and plans. The formalisation is characterised by: 1) the institutionalisation of ABE provision and delivery through PALCs; 2) the employment of schoolteachers as part-time adult educators; 3) the development of a unit-standards-based qualification (GETC); 4) the delivery of a national learning programme consisting of combinations of learning areas (old school subjects) and some specialisations; 5) the rather poor supply of books; 6) the establishment of an assessment system through UMALUSI that is similar to the current matric examinations; 7) the development of adult educator qualifications to support the professionalisation of the sector; and 8) legislation that is very similar, if not identical, to that for formal schooling.

PALCs have become 'schools' for adults. This second-chance education is modelled on the NQF levels which assume that adult learning and educational needs are similar to those of children. A closer look at the ABET curriculum shows very clearly that it is reproducing the curriculum categories of schooling and this is done through the delivery of a national curriculum consisting of school subjects. Poorly-trained and part-time adult educators, who are mainly schoolteachers, continue to be used to teach in ABET classes. Today, most PALCs can be described as dysfunctional institutions with few or no administrative and management systems (Nzimande 2003). The instability of these institutions is compounded by high attrition rates, deterrents to participation and a high turnover in educators.

The formalisation of ABET has also been shaped by a new quality assurance policy which suggests that providers be registered and accredited. This policy, which is highly prescriptive and burdensome, although it is not strictly applied to PALCs, has created a new bureaucratic system that has significant implications in particular for smaller NGOs. One of the key elements of this policy is the curriculum of providers which must comply with the national standards regime. This is clearly another mechanism that ensures control over providers of education in general and lends itself to the formalisation process of ABE in particular, as well as playing a key role in defining the role that education should play.

The level and quality of ABE provision

State provision of ABE has remained conspicuously weak even under the new democratic government. The number of PALCs declined from 1 440 to 998 during the period 1995 to 2002 (Baatjes 2003a), and the enrolment was estimated to be 250 000 learners by 2002 – far less than was anticipated in the MYIP. There are no reliable statistics on the level of provision by the private and NGO sectors. However, it is safe to say that, given the much-documented decline in the NGO sector (see Aitchison 2003; Baatjes 2003a) and the increase in unemployment which affects unskilled and semi-skilled workers (ABE candidates), enrolment in both these sectors combined is considerably low. This is excluding ABE provision that results from SETA delivery processes, which we discuss later. With the benefit of hindsight, the MYIP and the SANLI plan were both attempts by ABE activists to persuade government to prioritise and allocate necessary resources to ABET work.

Aitchison (2003) analyses the examination results and participation rates of the ABET Level 4 learners in PALCs in 2002 and identifies the following trends:
- Of the 40 974 learners enrolled, 21 148 wrote the exams and 17 926 passed between 1 and 8 learning areas;
- Compared to the enrolment estimates by the Human Sciences Research Council (HSRC) for 1999, the number of learners enrolled in 2002 in each province was less than 50 per cent;
- The number of learners who wrote the exams per province as a percentage of enrolment ranged from 36 per cent in Mpumalanga to 68 per cent in the Western Cape;
- The enrolment in ABET Level 4 as a percentage of PALC ABET learners in 1999 ranged from 11 per cent in the Western Cape to 52 per cent in the Free State;
- The lowest was 8 per cent (the Western Cape) and the highest 26 per cent (the Free State) of those who wrote as a percentage of those enrolled in 1999;
- Those enrolled in ABET in PALCs as a percentage of those aged 20+ with no schooling formed as little as 1 per cent in KwaZulu-Natal, the highest being in the Eastern Cape with 6 per cent; and
- A small number of approximately 790 learners qualified for a GETC although the quality of the assessment remains questionable (see Baatjes 2001 for discussion of portfolio assessments).

The above suggests a serious problem with learner retention in the state-driven ABET system. There is also often a positive correlation between high drop-out rate and poor quality of instruction. More than 50 per cent of adult learners drop out of ABET programmes run by the state. Poor quality of instruction can also be related to the employment of un- or under-qualified educators and lack of learning material. Many PALCs are simply dysfunctional (Baatjes 2003c). The situation is even worse when analysing the numbers of entries for learning areas and the number who actually wrote. The higher the number of learning areas, the lower the number of people who actually wrote for all the learning areas they entered.

There are currently two examination systems for ABET learners in South Africa – the state-run system (analysed earlier) and the one run by the Independent Examinations Board (IEB). While no statistical comparison of the two systems has been conducted, there is widespread belief among those in the field of ABE that the standards of quality of the two systems are significantly different in favour of the IEB system.

SETAs as delivery machinery of ABE

The *Skills Development Act* (SDA) of 1998 and the *Skills Development Levies Act* (SDLA) of 1999 respectively established institutions and set in place a system which requires employers to pay one per cent of their payroll to fund skills development of their employees. The Revenue Services Department collects levies, and the DoL and its subsidiary institutions manage the fund. The essence of this legislation is that it makes the training of employees a statutory requirement. Training is targeted at the employed, the unemployed and the employable. The SDA and all its subsidiary regulations constitute adult education legislation and therefore deserve a mention in this chapter. It also signals that, although adult education is still under-resourced, it should no longer be regarded as a marginal activity.

Among many institutions and systems introduced by the SDA, are the SETAs. Twenty-five SETAs were established to represent all economic sectors, with the main purpose of facilitating the implementation of the SDA across sectors. SETAs also have quality assurance of education and training in their respective sectors as one of their functions. In 2001, the DoL launched the NSDS, which identifies five key objectives and sets a number of targets that must be achieved by the skills development regime by March 2005. The most relevant of these is that by March 2005, 70 per cent of workers should have at least a NQF Level 1 qualification. The skills development regime and its institutional framework are new and it would therefore be unfair to judge them. However, there are design features of this system which, when scrutinised closely, leave us no choice but to question its ability to succeed.

Although detailed information about the successes and challenges of SETAs is not currently available, the overall picture is not a positive one. SETAs are having great difficulty with the implementation of the NSDS and are mostly likely to fail in meeting the set targets. They have become new bureaucratic structures preoccupied with the development of administrative and policy systems which have not only hindered the implementation of the NSDS, but also created barriers to providers to fast track education and training programmes and projects. Significantly, they have great difficulty in mobilising companies to support the implementation of skills legislation and the NSDS. This is evident in the small number of companies who have submitted Workplace Skills Plans and the increase of unspent money in the National Skills Fund (NSF). A small number of learnerships and skills programmes have been developed and the quality of these programmes requires investigation. A major hindrance to their success is the fact that education and training providers involved with unemployed and poor communities have great difficulty accessing funds from SETAs and the National Skills Authority (NSA) because of bureaucratic hiccups. And finally, although some SETAs and the NSA have allocated funds and discretionary grants to strategic projects, the effectiveness of these projects is unknown.

Mathe (2002: 90) argues that, given the rising rate of unemployment, the private sector is employing people with more than NQF Level 1 qualifications even for menial jobs, and that this will lead to those who have some training getting more, and those who have less, getting less or nothing. At the same time, those workers who would benefit from ABET are the most vulnerable to retrenchments. Workers with less than nine years of schooling in the mining and mineral sector are the first to be retrenched (Baatjes et al. 2002). This argument is corroborated by the *Human Resources Development Strategy*, which states that already '64.1 per cent of persons currently employed possess the GETC (equivalent to the current Grade 9 certificate) that is pegged at NQF Level 1' (DoL 2001: 38). This means that the 70 per cent target can easily be achieved (despite the apathy shown by employers[9]) without significantly altering the literacy profile of the country. This is especially so since there are no clear plans and specific targets set in the NSDS for reaching unemployed illiterate and under-educated adults. Also, the facilitation of skills development of the unemployed was initially made the responsibility of the DoL and financed from the NSF, which is made up of 20 per cent of the levies paid by enterprises. However, no institutional framework and infrastructure similar to that put in place for facilitating training in workplaces has been established for the unemployed. This responsibility was later shifted to the 25 SETAs whose main target is the formal (employment) sector, and given the fact that all 25 SETAs, with no exception, are struggling to meet challenges in their sectors, it is unlikely that they will do justice to this 'added responsibility'. It seems quite likely that, despite the enthusiasm and excitement generated in the ABE field, the *Skills Development Act* will be another empty promise.

The rise and fall of movements for social mobilisation in ABE

One of the constant features of the ABE sector is its lack of a powerful voice that represents its interests in national debates, especially around resources. The past decade has seen the demise of numerous ABE NGOs (see Aitchison et al. 2000; Baatjes 2003a for more details). The majority of organisations closed because of funding crises. As the next section will show, they do however seem to have re-emerged in new forms in the more recent period.

The weaknesses of this sector are a result of both internal and external forces, and have led to ambivalence within the funding community and the state about continuing to support or taking this sector seriously (see Morrow, this volume). Government is responsible for some of the reasons that explain the collapse of these organisations, particularly its involvement in the funding mechanisms to NGOs and their measuring tools of success. The NGO sector frequently views government as a gatekeeper that has failed to facilitate the effective channelling of donor funds to the NGO sector since 1996. It has also resulted in bureaucratic and accountability systems that do not suit the NGO sector. Although civil society could have a profound impact on shaping community development and democracy, governments might also perceive it as a potential site of counter-hegemonic learning.

The rise of the adult learning network and its renewed focus

A characteristic of the ABE sector is its resilience. This can be attributed to the long history of this sector in struggles against oppression, marginalisation and exclusion. Despite the high-profile collapse of organisations such as the National Literacy Co-operation, the Adult Educators and Trainers Association of South Africa (AETASA) and the World University Service (WUS) South Africa, the NGO sector has been able to regroup, reorganise and advance. It took no more than a year after the closure of AETASA for the new Adult Learning Network (ALN) to emerge as a new formation to: 1) provide a national networking structure for organisations working in the field of adult learning, basic education and development; and 2) promote redress and transformation, with the key focus on improving the status, quality and provision of adult education. Critics pointed out that, while this is a sign of resilience, it can also be a weakness to form organisations one after another without conducting a proper audit of why previous organisations have failed.

This criticism is justified. However, although the formation of the ALN was in response to requests from the sector and demands on those who had been part of previous networks, care was taken to take proper stock before formalising the organisation.

At the time of writing, the ALN was supported by eight provincial networks (no network existed in Mpumalanga). For its part, the network in KwaZulu-Natal investigated its formation and has decided to shift its focus towards campaigning for the constitutional right to adult basic education (see Membership Guidelines, *Talking Adult Learning* 2003). This change of approach requires a careful examination of the relationship between the state and civil society. A key element is informed by a more coherent approach to the study and practice of adult education and its links with new social movements and organisations within civil society. For now, it is clear that the struggle for ABE remains highly contested and is driven by different social, political and economic interests.

Summary and conclusion

In the decade since the first ABET policy was introduced in South Africa, there have been a number of significant policy developments and contributions to the field of ABE. At the time of writing, a well-founded policy was in place, as was a comprehensive, but partly dysfunctional system for ABET, with nine provincial programmes. The establishment of the evolving system has been created through literacy campaigns, projects and pressures from those within civil society representing the voices of the marginalised and excluded. Today, the state, business, and industry are playing a more dominant role in the provision and delivery of ABE programmes as a largely social and economic project. Although some loose rhetoric is heard regarding literacy, ABE for democratic participation and other forms of non-formal education continues to receive less attention from the state and the donor community. The NGO sector, which views ABE as a political project, has been in decline because of financial constraints but its resilience is shown in its reinvention and reorganisation and consistent attempts to maintain its role as a critical actor that is both defensive and offensive. Ongoing attempts are made to protect civil society from economic and political colonisation and to continue to exert influence and pressure on political society.

Enhancing the status and material wealth of the poor and marginalised population through ABE in South Africa reflects an ongoing struggle. Efforts by the state and business are increasingly being shaped by the human capital tradition and thus maintain the status quo, while the role and scope for emancipatory projects are ignored. The struggle for ABE remains a contested terrain of conflicting interests and ideologies. This tension exists between the two dominant ethics of adult education – emancipatory ABE and instrumentalist ABE. The emancipatory ethic recognises the importance of human resource development, but is mainly concerned with social justice and radical change. Its central position towards ABE is that it is an object of social policy and that literacy should be delivered as part of a political process that incorporates adult learners into democratic and participatory forms of citizenship and to fight against the colonisation of the lifeworld.[10] The radical tradition is critical of the instrumentalist tradition that is emerging as the dominant force currently driving ABE practices in South Africa. The terms 'ABET', 'FET' and 'lifelong learning' are increasingly being used to signal new concepts of adult education – particularly to support economic productivity and economic growth. There is greater emphasis being placed on linking adult education more effectively to the needs of the economy, concentrating on 'clients' needs', 'co-ordinating resources', 'effective delivery of services', and so on. These developments, according to Welton (1995), are indicative of the fact that adult education is becoming less marginal to the mainstream of education and the major preoccupation of the state. This neo-liberal tradition dictates that adult education become more and more relevant to the needs of the economy or corporate capitalism. Business and professional interests often invoke adult education as a means to increase efficiency and profitability, while many community groups look at adult education's potential as a vehicle for social reform. The neo-liberal tradition that has absorbed adult education into a 'cult of efficiency' (Collins's term; 1991) or instrumentalism is failing to create a more just and equitable society, therefore perpetuating asymmetrical power relations.

The human capital tradition has also shaped a number of developments in ABET in South Africa. Firstly, it precipitated the formalisation and bureaucratisation of ABE. This process has placed ABET policy formulation under the effective control of government. One of the key problems of this development is the role that ABET is playing in the reproduction of the curriculum categories of formal schooling. This is clearly reflected in the pre-packed curriculum being taught in PALCs and the emergence of formal qualifications for adult learners. ABET is hardly different to formal schooling and this is being reinforced by the systems adopted by state provision and delivery. ABET programmes, like schooling, are constantly being shaped by the market and it is highly unlikely that ABET will escape the narrowing focus of education on economic productivity.

Secondly, ABET provision and delivery in business and industry is also driven by human capital approaches and assumptions and will be increasingly linked to the workplace. However, the rather disturbing development in the workplace is the vulnerability of those with less education. Workers are constantly being lambasted and told that they lack the knowledge and skills for the new knowledge-rich society. We are not convinced that this argument is true because those with the least education are most vulnerable to retrenchment. The so-called emphasis on the skills-gap might well be a way to make people feel inadequate and a justification to cut jobs or to decrease the cost of labour and salaries of workers.[11] There are clearly not enough skilled or unskilled jobs for people to do and the use of screening techniques in selecting candidates for jobs is on the increase (see Payne 2000). For instance, a matric certificate has suddenly become a requirement to be employed in a low-skilled job.

Thirdly, there is the emergence of the private versus public ABET provision and delivery. Most of the NGOs in ABET have 'converted' to private providers or commercial providers as part of a strategy to survive. However, in the process they are abandoning the struggle for emancipatory possibilities and projects. Partly linked to the formalisation of ABET, these providers have to compete for resources made available through the NSDS-regime which services a small number of workers in mainly large companies at fairly high rates. On the other hand, public ABET continues to be poorly funded and the quality of programmes remains poor. Baptiste (2001) links the emergence of private versus public education to human capital approaches. He argues that greater pressure is being placed on poor and under-educated adults to pay for their education, which has become yet another commodity in the marketplace. The lifespan of these NGOs and commercial providers is very short given the current rate at which the economy is shedding jobs currently occupied by under-educated workers who could easily be displaced by the thousands of matriculants who enter the job-market on an annual basis.

Finally, but most importantly, is the value of ABET in the new knowledge-rich economy. We are increasingly being told about the lack of knowledge and skills amongst the South African population and that the 'promised' jobs would require higher levels of education. Both government, and business and industry do not appear to value ABET as an investment and an imperative for economic growth, but see it rather as an unnecessary and unwanted cost. ABET has very little economic currency and the state's inconsistent philosophy in approaching adult learning is reflected by its *laissez faire* attitude towards ABET compared to the interventionist attitude towards FET (Baatjes et al. 2002). It is highly unlikely that we will see an increase in support for ABET as shown through the current state of provisioning, SANLI and *Masifunde sonke*. ABET, however, remains a basic human right and the state needs to be pressured to fulfil its constitutional obligation towards the undereducated and to recognise alternatives such as those presented by the emancipatory tradition.

It is in relation to these alternatives that civil society and social movements are crucial. Radical adult educators continue to view ABE in the complexities of politics, social justice, economics and the intertwined issues of poverty, unemployment, racism, sexism, disease, crime, and moral decay. They foster the best and most suitable route to emancipation from the intricacies of exploitation, oppression, exclusion and marginalisation – a route that incorporates the themes of justice, freedom, care, equality, peace, stability and development (Baatjes 2003a; Welton 1995). An increasing body of literature (Apple 2002; Bello 2002; International Forum on Globalisation 2002; Kellner 2000; Morrow & Torres 1999; Murphy 2001; Ramadiro & Vally 2002; Welton 2001) on the role of civil society and social movements discusses the possibilities of how civil society and social movements should be organised and reinvented to confront the neo-liberal project and the growing global right-wing movement. One thing is clear: civil society and social movements that recognise ABE as a human right, a development imperative and an important aspect of social change, are re-emerging and already challenging governments and neo-liberal forces. It is evident that instrumentalist ABE in South Africa, if uncontested, will perpetuate marginalisation and exclusion. Close to ten million South African adults are so poorly educated that they cannot access the jobs on the market. The hope of being retrained or schooled for a new job in the elite knowledge sector is painfully out of reach for the majority.

Notes

1. Adult basic education is defined as all forms of organised education and training that meet the basic learning needs of adults, including literacy, numeracy, general knowledge and life-skills, and values and attitudes that they require to survive, develop their capacities, live and work in dignity, improve the quality of their lives, make informed decisions and to ... continue learning (Unesco 1997). Prior to 1996, ABE in South Africa consisted mainly of literacy in English and numeracy.
2. A fairly common and acceptable definition of literacy is the ability to read and write, not only by adults, but by children and youth as well. Literacy is a continuum of reading and writing skills. Often the term is used to include also basic arithmetic skills. It is widely accepted that an adequate level of literacy is achieved after seven years of schooling. Today, the term 'literacy' also includes various forms of basic knowledge and skills. These include knowledge and skills such as computer literacy, economic literacy, scientific literacy, technological literacy, political literacy, etc. Recently Unesco published literacy rates according to the number of people in a country who have gone to school. On the basis of this definition, South Africa has a literacy rate of 91 per cent. The South African government now targets the three million adults who have no schooling.
3. The first official government policy, namely *The Interim Guidelines*, was published in 1995. It was based on a range of policy discussions that took place during the period 1990–1994, including the *National Education Policy Investigation* (1992), COSATU's *Consolidated Recommendations on ABET* (1993) and the ANC's *Policy Framework for Education and Training* (1994).
4. In South Africa and in many other parts of the world, the provision of literacy and functional literacy is no longer enough and the need to provide ABE is increasingly being emphasised. ABE, which subsumes literacy, is increasingly emphasised as a vehicle to integrate poorly-educated adults in the emerging global society as parents, productive workers, participatory citizens and as fulfilled human beings. ABE is highlighted as necessary to stem the divisive and destructive forces of polarisation, marginalisation and exclusion.
5. The Ikhwelo Project was conceptualised in 1998 as a project that would provide ABET to approximately 3 000 adult learners in the Eastern Cape and Northern Province. The ABET programme was designed to provide adult learners with knowledge and skills in agriculture and SMMEs with the aim of encouraging self-sufficiency and self-reliance. The Ikhwelo Project was implemented in 1999 as a partnership project between Project Literacy and the DoE. The Rivoningo Project was also launched in 1999 as part of a strategy to develop good Public Adult Learning Centres (PALCs) in each of the nine

provinces. The Rivoningo Project was originally conceptualised as the Five PALC Project of the DoE, targeting five PALCs per province.

6. In terms of the new National Qualification Framework (NQF), the GETC is the first qualification achieved after the completion of the four ABET levels or nine years of general education in the case of schooling.

7. Safcert has recently been replaced by the Quality Assurance Body for General and Further Education and Training called UMALUSI. The Minister of Education launched UMALUSI on 11 March 2003 (see Muller, in this volume).

8. Asmal, K (1999) *Statement in the national assembly by the Minister of Education, Professor Kader Asmal, MP on the occasion of International Literacy Day*, 8 September 1999. <http://education.pwv.gov.za/Media_Statements/Aug99/Illiteracy.html>

9. Out of the 25 000 companies registered with the Manufacturing, Engineering and Related Services SETA (MERSETA) only 1 000 companies (four per cent) submitted Workplace Skills Plans (WSPs), which is the mechanism to fund education and training programmes (Baatjes 2002: 11) and of the 3 800 employers who pay levies in the Education Training and Development Practices (ETDP) sector, less than a third submitted WSPs in 2002 (Mathe 2002: 98).

10. Using Welton's (1995) definition of lifeworld, we use the term 'lifeworld' to describe the space in which we learn what life means and the practices – our interactions and organisations – that bind us together as human beings.

11. In recent instances where workers have been retrenched, they have been offered life-skills programmes that could increase their knowledge and skills so that they could access other jobs, including becoming entrepreneurs in the informal economy. This is part of a strategy to make people feel inadequate and that they need more education.

References

African National Congress (1994) *The Reconstruction and Development Programme: A Policy Framework*. Johannesburg: Umanyano Publications

Aitchison, JJW (1999) Literacy and Adult Basic Education and Training in South Africa: A Quick Survey. *Adult Education and Development*, 53: 99–120

Aitchison, JJW (2003) Struggle and Compromise: A History of South African Adult Education from 1960 to 2001, *Journal of Education*, 29: 125–178

Aitchison, JJW; Houghton, T & Baatjes, I (2000) *University of Natal Survey of ABE and Training: South Africa*. Pietermaritzburg: University of KwaZulu-Natal Centre for Adult Education

Apple, M (2002) *Educating, the 'Right' Way: Markets, Standards, God and Inequality*. New York: Routledge Falmer

Baatjes, I (2001) *Portfolio Assessment: A Report on the Use of Portfolio Assessment in the Northern Cape*. Kimberley: Northern Cape DoE

Baatjes, I (2002a) *The Challenge by Adult Basic Education and Training (ABET) and Adult Education Theory to the National Skills Development Strategy*. Keynote presentation at the CHIETA: Lessons Learnt from the Skills Development Strategy Conference, May, 2002, Durban

Baatjes, I (2002b) *A Baseline study of ABET in the Manufacturing, Engineering and Related Services Sector: A Strategy for ABET Provision and Delivery*. Johannesburg: MERSETA

Baatjes, I (2003a) The New Knowledge-Rich Society: Perpetuating Marginalisation and Exclusion. *Journal of Education*, 29: 179–204

Baatjes, I (2003b) *Reading in South Africa: An Overview of Policy, Programmes and Projects*. Paper submitted to *Innovation*. University of Natal

Baatjes, I; Aitchison, J & John, V (2002) *A Baseline Study of ABET in the Mining and Minerals Sector: Improving Provision and Delivery*. Johannesburg: MQA

Baptiste, I (2001) Educating Lone Wolves: Pedagogical Implications of Human Capital Theory, *Adult Education Quarterly*, 51 (3): 184–201

Burbules, NC & Torres, CA (eds) (2000) *Globalisation and Education: Critical Perspectives*. London: Routledge

Bello, W (2002) *Deglobalisation: Ideas for a New World Economy*. Cape Town: David Philip

Bird, A (1984) Black Adult Night School Movements on the Witwatersrand, 1920–1980. In Kallaway, P (ed) *Apartheid and Education*. Johannesburg: Ravan Press

Bond, P (2000) *Elite Transitions: From Apartheid to Neo-Liberalism in South Africa*. London: Pluto Press

Bond, P (2002) *Against Global Apartheid: South Africa Meets the World Bank, IMF and International Finance*. Cape Town: University of Cape Town Press

Brown, P (1999) Globalisation and the Political Economy of High Skills, *Journal of Education and Work*, 12 (1): 233–251

Brown, T (1999) Challenging Globalisation as Discourse and Phenomenon, *International Journal of Lifelong Education*, 18 (1): 3–18

Collins, M (1991) *Adult Education as Vocation: A Critical Role for the Adult Educator*. London: Routledge

Dale, R (1999) Specifying Globalisation Effects on National Policy: A Focus on the Mechanism, *Journal of Education Policy,* 14 (1): 1–17

Department of Education (1997a) *Policy Document on Adult Basic Education and Training. October 1997.* Pretoria: Government Printers

Department of Education (1997b) *A National Multi-year Implementation Plan for Adult Education and Training: Provision and Accreditation.* Pretoria: Government Printers

Department of Labour (2001) *Human Resource Development Strategy for South Africa. A Nation at Work for a Better Life for All.* Pretoria: Government Printers

Foley, G (1994) Adult Education and Capitalist Reorganisation, *Studies in the Education of Adults,* 26 (2): 121–144

Fragoso, A & Lucio-Villegas, E (2002) What Can We Learn From an Analysis of Adult Education Policies? *International Journal of Lifelong Learning,* 21 (3): 253–268

Freire, P (1970) *Pedagogy of the Oppressed.* London: Pluto Press

French, E (1982) *The Promotion of Literacy in South Africa: A Multi-Faceted Survey at the Start of the Eighties.* Pretoria: HSRC

French, E (2002) *The Condition of ABET: A Qualitative ABET Sector Review.* Contribution to the HSRC review of Education and Training for the ETDP SETA. Johannesburg, April

Harley, A; Aitchison, J; Lyster, E & Land, S (1995) *A Survey of ABE in South Africa in the 90s.* Johannesburg: SACHED

The International Forum on Globalisation (2002) *Alternatives to Economic Globalisation: A Better World is Possible.* San Fransisco: Berrett-Koehler

Kellner, D (2000) Globalisation and New Social Movements: Lessons for Critical Theory and Pedagogy. In Torres, CA & Burbules, NC (eds) *Globalisation and Education.* New York: Routledge Leask

La Belle, T (2000) The Changing Nature of Non-formal Education in Latin America, *Comparative Education,* 36 (1): 21–37

Lovett, T; Clarke, C & Kilmurray, A (1983) *Adult Education and Community Action.* London: Croom Helm

Mathe, K (2001) Who Sets the Agenda for ABET in South Africa? Unpublished paper presented at ABET Indaba: 3–5 September 2001. Johannesburg

Mathe, K (2002) A Policy Analysis of the Growth Employment and Redistribution (GEAR) Strategy with Respect to Social Development and Adult Basic Education and Training (ABET). A dissertation in partial fulfilment of the requirements for a Masters degree in Education. University of Natal, Pietermaritzburg

Morrow, R & Torres, C (1999) The State, social movements and educational reform. In Arnove, RF & Torres, CA *Comparative Education: The Dialectic of the Global and the Local.* Lanham: Rowman & Littlefield

Murphy, M (2001) The Politics of Adult Education: State, Economy and Civil Society, *International Journal of Lifelong Education,* 20 (5): 345–360

Nzimande, W (2003) Public Adult Learning Centres as Effective Sites of ABET Provision and Delivery: The Case of Jabu Ngcobo. Draft dissertation in partial fulfilment of the requirements for a Masters degree in Education. University of Natal, Pietermaritzburg

Payne, J (2000) The Unbearable Lightness of Skill: The Changing Meaning of Skill in UK Policy Discourse and Some Implications for Education and Training, *Journal of Education Policy,* (15) 3: 353–369

Ramadiro, B & Vally, S (2002) Testimonies from the Education Rights Project: From Abjectivity to Subjectivity. In Vally, S et al. (eds) *Quarterly Review: Human rights, neo-liberalism and education,* 9 (4)

Roux, E (1964) *Time Longer than Rope.* Madison: University of Wisconsin Press

Rule, P (2002) *Adults' Right to ABE and Basic Education in South Africa.* Centre for Adult Education, University of Natal, Pietermaritzburg

Talking Adult Learning. Newsletter of the Adult Learning Network. March/April 2003

Terreblanche, S (2002) *A History of Inequality in South Africa 1652–2002.* University of Natal Press & KMM Review Publishing

Torres, CA (1990) *The Politics of Non-formal Education in Latin America.* New York: Praeger

Unesco (1997) *Adult Education in a Polarised World: Education for All, Status and trends.* Paris and Stockholm: Unesco

Welton, M (ed) (1995) *In Defence of the Lifeworld: Critical Perspectives on Adult Learning.* New York: State University of New York Press

Welton, M (2001) Civil Society and the public sphere: Habermas's recent learning theory, *Studies in the Education of Adults,* 33 (1): 20–35

16 The education business: private contractors in public education

John Pampallis

This chapter examines outsourcing by state education authorities in South Africa since 1994 and its effects. Sometimes referred to as 'contracting out', this is not an altogether new phenomenon, but its increased scope and nature indicate a significant change in the way departments of education have functioned in the post-1994 period. This has been the result of various factors, including the context of globalisation and insufficient skills in the public service to meet the demands placed on government. A consequence of outsourcing has been the development of a market in educational services with the growth of various for-profit and non-profit organisations that provide a variety of services as contractors to government. The chapter argues that, for government, this trend has the potential of increasing its capacity and efficiency in the delivery of services, but that it carries certain dangers and needs to be guided by a comprehensive policy framework. The chapter draws on information gained by the author in the course of his work as director of the Centre for Education Policy Development, Evaluation and Management (CEPD), an NGO which, in addition to independent research, does contract work for education departments, often with other organisations, both NGOs and for-profit organisations.

Background

Towards the end of the apartheid period, the government, influenced by the neo-liberal thinking dominant in many sections of the developed world, started to consider greater privatisation of the economy – including the involvement of the private sector in the delivery of public services. The *White Paper on Privatisation and Deregulation* (RSA 1987) noted recent developments in Western countries 'towards the promotion of private initiative in order to improve the ability of the economy to perform'. This was accompanied by 'measures aimed at curbing or curtailing public expenditure ... and the privatisation of activities previously undertaken by (the public) sector'. The authors of the White Paper no doubt had in mind primarily the example of the UK under Margaret Thatcher, where the welfare state was under siege from an ideologically-driven programme of privatisation and a crusade to introduce markets and the private sector into the delivery of public services (Feigenbaum, Henig & Hammet 1998; Jackson & Price 1994). Other developed countries were also undergoing similar public service reform processes, contracting out public services to private companies (and, to a lesser extent, to NGOs), trying to stimulate markets and competition in these services, and generally trying to diminish the role of the state. Examples of countries where such reforms took place during the 1980s include the USA (Allen, Chi, Devlin, Fall, Hatry & Masterman 1989), the Nordic countries (Lane 1997), the Netherlands (Kickert 1997), New Zealand (Halligan 1997), Australia (Halligan 1997), and Canada (Lindquist 1997).

The 1987 White Paper accepted this course as desirable for South Africa and listed a number of methods for pursuing it. These included, *inter alia*, the sale of state enterprises and assets, partnerships between the state and the private sector, and contracting out. It stated that the government accepted 'that the private sector can undertake public services or activities on its behalf for a consideration ... Such contracting out can be justified if the public sector is not itself able to undertake the service or activity or if the private sector is able to undertake it just as or more efficiently or economically'. Although the area of education was not specifically dealt with by the White Paper, Annexure A listed a number of activities which had already been fully or partially privatised by government departments. Among these were transport of school children, and development and standardisation of psychological tests. Despite the policy set out in the White Paper, very little was done to increase private sector involvement in the public education system before the advent of democratic government in 1994.

Outsourcing after 1994

After 1994 – for reasons different to those put forward in the 1987 White Paper and which are discussed later – government increasingly engaged external educational agencies to undertake a growing range of tasks previously conducted by the education departments or not done at all. These agencies included a variety of education NGOs (many of which had developed during the last years of the apartheid period), parastatal organisations such as the Human Sciences

Research Council (HSRC) and the Council for Scientific and Industrial Research (CSIR), a growing number of new for-profit educational consultancies, individuals operating as educational contractors and university academics. They also included large multinational consultancy companies – formerly specialised in areas as diverse as auditing, information technology (IT), engineering or construction – which branched into various areas of public service consulting. Contracts are usually given through the processes of competitive tender which treat the various agencies on a more or less equal basis.

The work done by these various agencies includes the more general corporate functions of education departments that are the usual domain of the large consulting companies – for example, management and financial consultancy, IT systems consultancy, specialised software development. More significantly, perhaps, the work includes core education functions (see below) which are the usual area of operation of NGOs, parastatals, smaller companies and individuals.

This tendency towards a division of labour between these different groupings is not, however, hard and fast. Many projects are conducted by consortia of businesses and NGOs, or of more than one NGO, or of more than one business. A consultancy contract to advise on the restructuring of a provincial education department, for example, may require both specialist knowledge of education and expertise on the management of large organisations, making a partnership between an NGO and a private management consulting company ideal. Increasingly common are consortia between South African and overseas companies, particularly for donor-funded projects. In these cases, the overseas company tends to be the lead partner in the consortium. Occasionally, the management of donor funds for particular projects is undertaken on behalf of the departments of education by the larger NGOs or by private companies.

Education functions which are outsourced by national and provincial education departments include, amongst others:
- In-service training of teachers;
- Developing curriculum and learning materials;
- Training school managers and governors;
- Facilitating school improvement and institutional rationalisation processes;
- Assisting in the development of assessment instruments;

- Project management;
- Conducting adult education classes;
- Research;
- Evaluation;
- Organising educational conferences;
- Writing reports; and
- Aspects of policy development.

Contracting out by government in the post-1994 South African education system is not driven primarily by any ideological attachment to neo-liberalism or to a belief in the superiority of the private sector in delivering public services (although there are no doubt elements in government that share such a perspective). Instead, as Bobby Soobrayan, former Deputy Director-General in the Department of Education (DoE), put it, 'Outsourcing is meant to assist in the practicalities of development' (Soobrayan interview 2003).

This view reflects the report of the Department of Public Service and Administration (DPSA 2001) on the use of consultants. The main motivation for the report was the need to understand the reasons for the increased use of consultants by the public service and its impact on transformation and service delivery (DPSA 2001: 4). In other words, it is a study of an existing phenomenon which appears to have grown in the absence of policy either encouraging or discouraging it.

The report recognises the increased use of consultants in the public service and its necessity. It sees this, though, as largely the result of capacity problems, including a shortage of skills among public service managers, pressures of time and the need for rapid delivery of services. The report is concerned with 'unnecessary outsourcing', which is wasteful of public resources and inhibits the growth of capacity and efficiency within the public service, and makes broad recommendations to regulate the procurement, management and monitoring of consultants.

Another reason for the growth of outsourcing lies in the manner in which the major overseas donor agencies distribute their assistance, with contracts awarded directly to for-profit and non-profit service providers. This is in line with practices in their own countries and is discussed in more detail later.

Extent of outsourcing

The extent of outsourcing by education departments should not be exaggerated as it still forms a very small proportion of the national and provincial budgets for education. It is growing, however, and does help departmental managers to provide services and activities that they would otherwise be unable to offer.

While it is difficult to estimate the exact amount used by the education system to contract external service providers, the national DoE's Income Statement for the year ended 31 March 2002 shows an item for 'Professional and Special Services' which includes R41.7 million for 'Consultants and Advisory Services' and R7 million for computer services (DoE 2002: 146). Departmental expenditure funded from foreign assistance included R3.3 million for 'Personnel' and R15.7 million for 'Professional and Special Services' (DoE 2002: 152). Most of the funds in the latter two categories are likely to have been used for the purchase of short-term contract employees (probably consultants) or various forms of services of the kind listed earlier. In addition, the DoE also received R55.3 million 'in kind' from foreign donors – mainly, it appears, for goods and services (for example, the services of local or foreign consultants) purchased for the DoE by foreign donors, either directly or via grants management agencies (DoE 2002: 174).

These amounts do not include the contracting of external service providers by the nine provincial education departments or by public educational institutions such as universities, technikons, colleges and schools. The contracting out by public schools – almost exclusively with private funding from fees, donations, and so on – is an area in which further research would be enlightening. Anecdotal evidence suggests that the better-off public schools spend money on a variety of services, including extra tuition, in-service training sessions for staff, coaching for sports and cultural activities, and debt (fee) collection services. It is clear that the amounts spent in South Africa for these purposes, while still relatively small, are not insubstantial.

Probably larger than the amount spent by the education departments has been that spent *directly* by donors on projects agreed with the national and one or more provincial departments, often with a department providing co-ordination. The largest of these are projects funded by the United States Agency for International Development (USAID) and the British government's

Department for International Development (DFID). A typical *modus operandi* would be for the funding agency, after consulting with and obtaining the agreement of the national DoE, to agree with one or more provincial departments of education on the specifics of a support programme. The agency would then call for proposals from interested parties. Service providers, usually consortia made up of overseas and South African organisations, would then submit their bids and the agency would choose one.[1]

One of the biggest of such projects is USAID's District Development Support Programme (DDSP), which attempts to improve school and district performance in four provincial education departments. It provided US$20 million between 1999 and 2002 and was managed by the Research Triangle Institute (RTI), a non-profit US contract research organisation. It also involved a number of South African NGOs and companies, including the CEPD, the Joint Education Trust (JET), Khulisa Management Services, the Management of Schools Training Programme, READ, Link Community Development, the Education Foundation and the HSRC.

A DFID project in Eastern Cape, known as Imbewu, aimed to improve the quality of primary education. The first phase of this project ran for three years from late 1997, with a budget of £7.5 million.[2] A contract for the second phase, Imbewu 2, awarded in late 2001 to a multinational consortium of Dutch, British and South African organisations was worth £22 million over a seven-year period.[3] A contract for a similar project – the Khanyisa Education Support Programme, worth £7.7 million over three years – to provide assistance to the Limpopo DoE was awarded in early 2003 to a consortium in which the major partners were Cambridge Education Consultants of the UK and JET. The consortia who tendered for this included companies and NGOs from South Africa and a variety of other countries including the UK, the USA, the Netherlands and Canada. Clearly, these activities are taking place in an increasingly globalised market.

Both USAID and DFID also use other vehicles – for example, direct grants to particular service providers – to fund work done by for-profit and non-profit organisations for government or particular educational institutions. A USAID report (2003: 83–84) shows the total value of all programmes supporting education in South Africa between 1993 and 2003 as being US$397.8 million. Part of this would have been used for expenses other than paying contractors, but it is likely that the major portion of it was used for contracting service providers. Other foreign governments and foundations also fund education projects which are implemented with the use of contractors. These include, amongst others, the governments of the Netherlands, the Scandinavian countries, Switzerland and Ireland. Foreign-based charitable foundations include the Ford Foundation, the WK Kellogg Foundation, the Carnegie Foundation, the Open Society Foundation and others. Local corporate funders also donate money to assist education departments. The most prominent among these is the Business Trust, established with donations from 145 businesses, which has committed R95 million to three large education projects aimed respectively at primary schooling, secondary schooling and technical colleges.[4] These projects are also managed by NGOs, suggesting that the project model of the larger foreign funders is being adopted locally.

An interesting new tendency is that South African organisations are beginning to extend their operations to other countries. The author knows of South African education NGOs, private companies, parastatals and individual consultants that have worked in the past three years as contractors to funding agencies and multilateral organisations or as subcontractors to foreign companies in all the countries of the Southern African Development Community (SADC), a number of West African countries, Russia, the Republic of Georgia, Kazakhstan, Chile and even the UK. This work has included research, programme evaluations and technical assistance to state departments of education. Should this become a trend, it raises the possibility that South Africa could develop as a competitor to the developed countries in providing education services to public education systems, especially those in African and other developing countries. Furthermore, some foreign, notably American, companies such as the RTI, Aurora and Creative Associates have set up offices in South Africa and have taken, on occasion, to using skilled South African consultants (who are lower paid than American or European ones) to work for them in other countries.

A possible future source of growth of outsourcing is the prospective introduction of public-private partnerships (PPPs) to develop school infrastructure (Pampallis 2003: 27–31). It seems likely that South Africa will follow the British model – known as the Private Finance Initiative (PFI).[5] If so, the relevant education authority (in the South African case, a provincial education department) would appoint a private contractor following a competitive tender. The contractor, usually a consortium of companies, would normally be required to build a number of schools or substantially refurbish existing schools, to provide them with all the necessary furniture and equipment (for example, computers, laboratory equipment, and so on), to manage and maintain all the property, and possibly to provide additional services for a period of 25 or 30 years. The exact terms of an agreement would vary from project to project, but maintenance could include providing the caretakers, cleaning, heating, lighting, power, upkeep of the grounds, security, insurance and repairs. It could also include the costs of upgrading IT equipment and providing IT support services. The contractor would receive no money in advance and would be paid in instalments over the life of the project, starting when the school is ready for use (Glasgow City Council Education Services 2000; Thompson 2000).[6] A PPP agreement could thus include inbuilt outsourcing of substantial services for up to three decades.

By mid-2003, two provinces – the Free State and Mpumalanga – had decided to consider the possibility of using PPPs as part of their strategy to build schools.[7] If they go ahead with this and if other provinces follow suit – and the national Treasury appears keen to promote PPPs as a means of developing public infrastructure in various sectors (DoF 2000a, b)[8] – it could result in a major expansion in the outsourcing of school maintenance services (see Pampallis 2003: 27–31 for a fuller discussion of PPPs for developing school infrastructure).

Policy issues

The phenomenon of outsourcing by the state and the growth of a market in education services has grown in South Africa largely in the absence of a policy framework setting out the state's goals and objectives in this regard. The situation, as noted earlier, has developed largely as a result of public pressure on the state to meet the demand for the improvement of public services on the one hand and the absence of sufficient capacity in the state machinery on the other. In 2002, however, the national DoE commissioned a study on private involvement in public education, and is currently in the process of developing policy in this area (Deliwe interview 2003).

Such a policy would require a perspective on whether the state wants to encourage the growth of the market in outsourced services in the long-run or whether it sees contracting out as a temporary measure to help overcome the capacity shortages in the public sector. Whatever the long-term view, it seems inevitable that outsourcing will continue for some years to come. This requires the state to develop a more comprehensive and coherent policy than exists at present. It would need, for example, to give guidelines to individual managers on what should and should not be outsourced, how service providers should be selected, how outsourced activities should be monitored and controlled, what contractual obligations should be required from education managers and from service providers, and so on. In addition, the continuation of outsourcing has obvious implications for managers and the way that they work, and therefore the kinds of skills and training that they require in order to manage outsourcing most effectively.

In making a longer-term decision on whether contracting out of work is desirable, the government will have to take into account a number of other factors. Outsourcing could have a number of advantages. For example, there may be certain technical tasks which require skills that are not available in the public service and for which there is insufficient demand for departments to develop full-time capacity. In addition, there may be areas of expertise which may be more widely available in specialist institutions outside state education departments – for example, in universities or specialist research institutions. Independent evaluators may add credibility to evaluations of state programmes or institutions. Certain tasks may be done more rapidly or efficiently by outsiders – especially when the task is an unusual one or when departmental officials are engaged in other tasks. The education departments may also feel that it is diversionary to put their energies into developing capacity to undertake non-core work such as conference management, school transport or even facilities management.

A big danger of outsourcing is that the state may lose control of important education processes – especially where it involves large projects – or that officials may use outsourcing as a way of evading accountability by blaming service providers for non-delivery. If this were allowed to become common, it would constitute a violation of the democratic accountability of government and decrease the ability of stakeholders to influence the administration of education.

A clearly discernible feature of the South African market in education services, compared to those in many developed countries, is the preponderance of NGOs rather than for-profit companies among service providers. This is no doubt because of the growth of the NGO sector within a supportive funding environment during the decade preceding 1994 and the resultant accumulation of considerable professional expertise outside the formal education system. The shift in donor finance in the post-1994 period from the NGO sector to the state forced many NGOs to seek work as public service contractors. This created a lobby outside of government which sought to persuade the education departments to meet their needs by contracting out work to the NGOs.

In the absence of government policy to encourage the continuation of a strong NGO sector, it is likely that the proportion of private for-profit service providers will grow at the expense of the NGOs. This is partly because circumstances have become more difficult for the establishment of new NGOs, as very few funders are still willing to give the core funding that is normally required as capital to establish an NGO. This is not a constraint to the establishment of private companies, which will find the necessary capital if a market exists. It is also partly because it is possible – overseas experience even suggests that it is likely – that non-educational companies such as the large management consultancies and other services companies will start to move into the provision of educational services.

The questions arise: Should government seek to encourage and support the NGO sector by favouring NGOs in the awarding of tenders or by subsidising them in some other way? Is it socially useful to make a distinction between non-profit and for-profit sectors? Most NGOs would probably argue that they are more likely to subscribe to the government's stated vision of a non-racial, democratic and equitable society than the for-profit sector. Most NGOs have been established to fulfil a mission intrinsic to their particular work, such as improving the quality of education, promoting democratic practices, and so on. NGOs normally engage in commercial activities in order to sustain themselves in an environment where donor funding is no longer available or insufficient, and many would aim to use any surplus earned to subsidise non-commercial activities. For-profit companies may espouse similar aims to the NGOs, and do so sincerely, but their main *raison d'être* – the reason for which they invested capital – is to make a profit for their owners.

However, it is not at all clear whether the different outlooks of the two types of organisation actually make a difference to the quality and orientation of the work they produce, whether the role of NGOs is more socially beneficial than that of for-profit organisations, or whether they are more suited than for-profits to certain types of work. This would need to be determined through empirically-based analysis. It is not possible to discuss this in any detail here, but it should be noted that the fact that they have competed in a market to ensure their existence for several years has changed the ethos of many NGOs, shifting them towards a more entrepreneurial *modus operandi*.

The government's current attitude towards NGOs which tender for government contracts is rather ambiguous. In fact, the state favours some for-profit companies by awarding additional points in competitive tenders to companies with a substantial proportion of their equity owned by previously disadvantaged individuals. Non-profit organisations, not having equity ownership, do not benefit from this, no matter what the demographic composition of their governing boards, management or staff. However, many (probably most) NGOs do have the advantage of tax-exempt status.

Finally, in addressing the medium-term to long-term policy issues, the education authorities and the government need to engage in some reflection on what is to become of the small but growing industry that has been spawned. A whole cadre of skilled education professionals – consultants, trainers, managers, analysts, researchers, evaluators, assessment specialists and others – has developed outside of the public education system and is being supported to a large extent by foreign funding. This is clearly unsustainable beyond the period in which South Africa continues to be a recipient of foreign assistance. If – perhaps a better word is 'when' – foreign assistance to South African education ceases, what will happen to this group whose precise size is not known but who clearly number in the thousands? Will their skills be lost to education or be absorbed into the public service? Is there, indeed, a benefit to South Africa in having a group of education professionals working as independent contractors to support the education system and even providing services to other countries, particularly those in the southern African region?

There are no obvious answers to these questions which hinge, above all, on how government wants the public service to function, whether it wants NGOs and private businesses and individuals to continue in the longer term to play a role in the provision of public services, and, if so, what that role should be. Many constituencies have an interest in these issues – government, private and NGO service providers, teacher organisations, other education sector unions, and all who are affected by the education system. It seems necessary for public debate and further research on this neglected topic to begin to inform the development of policy in this area.

Notes

1. See <http://www.rti.org/ddsp>
2. See <http://www.jet.co.za>
3. See article by A Carlisle, 'R360m boost for schools', *Dispatch Online*, September 10, 2002. Available <http://www.dispatch.co.za/2002/09/10/easterncape/AAAALEAD.HTM> Also the speech delivered by MEC Stone Sizani at the launch of Imbewu 2 as a programme of the DoE, at JJ Skenjana Senior Secondary School in Idutywa, 10 September 2002. Available <www.ecprov.gov.za/speeches/education/2002/imbewu2.htm>
4. See: <http://www.btrust.org.za/education/>
5. See S Naidoo's article 'State seeks help with schools', *Business Day*, 5 July 2003.
6. Also interviews with Corsar 2000, Sava 2002 and Wright 2002.
7. See: <http://www.treasury.gov.za/> downloaded 12 June 2003
8. See articles by A Donaldson, 'Pukka PPP Provisions', *Financial Mail*, 16 May 2003 and S Singh,: 'Got the Foreman's Job', *Financial Mail*, 9 May 2003.

References

Allen, J; Chi, K; Devlin, K; Fall, M; Hatry, H & Masterman, W (1989) *The Private Sector in State Service Delivery: Examples of Innovative Practices*. Washington DC: Urban Institute

Department of Education (2002) *Annual Report, 2001/2002*. Pretoria: DoE

Department of Finance (2000a) *A Strategic Framework for Delivering Public Services through Public-Private Partnerships*. Pretoria: DoF

Department of Finance (2000b) *Guidelines for Public-Private Partnerships*. Pretoria: DoF

Department of Public Service and Administration (2001) *Use of Consultants in the Public Service*. [Online] Available <http://www.dpsa.gov.za/docs/reports/Report%20on%20the%20use%20of%20consultants%20-%2018%20June%2020011.pdf>

Feigenbaum, H; Henig, J & Hammet, C (1998) *Shrinking the State: The Political Underpinnings of Privatization*. Cambridge: Cambridge University Press

Glasgow City Council Education Services (2000) *The Future for Education: Project 2002*. Glasgow: Glasgow City Council Education Services

Halligan, J (1997) New Public Sector Models: Reform in Australia and New Zealand. In Lane, J-E (ed) *Public Sector Reform: Rationale, Trends and Problems*. London: Sage

Jackson, P & Price, C (1994) *Privatisation and Regulation: A Review of the Issues*. London and New York: Longman

Kickert, W (1997) Anglo-Saxon Public Management and European Governance: The Case of Dutch Administrative Reforms. In Lane, J-E (ed) *Public Sector Reform: Rationale, Trends and Problems*. London: Sage

Lane, J-E (ed) (1997) *Public Sector Reform: Rationale, Trends and Problems*. London: Sage

Lindquist, E (1997) The Bewildering Pace of Public Sector Reform in Canada. In Lane, J-E (ed) *Public Sector Reform: Rationale, Trends and Problems*. London: Sage

Pampallis, J (2003) Developing School Infrastructure through Public-Private Partnerships, *Quarterly Review of Education and Training*, 10 (2): 27–31

Republic of South Africa (1987) *White Paper on Privatisation and Deregulation in the Republic of South Africa*. Pretoria: Government Printers

Thompson, N (2000) Investing in Schools: The Experience of the Private Finance Initiative in Brent. In Lissauer, R & Robinson, P (eds) *A Learning Process: Public Private Partnerships in Education*. Southampton: Institute for Public Policy Research

United States Agency for International Development (2003) *Overview of USAID Basic Education Programs in Sub-Saharan Africa III*. [Online.] Available <http://usaid.gov/regions/afr/country.info/pdfs/south_africa.pdf>

Interviews

Corsar, Kenneth (2000) Director of Education: Glasgow City Council, 18 October.

Deliwe, Carol (2003) Director: Policy Support, DoE, Pretoria, 20 January.

Sava, Alex (2002) East Sussex Local Education Authority, UK, 15 November.

Soobrayan, Bobby (2003) Deputy Director-General: Policy and Monitoring, DoE, Pretoria, 12 March.

Wright, Fiona (2002) Head Teacher, Peacehaven Community School, East Sussex, UK, 8 November.

CHANGING CLASS

About the authors

Ivor Baatjes is a Senior Lecturer at the University of Natal, Pietermaritzburg, where he teaches Adult Learning, Curriculum Studies and Policy Studies in Adult Education.

Haroon Bhorat is currently Director of the Development Policy Research Unit (DPRU) at the School of Economics, University of Cape Town.

Linda Chisholm is a Director in the Child, Youth and Family Development Research Programme at the Human Sciences Research Council (HSRC) and an Honorary Professor in the Faculty of Education at the University of KwaZulu-Natal.

Edward B Fiske, formerly the Education Editor of the *New York Times*, is an education writer and editor.

Logan Govender is a PhD candidate in the School of Education at the University of the Witwatersrand in Johannesburg.

Suzanne Grant Lewis is Assistant Professor of Education at the Harvard Graduate School of Education and Director of the International Education Policy Program.

Ken Harley is a Professor of Education at the University of Natal, Pietermaritzburg.

Jane Hofmeyr is the National Executive Director of the Independent Schools Association of Southern Africa (ISASA).

Jonathan D Jansen is Dean of Education at the University of Pretoria.

Helen F Ladd is Professor of Public Policy Studies and Economics at Duke University and Associate Director of the Sanford Institute.

Simon Lee is the Communications Co-ordinator for ISASA.

Khulekani Mathe is the Executive Director of the Tembaletu Community Education Centre.

Thobeka Mda is Dean of Education at the University of South Africa.

Seán Morrow is a Chief Research Specialist in the Democracy and Governance Programme at the HSRC.

Johan Muller holds the Chair of Curriculum at the University of Cape Town.

Mokubung Nkomo is a Senior Research Fellow in the Assessment Technology and Education Evaluation Research Programme at the HSRC and Professor of Education at the University of Pretoria.

John Pampallis is the Director of the Centre for Education Policy Development, Evaluation and Management (CEPD) in Johannesburg.

Margaret Perrow is a Research Associate at the Bay Area Coalition for Equitable Schools in Oakland, California.

Kim Porteus is a Researcher at the Education Policy Unit, University of the Witwatersrand, Johannesburg.

Yusuf Sayed is the Education for All (EFA) Team Leader and Senior Advisor in the Policy Division of the Department for International Development (DFID), in the UK.

Crain Soudien is an Associate Professor in the School of Education, University of Cape Town.

Index

A

abbreviations x–xiv
academic workplace, changing nature of 20–21, 309–311
accountability
    for education services 429
    in higher education 296–298, 311–312
    and youth development organisations 375
administrative functions of universities 302–303
administrative progressivism 19, 223, 226
admissions policies, filtering mechanisms 71–72, 106–107, 109–110
adult basic education (ABE) 23, 393–415
    state-sponsored campaigns 405–406
adult basic education and training (ABET) 23, 395, 402–404
    as an investment 415
    youth policy 370
Adult Basic Education and Training Act 404
Adult Learning Network (ALN) 411–412
adult literacy 11, 396, 402
advocacy and education NGOs 327–331
Africa, education NGOs in 331–333
African languages 177
    and the Constitution 178
    as languages of learning 186–187, 191
    negation of 177, 182–187
African National Congress (ANC)
    and decentralisation of schools 64–65
    and discourse of resistance 372–373, 380–381
    and ECD policy 351–352
    and education funding 62
    education policies 57, 196, 222
    economic policies 279 *see also* Growth, Employment and Redistribution Programme;
    neo-liberal economic policies
    and NGOs 318
    and teacher unionism 268, 270–271, 282–283
African Teachers' Association (ATASA) 273
Afrikaans independent schools 162
Afrikaans language 177–178, 182
Afrikaans universities, private-public partnerships 305–306
Afrikaans-speaking teachers, and trade unionism 273
alternative language maintenance programmes 180–181
alternative schools 156
anti-apartheid resistance 271, 368, 372–374, 380–381
anti-racist education 95–96, 102
apartheid
    and language 177, 183
    and NGOs 317–319
    and racial discourse 91
apartheid education, resistance to 195–196, 372–374
Asmal, Kader
    on illiteracy 405–406
    regulatory powers 163
assessment, key documents 241–242
Assessment Policy for General Education and Training 231–232
assessment policy for learners 6, 19, 221–227, 231–239
assessment-driven evaluations 224–225
assimilationism 95–96, 102–105, 146
associations of independent schools 153
authority, decentralised 130–132
autonomy
    in curriculum development 258–259
    in higher education 296–298, 312

B

'back to school campaign' 372
basic education
  balancing resources for 57–82
  free 66
  sources of funding for 81–82
bilingual education 178, 182–183
'black' languages 186
black middle class 9–10, 17, 107–108
black students, access to higher education 300–301
black teacher training opportunities 248
boarding schools 162
Business Trust 427

C

capacity-building in youth development sector 380, 382
Catholic Institute for Education (CIE) 330–331
centralised/decentralised assessment 19, 221, 239
Centre for Education Policy Development, Evaluation and Management (CEPD) 233–234, 348
centre-based childcare 341, 346–350
child health 344–346
child rights 339, 342, 362
Child Support Grant (CSG) 344
childhood development 339–364
class (economic/social)
  as determinant at private schools 158
  as determinant in education 58, 65, 71–74
  inequalities 211
  and integration 105–110
  and notions of difference 90–91
  and race in SA 8–10
collective bargaining, teachers' rights 272
colleges of education 250–251, 253–256, 259, 295
Committee of University Principals, and Senior Certificate 228
Common Tasks of Assessment (CTAs) 224, 235
community development initiatives 166
community-based
  early childhood development sector 349–350, 352–353, 355, 356, 358, 360
  schools 155
compulsory education 57, 59
conceptual learning 205
conflict, and decentralisation policy 126–128
Congress of South African Trade Unions (Cosatu) 271, 278, 280, 351
Congress Youth League 367–368
Constitution, the
  and child rights 352, 362
  and independent schools 160–161
  and languages 178–180
constructivist theory and C2005 204
consultants to the public service 424
contingent model of integration 92–93, 111–112
continuous assessment (CASS) in schools 197, 200–201, 223, 231–232
contractors to state education authorities 421–432
core education functions, outsourced 422–424
corporate capital, and education change 7
cost-effectiveness of private schools 166, 170
Crouch, Luis 162
cultural capital 210
cultural challenges 170
curriculum
  for adult basic education 407, 413–414
  see also school curricula; teacher education
Curriculum 2005 (C2005) 19, 195–215
  in practice 199–205

teacher union involvement 283–284
terminology used in 206–207

D

De Lange Committee Report 152
decentralisation
  motivations for 6, 17–18, 116–119
  of school finance and governance 115–135
  of teacher education 259–260
decentralised/centralised assessment 19, 221, 239
degreed workers, and unemployment 45–47
democracy, and educational decentralisation 115–116, 121–123, 126–132
demographic profiles of learners 98–100
demographic shifts in higher education 300–301
Department for International Development (DFID) 426
deracialisation of schools 17, 89–112
development discourse in youth development sector 380–382
Directorate for Adult Education and Training 401, 403
distance education institutions 305–307
distance teachers' colleges 295
District Development Support Programme (DDSP) 426
diversity/difference *see* entries under class; race; racial; social
dominance and integration 105–106, 111–112
dominant factor model of integration 92–93
donor funding
  for education services 424
  for NGOs 21–22, 320–321, 324–325, 329, 334
drop-out rate at schools 71

dualist/monist tension 221, 223–226, 231, 239

E

early childhood development (ECD) 22, 339–364
  practitioner profile 349
  service provisioning 346–350, 353–354
economic considerations for decentralisation 116
economic growth, impact on employment 16, 32, 34, 37, 41
economic policy, influence on education 399–401
economically active population (EAP) shifts 35–37
education budgets 1, 5–6, 62–63, 79–80
education departments, restructured 1, 57–58, 60, 196
Education Foundation Trust 325, 333
Education Labour Relations Act 272
Education Labour Relations Council (ELRC) 6, 267, 272, 275, 279
Education Laws Amendment Act 128–129, 131, 163–164
education level
  and growth-employment relationship 37
  and unemployment rates 42–43, 48–49
education NGOs 317–334
education policy
  changes and continuities 14–15, 293–312
  and early childhood development 340
  reform 222–227
  and teacher unions 281–283
Education Policy Units (EPUs) 333
education professionals as service providers 23–24, 431
Education Renewal Strategy (ERS) 117–118
Education Rights Project 262
education service providers 23, 421–432

expanding from South Africa 427
education spending, influences on 79–80
Education White Paper 5 on Early Childhood Development 354
educational decentralisation *see* decentralisation
educational services, outsourcing of 421–432
educational trends and development 2–11
emancipatory ABE 23, 394–395, 397–399, 400, 413
employees, training of 409–410
Employment of Educators Act 128
employment expansion 34–35
employment preparation programmes 369
employment training programmes 377
employment trends 31–54
English language 177–178, 182
 and Curriculum 2005 203
enrolments
 changes in 97–98
 in higher education programmes 308–309
 impact of fees on 71–74
 in independent schools 158–159
entitlement to learning 272
equity
 and educational decentralisation 115–116, 122–126
 in independent schools 157
 and teacher education policy 250
external assessment activities
 government-initiated 232–237
 private sector 237–239

F

fees *see* school fees
female enrolment in private schools 159
finance *see* school financing policy
financial aid at independent schools 158–159
for-profit education service providers 430

Framework for Transformation, A 294
free basic education 66
funding
 for adult basic education 404, 411, 414
 for early childhood development services 351, 356–359
 for NGOs 320–322, 324–325, 334
 see also school funding; state funding for education
funding agencies for education services 424–428, 431
fund-raising functions in SGBs 127
further education and training (FET) 395

G

gender
 employment and EAP shifts 35–36
 enrolment in private schools 159
 representation on SGBs 127, 134
 unemployment rates 41–42
gender issues 10
gender politics, and trade unionism 275–278
General Education and Training Certificate (GETC) 235, 239, 403, 410
General and Further Education and Training (GENFET) 230–231
Global Campaign for Education 66
global economy affecting education spending 79–80
globalisation
 and adult education 395, 397
 effects on educational change 5, 14–15, 119
governance
 definition of 120
 see also school governance; teacher education systems
government *see* state
Grade 1 learners, C2005 Pilot Project 215
Grade 3 learners, assessment tests 232–234, 237–238

INDEX

Grade 4 learners, MLA Study 235–236
Grade 6 learners, assessment tests 238
Grade 8 learners, Mathematics and Science Study 238
Grade 9 learners, CTAs 235
gross national product (GNP), and education spending 62–63, 79–80
groupwork and outcomes-based education 200, 205
Growth Employment and Redistribution (GEAR) 79, 81, 270, 277
growth-employment relationship 35, 37

H

higher education 6
   autonomy and accountability 296–298
   changes and continuities 20–21, 293–312
   modes of delivery 305–307
   and teacher education 250–251, 253, 254, 259, 262, 295
higher education providers 298–300
Higher Education Quality Assurance Committee (HEQC) 254
historically advantaged schools, and C2005 205–206, 208–210
historically black universities 300–301
historically disadvantaged schools
   and C2005 204–206, 210–211
   and school fees 16–17, 58–59, 81
HIV/AIDS
   effects on childhood support 344–346
   effects on education 167–168
   impact on staffing 249
   response by teacher unions 277, 286
home learning 156
human capital theory, and education 3–4, 395–397, 413–414
human resource development (HRD) 395
   and Joint Enrichment Project 374–375
Human Sciences Research Council (HSRC), research on independent schools 146–149, 154–156

humanities enrolment at universities 308–309
Hunter Report 63–64, 81–82, 118

I

Ikhwelo Project 403, 404, 416
illiteracy 405–406
   and the unemployed 51
Imbewu 426
Impilo Project 353–354
Independent Development Trust (IDT) 383
Independent Examinations Board (IEB) 325, 333, 408
independent schools 6, 18, 143–171
   categories of 149–150, 154–156
   databases of 146–148, 154
   definition 144
   enrolment data 59–60
   erosion of independence 163–164
   key issues 163–164
   national associations 153
   racial demographics 98
   registration of 151, 153
   and school fees 16, 157
Independent Schools Association of Southern Africa (ISASA) 149, 153
   member schools 157
informal sector, employment trends 34
instrumentalist ABE 23, 394–397, 400, 413, 415
Integrated Approach to Youth Development (IAYD) 379–380
integrated knowledge system 197, 214
integrated youth development programmes 387
integration 95
   of education and training 7
   in private schools 159
   in schools 6, 17, 89–112
   and systemic reform 222–224, 226–227
Interim Policy on Early Childhood Development 352–353
international learners 162

International Mathematics and Science Study, Third (TIMSS-R) 224, 238, 240
Ithuteng 'Ready to Learn' Campaign 401, 403, 405

J
job creation 32
'jobless growth' 32, 33, 34, 53
　see also unemployment
Joint Education Trust (JET) 326
　Education Services 333
　Mahlahle tests 237–238
Joint Enrichment Project (JEP) 10–11, 368–387
Joint Matriculation Board (JMB) 228–229

K
Khanyisa Education Support Programme 426

L
labour demand patterns 39–41, 46–47, 54
Labour Force Survey (2002) 31
labour market trends 31–55
　statistics 32–34
language
　and African learners 183–187
　as a key to learning 177–192
　learner's right to choose 178, 180
Language in Education Policy (LiEP) 177, 179
Language Plan Task Group (LANTAG) 180
language policy 6, 18
　factors inhibiting implementation 182–188
　in higher education 177, 181–182, 184
Language Policy for Higher Education (LPHE) 177, 181–182, 184
　and multilingualism 188–189
language-teacher training 187–188
leadership roles in teacher organisations 276–277

learner migration 89–90, 97, 143, 165–166
　black 99–101, 106–108, 158
learner representative councils 131
learner-centred education 197–198, 200, 206, 208, 210, 214–215
　and teacher education 257–258
learner-to-educator ratios 74–78
learners
　assessment data 19–20, 233–234, 236, 238
　entitlement to learning 272
　foreign 162
Lesaka Holdings 275
liberation, education for 394–395, 397–399
liberation struggle *see* anti-apartheid resistance
life-skills 234, 236, 369, 380, 383–384
lifelong education 395, 402
lifeworld 413, 417
linguistic rights 177, 186
literacy 233–234, 236, 238
　of adults 396, 400, 402, 416
literacy levels of the unemployed 51
local control of schools 63–64

M
marginalised youth 375–376
market capitalism 11
matriculation examination
　pass rates 71, 75–78, 83, 230
　as systemic assessment 222–223
　see also Senior Certificate
meliorism 211–214
mergers in higher education 295–296, 301, 312
middle class, the 5–10
migration *see* learner migration
Model C schools (former) 65, 82
　and C2005 203, 206, 208–209
　governance structures 117–118
　and pedagogical progressivism 223

INDEX

principal's authority 130
modes of delivery in higher education 305–307
Molteno Project 332
monist/dualist tension 221, 223–226, 231, 239
Monitoring Learner Assessment (MLA) Study 224, 235–236, 240
mother tongue 183, 186
Multi-Year Implementation Plan (MYIP) 403, 405, 407
multicultural teaching 188
multiculturalism 96, 102–104
multilingual education 18–19, 177–192
multiplicity and notions of integration 92

N

Natal Education Department, and C2005 209–210
National Commission on Higher Education (NCHE) 294
National Education Crisis Committee (NECC) 117, 196, 372
National Education Policy Act 124–125
　and teacher education 253
　and teacher unions 272
National Education Policy Investigation (NEPI) 253
　and early childhood development sector 350–351
National Norms and Standards for School Funding (NNSSF) 118–119, 126
　effect on private schools 161
　and state subsidies 147
National Party, education policies 63, 149, 151–152
National Professional Teachers' Organisation of South Africa (NAPTOSA) 20, 272–275, 285
　and education policy 280–284
　and gender politics 276–277
　and labour relations 279

National Professional Teachers' Unity Forum (NTUF) 272
National Programme of Action for the Child 363
National Qualifications Framework (NQF) 7, 221–242, 281
　and multilingual education 188
　and youth policy 370
National Skills Development Strategy (NSDS) 54, 403, 404, 409–410
National Skills Fund (NSF) 410
National System of Teacher Education (NSTE) 248
National Union of Educators (NUE) 273, 274
National Youth Commission (NYC) 370, 378
National Youth Development Forum (NYDF) 370
National Youth Policy (NYP) 370
National Youth Service pilot programme 383
neo-liberal economic policies 7, 79, 81, 270, 277, 413, 421
'new' independent schools 150, 154
new managerialism in higher education 311
night schools 403
non-governmental organisations (NGOs)
　in adult basic education 11, 23, 404, 411, 414
　in education 21–22, 317–334
　as education service providers 23, 422–423, 429–432
　in transition 317–319, 323–327, 333–334, 386–387, 411, 412, 430, 431
　and youth development 368, 369, 371, 379
non-profit education service providers 430, 431
non-profit schools 156
Norms and Standards for Teacher Education (NSTE) 258, 263
numeracy 233–234, 236, 238

443

O

October Household Survey (OHS) 31
outcomes-based education 197, 201–205, 214, 395
  and teacher education 257–258
  training and implementation 200–201
output growth 34
output-employment relationship 34–35
outsourcing educational services 421–432

P

parent involvement
  in multilingualism 189–190
  in SGBs 108, 109, 122, 127, 130–131, 164–165
Parent Teacher Student Associations (PTSAs) 117
parental fees for ECD 358, 359
partnership funding 64, 82
pass rates 71, 75–78, 83, 230
  in independent schools 167
pedagogical progressivism 19, 222, 223, 227, 234, 236, 240
personal development for youth 375, 376–377
political agenda of C2005 198–199, 207–208
political change, and curriculum reform 195–215
political dynamics of integration 111–112
political economy 15
political motivation for decentralisation 116, 121–122
politics and notions of difference 90
population statistics 367
post-apartheid changes in education 1
poverty, effects on early childhood development 342–343
primary schools
  effects of fees on quality 74–76
  fees charged 60–62
  impact of fees on access to 16, 67–71

principals' authority 130–133, 165
private contractors in public education 421–432
Private Finance Initiative (PFI) 427
private funding of schools 59–62, 64–65, 81–82, 125–126
  effects on quality 74–78
private higher education providers 298–300, 301, 308
private international higher education 307–308, 311
private schools *see* independent schools
private sector external assessment initiatives 237–239
private teacher education providers 256–257
private-public *see* public-private
productivity, and youth development organisations 375
professional unionism 269, 271, 272, 278–280, 285, 286
profit-making schools 143, 155, 162
Project Literacy 325, 326, 328–329
Project for the Study of Alternative Education in SA (PRAESA) 189–190
Public Adult Learning Centres (PALCs) 403, 404, 406–407, 408
public education, outsourcing of 421–432
public funding of schools 59–63, 65, 81–82
  effects on quality 74–78
public schools
  contracting out by 425
  and fees 16
  financing 134
  racial demographics 98
  see also schools
public service reform, and outsourcing 422
public-private partnerships (PPPs)
  and Afrikaans universities 305–306
  for outsourcing education services 427–428

Q

qualifications, key documents 241–242
qualifications framework 19, 188, 221–242
quality assurance (QA)
    advent of 224–227
    for Senior Certificate 227–231
    and teacher education 259–260
quality of education
    impact of decentralisation 116, 132–133
    impact of fees on 74–81
quality management systems 225

R

race
    and class in South Africa 8–10
    employment and EAP shifts 35–36
    and notions of difference 90–91
    and unemployment rates 41–47
racial categorisations 90
racial demographics in schools 98–101
racial difference, concept of 89, 110
racial integration
    in private schools 158
    in South African schools 97
'Ready to Learn' Ithuteng Campaign 401, 403, 405
Reception Year education 22, 353, 354–356, 357, 358–359, 360, 361, 363
Reconstruction and Development Programme (RDP)
    and adult education 401
    and early childhood development 351
    and NGOs 318–319
religious schools 149, 150, 154–155
resistance movement *see* anti-apartheid resistance
resources
    and educational outcomes 75–78
    for implementing C2005 202, 203, 206, 207
    for implementing multilingualism 190
Restructuring of the Higher Education System in South Africa 294
retrenchment, and adult basic education 414
Review of the Financing, Resourcing and Costs of Education in Public Schools 134
Review of School Governance 115, 135
Revised National Curriculum Statement 187–188
Rivoningo Project 403, 404, 416

S

salaries
    college lecturer's 257
    in the ECD sector 349, 356
    teacher's 125, 168–169
SASA *see* South African Schools Act
Schollar and Associates, Eric, evaluation studies 237
school curricula
    discontinuity of 210–211
    integration 227
    policy and reform 195–215, 223, 283–284
    under-specification of content 237–238
school fees
    abolishment of 17, 66–67
    amounts and variation of 60–62, 73
    balancing resources 16–17, 57–86
    effects on historically disadvantaged schools 16–17, 58–59, 81
    effects on school quality 74–80
    exemption from 60, 65, 70, 71–74, 128
    impact on access to schooling 16–17, 67–71
    impact on enrolment patterns 16, 71–74
    for private schools 16, 157
    reasons for 62–65
school financing policy, and decentralisation 115–135
school funding
    balancing resources 57–86
    and equity redress 124–126

provincial differences in 125, 147
see also state funding for education
school governance 164–165
    and decentralisation 115–135
school governing body (SGB) 17, 60, 108, 117, 123, 164–165
    and financial resources 118, 129
    fund-raising function 127–128
    learners representation on 131
    perceived responsibilities 125
    and promotion of multilingualism 181
    and quality improvement 132–133
    and Reception Year subsidies 355
    reduced discretion and authority 128–130
    representativeness of members 127
    and school fees 126, 128
school infrastructure, outsourcing development of 427–428
school integration analyses 94
School Register of Needs 359
schools
    constitutional right to establish 160–161
    social character of 106–107
    and their communities 165–166
secondary schools
    fees charged 60–62
    impact of fees on access to 67–71
Sector, Education and Training Authorities (SETAs) 23, 54
    as delivery machinery of ABE 409–410
sectoral employment patterns 38–41
semi-skilled workers, share of employment 39–41
Senior Certificate
    and C2005 202
    qualifications and certification 227–231
service providers, NGOs as 325–326, 329
service provisioning for ECD 346–350, 353–354
SGB teachers 60, 75, 76, 78
skilled labour 24, 32–34, 39–41, 53–54

skills categories, and employment trends 39–41
skills development 7, 23, 409–410
Skills Development Act (SDA) 409, 410
Skills Training Programme 376
skills-biased employment 7–8, 16, 42, 47
skills-building for youth 375, 376
social change 11–15
    and adult basic education 399, 400, 401–402
    and decentralisation of education 115
social character of schools 106–107
social class in education 7
social class reproduction 210, 211–213
social difference, concepts of 89, 90–91, 110–112
social policy and integration 92
social reconstruction 89–112, 123, 211, 212
social science studies at universities 308–309
social security for children 343–344
social space 92, 93
socio-economic determinants for funding 119
socio-economic levels of private schools 149, 171
socio-political factors, against multilingualism 182–184
Soul City 333
South African Catholic Bishops' Council 372
South African Certification Council (Safcert) 229–231, 404
South African Congress for Early Childhood Development 361
South African Council of Churches (SACC) 372
South African Council for Educators (SACE) 258
South African Democratic Teachers' Union (SADTU) 20, 268, 272, 273, 274–275, 285
    and education policy 280–284

and gender politics 276–278
and professional unionism 278–279
South African National Literacy Initiative (SANLI) 403, 404, 406, 407
South African Qualifications Authority (SAQA)
  and integration 226
  and restructuring of teacher education 254
South African Qualifications Authority (SAQA) Act 222, 254
South African Schools Act (SASA) 17, 117
  attitudes to conflict 126
  and concept of participation 122
  and language rights 179
  and middle-class notions 108
  and right to establish schools 59
  and school funding 118
  and teacher unions 281–283
spontaneous schools 155
state
  and bureaucracy 14, 133–134
  control of independent schools 163–165, 169
  intervention in higher education 297–298, 305
  relations with NGOs 321–325, 329–330
state contracts for youth development 383, 384
state education authorities, outsourcing by 421–432
state education system 5, 58, 59, 60
state funding for education 5–6, 62–63, 79–80, 81–82
  and decentralisation 118, 119
state subsidies 119, 147, 169
state support for implementation of C2005 206–207
state-civil society relationships 21, 24
stereotypes and process of integration 92
'street academies' 151
strike action, teachers' rights 272

student distribution in higher education 300–301
student politics and organisation 303–305
stunting 345, 364
subsidisation
  for early childhood services 346–347, 348, 355
  in higher education 307
Suid-Afrikaanse Onderwysersunie (SAOU) 20, 273, 274, 280, 282, 283, 285
'system of provision' 3
systemic assessment 225, 232–237, 238–240
systemic reform 224–227

T

teacher education 20
  cost-saving changes 250–251
  curricula 248, 257–261
  decentralised 257
  moved to higher education sector 6, 250–251, 253, 255–256
  policy 252
  reconfiguration of 247–263
  training institutions 247–248
teacher education systems, governance of 248, 252–257
Teachers' Federal Council (TFC) 273
teacher identity 210
teacher training, for multilingual education 187–188
teacher unions 6, 20, 267–286
teacher-learner ratios 74–78, 251
teacher-state relations 267
teachers
  deficiencies of 251
  employment of 60, 75, 76, 78, 128–129
  funding for 82
  gender profile 276
  and HIV/AIDS 167
  new roles 258, 260–261

qualifications of 74–78
racial profiles of 101
salaries 125, 168
shortage of 168–169
technikon/university mergers 295–296, 301
technology and delivery of higher education 306
tendering process, effects on NGOs 321–322, 329, 430, 431
tertiary education, and unemployment rates 43–47
TIMSS 224, 238, 240
traditional independent schools 150, 154

U

UMALUSI 228, 230–231
Umsobomvu Youth Fund (UYF) 385, 387
unemployable, the 47–53, 54
unemployed, previous economic activity of 50
unemployment
  by education level 42–49
  by period of search 49–50
  by race and gender 41–42
  trends 22, 32–34
unions, teacher 20, 267–286
United States Agency for International Development (USAID) 425–427
United Teachers' Association of South Africa (UTASA) 273
Universal Declaration on Democracy (UDD) 121
universities
  admission requirements 228–229
  changing nature of 20–21, 309–311
  management and governance 301–303
  mergers of 301
  and teacher education 250–251, 253, 255–256, 259

university degrees, and labour demand patterns 44–47
university exemptions 230
university/technikon mergers 295–296, 301
unskilled workers, and employment 16, 39–41, 47–53

V

vernacular languages 177, 186
virtual schools 156

W

wage-earning households and unemployment 52–53
warehousing child care 341, 359
Washington consensus 3–4, 13
White Paper on Education and Training 118, 179
  needs of youth 370
  recommendations on ECD 352
White Paper on Privatisation and Deregulation 421–422
white teacher unions 270
women in education NGOs 323
workplace restructuring 395, 409–410, 414
World Bank early childhood development policies 318, 348, 361
World Conference on Education for All 57

Y

young adults, social issues confronting 367–368
youth development 22, 367–388
Youth Development Network (YDN) 385
youth development organisations 369–370
youth development sector 369–370
youth groups 368